Communicating in Business
THIRD EDITION

David N. Bateman
Southern Illinois University

Norman B. Sigband
University of Southern California

Brian K. McCarthy

Scott, Foresman and Company

Glenview, Illinois   Boston   London

Acknowledgments

Unless otherwise acknowledged, all photos are the property of Scott, Foresman and Company.

Positions of photographs are shown in abbreviated form as follows: top (T), bottom (B), center (C), left (L), right (R).

Front Cover   (T)   Scott, Foresman   (B)   Tom Grill/COMSTOCK

Back Cover   (ALL)   Tom Grill/COMSTOCK

vi TL, Ed Pieratt/COMSTOCK   *vi TC,* Chuck Mason/COMSTOCK   *vi TR,* Michael Stuckey/COMSTOCK   *vi T (INSET),* Tom Grill/COMSTOCK   *vi C,* Charles Gupton/Southern Light *vi B,* Tom Grill/COMSTOCK   *vii TL,* Tom Grill/COMSTOCK   *vii C,* Lawrence Migdale   *vii TR,* Charles Gupton/Southern Light   *vii BR,* Chuck Mason/COMSTOCK   *vii (INSET),* Charles Gupton (top)/Southern Light   *vii B,* Tom Grill/COMSTOCK   *viii T,* Bohdan Hrynewych/Southern Light *viii C,* Tom Grill/COMSTOCK   *viii B,* Tom Grill/COMSTOCK   *ix T,* Charles Gupton/Southern Light *ix C,* Tom Grill/COMSTOCK   *ix B,* Tom Grill/COMSTOCK   *x T,* John McKeith/Southern Light *x B,* Gerard Fritz/Southern Light   *xi T,* Chuck Mason/COMSTOCK   *xi B,* Billy E. Barnes/Southern Light   *xii T,* Gerard Fritz/Southern Light   *xii B,* Tom Grill/COMSTOCK   *xiii T,* Charles Gupton/ Southern Light   *xiii C,* Rod Mann/Southern Light   *xiii B,* Tom Grill/COMSTOCK   *xiv T,* Billy E. Barnes/Southern Light   *xiv B,* Tom Grill/COMSTOCK   *xv T,* Charles Gupton/Southern Light   *xv C,* Tom Grill/COMSTOCK   *xv B,* Lawrence Migdale   *xvi T,* Lawrence Migdale   *xvi B,* Lawrence Migdale

Library of Congress Cataloging-in-Publication Data

Bateman, David N.
   Communicating in business/David N. Bateman, Norman B. Sigband.
 —3rd ed.
    p. cm.
   Rev. ed. of: Communicating in business/Norman B. Sigband. 2nd
ed. © 1985.
   Includes index.
   ISBN 0–673–18998–8 : $30.50 (est.)
   1. Business communication.   I. Sigband, Norman B.   II. Title.
HF5718.S5297 1989
658.4'5—dc 19   88–23908
                                                          CIP

PREFACE

The third edition of *Communicating in Business* is truly different; while maintaining the structure of previous editions, it incorporates many new materials in innovative ways. In the rapidly changing world of business, both the substance and the implications of communication are changing dramatically. This edition provides an up-to-date, complete discussion of effective communication for people in organizations.

Part I presents the principles of business communication and links them to the productive movement of information in the organization, while Part II illustrates how to produce excellent business communications. Part III covers the unwritten elements of business communication, such as oral briefings and listings, and Part IV puts one's communications to work, showing how to implement employment strategies. Each chapter concisely covers important information and issues in a lively way. Helpful examples drawn from contemporary business issues support the text, and numerous new, full-page examples of business communications have been added. More detailed items are presented in the appendices—one on grammar, an expanded appendix on letter formats, and an appendix that illustrates various aspects of an actual long business report. The new edition includes other important features:

- *Actual letters from executives,* on their organizations' letterheads, introduce each chapter in an intriguing manner. These communications focus on key issues covered in the chapter, indicate the relevance of the material to practicing managers, and reveal that good communication is essential to managers of all ages and races as well as to both sexes.
- *Topical short readings* are incorporated into each part of the text; they have been carefully selected to supplement relevant chapters and eliminate the need for time-consuming trips to the library.
- *"Communication Checkups"* examine many common communication pitfalls. These challenging and enjoyable exercises, found at the end of each chapter, permit students to hone their communication abilities.
- *The end-of-chapter questions* have been expanded and provide a challenging, comprehensive review of the material. Instructors and students will find both short-answer and more comprehensive questions from which to choose; there are 35 various items for each chapter.
- *Executive summaries* conclude each chapter. These messages highlight the key practical points covered in the chapter.

Two chapters have been added in the third edition. "Communicating Across Cultures," Chapter 5, highlights the cultural aspects of communication managers face in their home offices in the United States as well as in situations abroad. "Making Sure You Look Good," Chapter 6, clearly presents the need for producing quality communications in today's marketplace. It addresses many practical, everyday communication concerns of the manager, such as memoranda preparation and strategies, copies to others, photocopying hints, binding considerations, and more.

Major revisions have occurred in most chapters. For example, the sales letter has been moved forward to the "number one" spot in the letters; after all, virtually every letter or memo a manager writes involves at least one element of sales. Motivation in communication has replaced the old credit-and-collection approach; the elements of needs and appeals are discussed as they apply to many communication situations—not just credit and collections. The topic of reading has been added to Chapter 21 on listening. Dictation techniques receive expanded coverage in Chapter 13 to meet the needs of today's manager. Employment communications have been thoroughly updated. Many ideas of an international expert in the field, William Morin, have been incorporated, and he introduces one of the employment chapters. In addition to demonstrating writing techniques, the examples throughout the text familiarize readers with contemporary business and organizational issues such as smoking policies, flex time, dual-career families, and changes in tax regulations.

Supplements

The supplement package is the most extensive available for any business-communication text today. It has been designed and developed by the recognized instructional designer, Dr. F. Dale Brown.

A teacher's manual, **Teaching Business Communication Effectively,** provides *Instructional Opportunities* for the communication issues in each chapter, *Scenarios for Success* that apply communication situations in common organizational contexts, *responses and suggested responses* for every discussion question, application, and "Communication Checkup" in the text, *Performance Expectations* for students, and *questions* for students with references to the text. A short booklet of **TIPS,** pedagogical tips for teachers of business communication from teachers of business communication, is also available. Three issues will be available over a year's time.

The printed **Test File,** also available in a computerized form, not only allows the instructor to easily select and retrieve questions, but also to design examinations to cover specific topics found in the text.

Transparency Masters enable the instructor to efficiently emphasize key communication concepts and issues for the entire class.

A student resource manual, **Business Communication Applications and Exercises,** focuses the student's attention on important business communication concepts and expands the coverage in the text.

Acknowledgments

The opinions and suggestions of dozens of business-communication faculty we have been able to meet at ABC regional and national meetings over the past three years have been incorporated in this edition. Numerous colleagues in business and education have contributed to the development of this text. Of special note is Dr. F. Dale Brown, who not only created the supplements but continually made suggestions on how the text could be strengthened to aid students and instructors. Besides the 23 executives who read, critiqued, and wrote about each chapter of the third edition, others who have made contributions include:

Lois Bachman, Community College of Philadelphia

Michael W. Bartos, William Rainey Harper College

James C. Bennett, California State University Northridge

Mary Joyce Burnett, Texas Wesleyan College

George Gebhardt, Essex Community College

Julie Hungar, Seattle Community College

Barbara Jewel, Fort Steilacoom Community College

Eva Kelly, Brevard Community College

Alicya Malik, Cochise College

Fern McCoard, El Camino College

Francis McGraig, Elgin Community College

Kevin F. Mulcahy, California State University Northridge

Carol A. Senf, Georgia Institute of Technology

Mary Williams, Clark County Community College

Continually, the Scott, Foresman team was helpful, encouraging, and professional in working with us. Jim Sitlington as usual provided his understanding of the business curriculum; John Nolan contributed his perceptive thoughts on the trends in business communication; Jane Steinmann, the developmental editor, made major additions to the content and solid suggestions for the final manuscript; and it was a pleasure to work with Marisa L'Heureux and Mark Grimes on a variety of editing details—they know how to make constructive suggestions, always in a positive tone. Then, too, there is Maggie Henry, the Business and Economics secretary at Scott, Foresman, who always treats you as though you are the only author.

The mechanical aspects of preparing a text can become substantial, but are eased when one can work with such competent assistants and secretaries as Donna Reynold, Wendy Teixeira, and Mary Ann Sexton in Illinois and Rachel Pearson in California. They continually went the extra mile not only to produce the manuscript but to work extra hours at inconvenient times and to make constructive suggestions.

The contributions of Southern Illinois University at Carbondale and the University of Southern California have been substantial. The understanding and cooperation of Dr. John Guyon, president, Dr. Thomas Gutteridge, dean, College of Business, and Dr. Uma Sekaran, chair, Department of Management, all of Southern Illinois University at Carbondale, and Dean John A. Biles and Associate Dean Phillip R. Oppenheimer of the University of Southern California, have all been superlative.

A revision as major as this one takes enormous amounts of time away from family and friends. We appreciate the encouragement of our wives, Marianne Webb Bateman and Joan Sigband; the Sigband children, Robin and Glenn Gotz, Shelley Wilkerson, and Betsy Seamans; and the Sigband grandchildren, Tami and Laura Gotz.

David N. Bateman

Norman B. Sigband

Contents

Chapter 3:   Putting Ideas Into Words: Activating Your Ideas   45

PART II

Producing Effective Business Communications

Chapter 7:   Communicating to Sell   137

Chapter 8:   Obtaining Information: The Inquiry   159

Chapter 17:   Aiding the Receiver Through Visual Aids   327

Readings

PART   III

The Unwritten Elements of Effective Business Communication

Chapter 18:   Preparing Oral Presentations   359

PART **IV**

Communication Strategies for Employment

Appendices

Dedication

To our wives, Marianne Bateman and Joan L. Sigband

Communicating in Business
THIRD EDITION

Communicating in Business
THIRD EDITION

David N. Bateman
Southern Illinois University

Norman B. Sigband
University of Southern California

Scott, Foresman and Company

Glenview, Illinois   Boston   London

Principles of Effective
Business Communication

Executive
Introduction

GE Management
Development Institute

General Electric Company
P.O. Box 368
Croton-on-Hudson, NY 10520
914 944-2100

May 11, 198_

Miss Sandra G. Williams, President
The Management Club
East Central University
Ada, Oklahoma 73021

Dear Miss Williams:

With many years of working with leaders in both the military and
industry, I have seen—again and again—the importance of communication.
There is no doubt that there is a high correlation between being an
effective leader and being an effective communicator.

The research study your organization is doing on the importance of
communication in management is vital and current in today's fast-paced
competitive market; it is a pleasure to lend my thoughts to the
materials you are collecting.

The competent leader is not only an excellent "sender" but also a good
receiver. He or she listens effectively and sensitively and then makes
a decision. In addition, that same competent individual plans every
communication carefully, from a three-line memo to a 35-minute oral
presentation to top management.

Beyond being an effective communicator, the outstanding leader is
knowledgeable about the field of communication. He or she can and does
analyze every communication breakdown to determine which barriers were
involved and whether they were on the sender's or receiver's part;
what roadways through the barriers could have or should have been
employed; and how to avoid a similar situation in the future.

You now have the opportunity to become an excellent communicator as
well as more knowledgeable about the field. Seize that opportunity;
communication will prove a vital tool in your future success.

Best wishes,

Eugene S. Andrews, Ph D.
Manager, Executive Education

1

Sensitizing and Coordinating Your Communications

WHAT YOU CAN LEARN BY STUDYING THIS CHAPTER

Writing a personal letter to a friend or a term paper in an English class is quite different from communicating in an organization, where communication has more than one purpose. The numerous dimensions of business communication are explored in this chapter. You will see that business communicators must be sensitive to others and must coordinate their messages with the people and activities around them.

YOUR COMMUNICATIONS REVEAL MUCH ABOUT YOU

You and your communications are inseparable.

New managers today, especially those educated in business schools, are sometimes criticized for being insensitive, ineffective, and exceedingly narrow. If this is true, it will certainly be reflected in their communications. After all, the way we communicate reveals much about ourselves.

You hear much today about the complexity of the world, the speed with which we can communicate, and the variety of new ways in which messages can be quickly transmitted inside and outside an organization and around the world. But even with the sophistication of computers and the emphasis on speed of communications, the

Individual communication is still important.

most basic and important element in business communication is the individual—that's you!

In isolation, communications are neither good nor bad. However, the way we communicate with others, and they with us, can have important influences on our

Be sensitive; coordinate.

lifestyle—making our activities, our relationships, our jobs, and our lives either difficult and upsetting or easy and enjoyable. That is what this book is all about: communication and you.

BUSINESS AND ORGANIZATIONAL COMMUNICATIONS

Business communication involves language that is different from basic speech and English. Although the basics such as articulation and grammar are important, they are assumed in the study and implementation of business communication. The business communication course emphasizes how the manager in an organization—a

The manager's job— move information effectively

business firm, a governmental bureau, or a nonprofit agency—can move messages and ideas *effectively*. In many respects, moving information within an organization is much more challenging than writing a paper in a college course. After all, in an organization, politics, personal sensitivities, and coordination of your activities with others' all play major roles. For over thirty years, study after study has indicated that the one key factor for managerial success is the ability to communicate—in both writing and speaking.

No area in business is exempt from the need for excellent communications. The top-notch accountant can write an understandable report for a person who has a scant understanding of accounting. The engineer on the way to the top is able to explain the ramifications of a design in a clear and concise manner to people who may not understand the intricacies of design. By recognizing the receiver of the message, the successful manager keeps communications on target. And this is done without upsetting the apple cart inside the organization, while at the same time meeting the needs of people outside the organization.

CURRENT AND EMERGING ISSUES IN BUSINESS COMMUNICATION

As with virtually all disciplines in the professions today, there are continual changes in business communication. Currently, there are many evolving issues that are important to managers. As you begin your study of business communication, you should understand and be able to discuss these issues.

Productivity. In the United States, improvements in productivity in the factory have become paramount. Likewise, productivity in the office and productivity of the individual manager are important. Since managers spend about 90 percent of their time involved in some kind of communication-related activity, the new manager must be not only a good communicator, but a faster, more productive communicator. Communication productivity can be increased in a variety of ways, some of which involve planning, dictating, and conciseness.

Productive communications

Overcommunication. In our information-oriented society, we are often overwhelmed with too much communication. Wading through lengthy reports and unnecessary memos is not productive. Therefore, knowing when to transmit information, what form it should take, and how much to include is crucial. As a general guideline, many companies today require that memos be limited to one page. The point is this: Don't clog the gears of the organization with too much paper or talk.

Beware of too much of a good thing.

Results. Managers are differentiated from operative employees in that they must analyze situations and recommend actions or make decisions. When they communicate their recommendations or decisions they can't beat around the bush or leave the receiver hanging—they must provide the results! Be results-oriented. Your goal should be to write memos and letters that solve problems instead of just listing them.

State the answer!

Employee Communications. With modern manufacturing technologies and the increased levels of education of operative employees, the need to communicate effectively with employees within an organization is growing. This must be done with more than just bulletin boards and company newsletters. Managers and supervisors must interact personally with employees in a clear, forthright, and honest manner.

People—not things—communicate.

Internationalization. Business communication is no longer just a *language* subject. Because of the tremendous flow of commerce among nations, business communication involves passing messages and images among people and organizations across cultures. Many "misunderstandings" arise from the nonverbal aspects of intercultural communication, such as how to greet people, how to initiate communication, and where to place yourself when communicating with others. Communication involves much more than just the words we use—it concerns our attitudes, our feelings, and how we relate to one another. (For a discussion of business communication in the intercultural setting, see "Communicating Across Cultures," Chapter 5.)

These trends and many others will all have an impact on you as a manager. These elements, along with sensitivity and coordination, are all illustrated in the tour of the Reynolds organization that follows. You will have an opportunity to see the fundamentals of communication in action and how they are used and sometimes misused in the modern organization.

REAL COMMUNICATION IN THE ORGANIZATION

Today, most managers work for nonmanufacturing organizations—hospitals, educational institutions, advertising agencies, and accounting/finance/tax/law firms, to name a few. Compared with manufacturing companies, service organizations have tremendous flows (perhaps floods) of communication. In fact, for many service organizations, the primary vendors are often the suppliers of paper, photocopying, and telephonic technologies. As we shall see when we tour the Reynolds facilities, service organizations are built upon communication. Clearly, the ability to be more concise, more productive, and results-oriented is going to enhance the effectiveness not only of the manager, but of the entire organization.

The Reynolds Association Management Company

The Reynolds organization does not make a product, but rather provides a necessary service. The Reynolds Association Management Company consists of a group of executives, junior executives, and various staff personnel whose job it is to manage the activities of professional associations, such as the American Accounting Association, the American Society for Personnel Administration, the National Consumer Finance Association, the National Association of Hospital Admitting Managers, and the Business Communications Association.

Providing services is big business.

Many groups find it efficient to hire a management firm like Reynolds to administer and organize their affairs instead of relying upon volunteers from their membership. Reynolds employs about twenty-five executives and junior executives who act as executive directors of the associations, with the assistance of an equal number of support staff. Located in Chicago, Illinois, Reynolds occupies two floors in a large downtown office building. Just envision this situation: Junior managers working in tiny cubicles, and upper-level managers working in spacious, enclosed office areas. Coordination among the various managers is essential, and as you can imagine, each of the executives must be in continuous contact and communication with the leadership of the associations that they manage. Reynolds handles the management activities for about 300 professional associations in the United States and abroad. The company has the advantage of centralized services, providing its clients with a variety of activities and services such as mailing, duplicating, and exhibit and convention planning.

A Tour of the Reynolds Company

The students in a local college's business communication course have been assigned to visit an organization to observe its various methods of communications. Jack Reiley made arrangements with the Reynolds organization to visit on a Tuesday afternoon. Suzanne Settlemeyer, a management trainee with Reynolds, meets Jack at the appointed time.

Suzanne has arranged to use a small conference room, where after appropriate greetings and pleasantries, she briefs Jack on the nature of Reynolds' operations and explains what they will be seeing. She also inquires about Jack's major in marketing and discusses his business communication course and career options. Suzanne, who graduated from college a year earlier, had also studied business communication. She looks forward to the time within the next twelve months when she will be assigned greater responsibilities, including actually managing some associations. Currently, she is assisting two managers in many of the routine aspects of association management. She explains that she will show Jack a variety of operations and that the success of the Reynolds organization is built on coordinated, sensitive, effective, productive, and efficient communication with clients outside the organization and similar interactions within the company.

An Oral Briefing.   During this briefing session, Suzanne makes use of a slide presentation to illustrate to Jack how the organization works and how they manage the professional associations. She mentions to Jack that instead of slides, she could have used a flip chart, overlays, or videotape to provide the overview. In this ten-minute orientation, Jack sees a real business briefing delivered in an interesting, extemporaneous manner. Leaving the conference room, he thanks Suzanne and remarks that he sees the importance of briefings. Suzanne notes that during the tour of the facilities, they will see numerous conference rooms and that managers are frequently expected to communicate orally—using appropriate visual aids. Further, because of the dynamics of their business, it is often not possible to plan thoroughly for these meetings. Therefore, the ability to organize thoughts quickly and deliver them concisely and effectively is vital to the success and smooth operation of the organization.

Briefing: Providing a quick overview.

An Effective Secretary.   Near the conference room they step into an area that is obviously special—the executive offices of the company. Here they are greeted by Ms. Herta Meckelroy. She is a senior executive secretary, who knows what is going on. As Suzanne points out some of the offices and activities at this high level of the

Executive secretaries are often communication gatekeepers.

organization, Jack cannot help but notice that Herta answers the phone quickly, kindly responds to questions, and directs inquiries to the appropriate people without bothering the executives. At her side is a personal computer and sophisticated telecommunications equipment. Leaving the executive area, Suzanne thanks Herta for her cooperation; Jack observes that these informal kinds of communication seem to be important in the organization. He notes that Suzanne speaks to everyone by name and is most considerate in greeting them and thanking them for their help.

Sensitivity is one of the requisites for successful interactions.

An Ineffective Meeting.

It would be rude to drop in on a meeting unannounced, so Suzanne has made arrangements for a fifteen-minute visit to a strategy session where one of the managers, Jonathan, is conducting an in-house conference with associates on how Reynolds can attract a new account. Jack observes that some of the managers are doodling, that the conversation jumps from one topic to another, and that managers are continually arriving and leaving. The chalkboard has materials from an earlier meeting; in this session, no visuals are being used. When the group starts to discuss a major-league baseball game, Suzanne suggests that she and Jack leave the meeting and continue their tour. Jack comments that the meeting seemed to be going nowhere. Without being critical of her organization, Suzanne suggests that because Jonathan is new, he needs to hone his organizational abilities and learn how to gain the confidence of fellow managers. Jack surmises that if these improvements do not occur, Jonathan will not be in the organization very long.

Meetings—where it is possible to take minutes and waste hours.

Moving down the hallway past several executive offices, Suzanne comments on the variety of academic backgrounds of the managers—majors in management, public relations, English, office administration, education, and even one in zoology. Although their backgrounds are diverse, business communication is important to them, both individually and collectively. At the end of the hall is a refreshment area where Suzanne suggests they have a cup of coffee before continuing their tour. Over coffee, Jack remarks upon the variety of managerial activities he has observed. Many managers were speaking on the telephone, several were dictating, and others were meeting with one or two colleagues in their offices. Jack added that his class recently completed an assignment on dictation and it was interesting to see it actually being done.

Dictation.

Continuing the tour, Jack and Suzanne notice one manager hunched over her desk attempting to rapidly write some kind of material longhand on a legal pad. That manager, Jackie Bentley, dashes out of her office to get a cup of coffee. Suzanne introduces Jack and he says that she is obviously working hard. Jackie responds that she certainly is, and says, "Look at the work piled up on my desk. I have to get this memo out to a client quickly, so I'm writing as fast as I can." She dashes back into her office. Jack says, "Isn't that strange; she has dictation equipment right on her desk." Suzanne responds by saying that every manager has his or her own style. Jack could not help but think that here is a person who is behind in her work and will be further behind by the end of the day because she is writing out material longhand instead of dictating. That's not only poor communication—it's bad management.

Dictation saves time.

Personal Computers.

Jack is now beginning to notice the personal computers on many managers' desks. Suzanne says that they are used for a variety of tasks, explaining that the network of PCs might be analogous to the communication glue that holds the organization together. The PCs can access the mainframe, interact with each other, and, of course, be used as word processors. This means that managers can access raw data in the mainframe and have it placed in reports in graphic form. Also, the PCs serve as an electronic bulletin board and electronic mail system within the organization. Suzanne comments that more and more managers are making effective use of computers in the organization. Although there are still some "old-fashioned" managers who seem to treat the PCs as decorative items instead of workhorses, many managers are using this modern technology to access information quickly and thereby improve their decision making and communication.

PCs—communication workhorses

Video Conferencing.

Taking the stairs to the next floor, Suzanne indicates that they will see several more things based on new technologies. Many of their competitors spend a great deal of time and money on travel. In addition to being expensive, traveling keeps the manager out of the office. For an organization like Reynolds, which maintains international activities, this could be very costly. However, with the company's uplink video-conferencing capabilities, it is possible to meet face to face with representatives of associations around the world.

Two managers are having a video conference with some colleagues in France, and Suzanne has permission to observe this discussion. As they enter the modern room, the conversation, primarily in English, is in full swing. The discussants are reviewing arrangements for a future meeting in France, and clearly cross-cultural factors are involved. The people making the initial arrangements in the United States have paid more attention to the substance of the meeting than to the social activities. The French want to have more receptions and dinners incorporated into the conference. Jack knows that in the United States, we pride ourselves on getting right down to business. But the French may have a better idea: Before directly moving into a business discussion, it may be beneficial to have some preliminary, nonbusiness exchanges.

International/inter-cultural uplink communications

Jack is amazed at the quality of the video picture and the ease with which the discussants are able to exchange ideas and to identify and solve problems. As the discussion ends, Jane O'Meyer, who is a vice president of Reynolds, comes up to meet Jack. She says, "Isn't that exciting—that twenty-minute meeting cost us about $750." Jack starts to say, "That's expensive," when Jane adds that in the old days, the managers would have had to fly to France, spend at least one week out of the office, and the total cost would have been in the thousands of dollars. Not only is the video conference efficient, it saves wear and tear on the managers and allows the organization to conduct much more business in the same period of time. The managers leave, and Suzanne takes some time with one of the technicians to show Jack the features of the company's uplink video capabilities.

Video uplink—saves money and time.

Other Communication Technologies.

Suzanne and Jack next head toward the centralized publication unit. Suzanne continues the discussion about communication technologies. She notes some of them, emphasizing that these are not executive gadgets—they are crucial tools. For instance, each manager is expected to carry a pocket-size dictating unit at all times for capturing ideas; to carry a pocket pager when away from the office, but within the complex; to use all of the features of the centrex telephone system; and, when traveling outside Chicago, to take a briefcase (kangaroo) computer, which allows the manager to access the centralized data bank of the organization through a normal telephone hookup from anywhere in the world. In this way, managers can continue to work while on the road almost as efficiently as when in the office. Furthermore, all managers have a credit card for Airfone so that if they are flying on a commercial aircraft across the country and have an idea to relay to the office or to one of the associations, contact can be made with the organization even at 30,000 feet. Top executive officers have mobile phones in their company-provided automobiles. Again, she emphasizes, these are not gadgets, but are ways for managers to communicate quickly and effectively. In their business, as in many businesses, timely communication is crucial, so the organization takes advantage of the latest technologies.

Managers can always communicate with the office.

Internal and External Communication.

In the publications unit, the organization produces the newsletters, bulletins, magazines, and mailings for the associations they manage. The unit has wide-ranging mailing lists and computer capabilities so that anything from a specific mass mailing to a letter to attract new members can be facilitated. Suzanne notes that Reynolds, which is so heavily involved in external communication, also does a good job of communicating within its own structure. Throughout the organization, there are clear, uncluttered bulletin boards that employees actually read. The organization has a good internal mail operation and soon will be installing electronic bulletin boards so that information of interest to employees can be communicated at strategic locations within the organization.

Mailings are sophisticated.

Information is vital inside too!

Word Processing.

Jack asks where all the dictation that he saw being initiated in the organization went. Suzanne tells him that Reynolds has a centralized word processing operation. It not only handles routine letters and memos, but also prepares extensive proposals for new clients. These proposals are initiated, proofread, and edited in this operation. Suzanne indicates that her organization applies the concepts for writing proposals just as they are often taught in business communication classes. She picks up a completed proposal that is going to an accounting association that Reynolds would like to secure as a client. Jack immediately notices the cover because of the art work, which is colorful and eye-catching. As Suzanne quickly flips through the proposal, Jack sees that it is neat, has clear headings, and is not exceedingly long.

Crisp reports

In about forty-five minutes, Jack has seen some fascinating elements of business communication. Suzanne suggests that they return to the conference room where they began, where she will summarize some of the elements of the business communication Jack has seen in action.

Business Communication: A Summary.   For concluding the tour, Suzanne had prepared a flip chart presentation summarizing the business communication situations that Jack would see in practice on the tour. The cover sheet has the words "Business Communication Issues" on it, and on separate sheets she has listed individual issues to discuss.

Flip charts are effective.

1. *Conference Rooms; Briefings; Extemporaneous Speaking.* Suzanne notes that although her introductory remarks may not have been brilliant, they were both extemporaneous and prepared. Although she had much to do that day— writing letters, memos, and reports—she still made time to plan this presentation. Conferencing, briefing, and various kinds of oral presentations are a part of virtually every manager's daily job.
2. *Courteous Support Staff.* Supporting the managers are superb secretaries, clerks, and technicians. Jack has seen that it is important that they interact cooperatively and efficiently.
3. *Working In-house Conference.* For the meeting, Suzanne has written the word "exchange." She adds that Jack may have seen some things here that were not very effective, and Jack ticks them off rather quickly: lack of planning, lack of organization, no agenda, lack of consensus, and no action.
4. *Dictation.* Jack comments that he did not realize how much managers use dictation. When he saw how Jackie was falling behind, he then realized the importance of dictation. Suzanne adds that dictating to a word processing unit provides an efficient way to dictate a draft, rework it, and then get the final copy.
5. *PCs.* Having data available is vital. It enables managers to communicate faster and more effectively. On the chart, Suzanne lists all the capabilities available to the manager using the PC:
   - access mainframe
   - interact with other in-house PCs
   - create graphics from data—incorporate them into reports
   - use as a bulletin board
   - use as a word processor
6. *Video Conference.* Video conferencing clearly saves time and money. One of the top female managers recently told Suzanne that video conferencing allows her to meet with colleagues around the world and still be home in the evening to spend time with her children.
7. *Communication Gains, Not Gadgetry.* In regard to technology, Suzanne lists equipment such as Airfone, briefcase computer, pocket dictation equipment, and pocket paging system.
8. *Intercultural Activities.* The need to have an understanding of other cultures in today's global society is important. In almost any industry or profession, international and intercultural communication will occur.

After Suzanne summarizes the presentation, Jack asks a few questions and then courteously thanks Suzanne for her time and for the thoughtful tour that was planned with a focus on business communication.

Afterthoughts.   Jack has had a thorough introduction to business communication in practice, and he departs to hit the rush-hour traffic home. As he takes the elevator down, he starts to consider the thank-you letter he will write. Driving back to the campus, Jack runs into a major roadblock along the way because of the heavy traffic. He realizes that the roadblock is partially of his making; he had had the option of visiting Reynolds in the mid-morning and returning home during the noon hour. As he thinks more about this, he recalls what he observed in the communications of the organization. Perhaps many of the roadblocks erected in our personal and professional lives are created by the initiator of the communication.

COMMUNICATION ROADBLOCKS

Who builds communication roadblocks?

When we think of roadblocks to communication we often think of the barriers created by other people. If we are honest, however, we find that most of the roadblocks to communication are ones that we make ourselves. Let's identify some of the roadblocks and see what we can do as students and managers to avoid them. The more roadblocks you can avoid, the better your chance for successful interaction.

Distractions. Clattering typewriters, nearby conversations, blaring TV sets, and even the presence of others can be distracting when we desire to communicate. While others may create the distraction, there is still much we can do to solve the problem—such as moving to a quieter office or establishing a strong mind-set to not be disrupted.

Besides noise, appearance can also be distracting. The speaker whose voice is squeaky, who jingles coins, and whose socks don't match is allowing appearance to distract the audience. Similarly, the page that is typed from top to bottom and from side to side with almost no margins and only two heavy block paragraphs, or the page that is full of misspellings and strikeovers, will create a negative impression on the reader because of its many distractions. As initiators of messages, we should take care not to allow such factors to interfere with our communications.

Lack of Knowledge. If, as the sender or receiver, we have insufficient knowledge, communication will be difficult. It is the responsibility of the person sending the message to be informed. As a receiver, you should not be embarrassed to say "I don't understand." That kind of feedback will be of substantial aid in improving communication.

Emotions, Biases, and Attitudes. Our emotions, biases, and attitudes can be barriers to understanding. If we let stereotypes and irrational beliefs get in our way, it will be very difficult to achieve meaningful communication. We must avoid jumping to conclusions before really listening.

Ineffective Listening. We are taught in school to listen for the facts. That is okay, but unfortunately it involves less than half of listening. You also need to listen for feelings. As a manager you must listen for and respond to feelings or it will be difficult to work with and lead others.

Differences in Perception. If the instructor sees the assignment as intriguing and the students see it as busy work, there are going to be problems. To achieve good communication, it is vital that the perceptions of the sender and receiver be similar. This does not mean that we have to agree on the perception. However, if we can understand how the other party sees it, it will help us improve communication.

Language. The words we choose to convey a message can be a communication barrier unto themselves. If you place an advertisement in the newspaper to read "House for Sale" and wonder why your real estate is not selling, it might be that you used the wrong word. Families don't buy houses, they buy homes. Be particular about the language you choose to relate your message.

Competition for Attention. In today's society, a multiplicity of things compete for our attention. It is a great challenge for the initiator of communication to gain attention, immediate reception, and closure. This means that when you initiate communication, *you must beat the competition.*

Feedback. Different modes of communication have different feedback response times. In an oral presentation to a live audience, we have the advantage of immediate feedback; in a letter sent using normal mail, feedback may be delayed for many days. In any situation, monitoring the feedback is helpful in combating the roadblocks to communication.

Although the treatment of roadblocks here is relatively short, it may help you recognize potential barriers. As you begin your study, work beyond the mechanics of the communication by striving not to place roadblocks in your own path.

QUICK REVIEW

Communication in an organization is more complex than most communication students have seen. This is because of the many relationships that are involved and the fact that as a part of an organization, you are representing much more than yourself— your communication represents your employer. The dynamics of interaction and the modes of exchange are many. The person who enters today's organizational environment must be able to manage these complexities.

EXECUTIVE SUMMARY

To: Business Communication Students

From: David N. Bateman and Norman B. Sigband

Subject: Sensitizing and Coordinating Your Communications

In organizations today, managers are concerned with communication issues such as productivity, overcommunication, the "results" orientation, employee-to-employee communication, and the internationalization of communication.

On any day, a visitor to a management firm (like the fictitious Reynolds Company) could see oral briefings, meetings, interviewing, dictating, use of personal computers, video conferencing, writing of reports, letters, and proposals, word processing, telephoning, and more. All of these forms of business communication have become very useful, and some are, of course, essential to today's businesses.

In any of these communication activities, breakdowns can occur, chiefly because people are involved. Roadblocks or barriers arise for many reasons, among which are distractions, lack of knowledge, emotions, biases, ineffective listening, differences in perception, language or semantic problems, and competition for attention. An awareness of the causes of these roadblocks can help business communicators avoid or eliminate poor communication.

DISCUSSION GENERATORS

1. *English vs. Business?* Compared to writing a term paper for an English course, what makes communication in business and other organizations different?

2. *Manufacturing vs. Service.* What, if any, are the differences between the communications of manufacturing companies and the communications in service-oriented organizations?

3. *Be Serious or Be Sensitive?* In what ways does a communicator in an organization need to be sensitive?

4. *Import to Numbers and Words People.* Why is communication effectiveness just as important to a "numbers person"—like an accountant or finance major—as it is to managers in public relations, personnel, and journalism?

5. *Productivity Increases.* What can be done to increase the productivity of managers who spend about 90 percent of their time involved in some kind of communication activity?

6. *Education and Communication.* If effective communication is so important to an organization, why do you suppose that our educational system has seemed to minimize communication effectiveness for students?

7. *Look at Your Productivity.* What could you do in your daily routine of communication to become more productive?

8. *Business Communication Is Changing.* The current and emerging issues in business communication are already evolving beyond those cited in this chapter; what other issues do you see in the forefront today?

9. *Just for Business?* This text is concerned with business communication. However, many of you are or will be employed in organizations that are not businesses, such as hospitals, public service organizations, educational institutions, and governmental or quasi-governmental agencies. Explain why the principles of business communication apply to these organizations just as much as to managers in what is often referred to as "traditional business."

10. *Personal Roadblocks.* How do the roadblocks to communication affect personal communication?

11. *Dodging Roadblocks.* For the communication roadblocks, cite a simple way an effective manager can overcome each.

12. *Only for the Young?* Why do you suppose some older managers avoid using the computer whereas younger managers use them effectively?

13. *Is Uplink in Your Future?* In this chapter, the use of uplink video conferencing seemed to work very well. What do you think might be some of the disadvantages of this process, especially when it is still relatively new?

14. *Message or Medium?* Do you agree, "It's not what you say, but how you say it"? Explain your answer.

15. *U.S. an Island?* What, if anything, are we doing in this country to improve cross-cultural relationships?

16. *Distractions.* What are several distractions that seem to affect your written and oral communications? List at least three for both oral and written materials.

17. *Extemporaneous.* Why are extemporaneous talks common in organizations like the Reynolds firm?

18. *Sensitivity.* What can the manager do to ensure she or he is being sensitive to others when initiating communication in the organization?

19. *Burdensome Communications?* Are there any problems in having managers "wired up" with pagers, centrex systems, and airfones?

20. *Perceptive Problem.* From your experience, give an example of a difference in perception that created a problem.

APPLICATIONS FOR BUSINESS

21. *Think About Sensitivity.* Cite three statements you have written or spoken to another individual that were not sensitive to the other person's feelings. Then restate each in a more sensitive manner.

22. *Cut Costs, Increase Quality.* Productivity is important today—producing more and maintaining or improving quality at less cost. Cite some ways that professionals in

your discipline are being productive. Then, as a manager within that discipline, explain how you could be even more productive.

23. *Multiple Faces of Feedback.* Feedback has at least two faces—a positive and a negative face. For instance, the athlete making an important score is cheered by the crowd, which encourages him or her to bring the team from behind to win. On the other hand, consider the manager who is making a presentation who stops to ask, "Does everyone understand me?" and sees only affirmative nods when several people are actually lost. This feedback is misleading. What can the manager do not only to receive feedback but to receive reliable feedback? Explain and justify your answer.

24. *What Are the Rules?* There are conflicting "rules" in some organizations. One says that you should always cover yourself with a memo that indicates what you intended to do and why. The other says that because the organization already suffers from paper overload, writing should be kept to a minimum.
   a. As a manager in a productivity-oriented manufacturing firm, which guideline are you going to follow? Why?
   b. As a manager in a governmental organization, which guideline are you going to follow? Why?

25. *Don't Let Me Distract You.* It's easy to *say* "avoid distractions." However, to *do* it is much harder.
   a. As a parent of a freshman son or daughter who is going to live in a college dorm, what specific suggestions would you make for avoiding distractions so that the student's assignments and other responsibilities are met effectively and on time? List at least five suggestions.
   b. As a mentor to a management trainee who has a desk in a large room with fifteen other new trainees, what specific suggestions would you make for dealing with distractions so that the trainee can do his or her work responsibly and on time? List at least five suggestions.

COMMUNICATION CHECK-UPS

This section will provide you with practice in spotting and correcting common writing errors in business communication. Many of the sentences are either incorrect or ineffective. Some are acceptable as they stand. If you improve the faulty sentences and identify the acceptable ones, you will increase your awareness of the elements of effective written communication.

26. Each and every person attending the seminar will receive a copy of Dr. Andrews' book, *How Women Can Survive in the Modern Corporation.*

27. I am writing you to thank you for speaking at our luncheon on June 15.

28. You will be pleased to know that the cite selected for our conference has all the ammenties we need.

29. The chairman of the session—Mr. James O'Danniel—is director of personal at the Raython Corporation.

30. The people involved, ie, operative employees, should understand the nature of the situation.

31. On the other hand, do not attempt to ruffle any feathers.

32. On Monday, January 29, 198___ you will make the keynote address at the convention.

33. There are numerous ways to contact high school seniors who may be interested in attending our college: through high school counselors, letters to high school principles in the region, alumni who are teachers in high schools, etc.

34. The assignment makes a person take a good look at their goals.

35. The questionaire should be distributed on a weekday.

Executive
Introduction

Post office box 1197
Paducah, Kentucky 42002-1197

502 442-8214   TWX 510546-2047

6 WPSD·TV·PADUCAH
AN NBC AFFILIATE

March 1, 198_

Mr. Jason C. Jackson
Bryant Hall, Room 223
Murray State University
Murray, Kentucky 42071

Dear Jason:

As you pursue your undergraduate degree in communications, I hope these comments will be helpful in explaining an assignment editor's job.

First, a quick explanation. My job is to come up with the majority of news stories WPSD covers, set the dates and times for each "shoot," and then assign each story to a reporter.

Planning. The "show must go on," and if I don't plan efficiently for news coverage on a particular day, we may not have enough stories for our newscasts. Planning is challenging because it is not possible to anticipate when a tornado will hit or when a dangerous inmate will escape from prison. But, if I don't plan and develop stories as much in advance as possible, time that could be better used critiquing the final product will be wasted looking for stories.

Communicating. Yes, we are in the communication business, but beyond what you see broadcast, it is vital that I communicate clearly with the people I set up stories with as well as the reporters who cover each story. The interviewee needs to know who he or she will be talking with, and the reporter needs to know the gist of the story as well as how much time there will be to tell it. The assignment editor is constantly communicating with people inside and outside the station.

If you would like to discuss these and other aspects of an assignment editor's job, please call and we can set up a time for you to visit our facilities and learn more about television newsroom operation.

Cordially,

Jane Tyler Arthur

Jane Tyler Arthur
Assignment Editor

Planning: The Manager's and Communicator's First Principle

WHAT YOU CAN LEARN BY STUDYING THIS CHAPTER

You cannot manage your affairs without planning, nor can you manage the activities of an organization without planning. Similarly, planning is an important part of written and spoken communication. Without a plan, communication is not likely to meet its desired goal. As a youngster you may have been told to put your brain in gear before moving your tongue. The idea was to think and plan *before* transmitting your message. That advice still holds. In the next few pages you can learn the practicalities of the planning process, discover the advantages of outlining, and hone your ability to develop a logical sequence for the ideas you want to communicate.

Planning is common to good management and to good communication.

Planning is the first and primary requisite of management. There are many parallels between the way the manager plans business activities and the way the manager should plan communications. An old adage about the necessity of planning may be trite, but it certainly is on target: "Those who fail to plan, plan to fail." Although there can be some disadvantages to planning, such as spending too much time on the plan instead of moving to action, they are outweighed by the many benefits of a thoughtful planning process.

THE PLANNING PROCESS

Using planning steps can keep your message on target.

There is much we can learn from how a manager plans. The steps involved in this process are both distinct and interdependent. They are as follows:

1. Establish the need;
2. Identify the goal(s), purpose(s), or objective(s);
3. Consider the policies and procedures;
4. Prepare a forecast;
5. Develop an outline;
6. Revise the plan;
7. Test the plan; and
8. Implement the plan.

Let's look at these steps as they relate to communication. To help us understand the planning process, we will examine the situation of Sophia Goldwater, owner of Sophisticated Bikercise, Ltd., who is considering expanding the manufacturing facilities of her company. We will review the process of expansion as it relates to management planning and as the same planning process relates to various kinds of communications. In this way, you can discover the linkage of management, communication, and planning in the business environment.

Establish the Need

More communication is not always the answer.

Before a manager decides to engage in an activity, like expansion, the need for that activity must be determined. Clearly, Sophia will not spend close to $1 million to expand the manufacturing facilities if she is not satisfied that there is an increased need for the specialized exercise bike her company produces. The same applies to communication. Why waste time and energy on writing a memo that serves no purpose? In assessing the need, consider factors such as the overall context, along with the advantages and disadvantages of developing and sending the communication. Textbooks on communication often suggest that situations always get better with communication. However, there are situations where choosing not to communicate may produce better results. It all depends upon the need. Just as in some cases it may be better not to expand, sometimes it may be better not to communicate.

TABLE 2.1   Stating the Communication Objective

TYPE OF MESSAGE	EXAMPLE OF AN OBJECTIVE
Inquiry Letter	*To obtain* the domestic sales figures for 1979 wheelbarrow sales from the Big W Co. by June 7, 198–.
Sales Letter	*To generate* 100 customer inquiries from the 1,000 letters sent to potential customers for the TopDesk photocopier by February 10, 198–.
Informative Oral Briefing	*To provide* the office staff with a clear understanding of the new ID badges in a five-minute briefing on November 18, 198–.

State the Goal, Purpose, or Objective

Specifying your purpose is probably one of the most important parts of planning. The executive must do a good job of specifying a precise objective: "To increase production of the Bikercise product by 15 percent by expanding the manufacturing facilities before July 1, 198-." That is a precise, measurable, understandable statement. The communicator should likewise be able to state the objective of the planned communication in a clear, probably measurable, understandable manner. Stating what you want to accomplish is a key factor in keeping your communication on target. Table 2.1 lists some goals for various kinds of communications—you should be able to add many more to the list.

An objective focuses your message.

Objectives such as those in Table 2.1 are not subject to multiple interpretations; they clearly state what the communicator desires to accomplish. They can establish a solid foundation for developing the message and for knowing if it achieved the desired result.

Consider the Policies and Procedures

A business person will review the policies and procedures concerning the plan to expand the facilities. For instance, what are the policies on transferring current employees to the anticipated facility? What are the procedures for notifying the union of the potential expansion? The same applies to the communicator. Communication policies are the basic guidelines (e.g., inquiries are handled expeditiously; company letterhead is used for external communication; telephones are answered politely and swiftly, in a manner that projects a positive image for the organization), whereas communication procedures are the steps or "how to do it" elements (e.g., incoming letters are logged in, response times are noted and recorded, photocopies are routed to appropriate persons). Table 2.2 presents some representative communication policies and procedures.

Policies are guides; procedures are steps.

TABLE 2.2   Communication Policies and Procedures

EXAMPLES OF COMMUNICATION POLICIES

Responding to Inquiries	Incoming letters of inquiry should be responded to within five working days.
Placing a Caller on Hold	Do not place any caller on hold for more than sixty seconds.
Approval for External Speeches	Managers making external oral presentations as an official representative of the firm should have speech titles and outlines approved ten working days prior to the presentation.

EXAMPLES OF COMMUNICATION PROCEDURES

Responding to Complaints	Use guide letters in responding to all complaints; have your supervisor approve all exceptions to the established guides; send a blind copy to all company officials affected by the complaint.
Use of Bulletin Board	Company information posted on company-wide bulletin boards should first be shared with supervisors via internal mail; whenever possible, provide the supervisors with additional information so they can respond adequately to employee questions.
Oral Briefings	In oral briefings to top executive officers: (1) state your purpose, (2) cover the material within the time limit, (3) use relevant visuals whenever possible, (4) do not wander from the purpose, and (5) anticipate and be prepared to respond to questions.

Prepare a Forecast

Forecasting is anticipating the receiver's response.

When managers consider expanding facilities they also make a forecast relative to the need. In the case of Bikercise, the forecast might be: Will there be a substantial long-term sales increase or just some temporary sales increase that could be handled by having employees work overtime? The communicator should also engage in some forecasting. What does the receiver really want to know? How receptive will the receiver be to the message? Is there a particular mode that is better for this recipient and a particular time that the message should be received?

Anticipating the nature of the receiver and how he or she will respond to your message can aid you in planning the presentation of your ideas. For example, if you anticipate the receiver will question the quality of your product, it may be advantageous to emphasize your commitment to quality; if you think a college official may think your student group is too inexperienced to host an "Executive Day" on campus, you might attach a program from last year's session along with copies of commendation letters from participating executives. Forecasting is a reflective process; you forecast and then prepare, revise, and alter your communication until the final message is in line with the prediction. Table 2.3 illustrates this point in preparing an introductory sentence to a letter of inquiry. The objective is to obtain information on maternity benefits. However, the forecast indicates that it may be more difficult in some cases—therefore, the wording is altered.

TABLE 2.3   Aligning the Message with the Forecast

THE FORECAST	THE MESSAGE
Information can be secured in a routine manner	For a college class in personnel, information on maternity benefits is needed.
Information not difficult to secure, but need to do more than say it is a college project	Your maternity benefits are considered by human resource experts as innovative and responsive to the changing role of women in society.
Difficult to gain attention and to get receiver to respond to outside requests	GM and IBM have responded and you should be included in this survey, too. Talbert Hanover, the noted authority on personnel policy, has said that your maternity benefit policy is excellent.

Choose the Mode of Communication

Another element of business forecasting is the mode of transmission. There are a variety of modes by which to communicate, and your choice of mode will depend upon the need and the factors derived from the forecast. You might choose to:

- Send a formal letter;
- Send a less formal memo;
- Send a very informal note;
- Telephone the individual personally;
- Have a secretary telephone;
- Use some type of electronic mail; or
- See the person face-to-face.

Your mode influences how your message is received.

The communication mode you choose and how it is implemented is directly tied to your forecast. For instance, you need some rather simple data from your organization's director of hourly employment. Generally, you would either make a quick telephone call or send a simple memo. However, the director has been under considerable pressure recently and a telephone call might provoke a hostile response, or the memo might go unanswered. Perhaps a pleasant face-to-face visit in this situation would work best. Tell the director you appreciate his work, understand the pressure his office is under, and are seeking a way to obtain the needed data.

Develop an Outline

If we look at some of our national leaders' outstanding accomplishments, we can see how they outlined their plans in very simple ways. For example, the president of

FIGURE 2.1   Outline on Scrap of Paper

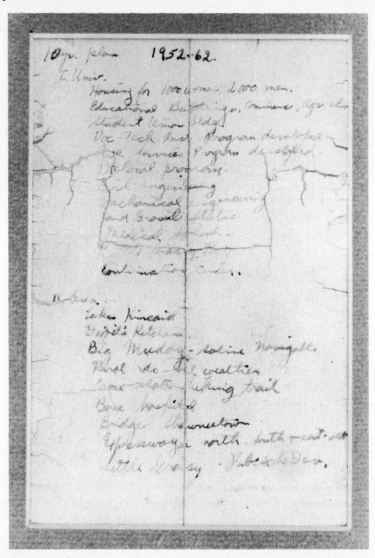

Outlining saves you time.

Southern Illinois University, who took a small teacher's college of a few hundred students and built it into one of the nation's largest comprehensive universities, outlined his plan on a scrap of paper (see Figure 2.1). Outlining goals and logical steps for a business activity is crucial for a manager. For a communicator, outlining the steps and progressions of thought is just as vital. Outlining is essential managerial work; it is not busywork, and it can be a valuable time-saver for the productive communicator.

Revise the Plan

As we will see later, the job of the writer is not so much to write as to rewrite. Similarly, the job of a manager is not just to plan, but to revise the plan. Revision is an ongoing part of the planning process. It's rare when we get the plan exactly right the first time. Therefore, as you review the forecast, analyze the receiver, and become smarter relative to the situation, it will be necessary to revise the plan. Since the plan is a simple outline, it is relatively easy to make changes. The adept communicator continuously receives input, develops it, and then revises the output. This may appear complex, but with patience and application, you can become capable of engaging in all of these acts almost simultaneously.

Most writing is not perfect the first time; revision is needed.

In planning to expand the Bikercise facilities, Sophia Goldwater has found that she can decrease the square footage of the actual manufacturing space (revises the plan) because new engineering developments have lessened the required assembly space. Sophia discovers that by saving space, she can now plan an attractive lunch/vending area for employees. Since the process is in outline form, this is relatively easy. It would be much harder to remodel if the walls and partitions were already constructed. Similarly, a speaker working from an outline instead of a word-for-word script can quickly revise his or her comments if a previous speaker has already covered a point. With a working plan, it is easy to make revisions and keep on target; without a plan, or if tied to a script, change can be difficult.

Test the Plan

Various kinds of marketing tests can be initiated to determine the need for the increased number of Bikercisers that will be produced. Similarly, there are ways to test messages for their potential to communicate effectively. The first draft of a letter can be a good test. Sometimes a letter may be shared with colleagues before it is sent. The oral communicator may test the communication by placing it on video or audio tape, listening to it, and perhaps having someone else critique it before it is developed to final form and delivered. Testing is clearly a part of planning; these activities, like forecasting and testing, are not just a step in the process. The information derived contributes to the final form of the communication.

It's beneficial to test a message before sending it.

Implement the Plan

One of the major disadvantages of planning is the tendency of some people to overplan. They work and work on the paper planning activities. The uninitiated plan is nothing but a piece of paper or a figment of someone's imagination. To overplan so that thousands of Bikercise sales are lost would be poor management. The letter that remains in draft form and is not sent certainly is not communicating. Eventually, the communicator must give the speech or send the letter or report. Do not treat the

Plan for action!

planning process as a list of steps to memorize; instead, strive to internalize the process and apply it. The application of the planning process will improve your management skills and your communication abilities.

SOME CRUCIAL PLANNING ELEMENTS

Beyond various steps in planning, other, related elements are of importance to the communicator. In an era of communication overload, a communicator should first determine if there is a need to send the letter or memo, place the telephone call, or make the oral presentation. If there is not an overriding need for the communication, don't plan it and don't initiate it. You can save time by refraining from communications that are not needed.

The Purpose

Exactly why are you initiating the communication? It is a good idea to be able to state your objective in a clear, simple statement; it need not even be a complete sentence. It can be helpful to review the communication objectives listed in Table 2.1 from time to time, because a communication without a guiding purpose is unlikely to be effective. Although a statement of the objective generally does not appear in the communication, the communicator with it in front of him or her will keep the communication on target. Objectives might be as follows:

Know (and be able to state) your purpose.

1. *To convince* the boss to upgrade the office word processing capabilities.
2. *To inform* the staff of an impending layoff.
3. *To brief* office personnel on recent sexual harassment regulations.
4. *To convince* my client, Mary Joneweather, to purchase a full-page advertisement in an upcoming edition.
5. *To explain* and illustrate the advantages of extracurricular activities to undergraduate students.

Outlining

To many, outlining is bothersome busywork. However, used for a purpose, it can be invaluable. An outline should be considered a working paper and generally not a perfect document. You use the outline as a working guide to aid you in accomplishing your purpose. It is not the outline but the eventual successful communication that is important. Therefore, it is wise to spend time in the conceptualization of the outline but not in making the outline a finished perfect product.

Outlining *speeds* your communication process.

    The outline of a response may be done in the margin of a letter you must answer (see Figure 2.2A); the outline of an extemporaneous speech or talk intended for a business conference may be jotted down on the meeting agenda (see Figure 2.2B); the

FIGURE 2.2A   Outline in Margin

September 3, 198_

Mrs. Jack O. O'Mally, Director
Human Resources
Sophisticated Bikercise, Inc.
7667 Garden Street
Memphis, TN 38101

Dear Mrs. O'Mally:

S Enjoys your excellent program.

Your founder's entrepreneurial spirit has been as long-lasting as it has been successful. Sophia Goldwater's enthusiasm for her company, her employees, and her community set a fine example for our students at Memphis Community College. As you know, we have a strong program in small business and Miss Goldwater has been kind enough to speak at our annual spring banquet twice. We appreciate all that she and other people in your organization do for our students and college.

Good asignment items ready.

You might like to borrow our video.

I would like my students doing case-study work in small business to have the opportunity to examine the Bikercise organization. In order for the students to pursue this in a realistic manner the following items from your company would be most helpful:

- <u>Brochures.</u> Twenty brochures that your public relations department has produced that provide a history of the company.
- <u>Company Newsletters.</u> Several copies of the last three editions of your orgasnization's newsletter.
- <u>10-K.</u> One copy of the most recent 10-K you filed with the government.
- <u>Organization.</u> If available, a representation of your organizational chart, or perhaps a listing of your primary managers and department heads.

Enjoyable to work with you and your students.

To be useful to our students, these items are needed by October 1; I will call your office in a week to see if they are available. If they are, I'll make arrangements to pick them up before the end of the month. Thank you, and be sure to relate greetings to Sophia!

Sincerely,

Marcia O. Kleinau

Marcia O. Kleinau
Instructor

FIGURE 2.2B   Outline on Agenda

S◯PHISTICATED
Bikercise, Inc.

7667 Garden Street
Memphis, Tennessee   38101

```
TO:        Department Heads
FROM:      Jack Monan, V. P., Operations
DATE:      February 4, 198_
SUBJECT:   Agenda

                Weekly Department Head Meeting
                     February 8, 198_

Time and Place: 7:30 a.m.-9:00 a.m.
                2nd Floor Conference Room

  I.  John Davidson:  Report on labor relations




 II.  Betty Washington:  Briefing on the National Exercise
                         Conference




III.  Sophia Goldwater:  Analysis of expanding manufacturing
                         facilities




 IV.  Dennis Hernandez:  Update on obtaining option for
                         adjacent land for possible expansion




  V.  Chuck O'Connell:   Report on orders and sales for
                         previous week
```

FIGURE 2.2C   Outline on Legal Tablet

P3-08868	**PUBLIX OFFICE SUPPLIES, INC.** 700 W. Chicago Ave. Chicago, Ill. 60610 312-226-1000

Advantages of Adding Vitamins to Our Product Line

I. Solid Reputation of Bikercise

    A. Loyal customers

    B. They look to us for counsel

II. Cash / Financial Situation

    A. The finances are right for some kind of expansion

    B. An investment in a new product can increase

        worth of the company

III. Current Customers as Purchasers

    A. 50 percent of current customers will buy our vitamins

    B. Establishes a solid base for locating other customers

    C. Family units will be a big market

IV. Distribution System Established

    A. Repackaging

    B. Distribution

    C. Point-of-sale

FIGURE 2.2D   Outline Prepared on Word Processor (Draft Quality)

Reasons to Upgrade Office Word Processing System

I. **Facility Update**

   A. We do more work than other offices.

   B. The current equipment is four years old.

   C. Today there are more managers (dictators) in office.

II. **Increase Productivity**

   A. Our staff is productive and conscientious.

     1. This conscientiousness is difficult to maintain with poor equipment.
     2. Let's strive to maintain the right attitude.

   B. New equipment can increase our productivity.

III. **Reduce Costs**

   A. Cost reductions include capital investment.

   B. Per-page costs decrease.
     1. Old 47 cents per page.
     2. New 32 cents per page.

IV. **Increase Employee Pride**

   A. Employees want to take pride in their work.

   B. Current quality of work is low.

   C. New equipment is a good investment for quality of work.

V. **Recommended Equipment**

   A. Text Reader

   B. Micro Manager

   C. Infowindow

FIGURE 2.3   Outlining Systems

Roman Numeral	Decimal	Roman Numeral
I.	1.0	A.
A.	1.1	1.
1.	1.11	a.
2.	1.12	b.
	1.13	2.
B.	1.2	B.
II.	2.0	1.
A.	2.1	a.
B.	2.2	b.
1.	2.21	(1)
2.	2.22	(2)
III.	2.23	(a)
	3.0	(b)
		(3)
		2.

report you are preparing for the vice president may be more elaborately outlined on a large, lined legal tablet (see Figure 2.2C). Sometimes the outline may be typewritten; then the word processor is helpful because outlines are working documents that are continually revised (see Figure 2.2D). Actually, *where* and *how* you outline are unimportant; sometimes the outline may be in your mind (when you dictate), but it is important that the effective manager and communicator outline.

Outline Formats

You may use any system of symbols in your outline that makes sense to you and that is easily expandable. Most people prefer to use one of the systems shown in Figure 2.3. If you design your own system, it should be logical, understandable, and expandable.

    The Roman numeral system is used most often in schools and industry. The decimal method is generally employed by technically oriented and engineering organizations. The alphanumeric system is often used by government agencies. The important point is to use *some* system to ensure logical organization.

Develop and use a simple outline system.

Logical Development

In outlining, you arrange your ideas. How logically you sequence ideas can influence the success of your communication. There are many ways to arrange ideas. Five common orders are topical, inductive, deductive, chronological, and geographical/spatial.

Have a rationale for how you sequence your ideas.

Topical.

The topical approach focuses on the basic subjects of the message.

The most common order of development of ideas in many business contexts is the topical sequence. This simply means that the communicator divides the topic into several subtopics or subjects. For instance, in the memo in Figure 2.4 to the boss on the advantages of upgrading the office's word processing activities, the writer gives several reasons. (Note that this memo evolved from the outline shown in Figure 2.2D.) The reasons can be clearly seen: updating the facilities, increasing productivity, decreasing costs, and increasing employee pride. Although there was no reason to place one subject before any other, the topical approach clearly lays out the reasons. Also note that headings can be used to highlight each reason for the receiver. The topical approach shows the rationale for the idea. The writer thought of the ideas, planned them, and then presented them in a coherent memo.

Inductive.

Induction leads the receiver to the conclusion *after* stating the facts.

Often a way to win a receiver over is to give her the reasons and then draw the conclusion. For instance, you know that the boss favors hiring John instead of Mary. However, you think that Mary is better qualified, and you want to make your point. You make an appointment with the boss, jot down your outline on your word processor, take the printout with you, and casually talk to the boss (see Figure 2.5). Notice the inductive approach—the reasons are cited *before* presenting the conclusion or recommendation.

Deductive.

Deduction states the conclusion and *then* presents the facts.

In the deductive approach, the conclusion is stated first and then backed up with the evidence. Note that while the inductive approach is often used when you need to win the receiver over, the deductive approach is often used when you know that the receiver is sympathetic to your recommendation. Therefore, you can state the conclusion at the outset and then offer the supporting data (see Figure 2.6). Notice how the subject statement states the conclusion and how the paragraph headings can support it. In comparison, if the memo in Figure 2.6 were to be written in an inductive order, two changes would have to be made. First, the subject statement would not include the conclusion (e.g., "Considerations for an Employee/Family Open House") and the positive recommendation would be stated in a clear and persuasive paragraph *following* the reasons for the event.

Chronological.

The chronological logic follows the clock—either forward or backward.

Sometimes information is best presented in the context of time. The chronological sequence works very well when it is necessary to review activities and to specify why a particular action was made. For instance, if you are asked to brief the dean's executive committee on the activities for the student three-day Career Orientation Seminar, you may find it helpful to explain the activities in a time sequence. Figure 2.7 shows an outline of such a briefing. In an extemporaneous manner, you would elaborate and explain each activity.

Geographical/Spatial.

The geographical logic is analogous to a map.

At times, the geography or the spatial arrangement of items or events will lend themselves well to the development and presentation of the idea. Your class is touring a company's manufacturing facility. Because of the layout of the plant, the host explains what you will see from a geographical perspective: "We

FIGURE 2.4 Topical Arrangement of Ideas in Memo Format

S⬭PHISTICATED
Bikercise, Inc.

7667 Garden Street
Memphis, Tennessee   38101

To: Jacquilyn Morganstern, Department Manager

From: Edward Webber, Office Administration *EW*

Date: July 7, 198_

Re: Why We Need to Upgrade the Office Word Processing System

Facility Update—Our office does more word processing than any other in
the organization. It has been four years since equipment for our increasing word
processing load has been upgraded. Because of the added responsibilities with the six
new managers in the department and the general increase in workload, it is time to
bring our equipment up to date.

Increase Productivity—A recent survey shows that our secretarial staff is
very productivity-conscious. However, it is difficult to maintain that attitude when
the current equipment actually hinders productivity. To handle the added work load
with the same secretarial staff, up-to-date equipment is necessary. We are fortunate in
having a staff that has the right attitude; it is extremely important not to negate that
attitude with inadequate equipment. We both know of departments in the organization that have very modern equipment, but poor personnel attitudes—therefore, their
productivity is poor. In our case, we know that new equipment will substantially
increase productivity.

Reduce Costs—With modern equipment our costs will rapidly decline—
even with the capital investment included. The proposed equipment for our
department would reduce the per page cost of word processing by 35 percent.

Increase Employee Pride—Combined with our strong, positive attitude,
the new equipment would increase our employees' pride in their work. We all like to
take pride in our work. However, if we are forced to work with inadequate equipment
for an extended length of time, it is possible for pride to decrease. On that basis
alone, the new equipment would be a worthwhile investment.

Recommended Equipment—To bring our current situation with five
secretaries up to date, the following equipment is suggested:

Equipment	Estimated Cost
Text Reader	$1,200.00
Micro Manager	$ 100.00 each unit
Infowindow	$4,200.00

FIGURE 2.5   Inductive Outline

1.   The situation—John or Mary?

2.   Job Requirements

    a.   Detailed interaction

    b.   Personality beyond the department

3.   Main Observations

    a.   Mary has six years of experience

    b.   John seemed to talk down to support staff

    c.   Mary's former employees give her the highest marks

    d.   Mary will probably be a long-term employee

4.   Therefore, suggest we hire Mary

FIGURE 2.6   Deductive Arrangement of Ideas in Memo Format

Remington Manufacturing

14499 Lotus Drive
Shreveport, Louisiana 71109

January 10, 198_

TO: Coleen Jacobson, Director of Public Relations

FR: Douglas Frazier, Manager of Personnel Дƒ

RE: The Need for an Employee/Family Open House this Summer

It has been five years since the company has had an open house for the employees' family and friends. The idea of having an open house this summer is excellent and is recommended to you for the following reasons.

Increase Pride	The evidence is clear that our employees and their families take greater pride in our company and their workplace when they have an opportunity to "show it off."
See New Facility	It has been two years since our new fabrication facility has been "up." It is operating efficiently and it should be shown to all our employees and interested family members.
Beneficial Socialization	Opportunities for employees and their families to get together on a nonworkday to socialize is a tremendous advantage and one that can be accomplished through the open house.
Improve Labor Relations	By involving members of the union in the activities, they are better able to understand the company's goals; this has positive spin-offs in our labor-management relations.

Will certainly be pleased to work with you in organizing the open house if we are able to have it this summer.

When a memo is relatively short and you want to emphasize the major points more than ususal, you can use a "reversed" format like this—the conclusion in the subject line and the supporting rationale in the headings.

FIGURE 2.7   Chronological Arrangement of Ideas in an Outline (Can Also Serve as a Handout for an Oral Presentation)

<u>Monday</u> Analysis of where the jobs are

9:00-10:00 a.m.	Dean's coffee for visiting executives this day
10:15-11:50 a.m.	Panel discussion of job opportunities
12:00- 1:30 p.m.	Lunch with student council
2:00- 3:50 p.m.	Executives attend selected classes to present ideas on job opportunities in their particular industries

<u>Tuesday</u> Techniques of developing one's job objectives

10:00-10:50 a.m.	Dr. Jackson of Career Services explains career testing for students
1:00- 1:50 p.m.	Dr. Brown on L.R.S. conducts session on writing the career objective
3:00- 4:50 p.m.	Mr. and Mrs. Irl Englehart—a dual-career couple —put their own job objectives in a realistic context

<u>Wednesday</u> Presentation by organizational recruiters

7:30- 8:30 a.m.	Dean hosts recruiters for breakfast and briefs them on this year's "crop" of graduates
9:00-11:00 a.m.	At individual tables, recruiters meet with students on a "drop-in" basis
11:00-11:50 a.m.	Recruiters meet in seminar setting with faculty; Dr. Hal Wilson is monitoring; the focus is on strengthening the campus/company connection
12:00- 2:00 p.m.	Luncheon and continued discussion among faculty and recruiters
3:00- 3:50 p.m.	Recruiters make formal presentations in structured classes
4:00- 5:30 p.m.	Reception for students and faculty to interact with recruiters
6:00- 9:00 p.m.	Individual student groups host a recruiter for dinner and beneficial social interaction

FIGURE 2.8 Geographical/Spatial Development of Ideas in an Outline of an Oral Presentation

<u>The Outline of the Speaker's Presentation</u>

1. <u>Orientation Room:</u> This is where we hold many executive sessions; you will noe that the room is designed for maximum interaction—every person can see every other person. There are a variety of audio and visual supports for the speaker(s) and participants. (Emphasize safety, wearing goggles, and staying with group.)

2. <u>Foundry:</u> Although many firms have eliminated their foundry operations, we have retained ours. Here the basic "guts" of our product are cast. It is a rather dirty and hot place to work.

3. <u>Assembly:</u> Here you see the product move along a line where pieces are continually added and the total product is assembled. Take particular note of the "stockless" production aspects of our assembly operation.

4. <u>Fabrication:</u> Of course, fabrication takes place before assembly, but on our tour it is easier to see the "fab" department after the product is assembled. In "fab" we produce many of the elements that are placed into our products; a substantial amount of the fabrication operation involves sheet-metal work.

5. <u>Shipping:</u> A well-made product must be packaged and shipped in a quality manner. You will see all kinds of packaging innovations and ways in which products can be shipped to customers nation-wide within eighteen hours.

6. <u>Orientation Room:</u> Back here our various department managers will join us to answer your questions.

will start here in the orientation room; move directly to the foundry; move next to the fabrication department; then see the assembly area; and finally overview the shipping area" (see Figure 2.8). This may not be the sequence in which the product is manufactured, but it is the geographical route of your tour. Pamphlets on vacation tours often put the sites in a geographical sequence: "you start in Germany, move south to France, farther south to Switzerland, and conclude the tour in Italy."

Formatting

Your format selection influences how your message is received.

It is difficult to plan an activity without envisioning the end result. When Sophia considers expanding her company's manufacturing facilities, she sees the addition to the building and initially what the factory layout might look like. The envisioning activity aids her planning. The same is true for communication. In the case of written communication, how we format the materials is crucial. As you plan a memo, for example, think through what the eventual memo might look like. Formatting will help you in focusing on the receiver and eventually getting your message across. Consider the letters and memos represented in this chapter. Each has a distinctive format. The ideas jump out at the receiver. That did not just happen—the format works hand-in-hand with the ideas being presented. Formatting is not an activity that is stuck on at the end of the planning process; it evolves in concert with the entire planning process. Compare the outline in Figure 2.2D with the memo in Figure 2.4. You can see the relationship between the ideas in the outline and the eventual headings and format in the resulting memorandum.

QUICK REVIEW

Planning is an integral part of management and communication. The planning process is simple and when employed will keep one's communications on target. The elements of identifying the purpose, outlining, and formatting the message are all part of effective planning for effective communications.

EXECUTIVE SUMMARY

To: Business Communication Students

From: David N. Bateman and Norman B. Sigband

Subject: Planning: The Manager's and Communicator's First Principle

Planning is the basis for effective communication.

This chapter presents a planning process that consists of a series of steps to ensure that the final communication will prove effective:

1. establish the need for the communication;
2. identify the goals of the communication;

3. consider the policy and procedures;
4. prepare a forecast (of the receiver);
5. develop an outline (a plan);
6. revise the plan;
7. test the plan; and
8. implement the plan.

Perhaps the most vital part of this process is the development of the basic outline or plan. That outline can be completed on a scrap of paper, a formal sheet, or in the margin of the letter or memo to which you are replying. The vital aspect, however, is to make a plan *before* you write that report, memo, or letter or give that speech.

There are several different ways to draw up an outline, as well as several different orders of development. Among these orders of development are topical, inductive, deductive, chronological, and geographical/spatial.

In addition to the eight steps listed above, the format (layout and appearance) of the communication should be included in the planning process.

DISCUSSION GENERATORS

1. *Why Plan?* Why is planning an integral part of both management and communication?
2. *Reducing Memos and Meetings.* How can planning help an organization reduce the number of meetings and memos it generates?
3. *Who Plans to Fail?* Explain the concept, "If you fail to plan, you plan to fail."
4. *Too Much Planning?* Give an example of a potential communicator taking too much time to plan a communication.
5. *Revised Plans.* Why is revision such an integral part of the planning process?
6. *Where Should You Outline?* Cite examples of when it would be advantageous to prepare an outline in each of the following forms:
   a. on a scrap of paper
   b. in the margin of a letter
   c. on a legal pad
   d. on a typewriter
   e. a word processor
   f. in your mind
7. *Relationships.* What is the relationship between the plan, the outline, and the eventual format of a document?
8. *Do People Really Plan?* If planning is so vital to management and to communication, why does it seem that many people don't plan? For instance:
   a. Do you have a clear plan for your current term?
   b. Does the student organization of which you are a member have a precise objective for accomplishments this year?
   c. Is there really a plan on how your current course work will affect your professional career?

   d. Do you have a workable plan for your career, or is it actually a case of "let's see what happens"?

9. *Forecast Before You Plan.* Cite an example of how forecasting relates to a communication you are planning; e.g., you desire to take a spring-break trip to a popular college vacation spot. However, you anticipate (forecast) that your parents will not be in favor of such a trip. How does the forecast influence your communication to your parents?

10. *A Trial Balloon.* Considering the situation in item 9, suppose you figure out a way to write your parents a letter about your vacation. How could you test the letter before you actually send it?

11. *Objectives.* You are to give a five-minute presentation to a group of transfer students who have recently arrived on your campus. State an objective for a talk you would give, and choose one of the logical orders of development. For instance, to inform the transfer students of professional organizations in the Business department, the topical arrangement would be: the Accounting Club; the Society for Advancement of Management; Alpha Kappa Psi; Pi Sigma Epsilon.

12. *Induction.* Why might it be best to use the inductive order of development in a communication to an audience that might be initially hostile to the conclusion you are going to draw in your communication?

13. *Deductive Subject Statement.* When using the deductive approach, it is possible to incorporate the conclusion in the subject statement of the memo. Why is this advantageous?

14. *Must the Outline Be Written?* Although it is not always necessary to prepare a written outline (you can do it mentally), there may be times when a written outline will be very helpful. What would be the advantages of preparing a detailed outline on a word processor?

15. *Objective Criteria.* What are the prerequisites for a good statement of an objective?

16. *Short Objectives.* Why should the objective of your communication be short—perhaps not even a complete sentence?

17. *Planning Is Time-consuming.* If it takes time to plan, and you are in a rush to get a memo written, isn't it counterproductive to work through the several steps of the planning process?

18. *What's Easiest to Revise?* Explain why it is easier and faster to revise an outline of a short report than it is to revise the actual report.

19. *A Quick Outline.* Time yourself—you have five minutes to outline a three-minute talk on "Common Communication Pitfalls of College Students." Prepare the outline.

20. *Inductive and Deductive Development.* Here is the conclusion of a talk you will present to college freshmen: "All college students, at some point in their college career, should live in a campus dorm." Develop two simple outlines using the deductive and the inductive orders of development, respectively.

APPLICATIONS FOR BUSINESS

21. *Objectives Provide Focus.* You are a senior majoring in accounting and are going to make a fifteen-minute presentation to a group of freshmen. Complete each of the following initial phrases of possible objective statements:

a. To persuade the freshmen to _____.

b. To inform the students about _____.

c. To brief the audience on _____.

d. To analyze with the students the _____.

22. *Wandering.* Sometimes we start to write without an objective and end up just wandering. The following letter seems to do just that.

a. First of all, prepare a simple statement of the objective for this situation.

b. Outline the communication.

c. Rewrite the letter.

```
                                        1776 Main Street
                                        St. Louis, MO  53207


Mr. Benson Washington, Personnel Director
Abbington Corporation
Box 66
Peoria, Illinois 61600

Dear Mr. Washington:

        In college this semester I am taking an exciting Personnel
course taught by Dr. Mary Jefferson. It is ironic that I have the op-
portunity to involve two important "names" in our nation's history as
I investigate some history of benefits in U.S.A. firms.

        Benefits have evolved in our nation. From a period when there
was hardly anything for an employee—except a minuscule wage—to a
situation today where employees receive a good wage plus excellent
benefits.

        My project in the course involves tracing the evolution of
dental benefits for employees and families. Because your firm has a
long history of providing this benefit, could you please provide the
following information:

    • Why?—What caused your firm to start offering this benefit
      to employees in the 1940s?

    • Children.—When were employee children included? Why is it
      advantageous to you to include them?

    • Cost Changes.—How have the costs of this benefit changed
      during the years; is there a marked difference in the
      costs between younger employees with teenagers and older
      employees?

    Your response to these items will be of substantial benefit to
me in preparing my class project.

                                        Sincerely,


                                        James Madison
```

23. *Observations on Logical Developments.* For each of the following, be prepared to describe the inherent order of the logical development.
    a. The full and complete address on an envelope to a corporate executive of a Fortune 500 firm.
    b. The table of contents for this text.
    c. The directions for a freshman on a snipe hunt.

24. *The Process.* The planning process is the same whether *planning* to add vitamins to the line of products at Sophia's Sophisticated Bikercise or *planning* to write a memo to the vice president of your college concerning the lack of parking spots for students. In a concise format similar to that below, clearly state your plan for communicating on one of the problems.

Add Vitamins to Product Line	Planning Process	Writing V.P. on Lack of Parking
Need for vitamins	Need	Need for memo
Sales objective	Objective	What you want to see happen
Laws	Policies/ procedures	Rules, regulations
Relationship of pills to peddling	Forecast	V.P.'s attitude is negative
Steps to accomplish goal	Outline	Major points
Hone	Revise	Edit
Test market in California	Test	Bounce draft off a faculty member
Set up sales organization	Implement	Send the memo

25. *A Business Plan.* You have an idea on how your student organization—Beta Beta Chi—can make money by printing and selling T-shirts for students at Halloween. Work through your plan in writing, employing each of the steps in the planning process.

COMMUNICATION CHECK-UPS

26. It is John's decision and *therefour* he must live with the ramifications.
27. Send the *questionaire* only to active employees—skip the retirees.
28. He said, "Implement to procedures immediately".
29. However, keep the policy intact while changing the procedures.
30. Her address is:

     Miss Susan C. Marriott
     1717 Conley Avenue
     Galesburg, IL 61401

31. Me and Ann plan to attend the conference.
32. Be prepared, be alert and don't forget to have enthusiasm.
33. Ask the speaker to be ready to give her talk at 7:15 p.m.
34. The proposed plant layout is ideal. (See attachment #2.)
35. Carnaghi University expects each student to have a personal computer and encourages students to purchase equipment that is compatable with the University's mainframe.

Executive Introduction

Southwest Texas
Methodist Hospital

MEMORANDUM

TO: New Staff Personnel

COPY TO:

FROM: Jill Olson, Administrative Instructor _J Olson_

DATE: July 10, 198_

SUBJECT: Activating Our Ideas & Using Appropriate Language

Communication is always important, but in our organization it is critical. A misused word can be upsetting or even life-threatening to a person who is already ill.

In a coming seminar, we will discuss communication in detail. Please review the enclosed material, which stresses the topics we will discuss in our seminar:

   You-Orientation. In all your communications, think first of the other person and present information considering his or her situation.

   Attention. Before providing detailed explanations, be sure you have the receiver's attention.

   Simplicity. Our goal is always understanding; therefore, use simple terms to explain your ideas.

   Courtesy. Be thoughtful and polite in all your interactions—with staff, visitors, and patients.

   Techniques. The techniques for effective writing are simple: avoid "fog"; be correct; and use effective formats, the active voice, and parallelism.

The entire staff of Methodist Hospital looks forward to interacting with you; by employing these communication guides our interactions will be efficient and meaningful.

Encl.

Putting Ideas Into Words: Activating Your Ideas

WHAT YOU CAN LEARN BY STUDYING THIS CHAPTER

Getting your good ideas accepted is generally dependent upon selecting the appropriate language to represent those ideas. It is not enough to say "I have a good idea." The effective manager and successful communicator have both good ideas *and* excellent language skills with which to express them. Regardless of your chosen vocation, the way in which you present your ideas to others will have a profound influence on your ability to succeed in your career. In this chapter, some easy-to-use concepts and techniques are provided to help you activate your ideas.

Make your ideas move.

For years, scholars have wrestled with ways of teaching language usage so ideas can move expeditiously. From the many ways that have been discovered, there are six key "action concepts" that are important in expediting your ideas. We will explore these concepts in an organizational context, because it is in the organization that you will continually strive to win people over to your ideas. These six concepts are nearly equal in importance, so the order of presentation is not significant. However, for your particular situation, you may feel that one concept, such as "interest and attention," is more important than the others. Following the six key concepts for activating your ideas, several techniques to aid you in smoothing the delivery of your ideas will be reviewed.

ACTION CONCEPT #1: THE YOU-FOCUS

I versus You

Consider some of the recent materials you have written—a letter to your parents, a memo to a colleague, or a report submitted in another class. How many of your sentences start with "I"? The I-orientation is a major roadblock to effective communication, and it is also a substantial squelcher in getting ideas accepted. It will be a challenge to turn your communications around after years of writing and thinking from an *I*-orientation. However, if you sincerely desire to have your ideas accepted by others, you must relate to other people—not to yourself; you need to adopt the *you-focus*.

Getting Things Done Through People

The you-orientation is good human relations and good management.

Too many I's may reflect laziness.

Management is often defined as "getting things done through others." If this is true, it is more important to communicate with others (the you-orientation) than to communicate to ourselves (the I-orientation). The easiest way to spot the I-orientation is to look for the words "I," "we," "me," or "our." But just getting rid of the personal references does not necessarily solve the problem.

What is so amazing about the I-orientation is that it is completely unnecessary. Read the following I-items; note that the personal reference from these letters can be removed and the message is still very clear:

Could you please assist ~~me~~ by providing information on the following items?
Your cooperation in getting ~~me~~ the information listed below will help in creating a quality product.

The You-oriented Thinking Process

In order to turn your thinking around you must think clearly about the receiver. Look at the I-oriented statements in Figure 3.1—can you turn them around? Remember, these statements are from letters—the writer has signed her name at the bottom—so there is no problem of the receiver wondering who is writing, who is asking, or who is thinking.

FIGURE 3.1   "I"—A Writing and Thinking Problem

"I"	VS.	**"YOU"**
I am writing you about the bank project; I feel it needs some clarification.		The bank project, which is of interest to you, needs some clarification.
I want to thank you for your support.		Thank you for your support.
We at Bellcraft appreciate your business.		Your business is appreciated by Bellcraft.
Bellcraft appreciates your business.		Your business is appreciated.
Our intent is to serve you well.		You deserve the best.
It is my opinion that your company would be most pleased with the modified system.		Your company will like the modified system.

You will not achieve the you-focus by simply eliminating the word "I." ~~You must change your perspective and attitude.~~ In this manner, you stand a better chance of activating (not just expressing) your ideas.

The I-focus reveals a logical pitfall.

FIGURE 3.2   Don't Be a Dull Communicator

Boring	Interesting
Introducing a speaker	
"It is a pleasure and an honor to introduce you to . . ."	"You have a special treat this evening."
Responding to a memo from your boss	
"Regarding yours of the 20th concerning the Dan Iltoff matter . . ."	"A probable solution on the Dan Iltoff matter is to . . ."
Transmitting a report to a manager	
"After three months of diligent work the results can be transmitted to you."	"The results show that. . ."
Congratulating a colleague on a promotion	
"I saw the article in the paper concerning you and wanted to write this note."	"You have done it again!"
Inquiring for information	
"For a project I'm doing at the University I need some information about your firm's finances."	"Your firm has been a leader in developing new financial strategies."

Do you get the feeling you didn't gain their attention?

ACTION CONCEPT #2: INTEREST AND ATTENTION

Most business communications should not be gaudy or too sparkly. At the same time, they need not be dull and boring. It is the responsibility of the communicator to gain the interest and the attention of the receiver. Whether you are writing or speaking, if you want to activate your ideas, you need to motivate the receiver. The concept is valid when you are writing a paragraph, a one-page memo, a long report, or presenting a one-minute oral briefing or a fifty-minute detailed spoken analysis. Look at the examples in Figure 3.2, and note how it is possible to enliven them and gain the attention and the interest of the receiver.

> **The sender does not have a right to bore the receiver.**

The you-focus and the concept of interest and attention tend to work hand-in-hand. Both of these concepts direct the message toward the receiver, not to oneself. After all, the objective of communication is not to create a cocoon of your own verbiage, but to gain the attention and spark the interest of the receiver.

ACTION CONCEPT #3: SIMPLICITY

It's Smart to Be Simple

To write in an understandable and forthright manner does not mean you are a simpleton or a dullard. It is the responsibility of the communicator to state ideas so that they can be easily received. If you want your ideas to be accepted, they should be stated in an understandable manner. The simplest language stands the best chance of being understood. Figure 3.3 shows some of the chief conspirators in making communication too complex—heaviness, wordiness, triteness, and stuffiness.

> **If you desire action, *keep it simple*.**

At one time it was thought stylish for the business person to write with complicated language. This may have increased the status of the communicator, but it did not contribute to moving ideas effectively and efficiently in the organization. The modern manager must rapidly move paper and ideas in the organization. The more simply they are stated, the faster they can be routed through the organization.

In the complex examples in Figure 3.4, consider the nature of the complexity and then read the first rewrite. Be sure to identify the clutter that we often place in our communications, such as words and phrases like "thus." In rewriting for simplicity, envision a streamlined automobile: It is flush, without awkward protuberances disrupting the flow; it is designed for speed and efficient movement; nothing is added to slow it down. Using language in that same manner allows you to activate your ideas.

Be Conversational

Another way of writing in a simple manner involves using a conversational tone. In the United States, business is conducted and communication is transmitted in a conversational manner. As a general rule, write as you talk. If your writing is stuffy and doesn't *sound* like you—stop—you are probably getting complex.

> **The conversational approach is understandable.**

FIGURE 3.3   Some Kinds of Complexity and How to Remedy Them

Complex First Draft	Nature of Complexity	Revised Statement
Each and every one of you should be happy, proud, and, last but not least, pleased that our department exceeded the goal.	Triteness	Congratulations! Your work allowed us to exceed our goal.
The aforementioned individual incurred and did not pay the tax liability on the property.	Heavy	She did not pay the property tax.
Thus, the rhetorical elements are in juxtaposition to the message.	Unconversational	The writing is confusing.
Therefore, it is simple to see that the elements of the benefit package are congruent with the needs of the employees.	Wordy	The benefits match the employees' needs.

FIGURE 3.4 Simplicity Can Be a Virtue

The Complex Communication	The Problem	A First Rewrite
Thus, the four (4) departments should utilize the beverage dispensers contiguous to their respective departments.	Heavy, wordy, overly formal, not conversational	The four departments should use the drink machines next to their departments.
Per your request on the Axley project, I am writing you to explain some additional options.	Wordy, nonsense words	Additional options on the Axley project include:

ACTION CONCEPT #4: ETIQUETTE

A sincere consideration of other people—relating to them at their own level and addressing them in a straightforward and personable manner—is not only courteous, but it helps you in getting your ideas accepted. In business and most other organizations, courtesy is never out of fashion. To be courteous does not mean being trite or always giving "yes" responses. But regardless of the message you are initiating, being considerate of other people and their feelings helps to establish rapport.

Courtesy and communication go hand-in-hand.

Timing

The "when" of your communication is important (see Chapter 12, "Communicating in Special Situations"). The busy executive cannot always respond to all requests immediately. Some organizations have response-time guidelines. However, it is generally the busy person who does a better job of getting things done on time than the individual with less to do.

Time the arrival of your message for maximum impact.

There are other aspects of timing to consider. For instance, try not to phone an executive the first thing Monday morning, because that is when she is attempting to get organized for the week. Generally, it would also be poor timing to phone the small-business owner at 5:00 p.m., when he is probably attempting to close down the operation. If the boss is in the office making last-minute preparations for an overseas trip, it is probably not the time to discuss some relatively minor "back burner" matter.

When a message is transmitted will affect *how* well the message will be received. Have you ever noticed the student who engages the professor in some personal conversation (e.g., last week's assignment) just as he or she is entering the lecture hall to give a major lecture? On the other hand, another student sees the professor during office hours. Who is going to get the better response and feedback from the professor?

Requisites for Courtesy

Guidelines for business communication courtesy.

Your ideas stand a better chance of being accepted when they are presented courteously. Some of the requisite considerations for attaining action with the courteous approach include:

1. *You-focus:* Developing a strong you-orientation with the receiver.
2. *Pleasing Language:* Using polite language such as "thank you," "please," and "sincerely" without overusing it or being trite.
3. *Respectfulness:* Indicating a respect for the other person and his or her ideas.
4. *Shoot Straight:* Communicating in a straightforward instead of a condescending or ambiguous manner.
5. *Conversational:* Establishing a friendly conversational tone instead of an impersonal, "to-whom-it-may-concern" approach.

A major factor in getting your ideas accepted in an organization is that people like you. Thoughtful communication can go a long way in aiding individuals to like you.

ACTION CONCEPT #5: THE ACTIVE VOICE

Don't slow your message down by adding molasses—the passive voice.

The passive voice slows the transmission and effectiveness of communications in an organization. The syrupy and slow passive voice does not reflect the aggressiveness or quickness of business. Also, the passive voice is generally wordy. It tends to hide ideas and therefore is generally not considered businesslike.

About the only time that you will want to use the passive voice is to side-step harshly criticizing another individual. For instance, for the sake of courtesy you may want to say "The material reviewed by Betty appears to have some flaws," instead of "Betty's materials are flawed." The active voice is more interesting, direct, and less wordy—it aids you in activating your ideas.

A few examples of statements placed in the passive voice are shown in Figure 3.5. Recognize how easy it is to activate the idea by placing it in the active voice.

Sometimes it is necessary to go from the active voice to the passive. The three statements in Figure 3.6 in the active voice are a bit crude and rude. Placing these statements in the passive voice can display a sense of courtesy.

FIGURE 3.5   From Passive to Active

Passive	Active
1. A sales increase was observed.	1. Company sales increased.
2. The firm was harmed by the recession.	2. The recession hurt the firm.
3. A negative reflection on the class was made by the poor exam scores.	3. The poor exam scores are an embarrassment.

ACTION CONCEPT #6: DEFOGGING YOUR LANGUAGE

For the most part, communication is an art. As such, there are subtleties that enter into making language complex. Although long sentences can be clear and understandable if well crafted, as a general rule, as sentences and words get longer, the reading becomes less comprehendable. And, we have already seen that the ultimate goal of communication is to be clearly understood the first time.

Lengthy words and sentences create communication problems.

In the interest of improving the efficiency and effectiveness of our language, scholars have developed readability formulas. The basis of these formulas is a technique of numerical analysis that can be applied to the written language to determine how it might be received by others. Determining the readability of one's own writing enables one to measure the effectiveness in advance, thereby becoming a more effective communicator.

In this field of study, there are two individuals who are the dominant leaders—Rudolph Flesch and Robert Gunning. Each proposes some relatively simple formulas for determining the complexity of language and, therefore, its readability. The formulas concentrate on two factors:

1. Sentence length (complex structure), and
2. Word length (complex words).

FIGURE 3.6 From Active to Passive (for Courtesy Considerations)

	Active		Passive
	Active		**Passive**
1.	Mary goofed on this tabulation.	1.	An error was made in this tabulation.
2.	Answer the phone properly.	2.	The way the phone is answered needs review.
3.	Retrenchment is needed today.	3.	Under these circumstances, a retrenchment program is necessary.

Gunning's Formula is one of the most widely accepted, and you can use this Fog Index to measure the readability of your writing.

As we look at the techniques for activating your ideas, it is beneficial to become familiar with the concept of readability formulas. The concept is to get the clutter out of your communication so you can move ideas more effectively in the organization. Again, as a general rule, short sentences and short words promote the movement of your ideas.

One of the most widely used readability formulas is Gunning's *Fog Index*. You can use this index to measure the readability of your writing.

The index has eight simple steps:*

Step	Procedure	Your Figures
1.	Select a passage with at least 100 words; stop your count with the sentence ending after you reach 100 words. The number of words is:	_____
2.	Count the number of sentences within the passage.	_____

---

*Gunning, New Guide, pp. 9–11.

3. Divide the number of words by the number of sentences.   _____

4. Count the number of "hard" words in the passage. These are words with three syllables or more. Do not count those that are capitalized, those made up of short easy words like *bookkeeping,* or verbs that are formed by adding *-es* or *-ed.* The result is the number of polysyllabic words.   _____

5. Divide the number of polysyllabic words by the total number of words in the passage.   _____

6. Multiply the answer to step 5 by 100; the result is the number of "hard" words per 100 (step 6).   _____

7. Add the average sentence length (step 3) and the number of "hard" words per 100 (step 6).   _____

8. To determine the Fog Index, multiply the answer to step 7 by .4. The Fog index is: _____

If the index is low (8–12), your writing will be read and comprehended easily, for it is at the eighth- to twelfth-grade level. If the index is at about 16 (senior college level), comprehension will be more difficult. If the index is at, say, 23, the writing is probably rather "misty"; and at about 28, "the fog is rolling in."

The differences in readability of the two similar pieces in Figure 3.7 are striking. Item "A" has an index of about 16.5; item "B" has an index of about 7.5. Compare the two pieces to see what makes the difference.

The Fog Index is recommended not only for analyzing writing in a business communications course, but also for your writing throughout your career and for helping your subordinates improve their communications. It has a variety of applications in business, such as monitoring the readability of letters sent to clients, company magazines sent to employees, warranties prepared for customers, and pension agreements for retirees.

The Fog Index has several uses.

The point is, indexing is widely accepted and widely used in business organizations. It is a simple, handy tool that you can apply to your writing so you can get your ideas quickly through to the receivers.

TECHNIQUES FOR ACTIVATING YOUR IDEAS

Beyond the six action concepts, there are also many techniques that you will find helpful in putting some oomph behind your ideas. Those cited here are the more common ones.

Parallelism

When presenting a series of ideas, you can draw attention to and bring unity and coherence to your writing with parallel words or phrases. If format is considered in conjunction with parallelism, it is possible to clearly communicate what you want the reader to do. In Figure 3.8, the cost-containment techniques are stressed not only with

Parallelism helps guide the reader.

FIGURE 3.7   Comparing Similar Messages with Different Fog Indexes

Item A Safety	FOG Contributer/Eliminator	Item B Safety
Since general safety conditions are one of the responsibilities you have within your department, we would appreciate your disseminating the following information.	← disseminating aware →	Safety in your department is your responsibility. Please see that your people are made aware of hazards and that they take measures to prevent them.
On a recent inspection of all areas, the most obvious hazard detected was the manner in which office equipment is placed or used in relation to personnel movement or traffic.	← relation to placed →	A recent inspection revealed a chief hazard to be office equipment placed in the way of people moving about.
All personnel in your area should be made aware of possible safety hazards and take precautionary measures at all times so that a high "safety level" may be maintained.	← irrelevant information	
1. Electrical cords on equipment such as typewriters, adding machines, etc., should not be permitted to lie loose on the floor where the possibility of someone tripping over them exists.	← long sentences short sentences →	1. Electrical cords of typewriters, adding machines, etc., should not lie loose on the floor. Someone may trip over them.
2. When not in immediate use, desk and file drawers should be kept closed at all times.	← wordy crisp →	2. Keep desk and file drawers closed when not in use.

FIGURE 3.8   **Techniques of Parallelism**

Costs will be kept in bounds in the following ways:

* <u>Increasing sales</u> will aid the . . .

* <u>Declining overheads</u> in the regional offices . . .

* <u>Promoting retirements</u> is another way to . . .

Items you should gain in reading this report include:

* <u>Learn</u> the costs involved in old inventories.

* <u>Appreciate</u> the new computerized accounting system.

* <u>Understand</u> the elements in the zero-based approach.

the parallel phrases, but also the emphasis in the format; the emphatic and clear objectives of the report jump out at the reader; you are to *learn, appreciate,* and *understand.*

Emphasis

You can emphasize an idea in a variety of ways, such as:

1. Using a word ironically, "Her idea is so 'dumb' that it will work." (Meaning the idea really isn't so dumb.)
2. Using a blatantly incorrect word or phrase, "You ain't seen half the benefits of this proposal."

Adding emphasis can make words, phrases, and ideas stand out for the receiver.

3. Using underlining (italics) or full capitalization, "The plan is *practical, reliable,*and *workable*" *or* "Please inform ALL EMPLOYEES of the new smoking policy."

Format

How you package your ideas is important.

The way that you format your material can help you in moving your ideas. Throughout this text, various formatting techniques are used (they are covered thoroughly in Chapter 6) but here are some simple format techniques:

- listing items vertically instead of horizontally,
- surrounding major ideas with more space, surrounding less important points with less space, and
- using headings judiciously.

You do not want to bury a good idea; the format can make your good idea stand out for the reader so your ideas can be accepted. With many word processors and printers it is possible to use other formatting techniques to add emphasis to ideas, such as bold print, right-justified margins, and various symbols.

Correctness

Errors like mispellings slow and harm communications.

Some may say that correctness is not a communication technique, but the incorrect statement or the incorrect figure is devastating when you are trying to have your ideas accepted. A president's nominee to a U.S. circuit court, the second-highest position in the court system, received tremendous criticism in the Senate because some of the briefs the nominee submitted had spelling errors. He may have had a keen legal mind, and he may have been a good person, but the lack of correctness in his materials brought him under severe criticism. The point is that the lack of correctness can hinder acceptance of you and your ideas; or, to state it positively, correctness is a technique that will keep your receiver on target.

QUICK REVIEW

Never assume your ideas will stand on their own; your choice of language, style, and communication techniques can do much to activate your ideas. The six action concepts can be employed to make sure you are not slowing down your ideas. The techniques of parallelism, emphasis, format, and correctness help the receiver latch on in order to grab your ideas.

EXECUTIVE SUMMARY

To: Business Communication Students

From: David N. Bateman and Norman B. Sigband

Subject: Putting Ideas into Words: Activating Your Ideas

Word choice and the use of language are important in having your ideas accepted. There are six key "action concepts" for success.

Action Concept #1: The You-focus. Make every effort to orient your communication from the reader's or listener's point of view. Rather than talking about what this action will do for you, indicate how it will benefit him or her. Think of the other person's need; avoid the frequent use of "I."

Action Concept #2: Interest and Attention. Arouse interest in the very first portion of your communication. This may be done by a variety of "attention" catching openings that involve the reader or listener.

Action Concept #3: Simplicity. For the easy assimilation of your ideas, keep your communication simple (easy to understand), and write in a conversational manner.

Action Concept #4: Etiquette. Establish rapport with your communicatee. Do so in a courteous and personable manner that is respectful as well as conversational.

Action Concept #5: The Active Voice. Make your communication come "alive" and "move" by using the active—not the passive—voice.

Action Concept #6: Defogging your Language. Make your writing and speaking easy to comprehend by using, on the whole, relatively short sentences and words. The Gunning readability formula will help measure the comprehension level of your writing.

In addition to the action concepts, note the importance of the following in achieving writing that is clear:

- use of parallelism
- use of emphasis
- format of materials: plenty of white space, generous use of headings, and listing of data where logical
- checking for correctness

DISCUSSION GENERATORS

1. *What Makes Fog?* What are the two factors in a sentence that probably contribute most to fog?
2. *Passive vs. Active.* Cite an example of when it would be best to use the passive voice instead of the active voice.

3. *Name the Short Word.* What is the short, simple word, which often starts sentences, that can turn a reader or listener off?

4. *Emphasize That Point!* Emphasis can be achieved in a variety of ways. Illustrate three ways to provide emphasis in the following sentence, "It would be nice if you would pay particular attention to the Fog Index."

5. *Writing and Talking Similar?* Are the authors serious when they suggest, "Write as you would talk?"

6. *Similar Concepts.* In what ways are the you-orientation and the concept of etiquette similar?

7. *Parallelism.* Place the following list in parallel form.

   The following students are to report to the ticket office:
   —students majoring in accounting
   —English majors
   —individuals pursuing Dental Tech. study
   —those who have an undeclared major

8. *Continuum of Language.* There are "degrees" of word selection somewhat similar to the degrees on the thermometer. That is, the same idea can be expressed with either a "hot" or "cold" word. For the following rather "neutral" words, present "cool" and kind words on the left side, and words that would be "hot" and more pointed on the right side.

Cool Word	Neutral Word	Hot Word
officer	cop	pig
	car	
	executive	
	professor	

9. *Eliminate the I-orientation.* Quickly rewrite or restate the following I-oriented statements, turning them into positive, you-oriented statements.
   a. I am writing you to express an interest in employment.
   b. Because I know your son John, it has been suggested I contact you about a project at school.
   c. I want to thank you for providing the information on your company.
   d. We are pleased to accept your invitation to attend the open house at the Mayfair Co.
   e. Our thoughts are with you as you open your new office.

10. *Just One Will Mess It Up!* Why does a single act of incorrectness (such as one misspelled word or one erroneous number) tend to diminish the worth of one's entire communication?

11. *Be Polite.* Why do business and other organizations tend to place such a premium on etiquette?

12. *Letter Etiquette.* How are the elements of business etiquette reflected in the communications from business organizations?

13. *Will "Smart" Ideas Stand Alone?* Accept or reject the following statement by a straight-A student: "Activating ideas with gimmicks like low fog and the you-orientation is for the less bright; my intelligent ideas will stand on their own."

14. *Can the Idea Be Separated?* If communication errors can ruin the idea, is it wise for teachers to give one grade "for the idea" and another grade "for the grammar and writing style?" Discuss this system versus giving one grade for the total message.

15. *Uninteresting Is Safe.* React to the following statement: "Business, by its nature, tends to be conservative. Therefore, it is inappropriate to use a writing style that creates interest and grabs the reader's attention."

16. *Is There More to the I-orientation?* True or false: Eliminate the "I's," and you will have automatically eliminated the I-orientation. Explain and illustrate your answer.

17. *High Fog Means High Intelligence.* Respond to a fellow student who says, "I'm going to be a graduate of this college, and my parents didn't send me here to talk like a simpleton; it is vital that the index of my writing consistently be at 18 or above."

18. *The I-orientation Beyond Writing.* What are some guidelines you might suggest to college students entering the corporate world for avoiding the I-orientation in their social interactions in business.

19. *Get It Right the First Time.* Explain and exemplify how the Fog Index can help the receiver obtain the message on the first reading.

20. *Where Else Can the Index Work?* For what communications besides letters, memos, and reports might you be able to successfully apply the Fog Index in your work? Please name them and explain.

APPLICATIONS FOR BUSINESS

21. *Turn on the Defogger.* The following sentences suffer from long words that increase their fogginess. Without substantially altering the meaning of these sentences, rewrite them using shorter words.
    a. The beverages were consumed by all participants.
    b. The utilization of the facility was substantial.
    c. Eleemosynary organizations can implement business principles also.

22. *Turn on the Defoggers Again.* The following sentence suffers from simply being too long. Shorten it.

    Therefore, it is recommended that the department alter its recruiting practices, institute an educational program, promote promotion from within, increase the opportunities for cross-department interactions, and strive for a more positive approach to human relations.

23. *It's Backwards.* The I-orientation looks at the communicator's perspective before looking at the receiver's viewpoint. Since the communicator is interested in winning the receiver over to his or her message, the I-orientation is not only rude, it's backwards. Turn the following messages around.

    a. I received your letter of October 19 and I want to thank you for agreeing to the matter.

    b. It is my opinion that your approach to labor relations is modern and refreshing.

    c. We at Reynolds are pleased to welcome you to our organization.

    d. Our perspective of the problem is that student fees should not be committed to extraneous factors—especially those of a very personal nature.

    e. Students, from our study, who speak a second language seem to have a better appreciation of world affairs.

24. *Action!* If you want your ideas to have action, they need to be stated in the active voice! Give the following statements a strong active voice!

    a. A sharp drop in productivity was noted from the results of our study.

    b. The competition was beat by the Bently Company's developing new production technologies.

    c. We were invited by the Bently Company to observe some of their production technologies.

25. *Know When to Be Passive.* The passive voice is not always wrong. When you desire to "hide" or not identify the source of action, it is desirable to use the passive voice. Place the following in the passive voice.

    a. George made an error in promoting this procedure.

    b. Your past-due bill means legal action must be taken.

COMMUNICATION CHECK-UPS

26. First, look at the college catalog. Secondly, study the requirements for your major. And finally, check the times that you are available to take classes.

27. Submit your budget recommendations for the next physical year by May 1.

28. The Reynold's Corporation is on the New York Stock Exchange and the corporation also is listed in the *Fortune* 500.

29. The article in *Fortune*, the Best Managed Firms in America Today, cited Reynolds at the top of the list.

30. In college you need to be prepared to work hard, study diligently, etc.

31. Guss' report was outstanding. OK

32. Her address is:

> Dr. Karen Kathre, Ph.D.
> Department of Physilogy
> Bentworthy College
> Bently, MA 01895

33. 6 people from our department attended the special session.

34. The file is unmoveable from the room.

35. The boxs should remain in the files until security grants approval for removal.

Executive
Introduction

Holiday Corporation
The leader in hospitality

3796 Lamar Avenue
Memphis, TN 38195 USA

HOLIDAY
CORPORATION

February 25, 198_

Dr. John Penrose
Department of Management
University of Texas
Austin, Texas 78712

Dear Dr. Penrose:

It will be fine to come to your campus on Tuesday, April 10 to (1) make a presentation to your class concerning "Excellence" and (2) interact informally with students interested in pursuing a career in hotel management.

In my discussion dealing with excellence in communication, the following topics are crucial:

Appearance: The element of appearance is vital. In order to get to first base, things must not only be good, they must also look good.

Proof It: In all of our operations we have ways to make sure work is completed to our standards. The same applies to our writing; we are all taught how to edit, and our supervisors periodically evaluate our writing to insure its quality. Remember, before sending anything out, take time to proof it meticulously. If it isn't done right, do it over.

Electronics: From our telecommunications system to our personal computers, we are highly automated. We all write on the word processor; it definitely speeds up the editing, polishing, and proofing processes.

Please call if you have suggestions on how the presentation could be improved to benefit your students. Giving your students the opportunity to learn of the current concern for corporate communication excellence is thoughtful - it permeates most of the manager's activities today.

Sincerely,

John Merkin

John Merkin
Consultant
Hotel Management Systems Implementation

Editing: Working to Produce Excellent Communications

WHAT YOU CAN LEARN BY STUDYING THIS CHAPTER

All things considered, writing is a relatively easy task. It's the rewriting that takes the communicator's time and effort. Learning to edit his or her own work is probably the hardest task for the communicator. First, it means that you must *look* at your writing in an objective and critical way; second, you must know how to *identify* your shortcomings; and third, you need to know how to *apply* the elements of effective writing to your work. The rewriting concepts apply to both your work and the work of others. As a manager, it would be ineffective to simply tell a subordinate to rewrite a memo. It is better to indicate the *specific elements* the person should improve. In this chapter, those specific elements are explained and illustrated for the communicator in business and other organizations.

GETTING ORGANIZED TO EDIT EFFECTIVELY

Just practicing is not enough.

To tell a ten-year-old piano student to just practice and the piano playing will get better is giving ill advice. To tell a little-league pitcher to keep throwing and the pitching will improve is giving ill advice. Likewise, to tell a writer to keep writing and somehow the writing will improve is probably not very helpful. With most skills, simply practicing is not enough. In order to improve, a person must be able to dissect the activity, study it carefully, and then put it back together in a better manner. This is certainly important when it comes to the rewriting and editing that precede the final written copy.

Knowing how to practice (how to edit) is vital.

The effective business communicator has a clear picture of the editing elements and is able to apply them. It is generally easier to apply them to someone else's writing than to one's own. However, if you want to be an excellent communicator, you must be able to dissect and analyze your own writing.

Word Processing: Making Rewriting Easier

Word processing is a substantial editing aid.

This chapter presents the elements of effective writing and rewriting. Fortunately, this job of rewriting is getting easier. The word processor provides you with a number of routines to assist you in rewriting. This does not mean that you don't have to think. Rewriting can be a mentally taxing activity, but word processing can be of substantial assistance. Three ways the word processor can assist and speed up rewriting are as follows:

1. *Instanteneous Change.* Editing a word processing document allows you to change a word or phrase and immediately see the rewrite in final form on the monitor. This process is very different from editing a page of manuscript with pencil, where one must follow handwritten insertions above and around deletions and various other editing marks.
2. *Language Assistance.* We saw with the Gunning Fog Index that there are some basic elements of poor writing that can be isolated—long words and long sentences. There are other elements of poor language usage that word processing programs will help you identify. For instance, the word processor can isolate misspelled words, innappropriate word usage, and the overuse of particular words and can also provide you with synonyms for a word you want to change.
3. *Formatting.* You can alter the format of your document to determine which format will be of greatest assistance in communicating your message.

Even with these aids, however, rewriting is still a rigorous mental task.

The Mental Activities of Editing and Rewriting

As we look at rewriting, it is important to recall the basic process of good communication. The process for preparing the first draft is as follows: recognize the purpose of the communication, have a clear picture of the receiver, know exactly what is to be accomplished, and have a cogent outline. Once the material starts to fall into place, you may revise the outline and some of the other elements. But the first draft is important because it begins to flesh out the skeleton outline. Before going any further, you should ask yourself the original questions you asked when you developed the materials:

Editing questions the computer can't answer

1. Is this communication necessary?
2. Has the purpose been accomplished?
3. Does this communicate effectively to the reader(s)?

These three original questions force you to take a macro view of the material, making sure that the communication is basically on target. Once you are convinced that this first draft meets the original objectives, you can start to attack the elements of editing—that is, taking a more micro approach to the work.

TEACHING YOURSELF TO EDIT: THE ELEMENTS OF EDITING

Learning to edit has many similarities to practicing in sports. For example, the rudiments and routines of a sport such as basketball can be a bit tedious. On the first day of practice, the eighth-grade team is on the court and all they do is dribble. The next day, all they do is shoot free throws. The third day of practice is devoted to defensive positioning. Then, of course, there is always the practice of running laps around the gymnasium. After a week of this rigor, a youngster might say "these isolated activities of basketball are rather dull and boring. When do we play the game?" Obviously, the actual game will require the use of all these skills, but before playing the game, it is important to have the fundamentals of basketball well in hand.

Apply the practice rudiments of your favorite sport to your editing.

The same applies to editing. Don't try to apply all of the editing elements at one time. Look at the various elements of the entire manuscript, working on just one of them at a time, such as clarity. Then spend an entire editing session on conciseness, gradually attacking each of the elements as you refine your writing. This is a laborious way to learn editing, but it is effective. You will find that over time, as a practicing manager, you will be able to do many of these activities simultaneously and quickly. But to learn them well you must practice them individually —editing for clarity, conciseness, organization, completeness, style, and format.

Editing for Clarity

Lack of clarity in communication is one of the greatest hindrances to productivity, understanding, and efficiency in business today. The responsibility for clarity rests with the initiator of the communication: Know your recipient and then communicate to that person in a manner that is crystal clear. A number of things can contribute to a lack of clarity. The main offenders include:

- writing long, superfluous sentences;
- separating related words;
- using unfamiliar language, and
- selecting words that have several meanings.

In the following examples, identify the clarity problems in the first draft. Then, before looking at the edited version, try to rewrite the material so that every phrase, every sentence, and every word is absolutely clear.

First Draft:
Colin, who had been working at the computer all afternoon and was exceedingly tired by evening, stopped.

Major Problem:
Long sentence; related words and activities not adjoining.

Final copy:
Colin stopped the computer work; he had been at it all afternoon and was exceedingly tired by evening.

First Draft:
Outstanding college students, for highest grades, easier goal attainment, and greatest personal satisfaction, should work to their full potential.

Major Problems:
Related words are dispersed and the language is excessive.

Final Copy:
Outstanding college students should work to their full potential for highest grades, easier goal attainment, and greatest personal satisfaction.

First Draft:
When one writes, it is wise to make adequate preparation for if this isn't done and one 5nds he or she is missing an item such as a dictionary or a thesaurus, or a word processing

```
program, then it is dif5cult to suddenly stop and get involved
in locating the item or items that would have been secured had
proper preparation been made before the task was begun.
```

Major Problem:
```
Long sentence with extraneous ideas and language.
```

Final Copy:
```
It is wise to make proper preparation before beginning the
task of writing. After beginning to write, it is inconvenient
to stop and look for missing items.
```

First Draft:
```
In preparation for the arrival of the board of directors,
please be sure the glass is clean in the washroom.
```

Major Problem:
```
Word with multiple meanings; what is ''glass''—a mirror or a
drinking glass?
```

Final Copy:
```
Because the board of directors is coming, please be sure the
washroom mirror is clean.
```

Editing for Conciseness

In the corporate world, information is processed rapidly and decisions must be implemented without hesitation. Consequently, there is a premium on solving a problem in a paragraph or summarizing an entire short report in one page. Unfortunately, some segments of our society do not put a premium on conciseness. If you listen to some of the popular vocal music today, you hear the same message stated in the same way six different times. Perhaps that repetition is acceptable in popular music. But for the business communicator, lengthening instead of shortening the message is not effective. The major factors contributing to lengthening messages are as follows:

> **Conciseness means that generally one word is better than two, a short phrase is better than a long one.**

- Extra words—verbosity (each *and every* person should attend)
- Nonsensical words (*per* your request)
- Triteness ("last, *but not least*")

In editing for conciseness, you may have to rework sentences and paragraphs several times to eliminate verboseness and triteness. But with those revisions, you are manufacturing a productive piece of communication. The drafted sentences displayed below are some examples of bloated material. First, see if you can identify the problems, and then rewrite them more succinctly before looking at the suggested rewrite.

First Draft:
Our store is large, compared with other stores in town, and we have many departments (twelve, to be exact). Most of our customers shop in the afternoon; that is, about 70 percent of our customers shop between 1:00 p.m. and 5:00 p.m.

Major Problems:
Verbosity.

Second Draft:
Our store is large, compared with other stores in town, and we have twelve departments. Most of our customers (about 70 percent) shop between 1:00 and 5:00 in the afternoon.

Final Copy:
Our store, with twelve departments, is one of the largest in town. Seventy percent of our customers shop between 1:00 p.m. and 5:00 p.m.

First Draft:
In order to have a complete understanding of all the requirements, obligations, policies, goals, and expectations of the company, we have decided that it is evident and quite clear that every employee (all workers in this company) needs to read the 5rst chapter of the 5fteen chapters in the company handbook. Those employees who don't meet this requirement will be terminated.

Major Problem:
Verbosity.

Second Draft:
In order to have a complete understanding of all company policies, we have decided that each and every employee needs to read the 5rst chapter of the company handbook or be faced with termination.

Final Copy:
Chapter 1 of the company handbook is required reading for all employees.

First Draft
```
Last, but not least, let me say that your work on this project
is appreciated by the people at the apex of the organization.
```

Major Problem:
```
Trite, wordy.
```

Second Draft:
```
Let me say that your work on this project is appreciated by the
people at the apex of the organization.
```

Final Draft:
```
The executive committee appreciates your work!
```
or
```
Your work is appreciated by the executive committee.
```

These examples demonstrate that editing for conciseness allows you to significantly shorten the length of your material without losing any meaning. When you consider that first drafts tend to be lengthy, the importance of editing becomes abundantly clear. These same principles can be applied to the spoken word. For example, an inexperienced manager preparing a first draft via dictation will naturally tend to be more conversational, inserting extra words and phrases. But, by applying the requisite principles of editing for conciseness, the barriers to effective communication can be eliminated. Editing for conciseness makes a difference not only in the appearance of your material, but also in the effectiveness of your business communication.

Editing for Organization and Proportion

Check your writing against your outline. Are your major points emphasized? Are your subordinate ideas taking less space on the page? Be sure that the proportional aspects of the actual writing align with your plan. In editing for proportion, be sure you know the point you want to get across and that it is fully developed (see Chapter 2, Figures 2.2D and 2.4).

Editing for proportion means matching your space to your plan.

Editing for Completeness

Your communication won't achieve its purpose if you haven't given your reader the necessary or requested facts. Figure 4.1A, for example, makes a strong recommendation to the reader but provides no facts to support it. The revised version in Figure 4.1B *proves* that sales have been declining by reproducing the year's sales figures. It is important to provide complete information.

Editing for completeness means providing the receiver with total information.

FIGURE 4.1A   Memo with Incomplete Information

Remington Manufacturing

14499 Lotus Drive
Shreveport, Louisiana 71109

TO: John C. Deterding   May 3, 198_

FR: Donald R. Patterson   *Donald Patterson*

RE: Looking for Trouble

Your idea of requiring each employee to purchase the new bar-coded ID card is ludicrous. First of all, the company has a history of not charging for such items; second of all, the new cards are primarily for the firm's benefit—not the employee's benefit. Such a requirement will just result in our nonunion employees becoming angry. It will probably result in a series of grievances from the union employees because such a payment for the right to work is not included in their contract. This idea is a bad one.

Abrupt—poor style.

Emotional and incomplete message.

Editing for Style

Editing for style means taking a you-orientation.

Sometimes in a hurry to get a communication written down on paper, we forget to pay attention to matters of style—courtesy and tact, the *you* attitude, and the other topics presented in Chapter 3. Be sure to edit for style, so that tactless communications like the memo in Figure 4.1A won't cause explosions. Figure 4.1B shows a better style and a more courteous way to communicate your message.

Editing for style is the most abstract of the editing elements. Besides considering tact, you are concerned with the grace, elegance, and zest you can bring to the language.

Editing for Format

Editing for format means making the appearance reader friendly.

Nothing will cause a busy executive to throw aside a report or memo more quickly than to find page after page of block paragraphs typed from top to bottom, side to side, with no headings, titles, or variety in appearance. Just a glance at such a format tells the reader he or she is faced with a time-consuming and formidable task—a task that he or she will gladly skip or put aside. Just as the speaker who drones on and on, with no variety or attention-getting statements, is sure to bore the listener, *heavy* pages are guaranteed to frighten away the reader.

The dictionary defines format as the "shape, size, and general makeup of a publication." When editing for format, we do so for the same reason that we edit for

FIGURE 4.1B   Memo with Complete Information

Remington Manufacturing

14499 Lotus Drive
Shreveport, Louisiana 71109

TO: Jack Deterding   May 3, 198_

FR: Don Patterson   *Don*

RE: Why We Should Not Charge for ID's

Although there are some costs associated with instituting the new bar-coded ID employee identification cards, it seems best for the company to absorb those costs instead of attempting to pass them on to the employees:

1. <u>Net Loss?</u>—From a pragmatic viewpoint, the costs to set up procedures to secure money would exceed the dollars collected.

2. <u>No History.</u>—The firm has a history of not passing such costs on to employees; this is probably not the time to start.

3. <u>Who Benefits?</u>—Primarily, the new cards are for the benefit of the company, not the employee. Therefore, it may seem unfair to the employees to be forced to purchase the ID.

4. <u>Grievances.</u>—Unionized employees would probably file grievances since such purchases, as a requirement to work, are not in their contract. Nonunion employees will become just plain angry!

At this time, on this particular issue, it seems best for the company to absorb these costs. In the future there may be other times where costs can be passed on, but this cost at this time does not seem to be the one that should be implemented.

If you have any questions—please check with me.

Good tone.

Complete information.

Format encourages readability.

Note how subject statements "frame" the communication.

organization, conciseness, or clarity—to improve the readability and impact. Figure 4.2A illustrates a memo before and after editing for conciseness and format. The format of the material often has an impact before the language is read. Therefore, editing for format is critical in moving information in the organization. Figure 4.2B shows how the information can have greater impact by deemphasizing narrative and giving careful consideration to format.

Some of the techniques that can be used to enhance the format of written material are as follows:

- short paragraphs;
- wide margins;
- topic headings and subheadings;
- listings or enumerations;
- indentation;
- underlining;
- a variety of typefaces;
- use of boldface;
- separations; and
- tables, charts, graphs, and other visual aids.

Remember, do not leave consideration of format until the end of the communication process. The alert communicator considers the format as he or she develops the outline.

With modern word processing and laser printers, you have a bevy of format tools available to enhance the appearance of your writing. The responsible communicator is aware of the technologies and their applications. You should be sure to recognize the different letter and memorandum formats (such as full block, modified block, and modified block with indented paragraphs). These simple format techniques can be strategic factors in getting your ideas presented and then accepted by the reader.

Editing and Time

How you allocate your time influences the success of your editing.

Today's efficient communicator allocates the time necessary for the editing process. Because it often takes longer to edit a letter or a memo than it does to prepare the first draft, a successful communicator plans his or her editing time wisely. How you allocate your editing time can influence the final work. For instance, on Monday you know that a comprehensive progress report must be completed by Friday to accompany a detailed analysis you and several other colleagues have written. You know you will need two hours to complete this important project. The ineffective manager allocates two full hours after work on Thursday evening and works diligently from 5 until 7 p.m. preparing the progress report (see Figure 4.3, Plan A). On the other hand, the effective manager/editor allocates the same amount of time differently, spreading the work over several sessions (see Figure 4.3, Plan B). The latter communicator gains the benefits of subconscious time for the mind to "work" on the project, along with the opportunity to get several fresh looks at the material.

FIGURE 4.2A   Editing for Conciseness and Format—Unedited Memo

C   C   C

CULVER COPIER CORPORATION

To: D. B. Frazier, Vice-President of Sales
From: J. D. Tinker, Accounting Director _JDT_
Date: April 2, 198_
Subject: 1st Quarter Sales and Expenses

Our sales in all districts were fantastic. Last quarter district A sold 108 Model I copiers, 170 Model II copiers, and 32 Model III Deluxe copiers. Not to mention 1,008 boxes of copying paper. The first quarter they sold 1,178 boxes of copying paper, 34 Model III Deluxe copiers, 200 Model II copiers, and 80 Model I copiers. District C sold 35 Model I copiers, down 12.5% over 4th quarter period; 90 Model II copiers, up 20% from last period; 16 Model III Deluxe copiers, up 33% from last period; and 480 boxes of copying paper, up from 400 boxes last quarter. District B sold 54 Model I copiers, down 10% from 4th quarter; 150 Model II copiers, up 200% due to the new Pacific Manufacturing contract for 80 copiers; 12 Model III Deluxe copiers, up 20% from 4th quarter; and 550 boxes of copying paper, up 10%.

Expenses have changed very little during the past quarter. District A spent $820 on meals, $580 on gas, $608 on lodging, $65 on brochures, and $20 on copying paper. Last quarter they spent $800, $600, $500, $62, and $20. District B spent $350 on meals compared to $300 last quarter, $285 on gas compared to $290, $260 on lodging compared to $220, $31 on brochures compared to $30, and $10 on copying paper compared to $9. District C spent $375 on meals last quarter compared to $405 this quarter, $245 on gas last quarter compared to $256 this quarter, $185 on lodging compared to $220 this quarter, $25 last quarter on brochures and $127 this quarter due to the business machine exposition, $7 last quarter on copying paper compared to $9 this quarter.

I suggest we divide district A into two districts starting next quarter. Sales in district A are double that of the other districts. I also suggest we introduce a new model to replace Model I.

421 Raleigh Road
Louisville, Kentucky 40238

This one page is rigorous reading.

Huge block paragraphs with no headings are hard to handle.

The recommendations do not stand out.

FIGURE 4.2B   Editing for Conciseness and Format—Final Edited Memo

C   C   C

CULVER COPIER CORPORATION

To: D. B. Frazier, Vice-President of Sales
From: J. D. Tinker, Accounting Director   *Jim*
Date: April 2, 198_
Subject: 1st Quarter Sales and Expenses

Sales

Sales Breakdown

in units	District A			District B			District C		
	4th Qtr.	1st Qtr.	% Chg.	4th Qtr.	1st Qtr.	% Chg.	4th Qtr.	1st Qtr.	% Chg.
Copier Model									
I	108	80	-26%	60	54	-10%	40	35	12.5%
II	170	200	18%	50	150*	200%	75	90	20%
III	32	34	6%	10	12	20%	12	16	33%
Copy Paper	1,008	1,178	16%	500	550	105	400	480	20%

*Due to the new Pacific Manufacturing contract of 80 copiers.

Expenses

Expenses Breakdown

in $	District A			District B			District C		
	4th Qtr.	1st Qtr.	% Chg.	4th Qtr.	1st Qtr.	% Chg.	4th Qtr.	1st Qtr.	% Chg.
Meals	800	820	2.5%	$300	$350	16.7%	375	405	8.0%
Gas	600	580	-3.3%	290	285	-1.7%	245	256	4.5%
Lodging	562	608	8.6%	220	260	18.2%	185	220	18.9%
Brochures	62	65	4.8%	30	31	3.35	25	127*	408.0%
Copy Paper	10	20	0%	9	10	11.1%	7	9	28.6%
Totals	$2,042	$2,093	2.5%	$849	$936	10.3%	$837	$1,017	21.5%

*Due to a demonstration at the business machine exposition.

Recommendations
1. Divide District A starting next quarter.
2. Introduce a new model to replace the Model I copier.

421 Raleigh Road
Louisville, Kentucky 40238

This format aides in moving the information.

Note headings, tables, and absence of personal pronoun "I."

Generally, the more succinct the recommendation, the better the chance it will be accepted.

FIGURE 4.3   Allocation of Time for Editing

Plan A The Inefficient Approach		Plan B The Efficient Approach
Monday		1/2 hour
Tuesday		1/2 hour
Wednesday		1 hour
Thursday	2 hours	
Friday		
Results of substance	C grade	A quality
Results of communication	C- grade	A quality
Overall quality	C	A
Total volume of time to be allocated to preparing and finalizing the memorandum	2 hours	2 hours

The Macro and the Micro Look

As you have seen, effective editing requires both an overall perspective of a written document and also an application of individual techniques. It is crucial that the manager/editor take both the big and the little look at his or her writing.

Proofing

Proofing is the communicator's responsibility.

You may want to rely on the secretary, the word processor operator, or anybody else, but it is the communicator's responsibility to proofread the material. Proofreading a document is part of the editing process. Read your writing carefully. Taking several fresh looks at your writing, during an extended editing session, will help you discover errors. When the entire editing process is too compressed, it is very easy to read right over simple spelling and grammatical errors. By employing the various editing concepts over time, note in Figures 4.4 and 4.5 how it is possible to easily improve a communication.

The Final Copy: Zero Errors

Apply the zero-error manufacturing process to your editing process.

In manufacturing today many firms are pursuing a *zero errors* policy—that is, producing or manufacturing a product that comes off the assembly line with absolutely no errors. As the product is manufactured, it is checked at every step against established standards. As consumers, we expect and demand that kind of performance in the items we buy. As communicators, we should have a similar standard of quality in the materials we create. At every step in the editing process strive to eliminate all errors, ensuring that the final product is error-free.

QUICK REVIEW

Editing is not a single-step activity. The alert writer *knows* what to edit out and the steps required to produce a polished paper. The word processor can certainly aid the writer in checking for repetitious use of words and spelling errors. However, there is considerable manual labor involved in good editing: striving for clarity; achieving conciseness; maintaining proportion; ensuring completeness; writing with style; and aiding the reader by providing a helpful format.

Time spent editing is generally time well spent. The time the writer takes to edit is more than saved by the reader who can access and act upon the information quickly.

FIGURE 4.4   Memo Drafted in One Sitting

Bikercise, Inc.

7667 Garden Street
Memphis, Tennessee   38101

Memo

TO: Sophia Goldwater   March 10, 198_
FR: Bob Meyers
RE: Land Options

The availability of an agreement on securing options on the land we desire for the proposed expansion of our manufacturing facilities can be consummated. There are several factors we need to finalize so that one of the options (attached) can be selected.

Length.—The length of the option clearly influences the price we will pay for the option. There is a substantial difference in whether we prefer a three (3) month option or a twelve (12) month option. Understandably, the option length will be influenced by our analysis of markets and sales. But, the sooner we can obtain the market data the easier it will be to make the decision on options.

Amount of Land.—Although we currently need, at the maximum, one-half acre of land for the proposed facility addition and related parking, the land parcels available make the purchase decision more difficult. The parcels available are:

a. one-half acre from Mercantile, $100,000; option basically 10%.

b. one acre from Mercantile, $160,000; option basically 12%.

c. three-fourths acre from Anderson, $150,000; option increases substantially with length.

d. one acre from Penrose,$150,000; no option available.

Projections.—Because of the amounts of land available that exceed our immediate needs, there are two added items we should consider:

1. Obtaining projections on sales and manufacturing capabilities for a longer time period—therefore allowing us to project the need for added land during the next ten years. Currenty we are only looking at a three to five year need.

2. Purchasing the greater amounts of land at a reasonable cost and using the "additional" land as an investment that could be sold at a later time.

April 1.—All of the parties involved expect to hear from us before the first of next month. After you take an initial look at the summaries and materials attached, I will be pleased to meet with you about them.

Is the subject statement clear?

Note the I-orientation.

Heavy language.

Narrative duplicates heading.

Is this paragraph concise?

This format hides the data.

Are the proportions off here?

Headings for listings are helpful.

Proof—did you spot the spelling error?

Is this clear?

FIGURE 4.5   Memo After Several Revisions

Bikercise, Inc.

7667 Garden Street
Memphis, Tennessee   38101

March 10, 198_

TO: Sophia Goldwater
FR: Bob Meyers
RE: Land Options: Why We Should Take the Penrose Offer Now

Subject statement
and first paragraph
provide good
overview.

The headings aid
clarity.

The format shows
the data.

The recommenda-
tion is concise.

    The original plan was to purchase a land option that would permit us to more closely review our business and expansion plans. Since it appears we will need expansion space in the immediate future, and certainly within the decade, it seems advantageous to make a purchase now. If we are going to make a purchase within a few months, it is best to secure the Penrose property because it is well-located land for our use and the price is excellent.

    Length and Cost of Options.—The longer the period of the option, the greater the price. Making a purchase now saves us the option cost.

    Available Land.—Although we currently need only one-half acre, the long-term market projections and prices on the available land favor purchasing a one-acre parcel. The land prices and option costs are:

Parcel	Amount of Land	Cost	Option Cost
A. Mercantile	1/2 acre	$100,000	10% of purchase price
B. Mercantile	one acre	$160,000	12% of purchase price
C. Anderson	3/4 acre	$150,000	10% + .05% weekly
D. Penrose	one acre	$150,000	No option available

    Time Limit Recommendation.—Because we will need the land during the next ten years, the amounts of land and the prices favor making an immediate purchase and not incurring the expense of the option. Since the Penrose land is very suitable to us and is the lowest price (and has no option available), the company should purchase that property on or before April 1.

    The attached summaries provide details that I will be pleased to review with you. Of course, I will want to discuss this opportunity with you and answer your questions concerning this recommendation.

Attachments

EXECUTIVE SUMMARY

To: Business Communication Students

From: David N. Bateman and Norman B. Sigband

Subject: Editing: Working to Produce Excellent Communications

"Writing is easy; it's the editing that is hard work."

Word processors can assist in the task of editing by permitting almost instantaneous change of words and phrases and by identifying misspelled words, inappropriate or repetitious word usage, and even overlong words and sentences. In addition, the word processor permits the writer to alter the format quickly and easily. But even with this mechanical assistance, the task of editing is still the writer's responsibility.

It is wise to develop a strategy for editing. Each element of editing should be practiced individually until the writer feels expert in the area. In the final editing process, all are brought into play: editing for clarity, conciseness, organizational proportion, completeness, style, and format.

Efficient editing always requires an adequate block of time. It is unwise to spend hours writing a report and then allocate only a few minutes to editing the document. Proofreading is also a vital factor in the editing process and should be carried through so the final copy contains zero errors.

DISCUSSION GENERATORS

1. *Editing Time.* Why do most successful writers allocate more time to editing their work than to preparing the first draft?

2. *PC Editing.* What are some of the advantages of editing on a word processor?

3. *Yours or Mine?* Why is it easier to edit someone else's writing than it is to rework a letter or memo you wrote?

4. *Clarity.* List and explain three factors you should look for when you are editing your writing for clarity.

5. *Conciseness.* List and explain three factors you should look for when you are editing your writing for conciseness.

6. *Format When?* Why is the following statement probably incorrect and inefficient?: "I don't worry about format until it's time to produce the final copy."

7. *Align Your Message with Your Emphasis.* How can your outline aid you in editing for proportion?

8. *Abstract Editing.* Of the various factors you can edit for, which one is most abstract? Why?

9. *How Should You Look at Your Writing?* What is the difference between taking a macro look and a micro look at your writing?

10. *Whoops, Just Missed It!* If you have a memo that is five lines too long to fit onto one page, what are some format factors you can use to get the memo to fit onto one page?

11. *Include Everything Important.* You are sending a letter to a high-school friend who has written you to inquire about procedures for attending your college. In editing your response, what are some quick and simple things you can do to ensure that your letter is complete?

12. *What Kind of Line Is It?* Under what circumstances can underlining be considered an element in formatting? Isn't underlining just used to either highlight a word or phrase or to indicate that a source is a book or newspaper?

13. *It's Tough to Proof.* Why is it difficult for you to proofread a memo you have written and edited three times?

14. *Editing Analogy.* In explaining how you can develop good editing skills the authors used a basketball analogy. What is another analogy that makes the points: (a) editing involves several different activities, and (b) editing is successful when those activities are combined in the final written product.

15. *Clarity, What's First?* When editing for clarity, what is the first factor to review in your writing?

16. *Etiquette Editing.* Which of the editing elements is most closely related to etiquette? What are some of the relationships?

17. *Format Speed.* Certainly, altering the format can change the appearance of a memo, but how can format enhance the readability of the material? Cite an example.

18. *The "Language" of Editing.* Would you agree that editing involves much more than words? Explain.

19. *Purpose.* In initially editing your materials, why is it vital to carefully consider the purpose you want to accomplish?

20. *Purpose, Proportion, Editing.* What is the relationship between the purpose of your memo and the activity of editing for proportion?

APPLICATIONS FOR BUSINESS

21. *Provide the Form.* This memo is well organized and meets the requisites of editing except for one—a readable format is almost nonexistent. Edit the material for format.

Allis, Inc.

312 Henderson Drive
Cleveland, Ohio   44112

TO: Jane Anderson

 FR: Bob Eddingfield *Scott Nerle*

RE: Proposal Review: The H.R.T Proposal

The attached proposal from an outside consulting firm concerns a market analysis of our situation. Since I will be out of the office the coming week, will you please review this proposal and have a one-page analysis of it ready for me on Monday, February 12th? Be sure your analysis includes a definite statement on whether we should pursue this proposal and have further discussions with H.R.T.

Three specific items I would like for you to carefully consider and investigate are (1) Has H.R.T. allocated enough time to do the study—or will they be coming back to us about mid-way and asking for an extension of time and additional monies? (2) Would it be more economical for us to hire the telephone surveyors instead of having H.R.T. do it; that is, we collect the data and turn it over to them for analysis? (3) Note that they really are not using current research techniques (like focus groups). For what they propose, is this a problem? Have they chosen the correct methods or are they just a bit behind the times?

We look forward to reviewing your written report. I'm sure I will want to have a follow-up discussion with you after gaining your insight. Thank you for taking on this quick project when I know you already have a "full plate."

Attachment : Proposed Review

22. *Nineteenth-century Style.* The writing style of this memo is stilted and certainly not conversational. Edit the material to bring it into standard twentieth-century, conversational English.

Remington Manufacturing

14499 Lotus Drive
Shreveport, Louisiana 71109

TO: Jackson C. Grayson, III

FR: Franklin Quinn Bradinford, Jr.

RE: Nonexempt Employee Participation in Profit Sharing

 Per your comments regarding the nonexempt employee participation in the profit sharing program, it should be graciously noted
that the company has, upon several occasions, made that offer to the
employees' representative. Because of the variable nature of its
profits, the problems to ascertain actually what a profit is, it is
recommended that we cease and desist from further conversation with
the employees' representative about this issue.

23. *A Lost Writer.* The creator of this memorandum got sidetracked and wandered
around a few mulberry bushes. The purpose of the memo—which could be stated

in one simple paragraph—is to brief the boss on the decisions reached at a meeting. Edit the memo for proportion, so that the purpose is accomplished in a precise manner.

THE FAST TRACK EXPRESS

1444 Walburg Avenue
Topeka, Kansas 66606

TO: Martha C. Jefferson

FR: Hank Lobowski

RE: Summary of United Fund Meeting, September 2, 198_

　　　The meeting was called to order by this year's chairperson, John Dillard of the Shipping Department. He got the meeting off to a very good start—I did not realize that John had such a delightful and captivating sense of humor. He then introduced Robert White, President of our company, who spoke impassionately for about twenty minutes on the benefits and services of the United Fund. He emphasized the role that companies in the community should play in supporting this worthwhile activity.

　　　This year the procedure for collecting the funds has changed in several ways.

1. *Envelopes.* The envelopes will be green instead of white.

2. *One Week.* Instead of dragging out the contributions time for three weeks, there will be a one week "bash."

3. *Supervisors.* Much more responsibility will be placed on supervisors this year to make sure that employees get their envelopes and get the message.

4. *Manager's Role.* All managers will report the results of their areas to the Executive V.P. on the Monday following the week of emphasis—they will have until the end of that second week to finalize "late" contributions.

　　　It was nice to be asked to attend the meeting—I especially enjoyed the delicious coffee and donuts that were served before and after the meeting. I didn't have to have lunch this day because I ate one roll before the meeting with a generous serving of coffee and then managed to eat two "goodies" after the meeting and drank two cans of soda with them.

24. *Gremlins.* This letter has some positive features, but unfortunately it was not carefully proofread. Rework this letter, concentrating on eliminating the various sloppy errors that remained in the final copy going to the receiver.

Andersen, Beaty, and Collins, CPAs

Betty C. Beaty
Anderen, Beaty and Collins, CPAs
Quincy, MA 02169

Dear Ms. Beaty:

Thank-you for serving as a discussent on the panel which our company sponsored at the recent career days for our female employees. Your comments were certainly germain to the group and many employees have commented on how they got so much out of your speach.

Appreciate you help in this project.

Sincerely,

John B. Gimenez
Personnel Assistant

bcc: Dr. James O'Daniel, Dean
     School of Business
     Williamson College
     New York, NY 10001

Quincy, Massachusetts 02169

25. *Stylistic Considerations.* Applying some of the techniques covered in this chapter, edit this portion of a memo. The writer is explaining the purposes of an employee communication program. However, the meaning, flow, and readability of the information would be much better if fifth-degree headings were used for each item and each introductory phrase was placed in parallel form.

- To attempt to explain the product line to employees.
- In an organized manner, show employees how products are used.
- Without getting too detailed, illustrate new features of our products.
- Show the employees comparisons of our products and the competitions'.

COMMUNICATION CHECK-UPS

26. It is beneficial for students to bring their workbooks, for students to have sharp pencils and also for the students to bring a calculator to the exam.
27. On the desk I noted the book.
28. The selection of a PC is difficult, there are several excellent brands available in our community.
29. The presentation of the students were excellent.
30. Hilta has reached the ripe old age of 65 and will now retire.
31. In the book, "Decision," James Henderson clearly illustrates the ways to evolve workable decisions.
32. The data in the report is clear and supports the conclusion.
33. On the other hand the manager should have considered other options.
34. 6 people are expected at the lunch.
35. The bookstore carries a complete line of computer materials, art supplies, textbooks, current novels, sports wear, and etcetera.

Executive Introduction

Ernst & Whinney

515 S. Flower Street
Los Angeles, California 90071-2283

213/621-1666

May 11, 198_

Mr. Jason C. Lundy
Stollard Hall-202
Cleveland State University
Cleveland, OH 43202

Dear Jason,

You ask about the need to study international aspects of business when you plan to be a CPA in the USA. It's a good question, and there are several reasons why it is vital to study other cultures and their communications if you plan to operate successfully in business. Our planet has become a global village. Business affairs conducted almost anywhere in the world often have repercussions thousands of miles away.

We in the United States are not only dependent on other cultures across the oceans, but also on the different cultures that now make up a large part of every urban center in the United States.

For those reasons, communication is vital to achieving our goals. But not any communication. It must be communication that appreciates the differences that exist among cultures; it must be sensitive communication; and it must be intelligent communication. To be effective, communication must reflect the perceptions, needs, and standards of the receiving party and of his or her culture.

These are the factors that you must keep in mind when you communicate with those whose backgrounds are different from yours. And this remains true for communications to anyone whose culture is not yours, whether written or oral communication, whether destined for overseas or for a business colleague five miles away.

I'm sure you will be successful in your efforts when you keep these suggestions in mind.

Cordially yours,

Yoshihiro Sano

Yoshihiro Sano
Principal

YS/myb

Communicating Across Cultures

WHAT YOU CAN LEARN BY STUDYING THIS CHAPTER

Because we expect that traveling abroad will put us in contact with cultures other than our own, we should anticipate and prepare for the differences we will encounter. But we need not go abroad to encounter other cultures: there is a great deal of cultural diversity in the United States. This chapter will help you become aware of aspects of communication that differ from culture to culture. You will learn how to avoid problems that can arise from these differences.

Commerce is very cross-cultural.

Twenty years ago, the label *Imported* on an item of clothing, food, or mechanical equipment signified that it was something special—a product of unusual merit or of special value that came from another country. But that is no longer the case.

Whether you are in your home in the United States or in an urban center on some other continent, you are probably surrounded by products made thousands of miles away. This situation is especially obvious in the United States.

Imagine the following scenario. After you awaken in the morning, you shower with soap made in Belgium, use high-tech faucets made in Italy, and finish off with a bit of French lotion. The tweed jacket you don was made in Scotland, Ireland, or England, the wool pants were manufactured in Australia, the shoes are from Milan, and the tie is from Paris.

Now for breakfast. The kitchen has a marvelous coffeemaker from Germany, and the omelet is whipped in a French mixer. The coffee, of course, is Colombian, and the delicious marmalade is Scottish.

You're a bit late, according to your Swiss quartz watch, so you hurry to the garage and slide into your Japanese sports car, or was this the day you were supposed to use your roommate's Swedish Volvo so you could have the French Michelin tires rotated?

Never mind. You're on the way to your office, which is located in one of the downtown Los Angeles high-rise buildings that is now owned by a Japanese investment group.

Finally you stand in your firm's office area marveling at how much of the furniture, decorations, equipment, and even people had their beginnings in another country.

The USA's heterogeneity makes cross-cultural understanding a necessity.

The thought startles you for a moment. Here you live in Los Angeles, one of the largest cities in the United States, with a population of well over three million, and yet last evening as you criss-crossed streets and neighborhoods, you felt sometimes you were abroad. Spanish signs, restaurants, and shops dominated many sections of the city. And why not? After all, almost 28 percent of the population of Los Angeles is Hispanic! You enjoyed a sushi dinner at a restaurant in "Japantown" with your colleague, Togo Tamashita, who told you that the number of Japanese living in the Los Angeles area was steadily rising, that there were more Koreans in the city than anywhere else in the world outside of Seoul, and that the Chinese and Vietnamese made up approximately 10 percent of the Los Angeles population.

What does all this mean to you—a student of management communications? Some of the answers are obvious. Your authors recognize the need for adapting to foreign cultures when traveling abroad. However, we also want to point out the need for you not only to practice effective communication according to the customs and culture of the nation you're in when you are abroad, but to do the same in the United States, where our growing heterogeneous population makes such action a virtual necessity.

CUSTOMS IN OTHER CULTURES*

How Time Talks

As a businessperson traveling abroad, you will discover that you must adapt to others' perception of time if you wish to be successful. If you expect Mr. Seiji Okura, your Japanese prospect, to get down to business shortly after you arrive, you are in for a surprise. First you will discuss a variety of nonbusiness topics, and perhaps you will share a meal or two and visit some type of entertainment center. And where is Mrs. Okura? Well, as a Japanese wife, she is usually not included in business social situations.

The same may very well be true when you open your sample case in Athens or Riyadh, Saudi Arabia: "Let's talk first so I may get to know you and perhaps—but only perhaps—develop a level of trust."

In the Arab Near East, making important decisions may require an extended period of time. And the more important the decision, the longer the time required to reach an answer.

Different cultures operate on different "clocks."

When you journey to Central or South American nations, you must recognize that time is much "slower." The North American who is kept waiting in an outer office for two hours before seeing the firm's president cannot interpret it as he would in New York ("you're very low on my priority list"). It's simply that time is viewed differently in Latin American cultures.

Even the time for meals comes not only as a "hunger shock," but also as a culture shock to the North American. If you expect to dine with your host or hostess at seven, you will be disappointed to find that dinner may not be served until 10:00 p.m. in Mexico City, Madrid, or Athens.

The Japanese concept of time is especially interesting. Although that nation, since World War II, treats daily time more and more like we do in the United States (schedules, appointments, airline travel, etc.), there are still major differences. A business venture suggested to a Japanese firm may not be forgotten simply because three years have passed. It's an important decision that must be carefully reviewed, discussed, and analyzed by all upper-level personnel. That takes time. And it takes more time to reach a consensus among those people, because a decision is seldom made by the one person in charge.

---

*One of the pioneers in this field is Edward T. Hall, whose article "The Silent Language of Overseas Business," *Harvard Business Review,* May–June 1960, gained wide exposure. His organizational pattern (of time, space, things, and so on) has been followed to some degree and supplemented in this chapter.

Even working time is viewed differently. White-collar (and even blue-collar) personnel in Japan seldom leave work at 5:00 p.m. Evening work and Saturdays on the job, elected to be carried through by the worker, are the rule, not the exception. Of course this says much not only about the perception of time but also about social and family customs.

Even the time we use in negotiation moves rapidly. We want to know about your product, your price, your guarantees, and your shipping information. Then we make our offer. You reply with your lowest price, and then an acceptance or rejection concludes the negotiation. This is not how things are done when negotiating with a Japanese firm. Your offer is heard. And then there is silence while your offer is being considered.

Be careful of how you interpret nonverbal time symbols in other cultures.

Unfortunately, most North Americans can't understand silence in conversation or negotiation. We usually interpret it as a sign that our price is too high or that our proposal is not acceptable. As a result, we may rush in with a lower price or a counterproposal. Time is thus used by the Japanese negotiator as a tool to secure an advantage—an advantage he or she deserves when we don't take the trouble to learn about foreign customs when we travel abroad.

How Space Speaks

Bob Baxter was absolutely delighted. He had been with his American computer company only four years and stationed in Topeka, Kansas, when he was chosen to accompany the sales vice president to the Middle East. Bob's first stop was the New York headquarters of the firm. He was really impressed with the V.P.'s large, beautifully appointed office on the twenty-seventh floor. The view of Manhattan was magnificent. And then the V.P. took him to meet Mr. Big himself: the corporate president. Of course *his* office was on the top floor of the building. But that didn't surprise Bob. Every president's office he had been in was at the top: the university president, the auto agency president, the insurance firm president.

Space communications are not always extra-terrestrial.

Nevertheless, he was a little surprised by the office of his firm's president. It was twice as big as the V.P.'s and was in the corner of the building, with high windows facing in *two* directions. Bob was invited to join the president and vice president for coffee, but first the president disappeared to "wash up" in his private bathroom. Then to Bob's surprise, they walked into a private dining room where a white-coated waiter poured coffee from an English silver service into fine china cups as the three men sat around an Indian rosewood table covered with fine Irish linen.

Two days later, the V.P. and Bob were in the Middle East, going to see Mr. Abdul Hakim, the president of a construction company. The building they found themselves in was old, the stairway unsteady, the smells far from savory, and the main office crowded, messy, dingy, and hot. And where was the president? They found Mr. Hakim sitting at his desk in the center of ten or twelve other people, each behind a desk—all of which were covered by stacks of paper and surrounded with more documents heaped on the floor or leaning against cabinets.

Bob's thought was, "Let's get down to business, close the deal, and get back to the Hilton." But that wasn't possible. It was first necessary to have several small cups of heavy, sweet coffee and discuss various affairs, none of which concerned computers or construction. Approximately an hour after their arrival, Mr. Hakim escorted Bob and his V.P. to their car and bid both farewell, but no business was discussed.

"Well," said Bob to the V.P., "I guess that was a wasted morning."

"On the contrary," replied the V.P., "I think we will get the order, but all in good time. For a few minutes there, however, I thought we didn't have a chance because of your communication, Bob."

"What did I do?" asked Bob.

"Well, you were almost the 'ugly American.' Your impatient drumming of your fingers was very rude. And when you asked Mr. Hakim about his wife, you were trying to be considerate but, of course, you were much too personal; that's why he didn't reply to your question. And when you reached across him to pass me the tray of cakes, you really committed a breach of etiquette. And the reason I moved my chair was to obscure the soles of your shoes, which you had pointing at Mr. Hakim—an almost inexcusable insult. However, he has traveled, and I think he was aware that your errors were not intentional. But, Bob, you really must learn how to communicate in the Middle East if you wish to be successful."

So Bob learned a lesson about how space and customs speak. But the lesson is different in various cultures. In France, the department or division head sits in the center, and his subordinates' desks circle his or hers. In Germany, the same executive may enjoy the privacy of a small office.

Even in the U.S., we have seen the concept of space utilization change. In our older buildings, most managers enjoy an office—sometimes small—with a door that can be closed. Then in the 1960s, the concept of the "open office" came along. An acre of space was used for many desks. The carpeting was bright, the chairs attractive, and the desks and file cabinets "modular" and available in "decorator colors." People were separated not by walls but by wall panels five feet high. And many workers were (and still are) unhappy because their personal space (privacy) was lost.

As a result, many organizations and companies have made changes. In other cases, individuals have made adjustments. It is safe to say, however, that most American managers treasure their space and privacy, both at work and at home.

Just as your parents have a particular space for every pan in *their* kitchen and for every item in *their* den, so too do *you* know exactly where you want the books in *your* room.

Of course space use varies from culture to culture. Have you ever watched a Latin American conversing with a North American? The former keeps coming closer as they talk, while the latter continues to back away. In many parts of the world, a father and son, or two unrelated men, walk hand in hand. But does it convey a different message if two men walk hand in hand down Sunset Boulevard in Los Angeles?

And even in our culture, the use of space varies. You cannot stand three inches from a woman you don't know in a department store, but in a crowded elevator, it is quite acceptable.

In the U.S. we usually think "big is better," from our homes to mountains to trees. But in Japan, where space has always been limited, small is made to be beautiful, whether in a home, carefully proportioned and designed in 800 square feet, a 3- by 6-foot square garden area, or a beautiful miniature bonzai tree.

Know the culture before you communicate or you may unintentionally be rude.

How Gestures and Customs Communicate

The position of your hands, fingers, eyes, and feet can relate different messages in different cultures.

Knowing what nonverbal, as well as verbal, communication is acceptable can prove valuable to the manager who travels abroad.

Obviously, a detailed list of customs and gestures cannot be presented here. However, business managers should be aware they exist, learn about as many as possible, and avoid them or use them, whichever is appropriate, according to the situation in which they find themselves.

Some customs and gestures have already been discussed. There are others that managers traveling abroad should learn about, such as the meaning of bringing white flowers to a hostess in Belgium (sign of mourning) or red roses to a hostess in Germany (love).

In the Middle East, crossing one's legs while seated or having the soles of your shoes face another person would be rude. In India and parts of the Middle East, passing food with your left hand would be offensive because the left hand is considered unclean. And although the upraised index and middle finger is a sign for victory in England, it may be looked upon as obscene in Scotland.

You should also take your hands out of your pockets when you speak to a German businessperson, or he or she will feel you are disrespectful. On the other hand, if the young Japanese manager doesn't look you in the eye, it isn't because he or she is being evasive, it's just a matter of respect *toward you* that he or she does not.

And if you expect young Japanese men or women to tell you about their accomplishments before you hire them, you may be disappointed. To extol or praise yourself, the Japanese feel, is much too forward and disrespectful. And as a matter of fact, if *you* praise young Japanese in front of their peers and colleagues, *they* may feel very embarrassed and not pleased at all. Each feels part of a group or team. The Japanese expression, "The nail which protrudes must be knocked down," may describe their feelings.

When you're in Italy or Spain, be careful if your host pulls at his or her eyelid. It may be that he or she is saying "I'm *on* to you. Let's have it straight." Touching, even embracing, is more common in many other cultures than it is in ours. This includes an embrace between men and even a perfunctory kiss on each cheek—all quite acceptable. To us a relaxed, lounging position in a chair is a signal of "Let's be friendly and relaxed while we talk." In Japan, and other nations, it may be interpreted as a lack of respect for your listener or a lack of interest in the topic under discussion.

We are aggressive, competitive, and hurried. But these qualities may upset harmony, a condition prized in most cultures.

THE LANGUAGE OF THINGS, FRIENDSHIPS, AND AGREEMENTS

In Western culture, *things* are very important and perhaps becoming ever more so. We tend to value highly items of material substance: an expensive car, a big home, a large diamond, a costly work of art, and so on. Many of us who own such objects display them prominently. This is not the case in many other cultures. Such displays are looked upon as ostentatious and, more importantly, in extremely poor taste. The status of the individual who attempts to impress others with such a display is lowered significantly. Although the English, Italian, or Arab home may display many treasures, they are not discussed or flaunted. They are there, but they are understated.

As for friendships, we make them quickly. In many parts of the world (England, Germany, France), friendships develop over many years. It is quite possible to live next door to an English neighbor for years and have him or her never express more than a daily "good morning." In the United States, we move often and quickly make "new" friends at school, church, and work. But the friendships are often superficial and without enduring qualities. An expression that applies in some areas of Europe, such as Italy, is "what you will do for friends you may not do for family."

Our customs or agreements in business may also be at odds with those in other parts of the world. We feel a contract, signed by both parties, finalizes the negotiations. However, a Near Eastern businessperson may say "It's only a piece of paper; if I tear it up, we will start our negotiations over. If, on the other hand, I give you my word and we shake hands, *then* we are both bound by our oral agreement!"

Cultural customs have an impact on commerce.

Keep in mind also that the Japanese reach agreements much more slowly than we do. Don't "drive" for an answer. We may look to a quick decision from our top officer. However, a Japanese group will discuss the proposal; the decision will result from consensus; then the spokesperson will announce the decision. But it does take time.

PHILOSOPHICAL AND RELIGIOUS DIFFERENCES IN CULTURES

Perhaps the major areas that comprise our understanding of other cultures are the philosophical and religious differences. How people view the position of parents and grandparents in the family unit, the obligations and responsibilities of children to the family, education, and the position of the worker vis-a-vis the employer vary dramatically from the Western world to the Eastern. And religion and religious background, training, and beliefs can be dramatically different from one culture to another, especially between the Western cultures and cultures of the Muslim, Hindu, Shinto, and a half-dozen other of the world's religions. Our Judeo-Christian concepts, compared to other religions' concepts of the Deity (or Deities), the role of the religious leader, the concepts of after-life, work, obedience, and other factors, are in many ways different and in other ways similar.

LANGUAGE

Certainly the primary way to avoid culture shock for businesspersons is to know the language of the nation in which they work. In this way, North Americans can converse easily and learn the values, perceptions, and feelings of those with whom they are doing business.

When one has no language facility, he or she is completely dependent on the understanding and English language ability of the foreign businessperson or the ability of an interpreter or translator. Any one of these will filter the message as translation takes place. Often that filtering—depending on the number of filters and/ or the translator's ability—will have an impact on the meaning of the message.

The answer is to learn the language. A little knowledge is helpful, but the more you know of another language, the better off you'll be. Surely your hosts and business colleagues will respect and appreciate your effort to speak in *their* language.

Strive to learn both the verbal and nonverbal language of different people.

But be careful. When going from one language to another, meanings can change, especially in translating colloquialisms. For example, "Come alive with Pepsi" was translated as "Come out of the grave" in Germany and "Pepsi brings your ancestors back from the grave" in Asia. "Body by Fisher" turned into "Corpse by Fisher" in another situation. And perhaps best of all, "The Spirit is willing but the flesh is weak" translated into Russian as "The ghost is ready but the meat is rotten."

There are problems even in "translating" British English to American English. A car hood is a bonnet in England, a car trunk is a boot, and a trash can is a dust bin. In spite of these unusual situations, knowing the language—even to a limited degree— will give you an advantage that is invaluable.

ACTION

What all this means is obvious. As we communicate more and more across cultures we must become more knowledgeable about the areas listed in this chapter and more: customs, language, the use of time and space, philosophy, religion, dress, food, and so on. More reading, training, and interaction among the cultures are all needed. Visit consulates, seek out foreign nationals, talk to knowledgeable people, and be understanding.

More specifically, try to:

- Speak more slowly in a foreign nation; enunciate carefully.
- Be careful about touching others.
- Don't stereotype a particular culture; keep an open mind and don't generalize even on the specifics listed in this chapter.
- Use standard English; avoid colloquialisms and jargon.
- Look for feedback to check understanding.
- Be alert to national and local customs; ask about what is correct in dress, food, and habits.
- Listen carefully.
- Be patient.
- Confirm conversations in writing.
- Be careful of your gestures and body language; theirs may not be yours.
- Eat in their restaurants, and enjoy the food and entertainment.

And before you go overseas, turn for help to agencies that can assist you. Here is a very short list. However, the U.S. Government Printing Office and the Department of State can supply you with others.

International Resource Directory
American Society for Training and Development
P.O. Box 5307
Madison, WI 53705

The Business Council for International Understanding
The American University
Washington, D.C. 20016

Intercultural Communications, Inc.
P.O. Box 14358
University Station
Minneapolis, MN 55414

Overseas Briefing Associates
201 East 36th St.
New York, NY 10016

The Society for Intercultural Education,
Training and Research
1414 22 Street NW, Suite 102
Washington, D.C. 20037

Intercultural Communication Network
1860 19th St. NW
Washington, D.C. 20009

Finally, be understanding, sympathetic, and empathetic. In that way, you will become the "Friendly American," not the "Ugly American."

QUICK REVIEW

In the United States, it is not necessary to leave the country to easily see and experience foreign cultures. In virtually every metropolitan area, and in many other locations, multicultural experiences abound. If you are going to do business in different cultures (and today that is virtually a given), it is beneficial to understand those cultures. Recognize that you need not pack a bag or leave the states to gain multicultural experiences—they are often right around the corner.

As you investigate and enter other cultures strive to not impose your ways and your values upon other people. Also, understand that different people do things differently, such as recognize different spaces, operate on different times, define friendship differently, use different gestures, and speak using different verbal and nonverbal languages. Just because things are different does not mean they are better or worse than your ways and your customs . . . they are simply different. Being a perceptive communicator will aid you in adjusting to the interactions across cultures. If you are going to succeed in today's business, cross-cultural understandings are vital.

EXECUTIVE SUMMARY

To: Business Communication Students

From: David N. Bateman and Norman B. Sigband

Subject: Communicating Across Cultures

Among the crucial points made in "Communicating Across Cultures" is the fact that we need not go abroad to encounter various cultures. Every urban center in the United States is made up of individuals whose national backgrounds may be very different from each of ours.

It is just as important to be aware of the habits and customs of these cultures when communicating in the United States as it is when communicating in Europe, the Orient, or the Near East, for example.

Cultural communication differences can be broken down into the following broad areas:

Time	Friendships
Space	Agreements
Gestures	Philosophy and religion
Customs	Language
Things	

For each of these areas, different cultures have different values and perceptions.

Some of the problems that may arise from different interpretations of time, space, customs, and so forth can be avoided by following these suggestions:

- Speak more slowly in a foreign nation
- Be careful about touching others
- Don't stereotype a particular culture
- Avoid slang and colloquialisms
- Look for feedback to check understanding
- Listen carefully
- Confirm conversations in writing
- Be careful of your gestures and body language

DISCUSSION GENERATORS

1. *Ugliness.* Cite ways in which you could inadvertently reveal yourself as a person like the proverbial ugly American to a member of a different culture.
2. *Colloquialisms.* Explain colloquialisms, illustrate several, and then indicate why they can confuse cross-cultural communications.
3. *Suggestions.* What are some of the suggestions the authors make for gaining familiarity with other cultures? What are two or three you could implement in the U.S. before interacting with a foreign culture?

4. *Their Language.* What are the advantages, when in another culture, of attempting to speak in *their* language? Is it still appropriate even if you are going to stumble?

5. *Values.* If the values are different from yours in a foreign culture, what should you do? For instance, if the standard procedure is to offer "finder's fees" to governmental officials for doing business in that nation, should you provide such fees? In the U.S. culture, we might call these bribes.

6. *Filtering.* Placing filters in your coffee maker may be a good idea, but placing a filter on the exchange of language when working in another culture is less effective. What are the disadvantages of having to rely upon others for your language when in a foreign culture?

7. *Employee–employer Relationships.* From your reading and from watching TV news, what are some differences in the employee-employer relationship in another country compared to the U.S.?

8. *Religion and Work.* If you are planning to manage an operation in another culture and are a member of a mainstream Protestant religion in the U.S., what must you be careful of in the "new" culture?

9. *Display Cases.* You are being transferred to a medium-sized city near Rome, Italy. Your firm permits you to take many household items with you, but does not provide you with a "suggested list" of do's and don'ts. You have beautiful curio cases to display your exquisite collection of antique Bateman silver. You and your spouse think it will be ideal to display it in your Italian home; it will be like taking part of your family with you. Is your decision correct? Why?

10. *Let's Be Friends.* Explain how friendships may change from culture to culture and how the "friendship clock" may run differently in different cultures.

11. *Friendships and Business.* How might the differences in friendship among people in different cultures influence your business relationships?

12. *Agreement.* What are the different ways to make a contract or agree on a business arrangement in different cultures?

13. *Interviewing.* In an employment interview in the U.S. you are generally expected to describe your attributes and accomplishments in a rather unboastful manner. If you are interviewing a person reared in a Japanese culture, what might you expect and how might you phrase such questions concerning the person's accomplishments?

14. *Sit Up Straight!* As a child you were probably told to "sit up straight in your chair." How does that advice relate to a business discussion in Japan?

15. *Say it with Flowers.* In many cultures, especially in Europe, it is polite to take a small gift when visiting another's home. If going for dinner you might take wine or flowers. If invited to the home of a German family for a business-related dinner, how could taking red roses send the wrong message?

16. *Open Office.* Although we still see a few open offices in the U.S., why did that architectural design really never catch on here? Why did most U.S. managers dislike this style of office?

17. *Don't Blow it Bob.* Bob Baxter in the computer company in Topeka just about

ruined some business dealings on his first overseas trip. What could Bob have done to avoid some of his cultural errors?

18. *Space Speaks.* Explain, in the business context, how space really does speak.

19. *Time Talks.* Explain, in a business context, how time really does talk.

20. *Foreign Influence.* From your personal or business life, illustrate the foreign influence on your activities—things you use, items you own, food you prefer, or an activity you pursue.

APPLICATIONS FOR BUSINESS

In the following situations, the context has been altered from those presented in the previous chapters. These applications permit you to carefully analyze and critique some special, but very realistic, cross-cultural situations.

AUF WIEDERSEHEN TO BOB

Situation

21. Bob Emory graduated from the School of Business of Northwestern University in 1981. He majored in Finance and minored in German. He had lived in Germany for three years when his father, a colonel in the United States Army, was stationed there in the early 70s.

With this background, Bob sought and secured a position with a German investment firm with headquarters in Munich. Because of his creative, conscientious approach and fluency in German and English, Bob rose rapidly.

Recently, Herr Gunter Kraus, the firm's president, asked Bob to join him and six others of the company's top managers for a Saturday morning of golf and lunch. Bob knew a vice president's position was open, and he was delighted to join the "brass."

By the fourth hole, he was quite relaxed and said to Mr. Kraus, "Gunter, I want you to know how much I enjoy working for your company. All of you are pretty terrific guys."

Some of the others, all older than Bob, seemed to be a little surprised at Bob's informality, especially with the company president, but Bob felt, "Why not; in the office we're formal, but this is the golf course, so let's lighten up."

Lunch was excellent and the wine delicious. Bob found himself laughing a good deal and enjoying himself tremendously.

At 2:30 p.m. each of the other six bid Bob and Mr. Kraus *auf Wiedersehen* and left. Bob called for another bottle of wine for "Good old Gunter and me," but Mr. Kraus also excused himself, and by 2:45 p.m. Bob found himself sitting at the large round lunch table by himself.

Bob was feeling quite good as he finished his glass of wine. When the waiters began to clear the table, he took the suggestion and rose rather unsteadily. A few minutes later, he left the club.

Sequel

Bob did not receive the promotion. Some nine months after the golf afternoon, he asked the executive vice president about advancement. To his amazement, the vice president suggested that Bob might wish to consider "broadening his experience by moving to another organization."

Bob took the hint and found employment in the international division of a New York bank three months later.

Discussion

In either a brief oral or written presentation, analyze the case, indicating what Bob Emory should not have done and why. Then suggest what he should have done to improve his relationships with his German company.

A JAPANESE DILEMMA

Situation

22. Approximately five years ago Nippon Hospital Equipment Company began to buy surgical instruments from Bert Baker's firm. The orders were not large, but they were steady, payment was prompt, and the relationship was satisfactory.

One day Baker's boss said, "Look, Bert, you deal with Nippon's buyer when he comes to Columbus—why don't you go to Kyoto, get to know the top people at Nippon, and see if you can get them to buy our entire line instead of just a few items? With some decent sales work, you should be able to increase their volume with us by tenfold. Take your wife, Bonnie, with you, and make it a business-holiday trip—all expenses on the company."

Bert's boss did not have to issue the invitation twice, and three weeks later Bert and Bonnie were on their way to Japan.

Bert had written to his contact at Nippon, Yoshi Takamura, and had invited him for dinner along with "several of your associates who would like to know more about our products."

When Baker and his wife arrived at their hotel from the airport, they were pleased to find a bouquet of flowers from Nippon Hospital Equipment and a message that Mr. Takamura had called.

Bert returned the call and was told that Yoshi and four of his associates would be pleased to meet Baker, as Baker's guests, at the White Lily restaurant at 7:00 p.m.

Although tired after a long trip, the Bakers showered, put on fresh clothes, and went off to the White Lily. When Bert walked in with Bonnie, Yoshi seemed surprised. "You have brought your wife?"

"Of course," said Bert. "I never travel without her. And where are your ladies—or are we going to your home and meet them there?" asked Bert.

"Well, no," replied Yoshi. "Our wives are all busy this evening."

"That's a pity," Bonnie said. "I would sure like to see them. Perhaps we could make it some evening later this week."

"Perhaps," said Yoshi.

"But before we have dinner," said Bert, "I have a small gift for each of you." And with that he gave each of the Japanese men a small pocket solar calculator. They thanked him but seemed embarrassed to receive a gift.

Conversation was polite and acceptable until it came time to order, when Bonnie made it known loudly and clearly that "I'm not about to eat raw fish. After all, *I'm* civilized, and raw fish or anything like that is yukky! But you all just go ahead."

As for Bert, he seemed to touch nothing but did make up for the food by imbibing in a good deal of sake. Throughout the evening, he continued to tell Yoshi's associates what an outstanding person, salesman, and individual Yoshi was . . . statements that drew only silence from Yoshi and his fellow Nippon employees.

At 9:30, when both Bert and Bonnie tried to make arrangements for subsequent evenings, everyone seemed "tied up."

However, the next day Bert did visit Yoshi at the Nippon Hospital Equipment offices. Unfortunately, after a half-hour, Yoshi excused himself, although he did agree to meet with Bert two days hence. That meeting was held but Bert was not successful in talking business to Yoshi or meeting any of his superiors.

Two days later, puzzled and confused, Bert and Bonnie left for Columbus.

Sequel

Orders continued to arrive from Nippon Hospital Equipment for the next few months. However, their volume steadily decreased, and after six months, no more were received.

Discussion

As an expert in international communication, what suggestions would you make, if any, to Bert if he visits another firm in Japan? Make your comments in either a brief oral or written report.

THE NEAR EAST IN DALLAS

Situation

23. Rachel Murphy graduated from the University of Texas at Austin in 1983 with a degree in petroleum engineering. One of her good friends and classmates, Hakim Abdullah, attended Rachel's wedding just three weeks after graduation and then returned to Riyadh, Saudi Arabia.

    Rachel and Hakim had kept in touch with an occasional letter. Both Rachel and her husband, Ben, were really excited when a letter arrived from Hakim indicating he would be in Dallas (where the Murphys had a home) in just ten days. Furthermore, Hakim indicated he would be accompanied by his father and his father's brother, both of whom were in the oil drilling equipment supply business.

    "If convenient," Hakim added, "may we plan to be together on our only free evening in the Dallas area, July 10?" Now Rachel and Ben planned the evening. They invited three of the professors from the University and their spouses (Drs. Wentworth, Goldberg, and Shannon), three couples who were close friends of the Murphys, and Rachel's parents.

    "Let's have something typically American," Rachel said, and Ben agreed. It was to be an outdoor barbecue in the Murphy's large backyard, which also had a swimming pool.

    The American guests arrived in mid-afternoon, and several of the men and women changed into swimsuits and cooled off in the pool. Others enjoyed cold beer and chips.

    Toward sundown, the guests from Riyadh appeared, and there were many handshakes, embraces, and greetings. Hakim's father and uncle seemed a little taken aback at the sight of bikinis, but once inside the air-conditioned house, they seemed to relax. They were especially pleased with the gifts Rachel had for each of the three visitors: very attractive Seiko travel alarm clocks.

    About 7:00 p.m. a clanging bell rang out along with the shouted announcement, "Chow's on; come'n get it."

    A bit puzzled, the three were led out into the yard by Rachel's father, who brought them to a buffet, handed each a large paper plate and plastic utensils, and said, "You have your choice of barbecued pork back ribs, hot dogs, or hamburgers, with all the fixins': lettuce, catsup, corn on the cob, cold beer, bourbon and water, Pepsi Cola, and apple pie á la mode."

    There seemed to be enough food for a hundred guests, but unfortunately Mr. Abdullah and his brother were not hungry and barely touched the buffet. They excused themselves with the apology of "an extremely large lunch and jet lag." Hakim, apparently in deference to his father, also ate very little, and at 8:30, making a variety of excuses for their early departure, they shook hands all around and left.

    Late that evening, after all the chairs were carried in and the yard put back in order, Rachel turned to Ben and said, "Well, honey, do you think our overseas visitors felt welcome and enjoyed themselves in a typical American home?"

Discussion

If you were to answer Rachel's question, what would you say and why? Present your comments in a brief memo or short oral presentation.

CROSS-CULTURAL LABOR RELATIONS AT WEBSTER ELECTRONICS

Situation

24. Assume you are the Vice President for Human Resources at the Webster Electronics Corporation, with headquarters in New York. Your firm has four plants: Hackensack, New Jersey; Chicago, Illinois; Dallas, Texas; and Los Angeles, California. Each plant employs 6,000 to 11,000 employees.

    Your products are primarily electronic components that eventually find their way into medical equipment, computers, appliances, automobiles, toys, and a score of other items, plus all types of Department of Defense products such as missiles, satellites, and armaments.

    Although your wage rates are excellent, labor relations in your four plants have been declining. There have been more and more grievances filed in the past few months and several costly work slowdowns.

    You feel it is largely due to supervisors and section chiefs who are attempting to manage the "old way" and have not recognized that 65 percent of Webster's work force today is made up of Hispanics and Asians. In the former category, the breakdown is largely between employees from Puerto Rico and Mexico. Among the Asians, the split is among Vietnamese, Chinese, and Koreans.

Discussion

Team up with one other student and produce a brief set of guidelines for Webster's supervisors concerning cultural differences among the members of the work force. You may wish to organize your paper or oral report into such areas as communication, interpersonal relationships, foods, designation of leadership and responsibility, use of time and space, etc. Or you may wish to make your comments general.

    You will find it helpful to do some research: newspapers and magazine articles, plus interviews with various ethnic representatives.

    Your goal is to improve labor relations at Webster.

SELLING TECHNICAL EQUIPMENT IN CHINA

25. Team up with one other student and present a brief oral or written report on "Selling Technical Equipment in China in 1988–90."

    What are some of the cultural factors with which North American sales representatives should be familiar to be successful when calling on buyers in China today?

    You will find it helpful to do some research: newspapers, magazines, Americans familiar with China today, Chinese in the U.S., official representatives (consulate or trade mission members), etc.

COMMUNICATION CHECK-UPS

26. Jogging and racquetball is my favorite forms of athletic activity.
27. He couldn't barely walk to the podium.
28. 937 people attended the evening meeting.
29. And, remember, the message and the media go together.
30. Not all firms list the recipients full names on the memo.
31. At times you may want to actually sign your name informally.
32. When you were new in business and the boss called for you to visit her office you responded immediately.
33. The ten commandments provide much guidance for commerce.
34. George was quite a Corporate president; his dog charlie guarded his desk and attended all business conferences.
35. The following organizations will be represented at our conference, Bently Inc., Clarion Hospital, Andrews University, New York Living Corporation, and Rexburger, Inc.

The Worst Best-kept Secret of Business

Tom Brown

Among the primary tasks assigned to every manager—budgeting, delegating, and appraising performance—at the very top of the list is communicating.

A manager may not desire to strive for the appellation of "the great communicator," but he had better be worthy of being called "a darn good communicator." I suspect that the manager who is building a great "communications spirit" in his organization—where employees and managers all know what's going on with customers and all seem to be willing to talk and write freely about their work—achieves this spirit because of the way he speaks of the job of communicating itself.

One of my first assignments inside a corporation was in one of those cavernous manufacturing plants that housed about a thousand engineers. My task? To help the individual engineers capture their thoughts and express them on paper. But not just any thoughts.

These men and women were specifically assigned to write sections of a voluminous proposal that would be sent to a potential customer as a competitive sales presentation on behalf of the entire company. Numerous companies would compile these thousand-page documents as "proposals," each competing to win contracts worth millions of dollars. Each company's proposal was, in essence, based on the same thesis: "Dear Customer, we have assembled all these data, all these ideas, all these thoughts, to prove, simply, that we understand you and your needs. Give us this contract!"

Tremendous amounts of marketing knowledge, based on years of working closely with the potential customer, was transformed into an intelligence profile containing such information as the customer's cost priorities, quality standards, and production horizons. This information was, in turn, transmitted to anyone who had to write a section of the proposal.

Then the really hard work began: getting scores of people throughout the company to squeeze their specialized knowledge into a few pages. The "few pages" from each of the people would be combined into a book-length sales document. Here was a chance for people to tell their story; to sit back and focus on their accumulated experience in industry.

Who's kidding whom? The reality, then and now, is that communication assignments such as this were intense misery for almost every person I met. Electrical engineers would weep over their five-page summaries due next Monday. Cost-accounting specialists moaned at how pointless all of this work was: "The customer ought to just know that we watch the nickels and dimes here."

Yet, the voluminous proposals were agonizingly completed. Too bad it has to hurt so much. The elements of communicating about how a business runs—whether it be a multivolume sales proposal or a simple sales letter—are the neutrons, electrons, and protons of the marketplace. Effective communication with customers is a key to any company's success.

Unfortunately, the attitudes of engineers and cost accountants (and all the others) toward communications haven't moved forward much over the last ten years.

How's Your Attitude?

I recall the manager who discussed with me an assignment in which he had to present the conclusions of his laboratory research. He paused as he frustratingly rearranged for a third time the points of his report. His jaw tightened; his cheeks turned red. "DARN," he growled. That word held the floor for a full minute. It captured his accumulated lifetime distaste for having to suffer through the communications end of his job.

Does that word capture your communications attitude? Much as a coach influences the way athletes hustle onto a playing field, a manager influences the way employees, and other managers, hustle toward a communications assignment. The best managers I have met seem to teach one basic lesson about the job of communicating: They don't classify it as drudge work.

A vice president who recently joined a computer chipmaking company was assigned to speak at the company's annual business meeting. Being new to the company, he could have taken the task as yet another necessary, but glum, assignment. Rather, he took the positive approach. Here are his words: "Here was a great chance for me to sell my ideas to this company! Plus, can I sell the services of my department? And, it is a great opportunity to project the sincerity and good humor that I hope to make my operating trademarks in this organization!"

The exclamation points were his. He added a final comment: "It was such an important speech, with several hundred of my company peers in attendance, that I chose to prepare so thoroughly that I could make the presentation without notes. It was great!"

Everyone in any enterprise has a responsibility not only to do his or her job, but also should be expected to freely, openly, and excitedly communicate how that job is making for a better company with better-served customers.

Business may be, at heart, about designing, building, selling, shipping, and servicing—but the best-kept secret about business is that no part of it should ever be a secret.

Manners Make the Manager

Edward Wakin

When a middle manager at a multimillion-dollar corporation barged into his vice president's office to find out why he had been passed over for promotion, he was hit with an explanation that rocked him. The reason wasn't his job performance: That was first rate. The problem was caused by his manners, his business etiquette.

The vice president expanded the indictment.

The manager continually interrupted others; embarrassed higher-ranking executives at meetings; and picked arguments with coworkers.

Dr. Milla Alihan, a New York City-based industrial psychologist and author of *Corporate*

"Manners Make the Manager" by Edward Wakin, *Today's Office*, June 1986. Reprinted with permission of Hearst Business Communications, Inc.

Etiquette (Mentor Books, 1974), summarizes what many management consultants point out: There is no guarantee that good manners alone will escalate a young hopeful to the position of chairman of the board. A business career can suffer, however, unless a person masters the art of courtesy.

Management consultant John Sauer, of the New York City office of management consultants Rohrer, Hibler & Replogle, adds, "When manners are forgotten, they become important in a negative way. They're like wallpaper. You don't notice it unless it's torn or defaced. Then, it sticks out."

Managers that ignore business etiquette overlook the fact that organizations are social settings in which people need to work together smoothly if company objectives are to be achieved in a productive manner. Managers can undermine their effectiveness when they forget that courtesy counts.

Allan Cox, head of Allan Cox & Associates, a Chicago-based executive-search-and-development firm, adds a relevant point: "Lack of courtesy reflects a negative outlook on people." And that puts a manager out of step with the emphasis that corporate America puts on people.

Business etiquette encompasses both courtesy and custom. Courtesy involves treating coworkers as they would like to be treated and requires sensitivity to the feelings of others.

Custom calls for awareness of how others conduct themselves. This involves paying close attention to the way people look, act and talk—specifically those at the top of the organization, since manners are influenced and shaped by those at the upper levels of a firm.

Further, managers must honor well-developed habits and traditions. Business manners are more than standard social etiquette; they also involve company culture.

Every organization has its own rules—some things are always done, others are never done. To fit in, managers had better learn those rules and follow them.

Unfortunately, it's easy to temporarily forget the rules in the day-to-day rush of getting the job done. Managers deal with many people during the day, and few of these meetings are especially noteworthy. But for the people working for these managers, each encounter with their supervisor stands out.

Fortunately, it is relatively easy to improve a manager's business etiquette. Sometimes, all it takes is a videotape to show a manager where he or she has gone wrong.

A consultant describes how he used this approach in a *Fortune* 500 company. A high-potential middle manager, who was sloppy in dress and manner, was having trouble fitting into the three-piece-suit style of his firm.

In the office, the manager went without a jacket, with his shirt half out of his pants and his sleeves rolled up. In addition, he was always chomping on a cigar.

When he saw a playback of the videotape in which he "starred," he was instantly cured. Now, the manager has become heir apparent to the chief executive officer.

Because codes of appropriate dress are obvious, violations are glaring. Businesspeople should dress and act in a manner that projects responsibility, respectability, trustworthiness and consideration for others.

In some offices, male managers are expected to work in jacket and tie. In others, shirt sleeves are permissible, but only with a tie in place and a long-sleeved shirt. For women, the same general rule applies: Dress in a professional and businesslike manner.

In addition to appearance and sensitivity to fellow workers, business manners touch on many other areas. For instance, a manager should be aware of company protocol about first names.

In some organizations, everyone is on a first-name basis; in others, the top echelon is addressed as mister or, if appropriate, doctor. When in doubt, use a formal greeting, and let the other person set the tone. Most authorities agree that Ms. is now the standard form of address for businesswomen.

Treat secretaries—yours and everyone else's—with respect. Avoid at all costs the lingering tendency to call secretaries my girl, honey or dear.

As far as socializing with those in higher ranks, the best approach is to wait for them to take the initiative. When making introductions, a lower-ranking person is usually introduced to a higher-ranking person, a younger person to an older one, a man to a woman. Handshakes are in order; hugs and kisses are not.

Giving business gifts is a tricky issue. Gifts should be signs of appreciation, not rewards for contracts, orders or assignments. That usually means limiting their value to about $25. Avoid personal items; instead, give gifts such as pens, desk diaries, lighters, key rings and wine.

A particularly delicate—and potentially explosive—area is etiquette between male and female colleagues. Should a woman be treated with chivalry or as one of the boys?

In *Mastering Business Etiquette and Protocol,* updated in 1985, the Research Institute of America, a New York City-based publisher and provider of business services, recommends the "offer and refusal technique" and the "understanding strategy." When men offer to extend courtesies, women accept those they feel are appropriate and gracefully decline others.

For example, when a man offers to open a door, the woman can either allow him to do so or say, "Thank you, but I've got it." The understanding strategy requires that a man observe the preferences of a woman colleague and respond accordingly—using chivalrous gestures when appropriate.

Some men still feel awkward when the woman pays the bill (or, more accurately, when her company does), but this attitude is passing. Waiters have become accustomed to the woman paying the check, particularly in restaurants that are noted for serving business meals.

Catalyst, the New York City-based nonprofit national organization promoting women's careers, has pinpointed the 10 "most fatal" business faux pas committed by both men and women in daily business life. The list of taboos, as noted in *Upward Mobility* (Holt, Rinehart and Winston, 1982), written by the staff of Catalyst, includes the following:

1. Assuming that all business associates want to be called by their first names.
2. Sending out sloppy-looking business letters.
3. Mistreating the secretaries of business associates.
4. Displaying a cavalier attitude on the phone—by not identifying yourself, putting others on hold, breaking off the conversation to talk to someone else and so forth.
5. Being lax about making and keeping appointments.
6. Smoking in the wrong places.
7. Giving conflicting signals on who pays for a business meal.
8. Talking only about business at a function that is both a business and a social occasion.
9. Inviting higher-ups out socially before they've taken the initiative.
10. Failing to put thank-yous in writing.

To keep up to date, *Emily Post's Etiquette: A Guide to Modern Manners* (Harper & Row, 1984) has added a section that distills the essence of etiquette at the office: "What your employer sees, aside from how hard you work and how well you perform, is how you present yourself to others. That is manners—good or bad.

"If you are courteous and sensitive to the code of etiquette and the unique rules and rhythm with which your place of business functions, you will communicate a positive image. If, on the other hand, you apply push-and-shove aggressiveness in your eagerness to get ahead and disregard what is considered acceptable behavior, you will project a negative image, that of a person who does not belong."

Executive headhunter Cox adds a tough-minded postscript: "Business manners are part of what you're supposed to learn in order to do your job and to get ahead."

User-friendly Correspondence

Adele Greenfield

Writing effective business reports, proposals and letters takes a little know-how. Many of these communications have become less formal and more conversational because business is beginning to recognize that doing business does not preclude the fact that real human beings actually talk to other human beings. For example, letters are now (to quote a computer term) "user-friendly" and sound natural. The guideline is simple: If you wouldn't say it, don't write it.

When you want to project a competent image, you can do it if you use contemporary phrasing. In fact, it is even better. Hackneyed sayings or old-fashioned clichés are absolutely and positively out. And so are redundancies like "absolutely and positively." One of these will do, since both mean the same and identical (here we go again) thing.

For example, does this sentence belong in the 1980s?

"Attached hereto, please find a memo pursuant to inviting the esteemed professor Dr. White to deliver a lecture on the date of our conference. Trusting you will read this . . ."

Slightly exaggerated? Maybe. No reader wants to wade through such gibberish. If you can barely read it aloud, look for another way of saying it.

"I'm enclosing a memo about inviting Professor White to speak at our conference."

Not only does the second version sound like an actual person wrote it, it gets rid of all that excess verbosity (or shouldn't I say wordiness?). It has a streamlined design, contemporary in style.

Since every designer has tools, here are a few in the form of three questions to ask yourself to help you design your writing:

Why am I writing this? The purpose should begin with a verb: to sell, to explain, to ask for something. Do not write it unless you are asked to state a goal, but keep it in mind as you work.

Who will be reading this? Who your audience is bears directly on what or how you write, since you are trying to make certain points. What kind of response do you want?

What do I need to say? The points you describe should support your purpose and be aimed at your audience.

Once you get the facts and write a draft, there are even more questions, concerning focus and image. In a sense, you are functioning as an editor.

- Is it complete? Check for omissions and consistency.
- Does it sound like it is written by a person or a machine? (Of course, if writing by machine is what you are after, reverse the question.)
- Is your topic clearly targeted?
- Is your work logically organized?
- Is it clear, concise and free of jargon, or does it have big, impressive and confusing words? If you must use the language particular to an industry or topic, go ahead. But, at least know better, and try to keep such usage as minimal as possible.
- Will the reader lose face or be put off in any way? If so, your effectiveness will be diminished.
- Is it "letter-perfect"—grammatically and typographically correct?
- Are the message and the professional image being conveyed the way you would like? Besides tone, correspondence must look good.
- Are there any redundancies, out-of-date language, wordiness, or stiff, "please-be-advised" phrases that sound as if they belong in a law book?

A design is not a design, however, unless the form is in some kind of order. In this sentence, for example, the repetition works for emphasis. If it is overdone, though, the impact will be lost. Structure will help you organize your thoughts into words. Here are some basics:

Develop your paragraphs. The first and last sentences are the most likely to be remembered. Usually, the first gives some clues on what the paragraph is about, and the last sentence either sums it up or acts as a transition to the next one.

Organize your paragraphs. What follows what? Paragraphs, like sentences, should flow from one another. They need to be clear and logically ordered. No reader wants to be jarred. Some common structures are:

- Chronological: Information is presented in order of occurrence.
- Ranking: Go from most to least important, or the other way around. Ranking is good for listing such things as recommendations, and is often used in persuasive writing.
- Discuss a problem: State the problem, analyze the factors, cause and other pertinent elements and then offer solutions, if any. Ask for input when appropriate.
- Look at pros and cons: State the options, then discuss each advantage and disadvantage. Close with the option you select and why.

Now comes the dessert—adding that certain polish. Getting down to specifics does not mean examining every word under a magnifying glass, but it does demand some attention to detail. These tips should help:

- If one word will do, use it. For example, instead of *at the present time,* use *now.* It is more compelling. *Soon* is better than *in the near future.* Do not use *the reason is because.* Just write *because.* Rather than *invisible to the eye,* use *invisible.* Everyone knows vision is through the eyes. The same applies to a *qualified expert:* The person has got to be qualified in order to be an expert. And never use *personal opinion.* All opinions (except expert) are personal. *Opinion* is fine.
- Use action verbs. They add more zip. Instead of *are going to,* use *will. Decide* rather than *make a decision.*
- To personalize a letter, you can use *you* or *your* instead of *we* or *our.*
- The English language is one of the most complicated. Although *affect* means influence or cause, *effect* refers to the actual result. *Assure, ensure* and *insure* might be interchangeable, but *compliment* is to praise and *complement* is to complete. Follow up with the dictionary to check your usage. (*Follow-up,* as in a *follow-up report,* has a hyphen when *follow-up* is not used as a verb. Whew!)
- If you are answering a letter, it is a good idea to have it in front of you for easy reference.
- Salutations should be as specific as possible; however, certain salutations are acceptable even when specific information is unknown. For example, initials such as *R. A. Brown* could mean male or female, so *Dear R. A. Brown* is acceptable, as is *Dear Leslie Brown.* Also acceptable are salutations according to title *(Dear Director of Advertising),* company name *(Dear ABC Nut and Bolt),* or classification *(Dear IRA Investor).*
- Contractions like *can't* are fine on occasion in formal business writing, but do not go overboard, especially with *can't.*
- Have standard letters or reports on hand to use as guides. Some letters can be copied almost word for word.

Books on effective written communication are everywhere. If you are in the market for one, make sure it is current. Look at the style. Do you like it? If so, it probably is a good investment.

Amid all the technique, however, do not lose your personal touch. Writing can be inhibiting if you ponder every word. Just write; let it flow naturally.

Later, you can fix it up.

PART

//

Producing Effective
Business Communications

BRIAN McCARTHY

Executive Introduction

Printing plant
606 South Illinois • Carbondale, Illinois 62901 • 618-529-3115

June 2, 198_

Margaret O'Malley, Director
Illinois Printers Assoc.
1703 Harcourt Bldg.
2223 LaSalle St.
Rockford, IL 61101

Dear Marg,

Those of us who operate "walk-in" operations complain about the poor appearance of materials customers bring us to reproduce. Of course, when we produce a sloppy copy, customers want to blame us—they forget, "garbage in, garbage out."

Because of these complaints, we must emphasize to our customers the importance of the appearance of copy. Some of the key points to emphasize are:

+ Print Quality: Use a good ribbon and avoid smudges.

+ Paper Quality: Use paper that has some backbone.

+ Cover-up: There are easy ways to cover your errors.

+ Binding: Think of the binding <u>before</u> you print.

These are things that relate to problems we face daily in our business; for a coming association newsletter, you may want to summarize these points. You might also want to pass along some hints on how to sign correspondence, use the correct memo form, and signify copies to others.

I look forward to seeing you at the annual meeting at Starved Rock; hope this information is useful and helpful to other members.

Sincerely,

Greg

Greg Vertrees, Owner

GV/wt

Making Sure You Look Good

WHAT YOU CAN LEARN BY STUDYING THIS CHAPTER

In the first five chapters you were introduced to the basic principles of business communication. These principles are applicable to all types of communication in all kinds of organizations. In Chapters 7 through 21 you will explore the various kinds of business communications. This chapter serves as a transition between the principles and the particular kinds of communications you will prepare in organizations. It will give you an idea of what and how you will communicate, together with examples of communications of the quality most organizations demand. You will learn some techniques for producing effective written and oral communications for any type of organization you may join.

You demand quality in what you buy!

Your employer demands quality in your communications.

In recent years, the quality of manufactured goods in the United States has been severely criticized. Many of your classmates own automobiles, stereos, and televisions that were manufactured in a foreign country. Why? Because, say those classmates, for the price, the quality of an American product is not up to that of the foreign product. They may be right. But what about the quality of those classmates' communications—and yours; are your communication skills up to the standard of the organization you want to hire you?

PREVENTION VS. DETECTION

Many manufacturers in the United States have recognized the quality problem and have changed their attitude. Quality is now a criterion imposed throughout the manufacturing process, not just tacked on at the end of the process. As Ford Motor Company says, "Quality is Job 1." To succeed in an organization, you must produce communications of first quality also.

The old-fashioned way to produce goods was to run the assembly line and then inspect for errors at the end. That is a quality detection system, and it is very expensive. Today, the emphasis is on prevention—establishing and applying quality standards so errors may be avoided. A similar quality prevention system can aid you in producing communications of outstanding quality. In manufacturing, quality must be considered at every step—in the market research, product development, manufacturing, distribution, and sale of the product. Many corporations today insist on *zero errors*.

Communicating with zero errors is the goal.

As a writer applying the concept of prevention you want to accomplish two goals. First, at every step in the creative process, you should strive to eliminate errors. Second, after drafting the material several times, you should try to produce a piece of communication that is completely error free.

At every step of the communication process, strive to prevent errors.

During the writing process, the concept of zero errors should dominate your thinking and the implementation of your communications. Therefore, let's look at some factors to aid you in ensuring that your communications are error free. After all, if it is possible for a team of individuals to produce a car or a computer with zero errors, certainly it's possible for you to prepare a letter, memo, or short report with zero errors. And remember, the communication you send that has zero errors makes you look good.

PRODUCING QUALITY COMMUNICATIONS

Having quality in your communications is *your job.*

Most of the problems in manufacturing are not created by operating personnel; they are created by management. As a future manager, you should make sure that you have zero errors in your communications. You may have a fine secretarial and support staff to assist you in producing quality material, but the quality standards and their implementation are your job. This means that you are responsible for the letters, memos, and reports you send. It is unwise and wrong for you to blame your communication errors on others—just as it is wrong for the management in a factory to blame its hourly employees for errors in a product. The quality of your communications is your responsibility.

Whether communicating with employees or writing a letter to a vendor, it is a manager's job to ensure that communications are of top quality with zero errors. This means the communications are neat, use up-to-date conversational styles, incorporate language that is understandable, and are correct in every detail.

Manufacturers have guidelines, checklists, and tolerances for employees to check as products move along the line so that errors can be prevented. You should develop a quality checklist, too. It might be similar to the one a business communication student developed, represented in Figure 6.1.

Do you have a communication checklist for monitoring quality?

With the concept of quality well in mind, let's look at the two dominant written forms of business communication—the memo and the letter—and then explore some suggestions you can apply to ensure that your written communications have a top-quality appearance.

USING THE MEMORANDUM EFFECTIVELY

The memo is a manager's most frequently used written medium of communication. At one time it was thought that because of its informality, the memo should be used primarily for internal communications—that is, the memo was not used for people outside the organization. Today, memos are often used inside *and* outside the organization.

Memos are used widely.

Memo Stationery

Many organizations print memo forms (see Figure 6.2), and some are a half-page in length or less; however, businesses generally use 8½-by-11 inch (standard letter size) paper; there is always a danger that smaller sheets can become misplaced. Printed forms often specify where the writer inserts names, subject, and date. The typed format of the memo itself follows the basic formats of letters. That is, the memo can be in full block, modified block, or modified block with indented paragraphs.

The narrative of the memo can be formatted like a letter.

Whose Name Appears Where

When the memo is going to individuals who have an equal interest in the subject, each person's name often appears at the top of the memo. However, if the memo is going primarily to one individual, such as a department head, and to some other tangential individuals, then the primary recipient's name appears at the top and the other names may be "copied" at the bottom. Some firms never want company managers and outsiders (like consultants) mixed together in the "TO" section. Be sure to know the policy of your organization before initiating messages.

Know your organization's protocol on listing names in a memo.

FIGURE 6.1 Analysis of Your Communication's Productivity

	Appropriateness	Specificity	Clarity	Tone	Correctness
I. Form/Format					
1. Salutation					
2. Subject Line					
3. Close/Signature					
4. Signed Name					
5. Typos/Spelling					
6. Headings					
7. Vertical Spacing					
8. Horizontal Spacing					
9. Proportion					
10. Margins					
II. Substance					
11. Organization Sequence					
12. Organization Clarity					
13. Organization Strategy					
14. Depth					
15. Clarity and Completeness					
III. Verbal Style					
16. Tone					
17. Jargon/Slang/Legalese					
18. Overuse					
19. Documentation/Proof					
20. Transitions					
21. It/There/Their Use					
22. Action/Passive Voice					
23. Sex-fair Language					
24. Triteness					
25. Variety					
IV. Non-verbal Elements					
26. Businesslike Appearance					
27. Tables/Charts					
28. Appendixes					
29. I-orientation					
30. Neatness					
V. English Usage					
31. Punctuation					
32. Capitalization					
33. Number Usage/Pg.#'s					
34. Abbreviations/Hyphens					
35. Subject/Verb Agreement					
36. Word Usage					
37. Adjective Usage					
38. Possessives					
39. Tense					
40. Pronoun Overuse					
41. Parallelism					
42. Paragraphing					
43. Sentence Construction					
44. Word Overuse					
45. Correct Contractions					

FIGURE 6.2   A Collage of Memo Forms

Continental Store

Inter-office

Date:
To:
From:
Subject:

ACCURADATA

To:

Fr:

INTER
OFFICE
MEMO

K
P   **Kalamazoo Plastics**

MEMO To:
FROM:
DATE:
SUBJECT:

Western Home Products

Fr: _____   To: _____
Re: _____   Date: _____

Get the Order Correct

In the "TO" section, it is usual to place the names in rank order, such as president, vice-president, manager, and department head. At times, you can avoid discriminating against individuals (especially if you are unsure of their rank) by placing the names in alphabetical order. Organizations, like people, have personalities. These "personalities" will be reflected in how they communicate. In some organizations, first names are not used: In the "TO" section you will see R. J. Benson, D. R. Demming, M. R. Ostrum, C. G. Rowland; in less formal organizations, you will see

FIGURE 6.3   Ways of Arranging Receivers' Names in a Memorandum

Formal, in Rank Order

TO: J. M. Penningworth, President
R. J. Bennington, Executive Vice-President
K. G. Andrews, Vice-President
L. V. Dietz, Sales Manager

Formal, in Alphabetical Order

TO: R. M. Benson
J. J. Evers
O. P. Hemingway
G. J. Munson

Less Formal, in Alphabetical Order

TO: David Conway
Donald Jennings
Janet Monroe
John Worthy

Informal, in Alphabetical Order

TO: Dave Conway
Don Jennings
Jan Monroe
Jack Worthy

Ray Benson, Donna Demming, Mary Ostrum, and Craig Rowland (this also aids you in knowing the gender of those involved). See Figure 6.3.

The same practices (use of the first name or simply the first initial of the first name) are also followed for the sender or "FROM" portion of the memo. Determine your firm's policy on the use of names in the heading portion of memos and adhere to it.

In addition, more and more firms are placing both the sender's title and the receiver's title immediately after the names. With more company documents "going to court" these days, the title is sometimes evidence that the writer (or reader) could or could not take such and such action (as stated in the memo), according to published company policy or governmental regulations.

Dates should always be written out as January 3 or 3 January. When a date is indicated as 1/3 or 1-3, it may very well be read overseas as March 1 and not as January 3.

The subject line should be concise, meaningful, and carefully phrased so the reader or the file clerk knows at a glance the subject of the memo. As a matter of fact, a good subject line can often save the sender the bother of writing an introductory paragraph.

In all cases, you should follow the memo format approved by the company for which you work.

USING THE LETTER EFFECTIVELY

The business letter is generally used for external communications; the letter may also be used for more formal internal situations. It is the writer's responsibility to know the various formats and to specify the format desired. Appendix B shows the letter formats, and Figure 6.4 indicates the two most common formats. There are several reasons for learning letter formats. First, it is the communicator's responsibility to know the medium by which he or she can communicate. Second, in order to meet certain space limitations, you may sometimes want to alter the format. Some employers will specify a preferred format, but you may need to deviate from the suggested format from time to time.

Copies: cc vs. bc

At times, you may send a written message to others beyond the addressee. When you do, you should normally indicate that a copy or copies have been sent by showing the recipients' names at the bottom of the communication. Although secretaries rarely use carbon paper today, the names are still often noted with a "cc: Donald Bates"; "cc" can also designate "courtesy copy." But the copy is probably a photocopy. Therefore, some writers use "xc." Yet, since not all photocopy machines are the Xerox brand, we sometimes simply see "c." Handling such notations is clearly a matter of individual preference.

The use of the blind copy ("bc") is even more intriguing. In Figure 6.5, the secretary of an organist association thanks a contributor for her contribution. But the secretary also wants the treasurer to know that contact has been made and that the check should be expected. In this case, it is easier to send a "bc" than to initiate an entirely new communication to the treasurer. But it would be in poor taste to indicate this information on the receiver's copy. Therefore, the blind copy is both an efficient and a private way to transmit this information. When you want to let someone else see a communication, but you do not want the primary receiver to know that you have

Think about how you handle routine items above the narrative in memos.

Knowing the various letter formats allows you to select the appropriate form for your message.

Recognize the functional and subtle aspects of copies.

"B.C.s" are quick ways of keeping others informed.

FIGURE 6.4   Two Common Formats for Correspondence

Memphis
Community
College

Memphis, Tennessee 38111

February 10, 198_

Mr. Leonard O. Hollmann
Executive Director
Trendex Engineering Company
1418 East LaSalle Street
Chicago, Illinois 60024

Dear Mr. Hollmann:

There are several different formats that may be used for typing
business letters.

This is an example of a full block style where every line starts at
the left margin. There are no paragraph indents. It is often preferred by typists because it is so easy to set up.

Note that the salutation is followed by a colon. In a more informal
situation where the addressee is a personal friend, the salutation
could be followed by a comma.

Sincerely,

Robert Jennings

Robert J. Jennings
Sales Manager

RJ/db

Enclosure

7667 Garden Street
Memphis, Tennessee   38101

October 19, 198_

Ms. Pam C. Cartwright
Abbott Corporation
100 West Fifth Avenue
Los Angeles, CA 90009

Dear Ms. Cartwright:

This letter is very similar to the modified block letter, except
that the first line of each new paragraph is indented five spaces.

As shown, the date and the complimentary closing start near the
center of the page. However, in some cases, the date might have to be
realigned to conform with the letterhead.

This type of letter is in common use today in many business
situations.

Cordially yours,

Clay S. Davis

Clay S. Davis
Customer Relations

FIGURE 6.5   Use of the Blind Copy

American Guild of Organists

July 1, 198_

Dr. Joan Jefferson, Dean
College of Communications and Fine Arts
Toledo University
Toledo, OH 43606

Thank you very much Joan . . .

. . . for your continued support of the Toledo Chapter of the American Guild
of Organists and specifically of the Chapter's Artist Subscription Series. This Series
allows the Chapter to bring outstanding organ recitalists to your campus. As you
know, with the exception of your generous gift, the funding for these recitals is
contributed by local organizations and individuals—primarily members of the
Chapter.

Now that the new fiscal year is underway, will you please have your financial
assistant send your contribution of $200.00 to the Chapter's Treasurer:

Mr. Edward Semmingson
711 East Heacock Street
Toledo, OH 43605

Of course, the College's contribution will be recognized in the program for the
recital as a Benefactor.

It is always pleasant to visit with you; it was certainly nice to get to see your
fabulous computer facilities—your students are certainly fortunate to have these
technologies right at their fingertips.

Sincerely,

Tim

Timothy C. Lemming
Secretary

TCL/mas

bc: Ed Semmingson

shared the communication, the "bc" designation is appropriate. Be certain that "bc" does *not* appear on the primary receiver's copy; however, you will want to place the "bc" notation on your file copy and on the copy going to the "bc" recipient. That way, the "bc" receiver will understand the context of the situation. Sometimes on the blind copy you will want to add a slight explanation (either typed or handwritten) updating the copied person.

THE NONVERBAL MESSAGE IN YOUR SIGNATURE

A factor often overlooked in business communications, but crucial to making sure your message is properly received, is how you sign your name on the document. Generally, letters and memoranda have your formal name typed on the correspondence. However, you can individualize and personalize the typed message by the way you actually sign your name. Look at the examples in Figure 6.6. What does the signature indicate? Although the name is typed identically each time, the signature indicates something about the nature and tone of the message.

How you sign your name *communicates*.

When you were a child, if one of your parents, using a stern voice, called you by all three of your names—"Jane Ann Snodgrass!"—you knew you were in trouble. On the other hand, when you had done something good and your parent wanted to praise you, the call would go out for "Janie." How you were named indicated the nature of the situation. The same idea applies in business correspondence. The way you actually sign your name indicates your relationship to the receiver, the tone of your message, the nature of the message, and the relationship you desire to establish. Give careful consideration to this factor—it is an important one for it has far-reaching communication implications.

IMPROVING YOUR COMMUNICATION IMAGE

In the rush of the business day, it is sometimes difficult to produce zero error correspondence. But the organization demands it. Here are a few techniques to aid you in producing excellent copy.

Print Quality

Whether you use a typewriter or a word processor, the quality of print is important. Using a manual typewriter with a worn-out cotton ribbon will not give you a crisp-looking message. Using a dot-matrix word processor can leave much to be desired, too. It is important to select your print medium carefully. There are a variety of considerations, but a carbon ribbon or a near-letter- or letter-quality printer can aid you in projecting an appropriate image on paper. Figure 6.7 indicates how different prints communicate.

Select a print that makes reading easy.

FIGURE 6.6   What Does the Signature Communicate?

TO: Betty Ford

FR: R. James Bennington   *R.J.*

RE: Analysis of Your July Sales

DT: August 10, 198_

TO: John Denton

FR: R. James Bennington   *R. Bennington*

RE: Analysis of Your July Sales

DT: August 10, 198_

TO: Lynn Johnson

FR: R. James Bennington   *Jim*

RE: Analysis of Your July Sales

DT: August 10, 198_

Congratulations on another banner month Lynn! Besides being impressed with just the total amount of sales, I was particularly pleased to see how you have expanded the market in your region. This kind of penetration is what we need; faster than any other technique, that is the way we can expand our market base.

TO: Joan Remmington

FR: R. James Bennington   *R. J. Bennington*

RE: Analysis of Your July Sales

DT: August 10, 198_

By this time I had hoped that your sales would be showing an increase. These summer months are our times when our sales should be very strong—in fact growing—in your district. Before the end of this month, will you please make an appointment with my secretary so we can seriously discuss your regional situation, your sales, and your performance in the market.

FIGURE 6.7   The Print You Select Also Communicates

<u>Cotton Ribbon, Electric</u>

For years, philosophers, teachers, and others have attempted to let people know that there is more to language than just the words--the appearance also has impact.

<u>Carbon Ribbon, Electric (Self-correcting)</u>

For years, philosophers, teachers, and others have attempted to let people know that there is more to language than just the words--the appearance of the words also has impact.

<u>Draft Quality, Word Processor</u>

For years, philosophers, teachers, and others have attempted to let people know that there is more to language than just the words—the appearance of the words also has impact.

<u>Near-letter Quality, Word Processor</u>

For years, philosophers, teachers, and others have attempted to let people know that there is more to language than just the words—the appearance of the words also has impact.

Paper Quality

If you have ever picked up a piece of stationery from a *Fortune* 500 company, you will note it has backbone. It is an excellent quality paper that has a high fiber content and when unfolded will stand erect. Corporations want to reflect strength and quality. Select paper of at least 20-pound weight, and consider using that which has a high fiber content.

Don't be a flimsy communicator.

Covering Your Errors

Most of us make errors when typing. Furthermore, those errors are going to show up on our final copy, even if we cover them with white-out. If you have a self-correcting typewriter, you can generally "lift off" your errors. If you are producing materials on a word processor, you can easily retype the copy. However, if you use a standard

Communication cover-ups aren't always bad.

typewriter, there is a technique you can use to eliminate errors without retyping entire pages. Use white-out or cover-up tape on your original. Then, using an excellent photocopier, have the original photocopied onto good paper. This can produce a professional-looking document. Also, when you use this technique, type the original on slick paper and photocopy it on the high-fiber paper. It is difficult to make neat corrections on high-fiber paper, and fiber papers often do not photocopy well.

Photocopying

Virtually every office has a photocopy machine. That photocopier can improve the image of your communication and speed your communications.

The photocopier can aid communication productivity.

Originals. As you have seen, a high-quality photocopying machine can be used to produce the final document. Sometimes it is possible to photocopy near-letter-quality print from a word processor on to paper at a dark setting to achieve "letter quality" print.

A Reserve. If you only have one form of a document you are to prepare, make several photocopies before you start to type. This will allow you to keep the original or a copy in reserve if you make an error.

Binding Problems. Sometimes you want to photocopy an item that has a spiral binding. The first photocopy is going to reveal that binding. However, by taking that copy and making an additional copy (after the "holes" have been covered or cut off), it is possible to remove the photocopied image of the binding. (See Figure 6.8.)

Covers and Binders

People do judge a book by its cover. The reports and other materials you prepare in the organization will be judged by their covers. Therefore, give careful consideration to how you cover your materials and how you bind them. Generally, because of their formality, long reports in the organization are bound. At the same time, the original is often left unbound in case there is a need to make additional copies.

Covers and bindings communicate.

There are a variety of bindings you can use. The type you select depends on the length, use, number of copies, and need to photocopy the material. The kinds of bindings and their advantages and disadvantages are noted in Figure 6.9.

FIGURE 6.8 Poor Photocopying Communicates the Wrong Message

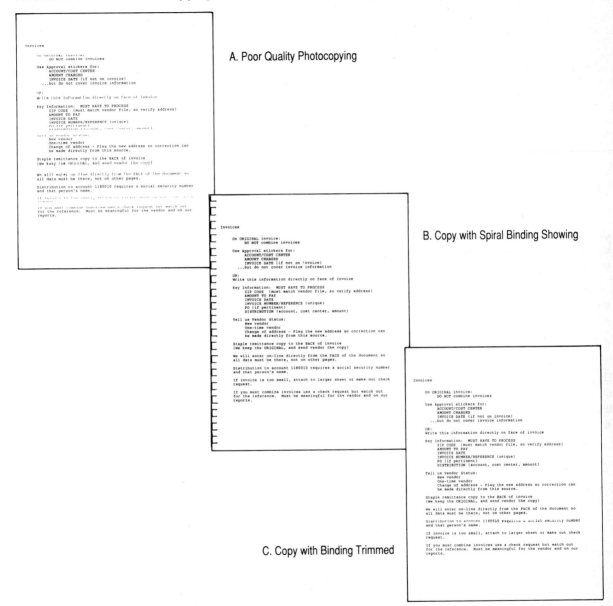

A. Poor Quality Photocopying

B. Copy with Spiral Binding Showing

C. Copy with Binding Trimmed

FIGURE 6.9   Collage of Common Bindings

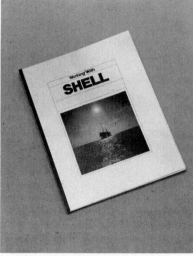

SPIRAL BINDING

Advantages
Neat
Useful for short and long reports
Lays open flat
Binding machinery generally available

Disadvantages
Pages cannot be easily removed
Difficult to photocopy

WELDING BINDING

Advantages
Pages are permanently bound, neat
    and secure

Disadvantages
Very difficult to photocopy
Pages cannot be removed
Does not lay open flat
Binding machinery not generally
    available

THREE-RING NOTEBOOK

Advantages
Easy to remove and change pages
Can create colorful covers by slipping
    sheet under plastic cover on front
No special equipment needed to
    implement
Easy to photocopy, but holes are
    unattractive

Disadvantages
Pages easy to lose if removed
Heavy and bulky
Holes tear with heavy use

In covering your report, give careful consideration to the use of clip art and other visual techniques. Chapter 17 presents information on visuals, but you should recognize in covering a report that the use of visuals and the color of the paper are important items. Do not leave the concept of the cover and binding to the last moment. Start to think of it well in advance so the ideas you have for covering and binding your report can be adequately implemented.

Using Word Processing

Today, a variety of word-processing programs are available to aid you in achieving your communication objectives. These programs can aid your communication image. A few of them are Spell Check, Synonym, Print Options, Overuse of Word, and Grammar Check.

USING THE ORAL MEDIUM EFFECTIVELY

An effective manager is also called upon for a variety of oral communications, from informative talks for groups to rather personal, one-on-one exchanges. Chapters 18, 19, and 20 deal with the elements of oral communication. Here are a few guidelines for quality oral communications.

Establish Rapport. In any oral situation, strive to quickly establish a meaningful relationship with others present.

Maintain Rapport. Having established rapport, don't lose it. One of the key elements is maintaining eye contact with others.

Don't Wander. In written communications, try to reduce words and gobbledygook. The same applies to oral communications—don't talk to simply hear yourself.

Be Yourself. Some people, when they sit at the keyboard, type words that are not part of their standard vocabulary. Similarly, when people start to talk they sometimes put on a different hat. Don't do that—just be yourself.

Most of the hints for writing also apply to oral communications.

Courtesy. When giving a speech, do not hesitate to express appreciation to others; when speaking in a discussion session, give others an opportunity to talk. Having the floor for a few moments does not mean you need to monopolize it.

Length. In written communications, one page is often enough. The same applies in oral communications. Have your audience wishing you had talked longer rather than hoping you will stop soon!

Image. Just as the memo must be neat in order to get to first base, so must the speaker be neat-appearing. Sloppiness is distracting and difficult for most people to accept in a person making a presentation.

Visuals. Be sure your visuals are easy to understand and readable from every seat in the room.

QUICK REVIEW

There is much you can do to project the appropriate verbal and nonverbal communication image. Think quality, strive to detect errors *before* they enter your work, and be sure to use appropriate memo and letter formats. Type neatly, use stationery with backbone, produce excellent photocopies, sign correspondence appropriately, and bind materials sensibly and cover them in a suitable fashion. When speaking individually or in a group discussion, apply most of the "look good" concepts—be neat, be brief, be interesting.

EXECUTIVE SUMMARY

To: Business Communication Students

From: David N. Bateman and Norman B. Sigband

Subject: Making Sure You Look Good

The primary message in this chapter has to do with securing "quality" in your written communications.

The memo is noted as a primary internal communication tool. Specific mechanics of the memo as well as the business letter are quickly reviewed.

The correct use of such mechanics as the "To" and "From" and the use of names in memos are discussed. Current conventions are also pointed out concerning the designation of "copies" in business letter use. Other items such as the signature, print and paper quality, covers, and photocopies are also reviewed.

The overall theme of this chapter is securing a zero level of errors in all oral and written communications. To assist the communicator, the authors also present a page with specific areas noted to serve as a checklist.

DISCUSSION GENERATORS

1. *A Cover-up?* Explain how "people do judge a book by its cover" in relation to business communications.
2. *Different Inkings.* Illustrate two different ways you might sign your name to identical business letters—although the language of each is the same, you desire to send different nonverbal messages.
3. *Letter Images.* Why are major corporations so concerned with their images— especially the image they project in the letters their employees send?
4. *Should You Be a Detective?* What is the difference between detecting errors and preventing errors in your written communications?
5. *Erasures.* What are three ways to cover up errors in your written materials?

6. *Zero Errors.* How does word processing help you achieve zero errors in the final copy of a written document?

7. *It's Your Fault!* The boss prepares a couple of drafts of a letter; they are typed and eventually the final copy is ready. The boss signs and sends the letter. Later the receiver points out that there was a group of words that was not a complete sentence. The boss "blows his stack" and blames the word processing staff and the secretary. Is the boss correct?

8. *Usual Errors.* What are the common errors that enter your written communications? What can you do to eliminate them?

9. *Your Checklist.* Figure 6.1 shows a checklist a student developed for evaluating communication quality. Noting your strengths and weaknesses, what would your checklist include that is not represented in this sample?

10. *"TO" Sequencing.* What are the options for arranging the names of six people in the "To" section of a memo?

11. *T. J. O'Hare.* What problems are created in firms that use first and middle initials plus the last name in the "To" section of the memo?

12. *Inside Letter.* In what situation might you use the letter format, instead of the memo format, when writing a person inside the organization?

13. *The "C's."* Explain the difference among "c," "cc," and "bc."

14. *Where's the "bc"?* The "bc" notation appears on the receiver's copy. Why doesn't the "bc" appear on the copy of the letter going to the primary receiver?

15. *What's Your Name?* You are vice-president of finance at a rather conservative corporation. Your name is Robert C. Swanson *III,* and those who know you call you "Bob." Indicate how you would sign your name on each of the following letters; in each case, your name is typed *Robert C. Swanson III:*
    a. A letter to college recruits that explains the financial operations of the company; the letter appears in a company recruiting brochure.
    b. A letter to a college friend who was just named the president of a firm that competes with yours.
    c. A letter to a government agency justifying a recent financial change your firm has instituted.
    d. A form letter to all employees in the finance area wishing them a Happy Holiday.

16. *Backbone.* Why is it important for your stationery to have "backbone"?

17. *Easy Copies.* What kind of binding makes it easiest to photocopy the bound materials?

18. *Don't Let the Errors Appear.* How can the photocopy machine save you time in producing zero error letters?

19. *Slick Type.* Why might you want to type the original material on slick inexpensive paper and then photocopy that material onto a higher quality paper?

20. *Not Necessarily a Pretty Ribbon.* What is the disadvantage of using a cotton ribbon on your typewriter?

APPLICATIONS FOR BUSINESS

21. *Quality Photocopies.* You are the lead student worker in an office on your campus. You note that rather frequently student workers make poor photocopies and also permit poor quality originals to leave the office. Develop some procedures for improving the overall quality of the photocopying and the quality of the item produced from a poor original.

22. *Training Manual.* You are in charge of arrangements for a training seminar the Oster Company Personnel Department is conducting for supervisors on non-discriminatory activities. Besides having the people learn items in the seminar, it is important that they take, read, and share photocopies of the manual materials with others in their department. All of the items in the manual are important and you don't want to have the participants separate them from the manual because some material may get lost.

      Develop a recommendation for how you would bind the thirty-five-page manual for the eighty people participating in the seminar.

23. *Immoral?* As a supervisor of the word processing department in your organization, you wrote a favorable letter of recommendation for Ronald, who had an opportunity to join your firm's computer department. Your letter was sent to Betty Benson, the head of the Computer Department. You also sent Ronald a blind copy. Ronald got the job, but Betty discovered that Ronald got a copy of the letter that she felt was written just to her. Betty feels that this is dishonest and actually immoral. Do you agree? Justify your answer.

24. *Image.* Corporations and other organizations want to project favorable images. Yet in some respects, the image is a value judgment. In this text and in the accompanying *Study Guide* are samples of stationery for a number of companies.
    a. From your perspective, which piece of stationery projects the most favorable image? Explain why.
    b. From your perspective, which piece of stationery projects the least favorable image? Explain why.
    c. Take your selection for "a" and find a good quality paper it could be printed on. What would be the weight and color of the stationery? Provide a sample and be able to justify your recommendation.

25. *Memo Formats.* As illustrated in Figure 6.2, there are a variety of formats for memos in different organizations. Some firms list the receiver first and others the sender first. Which do you prefer, and why?

COMMUNICATION CHECK-UPS

26. Betty works for Amdex and Jane is employed by WBS and they use their corporation's automobiles.

27. It was my sister's-in-law decision for them to make the transfer to Los Angeles.

28. The auditors, as well as the partner, did their jobs very professionally.

29. She errored on the side of conservative accounting.

30. Can Barbara Hemmingway attend the preconference meeting?

31. The coarse the firm sponsors for potential supervisors is rigorous and rough.

32. When the questionnaires were altogether they were transferred to data processing.

33. She accepted the complement graciously.

34. She took considerable flack on her decision to re-structure the department.

35. The photo copier is too be used only for business materials.

Executive
Introduction

A-Korn Roller, Inc.

3545 South Morgan Street
Chicago, Illinois 60609
Phone 312 254-5700

April 8, 198_

Mr. Patrick J. Koren, VP
A-Korn Roller, Inc.
4220 Milwaukee
Denver, CO 80216

Locating top sales reps is important to us, Pat . . .

. . . and getting the right people as our business expands is crucial
to our success. I've come across a chapter on sales in a business
communication text that makes some important points about sales. These
concepts can be helpful to us.

   Sales Orientation. In communicating, it is beneficial to
recognize the need for the total sales orientation. As we interview
and recruit sales reps, perhaps we should see if they have a solid
sales orientation—something beyond clever sales techniques.

   Indirect Sales. The aspect of indirect sales may be something we
need to emphasize. A great variety of indirect methods work in
communications, and they can surely work for us.

   Interest. It is essential for our reps to take an interest in
our products, their customers, and our company and to communicate that
interest. After all, from our viewpoint, there is nothing dull about a
printing roller!

   Prove It. The elements of proof are important to selling; how do
you persuade the customer to buy? It might be helpful for our sales
people to quickly review these elements; they are simple, but the
sales rep on the firing line has to remember them and employ them.

   You know it's odd for me to be sending textbook items to you;
however, these materials are on target for some of our problems. Enjoy
your snow, but please fall easy off your skis; we need you desperately
these next few months at A-Korn.

                              Sincerely,

                              Chuck

                              Charles Koren
                              Regional Manager

Encl: Sales Chapter

CHAPTER 7

Communicating to Sell

WHAT YOU CAN LEARN BY STUDYING THIS CHAPTER

Students sometimes say that since they are not going into sales, this chapter is not important. Some texts have chapters solely on sales *letters,* but this chapter goes far beyond sales letters. Why cover sales-oriented communication first? Because virtually every communication you transmit—regardless of your management position—will have some element of selling. Going beyond the traditional sales letter, we will examine the sales orientation in many kinds of written and oral communications.

Sales communications involve much more than sales letters.

There are two broad categories of sales communication we will explore. One is the traditional or direct, like the letter a sales representative for an office machinery company sends to entice you to purchase a new photocopier. The other, and more common, category includes most of the other communication, written and oral, you will be called upon to prepare. For example, you may make a presentation to your top management with the purpose of *informing* them about statistical process control, but your unstated purpose is to *sell* them on the idea that you are a capable and alert individual.

VIRTUALLY EVERY COMMUNICATION HAS A SALES ORIENTATION

Selling often means getting your ideas accepted.

Look at the list of business communications in Table 7.1, and consider how each might have some kind of sales orientation. This orientation may be either *direct* or *indirect,* but in either case, "selling" (or persuading) the receiver to accept you and your ideas is very important.

The communications in Table 7.1 represent various communications you will implement as a manager and that you will study in later chapters. Before looking at the right side of the table, consider how each communication might have a sales orientation. Consider the concept of the *shadings* of sales—how you "tone" the sales orientation can have a major impact on how the message is received and acted upon.

DIRECT SALES VS. INDIRECT SALES

Direct sales can be targeted to a specific audience.

It is important to differentiate what we might call the direct or obvious sales communication from the communication that has an indirect or more subtle sales purpose. The direct sales communication might be a letter that the automobile salesperson sends to some selected professionals in the community in an attempt to close out luxury cars at the end of a model year (see Figure 7.1). Clearly, the purpose of the letter is to attract inquiries for the luxury automobile and sell the autos. The sales orientation is obvious. Both the sender and the receiver understand the sales orientation. This example also contains a goodwill thrust that is not always part of all direct sales messages. Most of us receive many direct sales letters each month attempting to sell us magazine subscriptions, stereos, insurance plans, and a variety of other products and services.

Indirect sales often focus on selling the communicator.

Then there are those communications that have a more indirect sales orientation. For example, suppose that as a new manager in the accounting department, you need to prepare a memo to the department head recommending that a new computer software package be purchased. Here the obvious purpose is to persuade the boss to purchase the spreadsheet software. This has a somewhat direct sales orientation—you want to convince the boss to respond favorably. It also has an indirect sales orientation—you want to communicate that you are a capable individual; in essence, you are also selling yourself (see Figure 7.2).

TABLE 7.1   Shadings of Sales Orientation in Various Kinds of Business Communications

THE TYPE OF COMMUNICATION	THE SALES ORIENTATION
A mass-produced direct sales letter	Clearly a mass mailing; both the sender and receiver recognize the direct sales approach of this type of communication. (See Figure 7.3.)
A collection letter	It sells the idea of paying up at once; sometimes it may also attempt to sell the concept of continuing to do business with the sender, depending on the seriousness of the collection problem.
A direct sales letter	Clearly a sales letter, but with a personal touch: individualized address, salutation, and signature of sender. Besides "selling," the letter can maintain contact and strive to establish goodwill. (See Figure 7.1.)
An internal recommendation in memo form	Internal memos that make suggestions and recommendations can have both a direct and indirect sales thrust—direct in that the idea is sold; indirect in that your abilities are being "sold." (See Figure 7.2.)
A "no" letter written to deny a person credit	Even though the answer is negative—not the response the receiver wants—two concepts can be "sold." One is rather direct—please continue to do business with us on a cash basis; the other, more subtle, is to sell the receiver on the idea that the company is good, i.e., sell "goodwill."
A response to an inquiry	An inquiry response could have a very direct sales approach if the inquiry concerned something you sold. Or, when ideas and not products are involved, the sales approach is indirect. (See Fig. 7.4.)
An oral briefing	The emphasis here is on information, but a manager may want to "sell" himself or herself as alert, insightful, and competent.
A thank-you letter	The purpose is to express sincere thanks. At the same time, it can "sell" the receiver on an idea and create goodwill.

FIGURE 7.1   Direct Sales Letter with a Goodwill Message

Cameron Motors

Pleasanton, California   95928

December 1, 198_

(Name)_____
(Address)_____
(City, State, Zip)_____

Dear Mr./Miss/Mrs./Ms._____

You-oriented attention-getting opening statement.

    The new tax laws <u>require you</u> to lengthen the depreciation time on your business auto. Therefore, it is to your advantage to purchase your business automobile this year.

    There are several factors to consider on why you should select the luxurious Mercedes Benz from Cameron Motors:

Indented listings can highlight important points.

    +   In your income bracket, it is advantageous to consider the tax implications of your purchases. It is a good idea to buy an auto before the end of the year.

    +   The current models are not changing next year (and won't for the next several years), therefore the car you purchase this year will be in style for several years.

Modified block format with indented paragraphs.

    +   A Mercedes Benz from Cameron is not cheap. But because of the purchasing power we have, we can offer you a price that cannot be beat in the region.

    +   Our price and the tax implications add up to substantial savings for you.

Keeping action in sender's court.

    I will call you on Thursday, December 4, to arrange a convenient time when I can pick you up for an introductory drive in the glamorous Mercedes Benz.

Goodwill closing.

    During the holiday season all of us at Cameron wish you and your family the best.

Cordially,

Jan Meyers

Jan Myers
Sales Associate

Purpose of Communication: To have seven of the twenty recipients call back for a test drive.
Proof: Trial offer
Appeal: Economic advantage

FIGURE 7.2   Internal Memo with a Sales Orientation

Memo

TO: Bob Donnley, Director of Accounting Affairs

FR: Jane Perkins, Manager Internal Operations   *Jane*

DT: January 25, 198_

RE: Need for Faster Software (Quik:1-2-3)

Note the tone and familiarity in how the memo is signed.

The Situation

    With our new and faster terminals it is obvious that much more time could be saved if a new software package was purchased to aid us in establishing trial balances, reconciliations, and budget projections. The current system (Advance 100) is adequate and was good for the old terminals. However, with the new high speed equipment, Quik:1-2-3 would be much more advantageous.

Clear headings aid the reader.

Features/Advantages

    Compared to other somewhat similar programs, Quik has a variety of pluses for us:

    +Buy One. We need only purchase one package and then we are permitted to duplicate it for any pc in our department.

    +Speed. With our new pc's, the speed of the "set up" time and running our standard calculations would be cut in half.

    +Training. With the purchase, we receive training for each user, ongoing counsel, and tutorial modules.

    +Cost. The total cost for eighteen users in the department is $3,500. In the time saved alone, that expenditure would be recouped in less than one week.

The features are emphasized with the format: indented paragraphs each with its own heading.

Recommendation

    Because of the direct savings we would achieve and the advantages we would gain in developing comparable data, it is recommended that we purchase the Quik:1-2-3 and that the program be installed and our people trained on it during the first two weeks of March. In terms of work load and the fiscal year considerations, this would be an excellent time to switch to Quik.

The action desired is clearly stated in the recommendation.

Purpose: To persuade the boss to purchase Quik:1-2-3.
Proof: Comparitive analysis
Appeal: Economic advantage

Even thank-you communications can sell.

There are some "sales" communications that have an even more indirect sales orientation. For instance, imagine that you must send a thank-you letter to your boss and your boss' spouse thanking them for the kind and thoughtful dinner they had for you. On the surface, the purpose of the letter is to express appreciation for a fine dinner. On the other hand, you want to "sell" your boss on the idea that you are kind, considerate, professional, and have a future in the organization.

As you launch your management career, it is important to understand that the sales orientation is a part of virtually every communication you initiate. For that reason, it is important to understand the sales process, the various shadings of sales, and the different subtleties in the sales approach.

BASIC PRINCIPLES OF SELLING

Knowledge is key for successful sales.

Sales communications have a relationship to the sales approach you may have studied in a basic marketing course. Before attempting to develop a sales message (or have a professional firm write it for you), make sure you have satisfied the five basic principles of sales. These principles are applicable to both written and oral sales communications, and they work with direct and indirect sales:

1. *Know what you have to sell.* The communicator must know the strong *and* weak points of the item to be sold. What are its major advantages? How is it superior to competing ideas or products? What possible questions about the product or service might the receiver raise?
2. *Know your climate.* The "environment" is important in all sales situations. Who will find the product or service attractive? What will people pay for the product? In what geographical area will the major portion of the market be found?
3. *Know your receiver.* It is important to know as much as possible about the receivers. What are their specific needs and how does your idea, product, or service satisfy those needs?
4. *Know your competitors.* In most instances, the receivers will be well aware of competing products, services, or ideas. Therefore, it is necessary for the communicator to know the competition as well, whether it is other products or services—or even other ideas colleagues are attempting to sell in the organization.
5. *Know the appropriate proofs and appeals.* Once you know the product or service, the potential customer, and the market, you can select the proofs that will help receivers draw the appropriate conclusion. Determine the specific appeals the receivers will probably find attractive. The same product can have different appeals and different substantiating statements (proofs) for different people, depending on their needs or their economic, social, or educational status.

   Select a central appeal that will be attractive to your prospect and make your product or service "different" from competing items. There are a number of appeals, including pride, fear, and self-interest (such as economic security). These and other basic appeals are explained and illustrated more fully in Chapter 11.

DEVELOPING THE SALES-ORIENTED COMMUNICATION

There are four basic requirements for any sales communication: interest, description, proof, and action. Besides just knowing the sales steps, you should consider how the process applies to various kinds of direct and indirect sales. Review the examples in this chapter carefully, and consider the process in different situations.

Interest

There are two parts to capturing receivers' interest. First, the envelope must be interesting. Second, the actual message must immediately get the attention of receivers and get them moving through the content.

Ignore interest and the receiver will ignore you.

Getting the Envelope Opened—The Initial View.
Door-to-door salespeople must get the door open; direct-mail salespeople must make sure the envelope gets opened. Two techniques that can be used to motivate receivers to open the envelope are to (1) make it look as much as possible like a personal letter or (2) print an intriguing message on the envelope, such as the one used by an insurance company: "Insurance has never cost so little." Today mass-mail direct sales letters are sent to individuals by name instead of to "Occupant." The address is often typed with automatic memory typewriters, and sometimes a colorful commemorative stamp is used to add a personal touch.

Remember the "envelope" concept for other types of communications as well. The audience's first impression sets the stage. Do something at the very start of your oral presentation, briefing, speech, or short report to keep receivers with you. Just as the unread letter inside an unopened envelope is useless, so too is the oral briefing that the audience ignores or the report that no one hears. The sales orientation starts before the verbal message is received.

The "envelope" concept applies to written and oral communications.

Grab Your Receivers' Interest.
The average person receives an enormous amount of mail—much of it from mass mailings. We are also subjected to near bombardment by oral messages. Therefore, it is essential in direct mail to immediately arouse recipients' interest in reading the message. In organizations, the enormous number of internal and external mailings make the need to gain the reader's interest especially important. You need not be dull in attempting to win others over to your viewpoint. Good ideas become better ideas when they are communicated in an interesting manner.

A number of techniques can be used to attract interest.

Interest can be the "fly paper" of your communications—it attracts people to your ideas.

1. *An unusual opening statement* can entice receivers to read on or listen more intently. The opening might be a story, an interesting quote, or a startling statement. It should match the needs and desires of receivers, an approach that can be used in direct and indirect sales.
2. *A sample* can be provided, if feasible. In direct sales, a sample, such as toothpaste, might be included; in less direct sales situations (in your office, for example), a memo concerning a new computer print-out might include a sample of that print-out.
3. *Photos or sketches* can be used when it is not feasible to include the actual product or idea. In direct sales, a picture of the automobile, for example, can work well; in the office, a sketch of the layout of the new computer room can attract interest.
4. *Gimmicks* also attract attention. For instance, provide a pencil for marking a response in the collection letter—such as "payment enclosed." In indirect sales, gimmicks are rarely used, but sometimes intriguing questions or unusual computer graphics can help gain the interest of receivers.

Description

Create a good verbal picture.

Having gained the receivers' attention, you must next describe what you have to offer. Gaining attention should not take long in either direct or indirect sales. Obviously, it would not be wise to write a long paragraph or take a long time in a speech to establish interest. It would wear the receivers out. You want to get on to the "proof of the pudding" by describing the product, service, or idea. When dealing with more abstract concepts, be precise and detailed. To sell an automobile, for example, you might use glaring, rather nebulous adjectives for the description—"laserlike," "star filled," "fun," or "road master." On the other hand, describing the marketing strategy for a new, franchised fast-food outlet for towns under 4,000 in population must be exact: "4,000 in immediate area, cannot exceed 7,000 in market area; must be located in primary auto-traffic flow; older part-time help a key employee resource."

In Figure 7.3, note how the first sentence grabs one's attention, while the next two paragraphs describe the product and make an appeal to security. Finally, proof is provided.

Proof

Ideas do not stand alone; you must support them with proofs.

Although it's important to describe your product, service, or idea, that verbally painted picture is generally not enough to sell the idea. You must be able to provide recipients with proof that the product, service, or idea you are "selling" is worth the price or effort. In selecting your proof, carefully consider the audience. What approach will be most appropriate? For instance, in promoting a new word processing system for your office, the trade-in value of the current system, the increase in

FIGURE 7.3 Direct Sales Letter

HEMISPHERE
INSURANCE

May 31, 198_

Dear Young Professional!

You CAN put off to tomorrow a very important decision—but you may pay for it.

There is a simple way to secure your future and your family's security—by purchasing the Young Executive Term Life Plan (YETLP) from Hemisphere Insurance. This term-life plan allows you to continually set aside a standard amount of funds in order to achieve the level of confidence you desire.

Individuals on career paths similar to yours speak eloquently of YETLP:

Sue Markty, a single management trainee with a major department store, feels strongly that the insurance options provide her needed security.

Ben Jacobson, a newly married CPA, feels that the YETLP plan provides the added, and economical, security for his wife and their planned family.

Marg and Jim Washington, both working professionals, have found that the YETLP approach fits right in their budget today and their future financial plans.

If you will make arrangements to see one of our sales representatives before June 10, 198_, by calling Ted Huntley or Janet Benson at 309/654-3434, you will receive a gift certificate for a free meal on us at the fabulous Beachhead Restaurant.

Look at the many advantages that our plan offers for your future and then call so the Young Executive Term Life Plan can work to your advantage.

Cordially,

J.C. Rodgers

J. C. Rodgers

enc.

9225 W. KENMORE, BLOOMINGTON, ILLINOIS   61701

The use of the testimonial proof is targeted at the audience receiving the message.

Action is encouraged by offering a free meal.

Modified block format with indented paragraphs.

Purpose: To get 10 percent of the recipients to call before June 10.
Proof: Testimonials
Appeal: Security

productivity, names of other firms who have purchased the product, and the possibility of reducing one employee might be strong proofs. In selling life insurance, "no physical exam," additional coverage at a low cost, and the excellent reputation of the company may be "proofs" that will appeal to the receiver. In planning your communication, you need to carefully analyze the receivers: know their wants and needs; anticipate their questions. In selling a product, service, or idea, there are six common kinds of proof.

The Kinds and Uses of Proof.   In both direct and indirect sales, the communicator must support the idea being proposed. That idea might be to purchase a product, to hire a particular individual in your department, or to suggest the use of your bookkeeping service. The communicator should attempt to prove the value of the idea. The following kinds of proof are basic to any kind of management activity:

The Kind of Proof	*The Use of Proof in Direct and Indirect Sales Situations*
Testimonial	Citing the support of others can add credibility to an idea. Whether a quotation from a Nobel Prize winner to support a scientific idea, a public servant to support a social issue, or an athlete to support the use of vitamins, testimonials can be most persuasive.
Statistics	"Nine out of ten physicians recommend _____." Whether simple or complex mathematical representations, statistics allow the communicator to indicate that many people support the idea being presented. People are often impressed and persuaded by the magic of numbers.
Sample	The use of the sample is not limited to the small tube of toothpaste we periodically receive in the mail. In supporting ideas in the office, as in advertising, the sample can be a helpful proof: a sample of the redesigned package; a sample of the reconfigured letterhead; a sample of the gift to be awarded outstanding employees.
Guarantee	"Guaranteed for 90 days or your money back" is a familiar statement in selling products. It is a way to prove the worth of the concept. Similarly, in supporting an idea, a verifiable guarantee can help gain acceptance.
Trial Offer	People are often hesitant to adopt a new idea because they do not want to be stuck with it if it does not work. Therefore, the trial offer can be persuasive in getting people to give the product, service, or idea a try. "Try the photocopy machine for two weeks"; "use the courier

service for a month"; "set up a six-month trial run of flex-time." This persuasive proof allows the concept or product to be introduced with a "face-saving" way out.

Comparative Analysis	"Ours is ten times faster," " 'x' is more efficient and less costly than 'y.' " Comparisons, generally derived from one's own analysis, can be persuasive. You will find this element of proof useful and effective, especially in internal communications.

Three other keys to the sales orientation should be addressed in conjunction with proofs—the "picture," the element of selfishness, and brevity.

Painting a Verbal Picture.
Even though your communication may provide an actual picture of your product or concept, it is still necessary to create a verbal picture of your product, service, or idea. As you draw that picture, you should link it with the basic appeal or advantage you are offering receivers. What is the overriding reason receivers should be interested in the message? Focus upon it as you draw the verbal picture. Figure 7.4 paints a clear representation of a potentially complex issue; note the interesting use of the words "meat" and "bones" and the use of the faucet analogy. These techniques permit the receiver to envision your idea with you.

It is incumbent upon the communicator to paint the picture.

For another example, consider the many reasons for selecting a college to attend; different audiences will select the same college for different reasons. Whereas the young adult may be attracted by the social life and activities the institution offers, the parents may be more interested in the curriculum, placement of graduates, and the character of the faculty. In communicating with these different groups, you would want to carefully draw the appropriate verbal picture and then link it with the advantages offered the receiver.

What's In It for Me?
The receiver always wants to know, "What's in it for me?" Your verbal description should address this question and indicate ways to fulfill receivers' needs. You may prefer first to point to the product, service, or idea and then explain its benefits; or you may want to reverse the order and note the benefits before explaining the product, service, or idea. Either way, it is important to explain the advantages in clear terms with a you-orientation.

Let receivers know how they will benefit.

The One-page Maxim.
Although there are exceptions to most rules, effective sales letters are most often transmitted in one page. When selling a product, service or idea, however, there may be a wealth of other information you need to transmit. Therefore, various kinds of enclosures can be appended to the one-page sales letter. The sales letter strives to gain attention and briefly highlight the product, service, or idea, and then the attachments can provide the detail and supplemental information.

The one-page maxim is certainly transferable to oral communications. There is

FIGURE 7.4   Letter to "Sell" Ideas

Allis, Inc.

312 Henderson Drive
Cleveland, Ohio   44112

June 5, 198_

Mr. James Connelley, Manager
Human Resources
Antworp Corp.
P.O. Box 17
New Brunswick, NJ 08902

Dear Jim,

Your questions concerning our employee communications program are insightful
and challenging to answer. We recognized that to have good labor relations, our communications with employees had to be consistent, honest, and substantive.

These are a number of advantages in our approach to employee communications:

Supervisory Focus. Yes, we place considerable emphasis on the immediate
supervisor. In fact, we have eliminated communication activities that may tend to
circumvent the supervisor (employee hotline and the employee question box).

Meat. We don't toss our employees bones; we provide them with meaningful and
substantive information. Many times employers downgrade and denigrate their
employees by sending them nonsensical information.

Ongoing. Many firms treat their employee communications the way you and I
handle the faucet in the sink . . . we are continually turning it off and on. Consistency in
employee communications is vital. Information should be sent to employees regularly.

Thanks for your comments. Sure hope this information is helpful to you.

Sincerely,

John

John O. O'Malley, Director
Internal Communications

Because of the familiarity, note the salutation with the comma versus the colon.

Note the indirect sales, Allis is doing a good job.

Headings aid the sender emphasize the key points.

The closing paragraph is you-oriented.

Purpose: To answer Jim's questions and to inform him ("sell him") on the value of the employee
communication strategy.
Appeal: Workability—it works!

much the effective oral communicator can learn from the crisp 30–60 second announcements on radio and television. Effective and substantive communications need not be lengthy. In a well-planned and organized 3–5 minute briefing, a substantial amount of information can be transmitted and a hefty number of sales initiated.

You have seen many of these techniques used in direct sales. They will work in other kinds of communications, as well. In a memo to "sell" your boss on the idea of establishing a day-care center at your company or in a letter to a potential client to establish a retainer relationship with your accounting firm, these techniques of proof can be very helpful in winning the receiver over to you and to your ideas.

Action

As with planning (see Chapter 2), it is important with sales communications not just to memorize a list, but to understand the applicability of the concept. You can get started on the right foot—(1) provide a good first impression, (2) grab the interest, (3) describe the concept, and (4) provide proof—and still not make the sale. In sales communications, the most important measurement is not how fantastic the opening sentence was or how sophisticated your elements of proof were—it is whether you have convinced receivers to act and respond positively to your ideas.

Securing action is a key selling activity.

Align Your Action with Your Purpose.   Your communication has a purpose, and within a stipulated period of time, you can clearly see if you have accomplished that purpose. Note the following explicit sales purposes for various communications:

1. *To persuade* the boss (by March 2, 19--) to appoint a task force to consider the establishment of an in-house day-care center.
2. *To gain consensus,* install, and have operable in our office by September 10, 19--, a new, modern, and productive word processing system.
3. *To sell* the insurance offering to 7 percent of the recipients of the sales letter by February 15, 19--.
4. *To obtain* ten telephone call-back inquiries concerning a luxury automobile purchase by August 1, 19--.

Your purpose can focus the action you desire.

Knowing your purpose, you then need to design your communication to move the receivers to act. In direct-mail advertising, we see several ways to attempt this. For instance, "Respond within 15 days to get this low price" or "Offer available only to the first 800 telephone calls," or "Use the postage-paid postcard and respond today!"

In the sales-oriented communication, you are attempting to move the receivers to some kind of overt action. It is not enough for them simply to receive the communication. Having a purpose, knowing what action you desire, and then designing your communication to move the reader to action are crucial in any kind of sales-oriented communication.

Keep the Action in Your Court.   Do not relinquish the action to receivers in an unspecified manner. The following phrases are inappropriate because they give readers an "out"—a way not to respond. Your message is not sales oriented if it has any of the following phrases:

Don't promote inaction with trite statements.

1. Respond at your earliest convenience.
2. Hoping to hear from you soon.
3. Your interest in this concept is appreciated.
4. Let me know if you are interested in the idea.

You do not want to be too abrasive and you do not want to be too forceful. Yet, using ineffective phrases is not likely to stir action. Just think of all those employment cover letters you have seen that go unanswered and that end with the sentence, "Please call me at your earliest convenience." Trial balloons of that nature rarely work. Make sure your action statements result in the reader or listener "buying" your idea, product, or service.

USING PROMOTIONAL MATERIAL

Sometimes the sales-oriented communication will not provide you with sufficient space or time to adequately describe your product, service, or idea. In these cases, consider adding some kind of attachment or supplemental material that permits you to further describe and prove your point.

What Can Supplement?

Enclosures can enhance your sales strategy.

The enclosure to the sales letter or supplements to an oral communication can take many forms:

1. Product/service descriptions printed on 8½-by-11 inch paper.
2. A simple black-and-white folded insert with offset printing and pictures.
3. A full-color brochure, perhaps several pages in length, or a single-page, full-color enclosure.
4. Any variety of visuals for an ordinary sales presentation, such as slides, flip charts, handouts, or transparencies.

It may be beneficial to obtain some professional assistance from a printing house or an organization that specializes in such materials.

Several factors should be considered in determining how to approach the promotion item:

1. The number of promotion pieces needed. It would probably not be cost-effective to produce a color brochure if you need only five-hundred copies.
2. The nature and cost of the product or service being promoted. If the product sells for $2, you should not spend 50 cents to produce each promotion piece.
3. The class of mailing. A first-class letter is expensive enough; if a three-ounce brochure is included, the mailing cost soars.

Supplements can also be useful with other, less direct, sales opportunities. In "selling" an idea to the boss, an attractive, well-conceived "promotional" supplement (like a clear graphic that shows the responsibilities in a proposed structure for your department) can be helpful in the "sale" of your idea.

THE COVER SALES LETTER

When a promotion piece is to be sent, the writer should create a *cover* sales letter rather than a sales letter. Many times, the attachment seems more important than the letter. That is, the computer printout, color brochure, or fancy booklet clearly explains the product, service, or idea and contains many of the elements of proof. But it is a poor strategy to simply send that item without a message that provides interpretation. Even though the cover letter may be exceedingly brief, you should use that message to direct the reader to what you think is important to her or him. For example, a college catalog is often used as an attachment to a letter. Because the message is sent to different audiences, the letter changes but the catalog remains the same. For high-school seniors, the letter may emphasize extracurricular activities, the practicality of the curriculum, and the strong athletic program. For junior-college transfer students, on the other hand, the letter may emphasize the ease of transferring credits, how the school's curriculum "dovetails" with that of the former college, and the variety of career tracks available to entering juniors.

The cover letter can interpret, direct, and encourage.

If an enclosure clearly explains and fully describes the product, service, or idea and has a strong sales orientation, the cover sales letter should be designed to arouse sufficient interest to motivate the reader to examine the enclosure. In other words, a long letter is neither necessary nor advantageous in this situation.

In Chapter 22 we will consider one of the most important sales letters you will prepare—the cover letter for your résumé. All of the rules of sales and cover letters apply for that vital letter, in which you attempt to gain the attention of a potential employer, explain your "product," prove your worth, and move the receiver to action.

REACHING RECEIVERS BY MAIL

In general, reaching the receivers of indirect sales communications like internal memos is not a problem. However, getting your direct sales communications to the public can be a major problem. The message must get to the appropriate receiver. To send the message to the wrong person is a waste of money and inefficient.

The good message that is not received is wasted. A major concern in direct-mail sales letter operations is that the correct names and addresses are used.

Mailing lists can be obtained from a variety of sources. One's own customers are a possible source. Individuals who have done business with you may be most receptive to hearing from you. Public lists, like city directories, voting lists, tax lists, and auto registrations, can be used to build a mailing list. Also helpful in developing one's own list is the *Guide to American Directories for Compiling Mailing Lists.*

Developed properly, mailing lists can be most helpful.

Beyond "The List"

Obtaining the raw list is just the first step. You may feel that it is wise and inexpensive to use the city directory. But all these names and addresses have to be copied from the book and placed individually on each envelope. That can be a very time-consuming and costly activity. Also, if the list is transferred in such a way that it cannot be duplicated for future use, the process gets even more expensive.

One of the most expedient ways to secure a mailing list may be to purchase one. There are a variety of places to secure mailing lists for a fee: companies may have customer lists they will sell to you, and associations (like sales and trade groups) often will sell their mailing lists to responsible organizations. An advantage of the purchased list is that the names often come on individual labels that can quickly be placed on an envelope. Mailing list firms that specialize in selling lists also can be helpful. Many of these firms offer a very selective list of prospects. If you desire to send a mailing to widows over the age of sixty-five with an annual income in excess of $20,000 who reside in southern Arizona, such a list can probably be provided. If you want lists of electrical engineers, nurses, or auto mechanics, such lists can be purchased.

Reliability and Usability

Whether you compile your own list or purchase one, reliability and usability are important. Reliable lists are correct: they have correct addresses (20 percent of the population moves annually), correct spelling of names, and appropriate people (is the person really a prospect for your product or service?). Good lists are easily usable: they are organized into logical categories, according to economic levels, ethnic characteristics, sex, or age, for example. They are divided by zip code to meet current postal regulations. They are prepared in a way that is easy to use and reuse.

The actual preparation and mailing of the sales letter can be a sizable job in itself. Many businesses are not organized to handle mass mailings. Therefore, it may be wise to obtain the services of a specialized company that will print the letter and stuff, stamp, and mail the envelope—and just send you a bill.

The sales letter or sales cover letter and enclosed promotion piece should always arouse interest and attention, describe the product, service, or idea, prove the points made, and move receivers to action. Running throughout the effective sales communication is a central appeal specifically selected for the particular prospect(s) addressed and proofs that will cause receivers to want to accept your message. These basic elements are applicable to all effective sales communications, whether we are sending one letter or one thousand.

Be sure the mailing list decreases your work and increases your responses.

QUICK REVIEW

The concepts of the sales letter are applicable to almost all of the written and oral messages you will create as a manager. Therefore, be sure to learn, understand, and apply the sales process. It works with direct and indirect sales situations. The process is a logical way to move the receiver from one point to another. Remember that all sales communications need not be bombastic; there are shadings of sales, and sometimes the subtle indirect approach can work very well. But the basic elements from attention to action should all be incorporated.

EXECUTIVE SUMMARY

To: Business Communication Students

From: David N. Bateman and Norman B. Sigband

Subject: Communicating to Sell

Like the sales letter, almost every communication has an element of persuasion in it. Thus, almost every communication should have a sales orientation.

Among those communications that would fall into a "sales" (or persuasive) category are sales letters sent to a mass market, collection letters, a specific (or target) sales letter, an internal memo designed to sell an idea, a "no" letter that "sells" goodwill, a response to an inquiry, and an oral briefing. These categories are divided into direct sales or indirect sales or sometimes a combination of both.

The basic principles of both written and oral sales communication are:

1. Know what you have to sell: its qualities, advantages, and disadvantages.
2. Know your climate: who are the "prospects" and where do they live?
3. Know your receivers: their needs and their economic, social, and educational levels.
4. Know your competitors.
5. Know the appropriate proofs and appeals for the prospects.

Most sales messages are developed around:

1. Arousing interest on the part of the prospect.
2. Describing the product.
3. Proving the product is all you claim it is.
4. Seeking action on the part of the receiver—the sale.

All four points are selected to appeal to a specific type of prospect and his or her needs and desires.

When large sales campaigns are used, it is vital to make sure the mailing list of names is as accurate and reliable as possible.

DISCUSSION GENERATORS

1. *Are They Worth the Money?* Even though purchased mailing lists may be expensive, why might they be well worth the price to the communicator?
2. *Will Telephone Books Work?* What would be the disadvantages of simply using telephone directories to secure the names and addresses for a sales letter attempting to sell insurance?
3. *Letter Differences.* How is the cover sales letter different from a normal direct sales letter?
4. *"Earliest Convenience."* Why is it a poor sales strategy, in virtually every communication situation, to close with "Contact me at your earliest convenience"?
5. *Action.* Name and explain a technique to move your reader to action.
6. *Picture Painting.* What step in the sales process did the authors relate to painting a picture?
7. *Everything Is Sales?* Explain why virtually every communication is a sales communication.

8. *Action vs. Inaction.* Why is "Please call if you are interested" a poor action statement?

9. *Prove It.* Name the various proofs and exemplify one.

10. *Direct Sales Are Tough.* Why is it harder to get a direct sales-oriented letter opened than a letter in which you are attempting to persuade your boss to purchase some equipment?

11. *Interest vs. Proof.* What is the difference between arousing interest and proving your point?

12. *Create Interest.* Name the various ways in which the communicator can attract the interest of the letter receiver; give one complete example.

13. *Abstract vs. Tangible.* Why might it be more difficult to "sell" an abstract idea than to sell a tangible product?

14. *Selling Principles.* List the basic principles of selling.

15. *"Shady Sales?"* Explain the concept of the "shadings" of sales.

16. *Thanks.* How can a thank-you note simultaneously be a sales letter?

17. *Is a Letter Necessary?* Why should a cover letter accompany a descriptive brochure that illustrates your firm's products?

18. *Envelope and Attire.* How is your attire in the oral communication situation similar to getting the envelope of a written communication opened?

19. *What Source?* When would it be wise to secure a subscription list from a specific type of magazine to use as a mailing list?

20. *A One-page Speech?* How does the concept of the "one-page maximum" apply to oral communications?

APPLICATIONS FOR BUSINESS

21. *Sell This Idea.* You are president of the Young Manager's Association, a student group in the business department of your institution. Your group has decided that it would like to recognize outstanding graduates of your institution who have achieved some level of competency in their profession before reaching the age of thirty-five. The name of the award will be "(your college name) Young Manager's Recognition Award." In order to initiate this award, you need the approval of the chairperson of the business department.

   Prepare a concise one-page memorandum to the chair in which you sell this idea. Be sure you implement the various concepts of a sales-oriented communication, including such features as getting the attention of the reader, leading the reader to action, and using at least two discernible means of proof.

22. *Selling an Advertising Space.* The Young Manager's Association of your college, a student group, wants to sell advertising space in the program that it will distribute at the First Annual Young Manager's Recognition Award dinner (see number 21 above). Generally, it is best to make person-to-person contact with the advertisers. However, because the contact has to be made during the summer, and the membership is not on campus during the summer, you decide to send a sales-oriented letter promoting the ads to local businesses. Prepare that letter. Remember that the advertiser is going to be unfamiliar with the event and is going to have to be very clearly shown how placing an ad in this program would help generate customer flow and sales.

23. *The Thinking Hat.* The following is a list of purposes for various communications. For each, indicate how you could prove your point using one of these techniques—samples, guarantees, trial offer, testimonial, statistics, or comparative analysis.

 To persuade the company to institute an in-house day-care center.
 To persuade the college administration to start instituting a full-week vacation at Thanksgiving.
 To persuade students to sell their used books back through a student-government-run operation instead of the local bookstore operation.
 To persuade the college administration to provide parking spaces for students near classroom buildings.
 To persuade alumni of your academic program to make contributions for student scholarships at your institution.

24. *Freshman Mailing.* For a student organization on your campus you want to send a mass mailing to each first-year student. Compare the advantages and disadvantages of the various options; be sure to consider cost, time, reliability, and usability; and assume you will want to use the list twice—next month and again in four months. Use a situation on your campus; some of the options might be copying names and addresses from a student directory, obtaining a list from the registrar, or purchasing a set of printed mailing labels from the registrar.

25. *Communication and Sales.* Many of your colleagues on campus may not agree that many of the letters and talks they give in their professional careers will be sales-oriented. Select an academic student group (such as the Accounting Club or Student Management Organization) and (1) outline a talk you could give to them showing that many of the communications in their profession will have a sales thrust and (2) list specific examples of the kinds of sales-oriented communications these people will initiate on the job.

COMMUNICATION CHECK-UPS

26. Some of the report are well written.

27. The northwest is the place to test the new product.

28. The office manager paid seventy-five dollars for the table, $19.95 for the flower arrangement, and $1.98 for the table cloth.

29. It is estimated the land will produce 95 bushels of corn per acre.

30. All ready the report is on the way to the finance people.

31. "The analysis is complete . . . and correctly represents management's views."

32. A helpful publication for the job seeker is National Employment Weekly.

33. In the report she found a color graphic. Which came as a complete surprise.

34. The vendor is located at Twelve Industrial Drive.

35. If you see the secretary or the word processor, tell her the repair representative has arrived.

Executive Introduction

RALPHS GROCERY COMPANY
P.O. BOX 54143, LOS ANGELES, CALIFORNIA 90054

PATRICK W. COLLINS
PRESIDENT

AREA CODE 213
637-1101
605-4021

May 18, 198_

Janet Darling, Assistant Manager
Store #32
3410 W. Third Street
Los Angeles, CA 90020

Dear Janet:

Following the recent training session you asked the excellent question about how we should respond to inquiries. Giving your question additional thought, I wanted to respond more fully.

How clever we would be if we had all the answers whenever we needed them. However, the realities are that most of us do not have all the answers and, therefore, must turn to others for information. Those people can be retailers, suppliers, manufacturers, community members, government agencies, or any number of other resources.

Inquiries are a part of the successful conduct of business. There are questions concerning prices, deliveries, specifics of an incident, legal matters, and so on.

Effective inquiries must be structured clearly, concisely, and specifically. It is easy to see the possible loss when an inquiry is either poorly conceived or incomplete. Most often, the quality and value of the reply is diminished. Additional correspondence costs time and money.

Enclosed is a very helpful chapter on the inquiry from a business communication book. It covers the various types of inquiries you will be required to send out in the years ahead.

Cordially yours,

Patrick W. Collins

PWC:hg
Enclosure

CHAPTER
8

Obtaining Information: The Inquiry

WHAT YOU CAN LEARN BY STUDYING THIS CHAPTER

Whether in written form, such as a memorandum, or in spoken form, such as a quick telephone call, the most frequent kind of communication a manager uses each day, week, and throughout his or her career is some kind of inquiry. These communications aim to obtain information so the communicator can write a report, complete an order, or make a decision. Since this is the most common kind of business communication, it is important to know how to make inquiries efficiently and effectively. In this chapter, you will learn how to obtain information—using a variety of communication vehicles—and to do it in a manner that is easy for all involved.

Think before asking.

The purpose of any kind of inquiry is to obtain material or information. It is important to know precisely *what* it is you want, *who* has the information, *when* you need it, and *how* you need it. As we will discover, the dynamics of the inquiry—a two-way communication process—involve personalities, organizational contexts, and the pressures of time. The workhorses of information gathering in the organization include the memorandum, the telephone call, and the quick meeting. There is no one simple way to implement the successful inquiry—a number of factors must be carefully orchestrated if you are to be successful.

THE FIVE C'S OF COMMUNICATION

The five C's of communication—courtesy, clarity, completeness, conciseness, and correctness—are vital in inquiry communications. But, as you will note, they can and should be applied to all communications.

Courtesy

Tact goes beyond simply saying "please."

You are seeking information. You need it from an individual. He or she probably does not have to provide it. Therefore, it's common sense and good business to be courteous and tactful and to not place excessive demands upon the receiver. Remember, the receiver already has a full-time job, and you are encroaching upon the receiver's time with your request. Courtesy involves more than just saying the words "please" and "thank you." Tact is projected throughout your communication: its pleasant and undemanding tone, its clear questions, and its careful and accessible organization/format.

Clarity

Unfocused clarity results in poor responses.

An inquiry that is unclear can be frustrating to the receiver. If the message has to be read three times to be understood or if the receiver has to guess what the sender means, the communication is a problem. Clarity can be achieved in two ways. First, indicate exactly what you want. To state, "If the fan on the number 18 Norco exhaust system is satisfactory, send it out by service freight" is unclear—does the writer want the fan, the exhaust system, or both?

Second, the format of your request for information can be an aid to clarity. If, as illustrated in Figure 8.1, you are asking several questions, make it easy, through your format and heading system, for the receiver to see, identify, and later return (if necessary) to your questions. Notice the clear format and headings in Figure 8.1—the four items needing a response are headlined, helping the receiver to know what is needed and the sender to obtain complete information.

FIGURE 8.1　Routine Inquiry—Electronic Mail

```
################### START OF MESSAGE ###################
-----------------------) REPRINT (---------------------
DATE : 06:15:88          PAGE : 001          TIME : 15:14:53
TO   : D.N. BAXTER               FROM : R. JENNINGS
POBOX : MKEICTNG                  POBOX : MKEICTNG
TOPIC : $ALES MEETING
---------------- THIS MESSAGE WAS SENT TO 0010 LOCATIONS ----------------

ORIGINAL TO:   MKEICTNG        - D.N. BAXTER
CC:
  MKEICTNG    - K.L. CASTRO   | MKEICTNG    - M.G. HESTER
  MKEICTNG    - J.A. JONES    | MKEICTNG    - D.O. KING
  MKEICTNG    - J.M. MOSS     | MKEICTNG    - M.G. OLSON
  MKEICTNG    - C.H. PETERS   | MKEICTNG    - P.K. SMITH
  MKEICTNG    - F.A. VICTOR

THIS WEEK EACH OF YOU CONDUCTED SALES MEETINGS WITH YOUR TOP
CUSTOMERS.  ONE OF THE MAJOR ITEMS COVERED WAS YOUR INTRODUCTION
OF OUR NEW (LESS GENEROUS) CREDIT ARRANGEMENT.

FOR A MEETING LATER THIS WEEK WITH THE EXECUTIVE STAFF, I NEED YOUR
RESPONSES TO THE FOLLOWING QUESTIONS; PLEASE GET YOUR DATA TO ME BY
10 A.M., JUNE 12.

1. OVERALL REACTION.  IN A SHORT EXPANATORY PARAGRAPH, WHAT WAS THE
   BASIC THRUST OF THE CUSTOMERS' REACTIONS TO THE NEW CREDIT
   ARRANGEMENT?

2. CUSTOMER DRIFT.  WERE THERE ANY SPECIFIC COMMENTS CONCERNING MOVING
   TO ANOTHER SUPPLIER BECAUSE OF THIS CHANGE?  IF SO, WHAT SUPPLIERS
   WERE MENTIONED SPECIFICALLY?

3. SPECIFIC NEGATIVES.  IN RANK ORDER, WHAT WERE THE ELEMENTS THE
   CUSTOMERS LIKED LEAST ABOUT THE NEW SYSTEM?  RANK #1 IS THE LEAST
   LIKED FEATURE.

4. MAINTAINING PRICING.  DID THE CUSTOMERS APPRECIATE THE IDEA THAT BY
   INSTITUTING THESE NEW CREDIT PROCEDURES IT IS POSSIBLE FOR US TO
   MAINTAIN (NOT INCREASE) OUR PRICES?  (BRIEFLY EXPLAIN.)

YOUR HELP WILL AID US IN ASCERTAINING THE IMPACT OF THE NEW CREDIT
SYSTEM.

##################### END OF MESSAGE  #####################
```

TABLE 8.1   Inquiry Media and Factors to Consider in Selecting the Appropriate One

THE MEDIUM	FORMALITY	TIME AND COST*	FACTORS TO CONSIDER IN EMPLOYING THIS MEDIUM
The Memorandum	I	M/M	Informal, inside techniques; takes time to prepare; handy when inquiry is complex, lengthy, or involved. Provides a dated record of the request.
The Letter	F	M/M	More formal, generally used for outside inquiries; involves preparation time; when the inquiry is complex, lengthy, or involved, it is probably beneficial; it provides a record of the request (and the receiver can log the request in so it is known when it is received).
The Telephone	I	L/M	Often informal; can be very friendly; can be fast—especially when a very few pieces of simple data are needed and the receiver will have the data at hand. Eliminates the cost and time of preparing a written inquiry. Also, if telephone logs are not maintained, it is sometimes possible to initiate these inquiries without a record being maintained—in some situations this could be advantageous.
The Personal Visit	I	L/H	It is often easier and faster to obtain information in person than through less personal means. Generally, such visits should be scheduled (drop-ins can be disruptive); the actual cost can be high because two executives are involved in face-to-face time, which is expensive. Also, generally time is more limited.
The Telephone Conference	I	M/H	Generally some secretarial time is needed to arrange such conferences and some careful planning on the part of the initiator. Any time key managers are involved in on-line time, the expense is going to be high.

I = Informal   F = Formal   L = Low Time or Cost   M = Medium Time or Cost   H = High Time or Cost

TABLE 8.1   Continued

THE MEDIUM	FORMALITY	TIME AND COST*	FACTORS TO CONSIDER IN EMPLOYING THIS MEDIUM
The Video Conference	F	H/H	Probably the most expensive medium available (except the face-to-face meeting where travel is involved), the video conference has most of the advantages of the regular conference. Because the use of these meetings is still relatively new, it appears that more planning time is involved, they tend to be more formal, and the costs are high.
The Face-to-face Conference	I	M/H	Although it is difficult to categorize all such conferences, American business tends to make them generally informal. Our conferences and meetings might be more efficient and effective if more time were spent in planning and conducting them. The cost of such meetings is largely dependent upon who attends, the travel, the time involved, and the length of the conference.
Electronic Mail	I	L/H	The electronic medium is becoming very popular, and with its popularity, its formality is decreasing. Many messages are created "on line," but still the cost is relatively high.
The Postcard	I	L/L	For routine inquiries and responses, the simple postcard can move quickly. Just the "psychology" of the card enhances efficiency; everyone knows that the communication can be short—this can increase responses.
The PC Bulletin Board	I	L/M	The exchange of information on PC screens is growing; the notices are generally informal; the time involved is low and the actual cost is relatively inexpensive.

*Time refers to preparation time and the time involved in the actual communication. L = low time, M = medium time, H = time involved is high. Cost refers to the total costs of the medium, L = low cost, M = medium cost and H = indicates a high cost.

Completeness

To send an incomplete inquiry indicates that you have not thought through your question well and places a burden on the receiver. For instance, if you write to a large university and say "Send me information on your business program," what does that mean? Are you interested in the executive programs, one of the seven undergraduate programs, the M.S. in accounting, the MBA, or one of the two doctoral programs? The sender must consider the question(s) thoroughly; a complete question increases the opportunity to receive a complete answer. A clearer, more complete inquiry might say, "Please send the requirements for an undergraduate major in marketing for a student entering the university directly from high school."

C = C A complete question increases the opportunity to receive a complete answer.

Conciseness

When writing an inquiry, the one-page maxim should be observed if at all possible. If you want information, and you want it to move rapidly, be concise; this is not a time for verbosity. Listing your questions vertically on the page and striving to eliminate any extraneous information or words both enhance conciseness. Other techniques are introducing a series with a single phrase and placing the series in parallel form; for example:

Creative lists can aid conciseness.

What is your attitude on:

- *Requiring* athletes to pass all courses to be eligible to play?
- *Mandating* that athletes take periodic drug tests?
- *Programming* athletes to gain their degree?

You can also edit lists so that they are concise (note how the introductory phase can be altered) *and* interesting and attention grabbing; for example,

What is your attitude on insisting that athletes:

- *Pass* all courses to be eligible to play?
- *Pass* all drug tests to be eligible to play?
- *Secure* a degree or pay back their scholarship money?

Correctness

Incorrect data lead to incorrect responses.

If you ask the incorrect question, you will receive the incorrect answer. Be sure to double-check numbers, dates, sizes, and the like. Simple typos can be most confusing to the receiver and will either result in an incorrect or delayed response.

THE INQUIRY MEDIUM

Although we deal chiefly with letters and memos here, there are many other means of inquiry. As the initiator of the inquiry communication, you know the context best and must use your judgment in selecting your means of inquiry. The types of communication listed in Table 8.1 may help you choose an appropriate means of inquiry.

Some factors that may govern your choice of mode of inquiry are your relationship with the receiver, the time of day, your mood and that of the receiver, where the receiver is, how simple (routine) or complex (nonroutine) the request is, and time and cost.

The medium for your message can be important for inquiries.

THE INQUIRY PROCESS

Regardless of the medium and the type of inquiry, following a basic process can aid the communicator in eliciting a response from the receiver:

1. *Provide* information and the background of the inquiry for the receiver; set the stage.
2. *Inform* the receiver precisely of your question or the problem/situation you are trying to solve.
3. *Alert* the receiver of any urgency to respond, often giving a due date.
4. *Offer* confidentiality, if appropriate.
5. *Close* in a friendly manner.

There is a logical flow for inquiry communications.

The step in the process that may most frequently be skipped is the one concerning confidentiality. Many of your inquiries will have no confidential aspects. But when you request certain information (especially company-specific primary data), it is wise to offer confidentiality and to say why you need the data and how you are going to use it. For instance, asking to see a company's private survey of employee attitudes would call for a clear statement on confidentiality. Obviously, the firm would not want the data shared with others, but may be more willing to respond affirmatively if you offer confidentiality.

Plan Your Inquiry

Whatever medium you use, planning is important. Planning is not eliminated because you decide to "drop in" rather than send a mcmo or to call instead of sending a letter. Outlining your approach in order to make an effective telephone request can also be vital (see Figure 8.2).

Routine Inquiries

Much information is routine and ongoing in and out of the organization. Routine inquiries are made frequently: the small retail-business manager sends for catalogs from suppliers, a high-school senior solicits information from colleges, a major corporation receives requests for tours of its facilities, a government agency receives requests for basic information and brochures.

The most effective and easiest way to transmit a routine inquiry may be a quick telephone call or a simple postcard (see Figure 8.3). A formal letter that needs to be

FIGURE 8.2   Outline of Notes for Telephone Inquiry

Outlines can be
quick and provide
guidance for oral
inquiries.

Use this outline
technique and you
won't hang up the
phone and say,
"Whoops, I forgot to
ask . . ."

CALL BUZZ RE. LEASE OF PCs

1. OUR CURRENT SITUATION
   a. #
   b. NEED TO UPGRADE
   c. CASH FLOW

2. BUY OR LEASE
   a. FLOW
   b. TECHNOLOGY

3. WHAT DO YOU HAVE FOR LEASE
   a. TRADE-IN
   b. LENGTH
   c. BUY-OUT OPTIONS
   d. TIME FRAME

prepared, mailed, opened, filed, and recorded is not necessary. The supplier does not
need a detailed memorandum from a small business entrepreneur indicating a
problem when all that is desired is a new catalog of the supplier's products. Even when
a letter is necessary, you may desire to provide space for the receiver to write a quick
answer and simply return the letter to you. In other words, sometimes the quick,
informal manner is most effective and efficient for everyone involved.

Personalizing the Inquiry

Sometimes personalizing the routine inquiry can speed it up and guarantee a good
reception. The sender of the communication should know the name and title of the
receiver and certainly the correct address. If Janet Myers has been the Director of

FIGURE 8.3   Routine Inquiry—Postcard

Wilson Electric Co.
P.O. Box 1717
White Plains, NY ZIP
Catalog Manager

For our sales staff, please send us six Distributor Catalogs immediately.
Thank you.

George Abrahams
Sales Manager

Often simple communications like postcards can speed inquiries.

Manufacturing at the Rayburn Corporation for four years and is listed in all of the major manufacturing directories, she is not going to be impressed nor moved to provide information to a college student seeking information about her manufacturing processes who has addressed her "Dear Sir"!

Some of the basic sources for names of top managers in organizations are listed in Table 8.2. Other ways to get the name you need include:

Having correct names, titles, and addresses is crucial for successful inquiries.

- *Calling* the organization and obtaining the name; this can generally be done simply through the organization's switchboard or through a secretary in the appropriate department.
- *Locating* a directory for the relevant professional organizations, like ASPA for Personnel Directors, which identifies people by geographical region, industry, and company.

TABLE 8.2   Sources for Obtaining Names of Managers in Organizations

Ward's Directory of 55,000 Largest U.S. Corporations   Provides name of CEO along with address and phone number.

Moody's Manuals   Lists 20,000 U.S. and foreign companies, provides cities of principal plants along with officers and directors.

Standard & Poor's Register of Corporations, Directors and Executives   Volume 1 is an alphabetic listing of over 36,000 U.S. and Canadian Companies—listing officers. Volume 2 lists executives and directors with data about each.

Dun & Bradstreet Million Dollar Directories   Volumes 1–3 are alphabetic listings of U.S. and Canadian companies; includes listing of officers for each company.

Nonroutine Inquiries

Nonroutine inquiries take more time for both the sender and receiver.

Both senders and receivers use the nonroutine inquiry less frequently than the routine. By its nature, the nonroutine inquiry deals with more specialized subjects and can be rather complex. Nonroutine inquiries require more time from both the sender and the receiver. The sender will probably have to go through *all* of the steps in the process (except perhaps the offer of confidentiality), and the receiver will not be able to respond routinely—by just placing a catalog in the mail, for instance.

The Request

Requests call for overt action.

Similar to the nonroutine inquiry, the request goes one step further and asks for *added action*. It asks the receiver to take an action that goes beyond just writing a letter or responding with already prepared information (see Figure 8.4). Typical requests are asking a person to serve on a task force, to chair the Better Government Committee, or to keynote a career week on campus. These communications need to provide a strong justification to entice the receiver to take the action you desire. You generally must explain the benefits involved. In many respects, the request communication is like the sales communication. It must gain the receiver's interest, inform and describe, suggest the urgency, and move the receiver to respond affirmatively to your proposal.

INQUIRY RESULTS

The inquiry that does not get the response you need is a very costly communication. It took you considerable time to prepare the communication, and you have nothing to show for it. Your ability to initiate effective inquiries affects your success in the organization.

Checking Your Success

With inquiries, it's the results that count.

There are several ways in which you can measure your success in gaining the correct responses to your inquiry communication. Some of the ways include

- *Speed.* How fast did the response get back to you?
- *Correctness.* Was the response what you wanted, or did it require you to initiate a follow-up?
- *Completeness.* Was all of the needed information included, or was some missing—requiring some kind of follow-up?

Try to discover why you were successful or unsuccessful. For instance, was the speed enhanced because you listed a due date or was it because the simplicity of your request? Was it delayed because of poor return-mailing instructions? Were the returned data correct because of the precision of your questions? Were they incorrect because the questions were ambiguous? Were the returns complete because of the

FIGURE 8.4   A Request—Interoffice Memorandum

Memo

TO: Daniel Robinson, Manager
        Factory-in-the-Factory (F-i-t-F)

FR: Jamie Jones
        Supervisor, Fabrication

SUBJ: Information Needed in F-i-t-F

DATE: May 2, 198_

Good Publicity on Operation. The press has been generous with their comments on our new factory-in-the-factory operation. The F-i-t-F is certainly an innovation that can have enormous impact on the way companies go about producing their products.

Problem/situation.

Security. It is certainly understandable that the current security is needed so that un-authorized people do not wander through this sophisticated operation. At the same time, the press has seen the operation and many outsiders have toured the facility.

Problem. Each day my employees ask me, "When do we get to see the F-i-t-F?" They continually make the following points:

Information.

a. I'm proud of what my company has done . . . when can I see it?
b. How come I have to read this in the magazines? I work here, and I haven't seen it.
c. How is this manufacturing system going to affect me; will it eliminate my job?

Positive Motivator. The employees have a good point. By not responding, the company can aggravate a situation that should be a very positive one.

Urgency.

Therefore, would it be possible for a group of fourteen employees and me to tour the facility at some time during the next month? As part of our brief tour (about 30 minutes) could we also (a) receive an explanation of the system and (b) be informed of how this helps our employment security, instead of diminishing it.

I appreciate your taking the time to consider this request. I'm sure if you agree to our group's coming through, many more supervisors will want to bring their employees. However, these brief tours could be most advantageous to our in-plant morale.

Friendly close.

cc: Betty Fohr, Director
        Labor Relations

way all the questions were placed on the inquiry letter? Were they incomplete because your format tended to "hide" some of your questions? Your analysis will aid you in the next inquiry to send.

QUICK REVIEW

Inquiry communications are not simple; they are complex two-way communications that call for careful planning and implementation on the part of the initiator. Besides just determining what is needed, one must also consider how the inquiry will be delivered to the individual. Before you write a quick note asking for information, take a moment and think through *all* the factors involved—remember, excellent planning and thinking on your part at the very start of the process will enhance the quality of the answer you receive.

Considerations	*Medium*
What is needed	Memo or letter
Who has it	Orally (face-to-face, phone, or meeting)
When do I need it	Electronically (fax or electronic mail)
How do I need it	

EXECUTIVE SUMMARY

To: Business Communication Students

From: David N. Bateman and Norman B. Sigband

Subject: Obtaining Information: The Inquiry

Organizations are highly dependent on information to carry on their daily activities. Much of this information is secured through a variety of different inquiries.

In all cases, the inquiry communication should follow the five C's: courtesy, clarity, completeness, conciseness, and correctness.

The inquiry process should offer or provide the receiver of the message with

- Information and background for the inquiry
- Information on the problem or situation under discussion
- A due date for the reply, if needed
- Confidentiality, if appropriate
- Appreciation for the assistance to be provided

DISCUSSION GENERATORS

1. *Kinds of Inquiries.* Name and differentiate the different kinds of inquiry communications.
2. *What Medium?* Name and briefly explain the factors to consider in determining what medium to use for an inquiry.
3. *Walk or Phone?* You need some simple information from a colleague who is just

down the hall. Explain why you may stop by the person's office instead of telephoning her.

4. *What's Your Name?* Why is knowing the receiver's name a basic element of courtesy in inquiry communication?

5. *Is It All Here?* Why is a lack of completeness a hindrance to both the receiver and to the initiator of the inquiry communication?

6. *Just Send a Card.* Name and briefly explain three situations in which it would be appropriate to send an inquiry on a postcard.

7. *Linking Sales and Nonroutine Inquiries.* What is the relationship between a sales letter and a nonroutine inquiry letter?

8. *What's the Difference?* What makes the communication of a request different from the nonroutine inquiry?

9. *Misinformation.* How can including incorrect information in the inquiry make the inquiry less effective?

10. *Your Inquiries.* For your intended career/profession, give an example of a routine inquiry.

11. *How Formats Help.* Illustrate how your letter or memo format can help the receiver in responding to your inquiry.

12. *Typos and Beyond.* List a half-dozen kinds of correctness errors that can create havoc in inquiries.

13. *Total Cost of No Response.* What is the total cost involved in inquiries that receive no response?

14. *Total Cost of Incorrect Information.* What is the total cost involved when the original inquiry has correctness problems, resulting in an incorrect response?

15. *Superfluous.* Why is it often unnecessary to indicate that you will hold the response to your inquiry in confidence?

16. *Basic Management.* Why is the inquiry communication a key management tool?

17. *Other Courtesy Considerations.* What are some aspects of courtesy beyond using the words "thank you" and "please"?

18. *How Conciseness Helps.* How does conciseness aid the sender in obtaining a response?

19. *Need It May 1!* Why is it in the sender's best interest to inform the receiver of deadlines involved in the inquiry?

20. *The Long and Short of It.* Why will nonroutine inquiries generally be more lengthy than routine ones?

APPLICATIONS FOR BUSINESS

21. *The Who.* You often hear that it's not what you know, but who you know that counts in business. When it comes to inquiries, that *what* and *who* are vital. You are a management intern in one of the following offices in a major corporation:

comptroller's office; manufacturing engineering; market research; personnel. Your supervisor asks you to write three other firms to obtain information. Below is the question for each of the listed offices. Identify the area in which you are working and then obtain the names and addresses of people you could contact. Cite the complete "who" as it would appear on the inside address of a letter.

Functional Area/Question

Comptroller	"What effect will the continued increase in imports have on your firm's profitability?"
Manufacturing Engineer	"As factories become more automated, is it your experience that accident rates fall?"
Market Researcher	"How do you use focus groups in conducting research in your industry?"
Personnel Director	"Will the apparent new government procedures concerning leaves for employees who have babies influence who you hire among recent college graduates?"

22. *Format Aids Communication.* As vice-president of the Executives Club—a social group in your business school—you need to write the Dean with three questions. In your letter or memo you have set the stage and are now going to present the three questions listed below. Illustrate two different ways you could format the questions so that they will be clear to the Dean and will encourage a complete response. Be prepared to discuss how your formatting techniques aid and support the inquiry-response process.
    a. May the Executive Club hold a formal dance for members, alumni, and selected local business executives on the terrace of the business school?
    b. May the Executive Club serve wine and cheese at a social hour prior to the dance in the lounge of the business school?
    c. May the Executive Club decorate the basement hallway to look like a diner where a light meal will be served following the dance?

23. *Be Complete.* Incomplete and incorrect responses to inquiries are generally the result of incomplete, poorly designed, and vague questions posed by the initiator of the communication. Improve each of the following ineffective questions so that the information you desire can be obtained on the first try.

To	*Question*
a. Director of Employee Health Fitness Program	a. What does the health fitness program at your company cost?
b. Director of Manufacturing	b. How does the just-in-time system work?

c. Vice-president of Finance

c. Did the changes in the tax laws alter any of your procedures?

d. Manager of Human Resources

d. What is new in personnel recruiting?

24. *The Sales of the Request.* The letter of request often requires a heavy sales orientation if you are to achieve your goal. Prepare a letter of request to convince Ms. Goldwater to speak. On an attached sheet, explain and give an example of how you used elements of the sales process to achieve the desired result. As you will see, you are going to need to do some "selling" in order to achieve this request. Purpose: To gain Ms. Sophia Goldwater's agreement to speak at the Entrepreneur Banquet on May 2, 198—. (You became familiar with Ms. Goldwater in Chapter 2; review the nature of her operations as explained in Chapter 2. Figure 2.2A will also aid you in getting to know the receiver.)

25. *Planning: Inquiries Can Help.* As the newly elected program chairperson of the Zodiac Association, a national organization with over 2,000 members, you must arrange the national convention to be held in Atlantic City in March three years from now. Before you begin planning, you would like advice from someone who has been in charge of a similar convention in Atlantic City. You know that Jeff Lawson, former chairman of the New Jersey Starwatchers Club, was in charge of their convention last year in Atlantic City.

   Write to Mr. Lawson and ask him for advice. What did he find good or bad about holding his convention in Atlantic City? What hotel did he use? Was he happy with the accommodations? What advice can he offer as you begin your preparations? Tell him that he may write to you at your home address.

COMMUNICATION CHECK-UPS

26. Mrs. Goforth, whom I am informed is an excellent accountant, will perform the internal audit.

27. Its too late to submit the budget request.

28. Canvas the employees well to obtain many contributions.

29. She is confidant of your ability to do the job.

30. He will receive the PHD in the June graduation ceremonies.   Ph.D.

31. He was different than all the other applicants.

32. Per your request the annual report is being sent.

33. Sincerely Yours,

   Kate Morgan

34. And finally, I want you to know that James did an outstanding job on the marketing research project.

35. The secretaries desk was filled with candy wrappers.

Executive
Introduction

Product Development & Distribution
11011 S.W. 104 Street
Miami, Florida 33176-3393
(305) 347-2158

MIAMI-DADE
COMMUNITY COLLEGE

Number one in America.

September 7, 198_

Debra Stonnington, Sales Manager
Eastern Region
Allied Products, Inc.
P.O. Box 17
Athens, Georgia 30601

Dear Deb:

To follow up on our telephone conversation about how we interact with our clients, I've found that saying "yes" opens up the opportunity to say more than yes. You might try it in your correspondence with your clients. It is always interesting, Deb, to exchange and compare promotion ideas with you. Although we serve diferent markets, the principles remain constant from one market to another.

Recently, in a campus bookstore I perused the book <u>Communicating in Business</u> and found some additional points on the strategies for saying "yes":

+ Don't beat around the bush.

+ Provide the needed information clearly.

+ If necessary, provide suggestions.

+ Attempt to promote goodwill.

+ Remember to sign off in a positive manner.

In our office we do a considerable amount of correspondence, and I want to make sure we are taking advantage of situations where we can say "yes" and maximizing the positive impact.

I am always pleased to share ideas with a colleague. I look forward to sharing more experiences and ideas on positive sales!

Yours truly,

Cindy

Cindy Elliott
Manager

CE:mp

Responding to Inquiries Positively

WHAT YOU CAN LEARN BY STUDYING THIS CHAPTER

Although the inquiry communication is the workhorse for the manager, *responding* to inquiries makes up a considerable amount of his or her daily writing assignments. Therefore, whatever the manager can do to be efficient—and still not appear abrupt or trite—in responding to inquiries will result in more time for his or her "real" job. Although you may see inquiries as disruptions and interferences with your work, responding to them effectively can be an important part of your job. In this chapter, the basic categories of inquiries you are likely to receive are identified, the process for providing a "yes" answer is outlined and explained in detail, and procedures for being effective, efficient, and tactful in responding to them are discussed.

In Chapter 8 you learned some strategies for encouraging receivers to respond to your information needs. Now you place the shoe on the other foot—the inquiries are coming to you. To some you can respond affirmatively, and to some you must respond negatively. In this chapter we look at the "yes" response, but first we'll generally explore inquiries that come to individuals, managers, and organizations.

WHY EVEN RESPOND?

We are all familiar with the "I'll get back to you later . . . " that never gets acted on. Some organizations and some individuals don't respond to inquiries—perhaps they see nothing in it for themselves, and therefore they won't take time to respond. For them, probably none of the approaches discussed in Chapter 8 will do much good in encouraging a response.

Informational exchanges are very common in commerce.

Fortunately, the business community of the United States is generally willing to share information and ideas. Competitors, when not restricted by legal limitations, very often share information with each other. For instance, groups like the Rubber Manufacturers Association of America hold conferences and exchange ideas on human resource management. Following such conferences, members commonly seek added information from one another by letter, memo, and phone. If the Good Day Company has implemented a successful no-smoking program, it will probably have no objection to sharing its program with competitor Fire Rock Company or anyone else.

The reasons for being willing to share information include:

1. *Helpfulness:* The simple desire to be helpful.
2. *Goodwill:* To aid the organization's goodwill efforts.
3. *Public relations:* To promote the organization's public relations efforts.
4. *Professionalism:* To share ideas with professional colleagues.
5. *Selfishness:* Recognizing that the person who sends you an inquiry today may be the person who can respond to your inquiry tomorrow.

Sometimes, for competitive reasons or because of labor relations or other sensitive issues, it is not possible to respond as fully as either the sender or receiver would like. But even with limitations, it is often possible to provide some kind of response or to direct the inquirer to other sources that may be helpful.

THE "YES" RESPONSE PROCESS

There is a logical flow for the "yes" response.

When it is necessary to respond with more than a brochure, price list, or form letter, follow the steps below for the "yes" response. Sometimes you may find it necessary and advantageous to alter these steps, but they generally work well for situations when you can say "yes."

The Steps of the "Yes" Process	*Some Dos and Don'ts for Each Step*
Acknowledge the inquiry	Use a strong you-orientation, and avoid trite language like "Per your request" or "Responding to yours of June 3rd."
Say "yes"—grant the request	There is generally no advantage in holding off the good news. As clearly and positively as possible, provide the affirmative answer. It is not poor taste to reveal some sincere enthusiasm in your positive response.
Provide the needed information	With the narrative of your response or through various attachments, supply the requested information. As it is advantageous to use headings to outline the request, it is similarly beneficial to use these signposts in the response.
Add a constructive suggestion, if appropriate	Sometimes you can provide hints or other information that will benefit the receiver, such as, "You may want to phone Jan Wentworth at Remington—they instituted a similar program recently" or "If you write others seeking this information you may want to change the term 'fringe benefits' to 'total pay.' " (See Figure 9.1.)
Consider a sales or goodwill appeal	In responding to a purchase request for file cabinets, for instance, you may want to emphasize that the file holders are currently on sale and/or that for speedier service in the future, the individual may want to explore opening a charge account. (See Figure 9.2.) Goodwill statements that promote the good name of the organization are often effective: "Thank you for your order. As we look forward to the July 4th weekend we join you in celebrating our freedoms and hoping that we have a safe and happy holiday."
Close with a friendly statement	Beyond the normal closing in a letter or a goodbye on the phone, a pleasant and friendly closing short paragraph may be beneficial. Try to alter these to fit the particular situation—continually closing with "Best wishes to you" followed by the obligatory "Sincerely," becomes hackneyed. On the other hand, a short closing paragraph can be friendly and encouraging; for example, "Your tour of our facilities with ten blind children will be the first of its kind in our plant; although some very special precautions will be necessary, the children will gain some insights into our operations that we often miss—the various sounds, smells, and touch senses of our manufacturing process."

FIGURE 9.1   Saying "Yes" to a Request with an Emphasis on Constructive Suggestion

S◯PHISTICATED
Bikercise, Inc.

7667 Garden Street
Memphis, Tennessee   38101
January 9, 198_

Ms. Joan C. Murphy, Executive Director
Silver City Regional Chamber of Commerce
P.O. Box 1
Silver City, NM 88061

The Entrepreneurial Spirit is Vital . . .

Acknowledgment.

Yes.

. . . to America and to me; if we are to continue our economic miracles in this nation, it is important to continually bolster the entrepreneurial effort. Therefore, I am delighted to accept your invitation to speak at the Regional Entrepreneurial Banquet in Silver City, New Mexico, on Monday, May 3, 19__, at 7:00 p.m.

Information.

As plans stand now, my aircraft will set down at the S. C. Regional Airport at 6:15 p.m., allowing me to arrive just in time for the dinner; it will not be possible to participate in any predinner activities. However, if you could arrange a press conference following the dinner speech, that would be excellent.

Constructive suggestions.

For the dinner speech, please be sure to arrange the following:

+ <u>Podium:</u> A podium with adjustable height, a bright light that works, and a rack to hold materials on the podium.
+ <u>Room Lights:</u> Please adjust the room light to allow me to see the audience.
+ <u>Internal Distractions:</u> Dishes should not be distributed nor removed from the tables, and the audience should not be moving about the room during the speech.
+ <u>External Distractions:</u> The room should be protected from outside distracting noise.
+ <u>PA System:</u> Please have a clear, adjustable, and "unsqueaky" public address system in operation and someone on hand who can operate it.

Friendly close.

This will be my first trip to Silver City; I'm looking forward to meeting members of your campus community and business leaders from your region.

If you have any questions, please contact my arrangements secretary, Mrs. Joan Roethe 312/767-0002.

Don't

Sincerely,

Sophia Goldwater

Sophia Goldwater, President

FIGURE 9.2   Inquiry Response with Direct Sales Appeal

FELTON   *240 Burton Street*
FURNITURE   *Bainesville, Iowa   50001*
CORPORATION   *(319) 338-8684*

March 17, 198_

Mr. Benjamin Sendworth
Vice President, Building Operations
Seabrook Corporation
Trenton, NJ 08601

Dear Mr. Sendworth:

Your intriguing request for specially designed console platforms for portable computers has been carefully reviewed by our design department. The consoles can be manufactured by us, and we look forward to working with you in this creative activity. — **Acknowledgment.** / **Yes.**

The drawing you sent us is most adequate and will permit us to build a mock-up of the console platforms. The specifics concerning the consoles are: — **Information.**

1. <u>Number</u>: We will produce 80 identical consoles.
2. <u>Material</u>: Each will be built of solid mahogany.
3. <u>Surface Treatment</u>: External surfaces will be treated to resist marks from pens and water.
4. <u>Manufacturing Time</u>: The 80 consoles can be delivered to you 16 weeks following your acceptance of this offer.
5. <u>Cost/Financial Arrangements</u>: The cost of the first 80 consoles is $185 each; within the coming year, identical consoles, ordered in groups of 10 or more can be shipped to you for $150 each. If you forward a 20% deposit, we will start work on this quality piece of office furniture immediately.

We will manufacture the consoles with the same care we have given other specially designed furnishings for firms like Ford Motor, IBM, and other major corporations here and abroad. — **Sales appeal.**

Call me collect, Mr. Sendworth, if you have questions concerning the manufacturing process, delivery dates, or financial arrangements. We like new projects and will enjoy preparing these consoles. — **Friendly close.**

Sincerely yours,

Stanley Morgenthaw

Stanley Morgenthaw, Vice-President
Manufacturing Operations

THE THINKING AND PLANNING PROCESS

Don't shoot from the hip when responding to inquiries.

To respond effectively to an inquiry, the business communicator must do several things:

1. *Read or listen carefully* to the inquiry; many responses do not prove satisfactory because the receiver misunderstood the inquiry.
2. *Outline the response* to ensure a logical and complete flow of information.
3. *Double check* the completeness of your response; literally check off each question in the inquiry to ensure it is answered.
4. *Prepare the response,* adhering to the process for a "yes" communication.

To see how this process works, read the inquiry in Figure 8.1. Next, prepare an outline for a response (see Figure 9.3). Check the outline against the inquiry for completeness; then prepare the response (see Figure 9.4), attempting to follow the "yes" response process, "acknowledgment" through "goodwill/friendly close."

THE "YES" PROCESS IN ROUTINE AND NONROUTINE SITUATIONS

Many organizations have precise procedures for handling inquiries so that the public (or customer) gets a fast response: The inquiry is logged in and routed to the appropriate individual and deadlines are often established for when responses should leave the office. As we will see, if the inquiry is routine, the turn-around time should be very short; responses to nonroutine requests generally take longer.

Responding Affirmatively to Routine Inquiries

There are advantages to having procedures for responding.

By definition, the routine inquiry is anticipated; therefore, the response is often already prepared or well in mind. The organization need not reinvent the wheel each time a routine inquiry arrives. Either

1. *a standard response* (stick a brochure in an envelope and send it),
2. *a form letter response* (here is our annual report—thank you for your interest in our organization), or
3. *a guide-letter response* (you are welcome to tour our facilities on _____; because of the age of your group you will need to _____; and [add any particulars that are unique to the situation])

should be in the standard operating procedures of the organization.

FIGURE 9.3   The Outline: A Crucial Step in Preparing a Complete Response

Outline *Jimmy's memo*

I. Reaction
   A. "Understand"
   B. Don't like it
   C. Long-term let down
II. Drift
   A. Long-term customer comments
   B. "For sound business reasons"
III. Negatives
   A. Lead time
   B. Poor timing
   C. Dumping
IV. Maintaining Prices
   A. Doesn't fly
   B. Credit is key factor
V. Conclusions
   A. More negative than expected
   B. Long-term customers boisterous
   C. Possible new-customer rip-off
   D. "Steam" vs fire
   E. Strong customer rapport

FIGURE 9.4   Positive Response to an Inquiry

Memo

TO: Robert Jennings, Marketing Manager
FROM: Jill Olson, Midwest Regional Manager *JO.*
DATE: June 11, 198_
RE: Customer Reactions at Recent Sales Meeting

Acknowledgment/
yes.

Your request for information on the customer meeting we held on June 8 arrived just as we were discussing and evaluating our session; your inquiry provided a good focus for our meeting. Here are your data in brief:

The information is
provided.

1.   Customer Reaction: Because of recent and ongoing changes in our economy, our customers "understood" the need for and concept of the less generous credit arrangements--but, like all of us in that situation, they don't like it. The most perturbed customers are the long-term customers--they seem to feel that we are letting them down.

2.   Drift to Other Suppliers: A number of customers, again primarily our longer-term customers, commented that just as we had to alter our credit arrangement for "sound business reasons," they would have to look at other suppliers "for sound business reasons."

3.   Specific Negatives: The three dominant negative concerns were:
     a. Lack of lead time; they felt the change was being thrust upon them suddenly.
     b. Poor timing; most of our customers' fiscal years end within six weeks, and the change does not permit them time to get reoriented for the next fiscal year.
     c. Dumping; there was a feeling that the company was "dumping" on them. The customer was not being treated as a partner; they would have preferred discussion prior to implementation.

4.   Price Maintenance: Maintaining the prices did not impress our customers. Credit with their supplier is more important to them than product cost currently. Product costs can more easily be passed on, but the changes in credit affect their entire operation (from inventory to banker) and makes their world much more complex.

Goodwill/friendly
close.

Overall the reaction was more negative than anticipated; particularly discouraging was the boisterous objection from long-term customers. If they remain unhappy and it "rubs off" on newer customers, the new credit arrangements could make life difficult for us. On the other hand, there was probably more letting off steam than serious rejection of us. We have a solid rapport with our customers, and we will be striving (through our service and other features) to maintain positive relations with them.

Responding Affirmatively to Nonroutine Inquiries and Requests

Because nonroutine inquiries by definition arrive less frequently and tend to be highly individualized, it is not cost-efficient to have a standard response. These communications will have to be developed and designed individually. For instance, unless you are a professional speech-maker who receives three requests a day to give speeches, you are unlikely to have a routine response to the "can you give a speech" request that arrives once a year.

Whether the response is routine or nonroutine, the "yes" process is still applicable. The goal is to get the information to the individual, make him or her feel good, and make you and/or your organization look good.

COMMON CATEGORIES OF INQUIRIES

It is impossible to anticipate the variety of inquiries you will receive in your professional life. Yet, there are some common, general categories of inquiries. Let's look at each briefly, considering the implications of responding in the affirmative.

You can anticipate responding to these kinds of inquiries.

Responding to Order Inquiries

In business, you hope to receive orders from customers or individuals who need the product or service you provide. We are familiar with mail-order houses to which we send in an order blank and receive a simple response—the goods arrive. But at times, an explanation or addition to the basic "yes" is necessary.

1. *Multiple Deliveries:* The order will arrive in different packages over a several-day span.
2. *Incomplete Order:* Because of an unexpected influx of orders, the request cannot be completely filled at this time, but "yes," the complete order will be filled by March 10.
3. *Special Acknowledgment:* The order is of such magnitude that besides sending the material, you want to communicate a special "yes" to the customer.
4. *Special Packaging:* The customer requests nonstandard packaging and you are able to accommodate the customer.

Responding to Claim Inquiries

If you sell a product, periodically something will go haywire with its delivery or performance. You will receive requests to make some kind of adjustment. If your decision is to agree with the individual making the inquiry, generally some kind of direct communication is needed.

If you, the seller, are at fault you should emphasize the "yes" aspects and not belabor "why" the service was defective or the product malfunctioned—after all, that will only put egg on your face. Instead, you should strive to build confidence and goodwill for future offers.

If the buyer is at fault, and for future business reasons you desire to grant the request, you need first to indicate tactfully that you are not accepting responsibility and that, in fact, it is the buyer's fault that the product malfunctioned. Then, perhaps because the individual is a long-term customer you want to retain (or a new customer you want to cultivate), you provide a positive response to the inquiry.

Responding to Information Inquiries

The depth of your response and the time you take to respond will be influenced, to some degree, by who is making the inquiry for information. The most costly response is the one you need to research and dictate. The cost of the response and the time involved diminish substantially if you can dictate an overview and enclose some brochures or other printed materials.

Focusing on the key statement from two separate information inquiries, let's examine this aspect of responding.

Inquirer	*Key Request to Firm's Director of Benefits*
Andrew Bernhart, Student, Conway College	Evidently you are having success in having your employees comprehend their total pay. Can you share with me how you are accomplishing this?
Marion Koehn, Manager, Employee Benefits, Jetway Corporation	Your success in explaining total pay to your employees is superb; we would like to attempt to match your success. Can you please explain how you have developed and implemented your program?

Because the requests are different, the depth of response each needs is different, and because of professional courtesies, the detail and time involved in preparing the responses is different (see Figures 9.5 and 9.6).

Responses to Tour Inquiries

Virtually every business receives requests from all kinds of groups, for all kinds of reasons, to tour the facilities. If your organization is set up to handle such tours, the request is routine; if not, the request is nonroutine. Most organizations, especially those where safety is an issue or the work is sensitive, have very detailed instructions and admonitions when responding affirmatively. Because of safety and work flow and other activities of the office or factory, such "yes" responses are very detailed, often involving legal factors as the organization attempts to reduce its liability for mishaps.

FIGURE 9.5   Positive Response to an Information Inquiry, Maximizing Use of Enclosures

Remington Manufacturing   14499 Lotus Drive
                                               Shreveport, Louisiana 71109

Mr. Andrew Bernhart   October 3, 198_
Stevenson Hall, Room 303
Conway College
Conway, AR 71606

Dear Mr. Bernhart:

    Your inquiry concerning our Total Pay program indicates that you must be taking an
exciting and very practical course at Conway College. It is always worthwhile to take
time to share activities and findings with college students who are studying ways in which
business operations can be improved.

    Employee Communications. The basis of our success is the way we communicate
with our employees. This communication process is explained in detail in the enclosed
memo and attachments, "Communications at Remington."

    Setting the Record Straight. For too long, companies have hoodwinked themselves
by labeling, and allowing others to label, their benefits as "fringes." This is simply not
true. Therefore, we have been careful to ensure that our employees understand the reality
of the situation.

    As part of our ongoing communication effort we have explained "fringes" to our
employees. Enclosed are a variety of materials—the supervisor's briefing booklet, the
supplemental information for supervisors, and the postings that appeared on the company
bulletin boards. These items will clearly reveal how we are making sure our employees
comprehend their total pay.

    Your professor is to be commended for having you explore these current business
issues; I certainly hope you and your class colleagues are finding your studies invigorat-
ing. If your class needs additional copies of these materials, please let me know.

                          Sincerely,

                          Jodi Engres

                          Jodi Engres, Director
                          Employment Benefits

Enclosures

-Communications at Remington
-Supervisor's briefing booklet
-Supplemental information for supervisors
-Bulletin board postings

Margin annotations:

Acknowledgment.

Yes.

Goodwill.

Friendly close.

Enclosure detail.

FIGURE 9.6   Positive Response to an Information Inquiry—Detailed

Remington Manufacturing

14499 Lotus Drive
Shreveport, Louisiana 71109

October 4, 198_

Ms. Marion Keohn, Manager
Employee Benefits
Jetway Corp.
P. O. Box 10
Clinton, IN 47842

Dear Marion:

Acknowledgment/
yes.

    It was nice to hear from you; I clearly recall meeting you at the conference two years ago. Let me briefly highlight our Total Pay program.

Information.

Communication Premise. With an ongoing communications program it is relatively easy for us to get information to our employees. The total pay issue is just one of many topics we regularly communicate. (A list of the topics covered to date, our employee communication philosophy, and the briefing booklet on Total Pay are enclosed.)

Benefit Misinformation. As at many firms, our employees thought benefits were (1) often paid by the union, (2) added only about 3 percent to their wage, and (3) therefore rather inconsequential. There were several reasons for the misinformation:
a. Terminology: the term "fringe" benefits is hardly correct; they add over 60 percent to each employee's basic wage! We got the term "Total Pay" into everyone's vocabulary.
b. Understanding: Benefits are paid by the employer, and there are many benefits that employees take for granted. For instance, every time we add another free parking slot to a lot, it costs us over $10,000. That's a benefit.

Beyond Standard Booklets. Most employees don't read slick booklets on benefits. Therefore, we started at ground zero to build a realistic understanding of benefits. As you see in our enclosed bulletin board postings, the information is highly visual (instead of verbal) and the basic issues are addressed in very small doses. This holds everyone's attention span and maintains interest. Also, we made sure that the supervisors were informed so that they could respond appropriately to employee questions.

Goodwill.

After you have studied these materials, please call with any questions or comments—any of us in the department will be pleased to help you explain Total Pay to your employees.

Friendly close.

Sincerely,

Jodi Engres

Jodi Engres, Director
Employee Benefits

Encl.

Responding to Meeting Inquiries

When you are invited to attend a meeting, for instance a Lions Club Planning Conference, it is appropriate to respond. When your response is "yes," your communication becomes even more important if you must place certain limitations on it. Let the leader know if you will arrive late or will be unable to join the group for cocktails following the session. It is also the courteous thing to do. American business wastes too much time waiting: "I wonder if Tom is coming—let's wait another five minutes before starting."

Responding to Speech Inquiries

Pay particular attention to the constructive suggestion part of the "yes" response when you agree to speak. If you need certain kinds of equipment or insist on certain conditions, be sure your communication spells them out. The speaker has enough to worry about when giving a speech without having to handle, often unsuccessfully, last-minute details. When you say "yes," you should be clear about what you are saying "yes" to (see Figure 9.1).

Responding to Employment Interview Inquiries

In the employment arena, the first requisite is that your communication meet the letter and spirit of the law and not be discriminatory in any manner. The response should be very up-beat and strive to establish goodwill with the receiver. Further, be precise on how travel costs, lodging, and meals are to be handled and when and where the person is to report. Some employers today add one step beyond the formal "yes" letter. They assign an employee as the host. This person phones the interviewee after the candidate receives the interview invitation to check if he or she has any questions or concerns. Some firms even follow up several times via phone as they strive to establish a favorable rapport with interviewees prior to their arrival.

QUICK REVIEW

Responding to inquiries can dominate your time; that is not efficient management. However, by understanding and employing the thinking and communicating process, it is possible to say "yes," be a conscientious manager, and also be able to pay close attention to your regular job.

Before moving to the communication process, be sure that you work through the thinking and planning process; as emphasized in Chapter 2, planning and outlining are important. Then you can kindly and courteously provide complete and accurate information to the person making the inquiry.

EXECUTIVE SUMMARY

To: Business Communication Students

From: David N. Bateman and Norman B. Sigband

Subject: Responding to Inquiries Positively

Responding efficiently and effectively to inquiries is an important part of any manager's job. Among the reasons for responding to inquiries at all are good public relations and self-interest.

Many "yes" responses can be made efficiently with form letters and other printed materials. But many require nonroutine, individually prepared letters. Before you write your response, be certain you understand the inquiry and outline your response, double checking it to be sure it is complete. In preparing the response itself, you should follow the steps of the "yes" process:

Acknowledge the inquiry.

Say "yes."

Provide needed information.

Add helpful suggestions, if appropriate.

Add a sales or goodwill appeal, if appropriate.

Close with a friendly statement.

Business inquiries fall into many categories, like order or claim inquiries. Responding positively requires variation in strategies for each category.

DISCUSSION GENERATORS

1. *A "Yes" Propensity.* Why is there generally a willingness on the part of most organizations in the United States to respond affirmatively to most inquiries?
2. *Sorry.* What are some reasons why organizations sometimes cannot respond to inquiries with a "yes" answer? Cite examples for each reason.
3. *Think!* Before grabbing the dictation machinery or placing the stationery in the typewriter, what are some of the thinking and planning activities that need to be considered and implemented in a "yes" response?
4. *A Quick "Yes."* Give examples of satisfactory "yes" responses that are simply a flyer, brochure, or the ordered product sent to the individual making the inquiry.
5. *Acknowledgment.* Why is it ineffective to start a "yes" letter with statements like the following:
   a. Per your request for information on felt wallpaper ...
   b. We received your letter yesterday inquiring about ...
   c. I want to thank you for your inquiry concerning ...

6. *Enthusiastic Yes*. Does the "yes" response of Sophia Goldwater in Figure 9.1 reflect a sincere enthusiasm? Is the approach more interesting than responding, "I can come to Silver City to speak on May 3"?

7. *Provide the Info*. Why is it beneficial to use headings in providing the requested information; how do headings aid you in ensuring that your response is complete?

8. *Suggestions*. How can adding a constructive suggestion aid both the sender and the receiver of the "yes" communication?

9. *Sales and Goodwill*. What is the difference between the sales appeal and the appeal to goodwill? Illustrate each.

10. *Friendly Close*. What is the difference between the friendly close and the complimentary close? Give some examples of trite friendly closings that may make your communication appear insincere.

11. *Completeness*. What are some simple procedures you can implement to ensure that your responses to inquiries are complete?

12. *Common Categories of Inquiries*. The text lists seven common kinds of inquiries managers often receive. Select three that you feel are ones you will receive in your professional life and clearly explain their use on your job.

13. *Fault*. How does the assignment of fault, be it on the part of the seller or the buyer, influence the nature and tone of the "yes" response?

14. *Inquiries to Tour*. Why do communications responding to inquiries to tour an organization's facilities often have to be rather detailed?

15. *Employment Inquiries*. To promote goodwill and to ensure that all goes well, what are some employers doing today besides just sending a "yes" letter? What are some of the benefits of these "extras"?

16. *Who*. How does the identity of the sender influence the response to inquiries for information?

17. *Enclosures*. How can attachments and various enclosures save preparation time for the person preparing the "yes" response?

18. *Provide the Answer*. What do some organizations do to ensure that their managers answer inquiries?

19. *Systems*. What are some common systems that organizations have to respond to routine inquiries?

20. *Help a Competitor?* Why, and under what circumstances, would a firm be willing to respond with a "yes" response to an inquiry from a competitor?

APPLICATIONS FOR BUSINESS

21. *Tired of Triteness*. As a vice-president at Reynolds, you have just discovered the triteness of many of your managers' responses to inquiries. Often they start with "Per," "I," or "Responding to," and sometimes the writer thinks it important to let the receiver know the time of the day the letter arrived, "Your letter arrived this morning. . . ." Who cares and what difference does it make whether the inquiry

arrived at 11:55 a.m. or 12:01 p.m.! Here is a typical inquiry your firm is currently receiving; in response to it, develop at least three you-oriented first sentences that are fresh.

> Your firm's success in creating and implementing a workable in-house day-care center for employees' children (ages 6 months to 5 years) has received rave reports in *Time* and other publications. Can you please send detailed information on how you organized the resources of your firm to develop this beneficial service?

22. *Labor Limitations.* As director of labor relations at Allis Inc. you like to share your insights with college students on developments and trends in labor negotiations. You are currently engaged in some publicized negotiations with one of your unions—a major issue is your firm's use of unorganized, at-home computer programmers. You have received several requests from college students asking you to comment on the trend to use out-of-plant (unorganized) rather than in-plant (organized) employees. It is an intriguing issue, and you would like to be able to comment. However, because of the negotiations, anything you might say (even in an individual letter) could upset the tenor of the labor discussions. You want to provide these students with a "yes" response; since you cannot comment on your situation or anything resembling it, how can you still respond affirmatively? Explain your approach, and then write such a "yes" letter.

23. *Tour de Force.* Responses to requests to tour manufacturing facilities must be explicit, detailed, and clear. Firms receive tour requests for uncontrollable young-sters, unpredictable adolescents, overly nosy executives, and sometimes tottery old people. For Oster Manufacturing Company,
    a. prepare a guide letter for responding to tour requests;
    b. prepare, from the guide, a specific letter that would go to one of the categories of people cited above.

24. *Employment "Yes" Responses.* College students love to receive "yes" responses from potential employers that invite them to come and interview at the firm's headquarters. As a person looking forward to receiving such a letter, create the following lists.
    a. The specific items you would like to see covered in the letter.
    b. Other kinds of courtesies you would like to have the employer extend in order to make your visit as relaxing and enjoyable as possible.

25. *Goodwill Is Good Business.* Although the aspect of goodwill is near the end of the inquiry process, it is not unimportant. However, too often it appears that goodwill is just "stuck on" or routine in communications.

    As assistant director for public relations for the Remington Company, you receive many requests from all sorts of people for copies of your firm's annual report. You could just stick the report in an envelope and send it, but you have a guide letter that individualizes each letter for the situation. In your guide letter you want to enhance the goodwill aspect. Prepare a paragraph or several sentences for each of the following situations that you can consider incorporating in your standard letter.

Suggested Goodwill Statements for Different Contexts
a. For reports sent December 1 through December 20.
b. For reports sent June 25 through July 1.
c. For reports sent one week prior to Thanksgiving.
d. For reports sent during the first 10 days of January.
e. For reports sent to individuals who indicate they are concerned with environmental protection.
f. For reports sent to individuals who indicate they are concerned with fair employment practices.
g. For reports sent to individuals who indicate they are concerned with women's rights.

COMMUNICATION CHECK-UPS

26. Because she is your sister in law she is not eligible for the college internship.
27. Janice Bright is a woman whom will do well in the management environment.
28. A review of the report.
29. We at Bellcraft want to welcome you as a customer.
30. In order to proceed an procedural statement is necessary.
31. Being Monday morning the cafeteria was crowded.
32. Neither of the men paid their bill.
33. It was him who received the reward.
34. The supervisor suggested, "effective communication is *key* in successfully working with employees."
35. The apprentice graduates of 80 will be honored at the annual company banquet.

Executive
Introduction

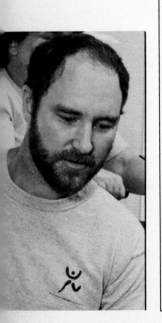

Tenneco Inc
Health and Fitness

Tenneco Building
P.O. Box 2511
Houston, Texas 77252
(713) 757-5704

June 19, 198_

Scott Hayden
126 Bertl Street
Los Alamos, New Mexico 87544

Dear Scott:

We appreciate your interest in the Tenneco Health and Fitness Program. Your experience suggests that you have many of the talents necessary to work within a corporate environment.

There are no positions open in our department now, nor do I see any professional positions opening in the near future. The field of corporate health and fitness, although steadily growing, currently has a very competitive job market. I would encourage you to continue to search for a position within a corporate setting or an adult fitness program where you can grow toward your goals. Some of the important organizations to help in your search are:

AFB
1312 Washington Blvd.
Stamford, CT 06902

ACSM
P.O. Box 1440
Indianapolis, IN 46206

AAHPER
Recreation Dance
1900 Association Drive
Reston, VA 22091

La Crosse Exercise Bulletin
University of Wisconsin - La Crosse
La Crosse, WI 54601

Thank you for giving me an opportunity to look at your resume, which I will keep on file. I wish you the best of luck in finding an opportunity to use your skills and experience.

Sincerely,

William B. Baun, Manager
Health & Fitness

WBB/sm

Responding to Inquiries Negatively

WHAT YOU CAN LEARN BY STUDYING THIS CHAPTER

Part of graciousness is knowing how to convey negative news in a considerate manner. Psychology plays a major role in "no" communications. In this chapter you will learn how to structure the "no" response, temper its emphasis, and leave the receiver with something other than a bitter taste in his or her mouth. You will also learn that "no" communications need not be a complete closing of the door. Through the use of options, sales appeals, and statements of goodwill, it is possible to say "no" today and still leave room for some positive relations in the future.

Establish the appropriate attitude.

Of all the letters explained and illustrated in this text, the two types that people dislike writing the most are probably letters of sympathy and "no" letters. *Management* is defined as getting things done through people, and clearly it is not possible to always say "yes"; neither is it acceptable to avoid communicating information that may be unpleasant. Therefore, the attitude you project in your "no" communications, including the unwritten aspects, becomes very important. Remember, just because the message may be unpleasant, the language and the attitude of the communicator need not be unpleasant. In fact, a good guideline is that as the unpleasantness of the message increases, the responsibility of the communicator to be pleasant in tone, tact, and temperament increases.

You will be called upon to say "no" in a variety of situations. After all, for each of the categories of "yes" letters presented in Chapter 9, we must recognize that sometimes the answer must be "no." After exploring the elements of creative "no" responses to inquiries, we will review a variety of examples in order to gain an understanding of how to prepare and deliver these messages.

PROMPTNESS: DON'T SIT ON IT

Delaying the "no" response aggravates the situation.

It is beneficial for neither you nor the receiver of the communication for you to sit on the "no" response after the "no" decision has been made.

First of all, it is inconsiderate for the individual making an inquiry. If a junior college business instructor inquires about bringing a CAD/CAM group of students to tour your computer graphics facility, it is going to disrupt the instructor's plans to not receive your answer within a reasonable period of time. The company may have some new experimental equipment that it cannot allow outsiders to see. There are no other feasible alternatives. The response must be *no*. To wait to communicate the "no," however, may prevent the instructor from making arrangements with another firm to tour its CAD/CAM facilities. Even though it may be more gratifying to prepare "yes" communications, if you have a stack of letters and phone calls needing "yes" and "no" responses, you should initiate the "no" communications first.

Second, the "no" letter should be prepared (perhaps drafted) promptly because in some "no" situations, legal factors may constrain your response and language. You may want to prepare a draft letter and check it with counsel. If you keep putting off such communications, you are more likely to prepare a "no" response that may create some legal problems.

Third, some people are generally negatively influenced when they are faced with communicating negative news. People have reported that it is difficult to live with their spouses when they know the spouse is going to have to terminate an employee. Many people lose weight, lose sleep, and become edgy when such negative clouds are hanging over their heads. The clouds continue to linger if you don't hold the meeting, don't make the phone call, or don't write the letter. So, it is beneficial and helpful to others and to yourself to promptly and judiciously prepare and communicate the "no" responses.

THE PSYCHOLOGY OF SAYING "NO"

Consider the college instructor who wants to bring her computer programming class to your firm's computer installation for a practical on-site visit. Looking at it from her point of view, she probably sees herself as a dedicated teacher who is going beyond the call of duty in making the appointment, arranging buses, and taking care of the dozens of details involved in transporting thirty-five students from the college to the company's offices. She feels her request for a visit is reasonable and desirable for all parties concerned. If we open our reply with a "No; sorry, we can't accommodate you," it is easy to understand her irritation and even anger. If, on the other hand, we open with an explanation of the situation, permitting her to conclude that the answer *must* be no, we may retain her friendship and goodwill.

In all refusals—whether they are oral or written, whether they are made to an employee, a customer, your parent, spouse, child, or friend—explain before you refuse.

Explanations often benefit "no" responses.

In almost every situation in which a refusal or unfavorable answer must be given, there is a good reason. If that reason is tactfully, sincerely, and courteously presented, most readers or listeners will say, "I can understand; I can appreciate the situation."

THE PROCESS OF SAYING "NO"

You will recall that in the "yes" letter, it was sometimes possible and polite to communicate almost abruptly—even just sending the individual the product ordered, for example. Such efficiency and straightforwardness is generally not advisable in the "no" response. As with the "yes," the process for communicating the negative answer has six steps, but with a basic difference. Whereas in the "yes" response you should say "yes" (grant the request) as quickly as possible, in the "no" communication you should delay the refusal. In fact, in some situations it may be possible to say "no" implicitly and avoid the harshness of the negative language.

The rationale of the "no" process.

Let's look at the process for responding with a "no." This process generally works, but in some situations you may have good reason to slightly rearrange the sequence of the steps for specific individuals and contexts.

The Steps of the "No" Process	*Some Dos and Don'ts for Each Step*
1. An introductory statement of acknowledgment	The you-orientation is important; recognize the needs of the receiver, and get in step with them. Avoid triteness.
2. An explanation	Without prolonging the narrative, explain the situation that makes the refusal necessary. Beware of making this too long or the receiver will think, "I know the answer is no" and then

jump to inappropriate conclusions without hearing or reading your message.

3. Communicate the refusal

In areas that have legal implications, the refusal should be stated explicitly. In some other situations, the "no" may be implied—this works especially when you are proposing alternative options.

4. Consider a constructive suggestion or alternative plan

Sometimes the impact of the "no" response can be tempered by providing a suggestion, "Although it is not possible to tour our facilities at this time, you may want to contact nearby companies like Atwood Co., Menning Mfg., or Pinckneyville Plastic—they may be able to accommodate you." Alternative plans, such as "Although we cannot currently provide a tour of our CAD/CAM facilities, it would be possible for one of the managers of that operation to visit your classroom, show a video of our operation, and respond to questions." (See Figure 10.1.) However, it is not always incumbent upon the communicator to suggest alternatives; the realities of business sometimes demand a clear and simple "no."

5. Sales appeal and/or goodwill

When denying credit or rejecting a potential sale, sometimes it is still appropriate to make a sales appeal— you still want the individual who was denied credit to give you his or her cash business. Or you may not be able to supply the product or service to a customer this time, but you may still want future business.

6. A friendly close

A friendly approach is always in order; you should attempt to build it—it may pay a bonus for you in the future.

The requisites for a friendly close are identical to those for the "yes" letter; strive to be sincere without being trite.

FIGURE 10.1   Saying "No" to a Request, but Offering an Alternative

WISCONSIN FARM EQUIPMENT

Parkside, Wisconsin 53467

April 3, 198_

Dr. F. Brewster, Assistant Dean
Parkside Community College
Parkside, Wisconsin 53469

Dear Dr. Brewster:

You and your colleagues at Parkside Community College deserve high
commendations for all your efforts in arranging the County Fair each
year. The service you perform for our area is extremely valuable.

We are very appreciative that you have given us an opportunity to
display our equipment and products in one of the booths. However, we
have already committed our personnel and display equipment for the same
weekend to the College of Agriculture at the state university.

Last year, at your request, we had one of our drivers use a Cable field
mower to cut grass and brush in the exposition area. If we can assist
again this year, in the same capacity, we will be happy to do so. Just
call and we will set a time at your convenience.

Thanks again, Dr. Brewster, for inviting us. We hope we may use our
"rain check" for next year.

Cordially yours,

Thomas H. Benton

Thomas H. Benton
Area Manager

Introduction/
acknowledgment.

Note the you-
orientation.

Explanation/
refusal.

Suggestion/
alternative plan.

Goodwill.

Friendly close.

OTHER GUIDELINES TO SAYING "NO"

These guidelines can aid in not making a poor situation worse!

We recognize that "no" communications can rarely result in everyone's being pleased. Here are some pitfalls to avoid so you don't aggravate an already negative situation.

> *Avoid Lecturing:* In denying credit to a potential customer, for example, nothing is gained by hinting that it would have been beneficial to pay bills on time.

> *Don't Hide:* Avoid erecting verbal barriers that will be meaningless to the receiver, such as "your request cannot be granted because of company policy." Remember, the receiver does not have your firm's policy manual at hand.

> *Watch Negative Words:* The explicit or implied "no" is clear enough without exacerbating the situation with words and language like "your fault," "your surprising request," or "because of the rambunctiousness of your children."

The letter in Figure 10.2 is a good illustration of a negative response that avoids these pitfalls.

CATEGORIES OF "NO" COMMUNICATIONS

Refusing Orders

In refusing one order, you may want to try for another order.

At first glance, it may seem impossible that there would be orders that must be refused. But it does occur. The following are some of the situations in which an order is received but the sale must be declined.

1. The buyer is a poor credit risk.
2. The buyer has exceeded his or her credit limit.
3. Company, local, or federal regulations involving sales, franchising, or distributorship might be violated.
4. The merchandise requested is not handled or stocked by the seller.
5. Filling the order would prove unprofitable because of the limited quantity ordered, the distance to be shipped, or modifications requested.

Figure 10.3 exemplifies a letter refusing a potential buyer's order. Note that a brief and courteous explanation is made before the refusal. And the refusal itself is handled courteously and tactfully. In addition, the tone is positive and the sales approach quite strong. The letter seems to say, "This is the situation; it isn't good, but we feel you will understand. Now let's continue on a businesslike basis in the future."

FIGURE 10.2   Saying "No" to a Request for Credit

TECH OFFICE PRODUCTS

58 ADRIAN STREET   CHICO, CALIFORNIA   95928

April 29, 198_

Mrs. Lillian Miller
5600 Talman Avenue
Fayetteville, AR 72701

Dear Mrs. Miller:

As a community leader, your business is especially valued to us—we are flattered to include you as a regular customer.

The information you supplied has been carefully evaluated and it is in everyone's best interest for you to continue as one of our valued cash customers. In this way you will avoid the task of end-of-month bills and the keeping of records.

On June 10 we will hold our annual salute to city leaders. Honored will be six carefully selected leaders from the public and private sectors. Enclosed is a card that will admit you to the reception and luncheon. Please let us know if you will be present.

Also enclosed is a "Preferred Customer" card that will entitle you to an additional ten percent discount off any sale item purchased at our "Annual Bonanza Sale," May 8-10.

Thanks again, Mrs. Miller, for your interest in Tech Office Products. We look forward to hearing from you.

Cordially yours,

Lester Jameson

Lester Jameson
Sales and Credit Manager

Encls.

Sidebar annotations:

Friendly introductory opening (acknowledgment implied).

Explanation.

Implied refusal.

Positive goodwill message.

Friendly close.

This kind of letter could not be used routinely, but for those special situations that face managers periodically that call for the nonroutine response, this type of approach can be effective.

FIGURE 10.3   Saying "No" to an Order

PLAZA
DEPARTMENT   STORE

February 21, 198_

Mr. Dana P. Ortinau
Chips and Fish Corp.
One Wilshire Blvd.
Los Angeles, CA 90067

Dear Mr. Ortinau:

Acknowledgment.

Thanks for your first order with us—we certainly want to serve you.

Explanation.

Several years ago, we established a policy designed to save you and
other customers significant amounts of money. This policy, which is
described in more detail in our catalog, basically consists of eliminating such extras as drop shipments, advertising allowances, and store
demonstrations in order to offer our customers the lowest possible
prices.

Constructive
suggestions.

Your order, requesting drop shipments of various quantities to each of
your eighteen outlets in Southern California, would increase our
shipping costs substantially. You can appreciate our situation; we do
want to send you the merchandise at the special prices quoted, but we
can ship the order to only one address. If you do not have a warehouse
facility, perhaps you might designate one of your outlets as a receiving
point.

Sales appeal.

Please call me collect, today, Mr. Ortinau, and we may be able to ship
your order at once.

Sincerely yours,

Mike Huesenkraft

Mike Huesenkraft
Shipping Manager

5592   FAIRVIEW   AVENUE
ROANOKE, VIRGINIA 24018

Refusing a Claim

Most companies find that each day's mail brings in a certain number of requests for adjustments. In cases where a review determines that the fault is not the firm's but is the buyer's, the company will want to refuse. In addition, in some instances a refusal must be made because of local or national statutes. For example, medical prescriptions, once received by the buyer, may not be returned to the place of purchase for credit. In many states, undergarments or other personal items may not be returned once they have left the store.

In Figure 10.4 notice how the positive closing paragraph makes a strong effort to lessen the impact of the refusal. The tone is friendly and businesslike. In addition, the explanation of how the buyer is at fault—always made before the refusal—is conveyed tactfully.

Refusing to honor a claim need not be all negative.

Not Offering Employment

As you will discover in the employment-letter section of this text, applicants for employment spend considerable time preparing résumés and cover letters, and they seem to do all of this in order to receive what is commonly referred to as "rejection letters." For firms that do considerable recruiting, the letters will be in their form or guide letter system. As with other negative responses, the "no" process applies to these communications.

It is important to not stumble over one of the laws or regulations relating to employment in communicating with the individual denied employment after an interview. Remember, the "rejection letter" will be the one printed item the individual has that says "no," and you don't want to see that letter again, in court. Avoid the following in writing this "no" letter.

Watch for the "sandtraps" when denying employment.

Referring to sex, marital status, children, or age.

Implying that one of the above might diminish the person's effectiveness.

Stating that the individual does not meet the requisites—when he or she actually does.

In Figure 10.5 there is an example of an actual letter a business-communication student received from an employer after responding to an advertisement in a major metropolitan newspaper. The communication meets the requisites of the "no" letter and also clearly illustrates how such letters can bolster the feelings of the recipient.

Rejecting a Job Offer

Students often wonder if they will ever get a job offer; that is a problem. However, another big problem arises when they have several offers; all but one must be rejected. For several reasons you should say your "no" in writing, perhaps preceded or followed up with a personal telephone call:

Saying "no" to a job offer may be a positive step for the future.

FIGURE 10.4   Saying "No" to a Claim

a & c

Distributing, Inc.

March 10, 198_

Mr. A. J. Werner
Computer Center and Sales
121 South Farnsworth
Des Moines, IA 53201

Dear Mr. Werner:

Friendly opening.

It was good of you to write concerning the Technical Home Computer (Model 211) with the cracked cabinet.

Explanation of the situation.

You did what you felt was proper under the circumstances. However, we would have preferred for you to have given us an opportunity to replace the entire unit for your customer rather than simply giving him a $100 refund and having the cabinet repaired.

Neither we nor Technica Corporation likes to have a damaged product in the hands of a user. This policy was established for the benefit of you and other retailers.

Refusal.

Also, as noted on all our sales literature, items may be returned within 30 days for full refund or replacement. Since this was not done in this case, and in fairness to all our other customers, you can understand why we cannot credit your account for $100.

Sales appeal and goodwill.

You may be sure, Mr. Werner, that we want you to have the best in-home computers available for sale to your customers. For that reason, we handle all the major brands at prices that can't be beat. Please call us at any time if we can assist you.

Cordially yours,

Joan L. Meyers

Joan L. Meyers
Dealer Services

399 Zenith Avenue
Clinton, Iowa   52732

FIGURE 10.5   Saying "No" to a Request for Employment

Pachmayer

Data   9590 *Clyde Avenue*

Services   *Wheaton, Illinois   60188*

Ms. Kimberly Benning
2035 Edith Street
Murfreesboro, TN 52701

Dear Ms. Benning:

Your recent letter caught our attention; with the abilities
reflected in that letter and backup material, I am confident
that you will have considerable success in securing a position
in marketing research. Unfortunately, your educational and work
background is not in line with the opening we have at this
time.

You should know that when we place advertisements like the one
to which you responded, it is not possible for us to attempt to
respond to every inquiry. But, I'm writing to you because yours
was one of the best letters of application I have seen in
fifteen years of personnel recruiting.

I know you will be successful in finding permanent employment;
thank you for your interest in Pachmayer Data Services, and
also congratulations in learning to communicate so well—those
skills will be invaluable to you as you launch your professional career.

Yours sincerely,

Judith Toat

Judith E. Toat
Director of Recruiting

Acknowledgment.

Refusal implied.

Constructive
statement.

Goodwill.

Positive close.

FIGURE 10.6 Saying "No" to a Job Offer

You-oriented
acknowledgment.

Explanation.

Implied refusal.

Friendly close.

April 10, 198_
302 Tenth Street
Utica, NY 13502

Mr. Albert Tomasaki, CPA
Cohen and Tomasaki, CPA's
1111 West Marine Avenue
Elmira, New York 14902

Dear Mr. Tomasaki:

Your offer of employment for a position as a junior accountant was
flattering and most satisfying. Thank you very much.

Just yesterday, another organization also contacted me concerning
employment. Although Cohen and Tomasaki, CPA's offers many advantages,
the lure of a brief five-minute ride to work, plus tuition remission
funds toward an MBA degree, motivated me to say "yes, thank you" to
the other organization.

I'm well aware of the success of Cohen and Tomasaki, CPA's, and I wish
you continued progress in the business arena.

Very sincerely yours,

Eugene

Eugene Taylor

1. *Networking* is crucial in any profession. You might as well start to build your network with those who thought you good enough to offer you employment.
2. *Consideration* reflects well on you, and the letter will permit you to build goodwill.
3. *Closure* is brought to the situation—both you and the firm making the offer know the offer is rejected.

This type of letter need not be long—but the basic steps of the "no" response can be covered and done so to your advantage. (See Figure 10.6.)

QUICK REVIEW

Regardless of the context, the process for communicating "no" basically does not change from situation to situation. As you can see, often the problem is not in how to say "no" but how to do so kindly and with tact. The "no" communications call for a strong you-orientation—a you-orientation where you get in step with and understand the receiver's situation and then communicate meaningfully and kindly to that individual.

EXECUTIVE SUMMARY

To: Business Communication Students

From: David N. Bateman and Norman B. Sigband

Subject: Responding to Inquiries Negatively

Most people dislike having to say "no," but managers frequently must do so. The effective business communicator is especially tactful and thoughtful in conveying negative messages. Maintaining the *you*-orientation is crucial. In sending the "no" response, it is essential to respond promptly, following these steps:

Acknowledge the inquiry.

Explain.

Say "no" (or imply it clearly).

Offer constructive suggestions or alternative plans, if appropriate.

Add a sales/or goodwill appeal, if appropriate.

Close in a friendly manner.

The thoughtfully written refusal is direct but avoids lecturing the receiver and the use of negative language.

The major categories of inquiry that may require a negative response are orders, claims, and denial of employment. Although each of these categories can be approached with special strategies to ensure clear communication and continued good relations, the basic process of communication is the same for all.

DISCUSSION GENERATORS

1. *Dark Clouds.* Explain the "dark clouds" that can hang over the communicator who does not respond promptly with "no" letters.

2. *Legal Advantage.* What is the legal advantage to the writer of the "no" letter in promptly drafting a response?

3. *Bothersome.* If you are a personality type bothered by having to relay negative news to individuals, what can you do to reduce this frustration when faced with having to communicate negative news?

4. *The Writer's Viewpoint.* Why is it important to attempt to get in step with the person making the inquiry before preparing the "no" response?

5. *Happiness.* Is a goal of most "no" communications to make the recipient happy? Explain your answer.

6. *Avoidance.* If you do not like to say "no," what is wrong with always trying to imply the "no" in your communications instead of saying it explicitly?

7. *Explain Before You Refuse.* What is the reason behind explaining the situation before you say "no"?

8. *Teenage Communications.* Take on the role of a parent. A teenage son or daughter will sometimes have to receive "no" responses from you. Illustrate how the various steps of the "no" process can aid you in communicating the following to them:
   You can't have the car tonight.
   You cannot stay out until 3 a.m. on a school night.
   You cannot wear your shorts and tank top to church.

9. *Let Me Tell You How It Is.* Explain why it is a poor strategy to lecture or preach in a "no" communication.

10. *Absolutely No.* Cite two or three situations where an organization would have to respond "*absolutely no* . . . there are no feasible alternatives or options."

11. *Understanding and Happiness.* Why is it that although your "no" communication may be strong on creating "understanding," it may be weak on creating happiness?

12. *Timing.* Why should refusal communications be prepared and sent even more promptly than "yes" communications?

13. *I Won't Accept Your Order.* Name and explain various situations in which a retailer may turn down an order; why, in these cases, is the decision to not make a sale good business?

14. *Don't Do It.* What are some traits that a considerate "no" communication will not contain?

15. *Politely, the Answer Is No.* Explain why it is courteous to say "no" promptly instead of waiting for a better day.

16. *What Does "Acknowledgment" Mean?* Some "no" letters begin as if "acknowledgment" means you must say you received the letter, and then specify the day, time, and place you received it. Obviously, that is ridiculous. Illustrate how the acknowledgment step might be implied and how you can quickly move on to introducing your material.

17. *Why Bother with an Alternative?* As represented in Figure 10.1, organizations sometimes go to great lengths to attempt to satisfy the inquiry when the answer to the request must be "no." Why do organizations do this?

18. *Really Friendly?* Why might the following phrases not be considered friendly by the receiver and actually not meet the requisites of a "friendly close" as suggested in the "no" process?
    a. Best wishes.
    b. Good luck to you in the future.
    c. Merry Christmas and Happy New Year.
    d. My sincerest best to you in your future endeavors.

19. *Rewrite the Litigious Items.* An incorrect statement made in a letter refusing employment can create legal problems for the employer. Rewrite the following statements to make sure they avoid such problems.
    a. Because you are very young, it would probably be more advantageous for you to seek employment at the plant-level rather than the corporate level.
    b. Because all of our customers are men, Alice, it does not seem advantageous to our business strategy to bring you aboard in our sales department.
    c. John, your typing skills and other office management abilities are fine, but we feel you would find it difficult to "fit in" as the lead secretary in our unit.

20. *Interpersonal Applications.* Illustrate how avoiding lecturing and negative words and not hiding behind mysterious words can aid people in getting along at home, work, and play.

APPLICATIONS FOR BUSINESS

21. *No by Implication.* You are asked to return to your college campus to speak to honor students on Honors Day. In just seven years out of college you have been inordinately successful in your profession, and it would be gratifying to return to the campus under these circumstances. Unfortunately, you will be in Europe at that time; it is not practical to rearrange the important European business trip. In a letter to the Dean, accomplish all of the objectives of a "no" letter using an implied "no," and offer an intriguing alternative that can get you back on the campus at a different time.

22. *Don't Mail This Letter.* The following letter does nothing but insult the receiver and create disharmony. Rewrite the letter to establish goodwill.

Dear Mr. Hernandez:

Your request for one of our new "Back to School" signs for use in your store display was received today.

Unfortunately, we must refuse your request because the size of the order that accompanied the request was far below the $800 minimum required.

Our fall catalog indicated the terms by which it was possible to obtain the sign. Perhaps you missed the explanation. However, they (the signs) are very costly to us, and we can't just give them out to everybody.

If you would like, we can send you our fall poster collection, which you can use to advertise twelve different sale items. Or, if you can call in an increase in your last order and bring it from $350 to $800, we can make arrangements.

Please let us know.

---

23. *Antagonism Reduction Therapy.* Making sure your "no" communication is actually heard can be helped by not heightening the antagonism of the receiver. Understanding the receiver's position and getting in step with that individual are two common ways of reducing antagonism. For the following situations, illustrate how you would respond to accomplish this anti-antagonism approach. Clearly the initiators of these communications are angry. Sticking to your "no" response will call for a great deal of tact.
   a. A student writes a professor: "I not only work hard in my college courses (study at least four hours each evening), I'm holding down a thirty-hour per week job that often calls for overtime on top of that. For these reasons alone, you should be able to give me the 'B' grade I missed by just 3 percent."
   b. A taxpayer writes a government official: "The county is unfair in charging my family $78 for the ambulance trip it made to the hospital on May 23rd—my Grandmother died before the ambulance ever arrived at the hospital. Can't governments show sympathy?"
   c. A loyal fan writes the team's management: "As a season ticket holder, I should be able to have my regular seats for the championship game. It is unfair of you to give my seats (and those around me) to a bunch of politicians and VIPs—if they are so interested, why haven't they been at the games all year?"

24. *The "Yes" and "No" May Be Similar.* Compare the organization of a letter that says "yes" with the organization of a letter that says "no" by giving the outline you would write for each of these situations.
   a. A recent high-school graduate has applied to your college for acceptance in the nursing program. You can accept the graduate.
   b. The same situation as above except the class list is already filled and you cannot accept the graduate.

25. *Not Yet You Don't Get the Promotion.* In management and personnel relations you will often have to relate negative news to subordinates. You have one slot open for a unit head and three individuals in your department have applied. Orally, you need to relate the bad news to two while attempting to maintain morale in the department and encouragement for those that have not been selected. Review the "no" steps and be prepared to explain in class (perhaps role play) how you will do this.

COMMUNICATION CHECK-UPS

26. They are paying about 3,500,000 dollars for the plant.
27. The Finance Department has one third of the project completed.
28. Place the first Monday after Christmas on your calender for our budget review meeting.
29. The censor will detect anyone entering your office.
30. "English is a very important subject," Mary remarked, "so I spend a substantial amount of time reviewing the subject."
31. The word processor was sold for half it's value.
32. He purchased three shares of AT&T, seven shares of Sears, and 55 shares of Zenith.
33. She is the first southerner appointed as a regional manager in our area.
34. Neither the smokers or the nonsmokers were pleased with the new policies.
35. Her address is in Ill someplace. IL.

Executive Introduction

 CATERPILLAR INC.

Peoria, Illinois 61629 -5440

January 15, 198_

Mr. Charles A. Walker
C. A. Walker & Associates, Inc.
2950 Los Feliz Blvd.
Los Angeles, CA 90039

Dear Charlie,

Surely you would like to have more marketing-research projects from
Caterpillar like the Service Quality mail survey we recently assigned
to you. We will be looking closely at the response rates to your
mailings in evaluating your performance. As you know, Charlie,
achieving high response rates does not require magic—just careful
application of fundamentals.

Receiver analysis and identifying the appeals are critical tactics.
Choose words that make the receivers feel important (no one wants to
feel he or she is just a number). Tell them how their response to the
survey will benefit both them and the industry.

Of course, you'll develop a series of communications; follow-up
mailings usually produce as great a response as the initial one.

These techniques work. I know that as an "old pro" in the business,
you'll apply them to get great results.

I'm looking forward to receiving your reports on this important
project.

Very truly yours,

Senior Marketing Consultant
Product Support Development G.O.

RJBateman
Telephone: (309) 675-5178
kh

65rjb80150800

Motivating the Receiver to Act

WHAT YOU CAN LEARN BY STUDYING THIS CHAPTER

It is not just the format, grammar, and style of communications that make them effective. Your appeal to the receiver also plays a major role in successful communication. This chapter will examine various appeals and how they can be used in business communications. We will consider credit and collection letters, because they use not only the basic appeals, but also some special kinds of persuasion. We will also consider other, wider uses of appeals. When combined with the strategy of placing communications in a series, some very potent communication techniques are available that will be useful to you throughout your career.

If we accept the notion that many communications are "sales" communications (either directly or indirectly) and that the final step in the sales process is action, then identifying the "carrots" or the appeals that will stir that action is important. It is important, therefore, for you to recognize the appeals and to learn how to include them in communications.

The correct appeal can move the receiver.

As we know, there are all kinds of situations in which you will want to encourage the receiver to act, that is, to *accept* your viewpoint, to *implement* your recommendation, or to *purchase* your product. Just stating the case and rationale often is not enough; but an appeal targeted for the receiver can be the deciding factor in accomplishing that action goal. For instance, a simple printed "past due" notice on a bill may not motivate many people to pay; however, the same bill attached to a letter that appeals to the need to maintain a good reputation may move the receiver to action. A request from your boss to join other department members in sponsoring a Junior Achievement company may initially seem relatively unimportant; the same request based on the need for team play may shed a different light on the situation.

Good reputation, self-interest, and team play are just some of the possible appeals for structuring communications so that desired action can be achieved. Appeals are often crucial to communication because they aid you in actually linking the message with the objective. As we turn to an examination of different kinds of appeals, remember that much more than just "letter perfect" grammar, structure, and syntax are necessary in effective business communications—the communication should stir the appropriate action and achieve the communicator's desired result.

Appeals can link your objective to the desired action.

ACTION AND APPEALS

Appeals and action go hand-in-hand.

Everyone communicates. Successful communicators are the ones who get the desired results from their communications. Sometimes the logic and the outline of communications from two individuals may appear similar, but one gains the appropriate response and the other doesn't. Why? Because the successful message struck the right chord in the receiver. The message was intertwined with an appeal that was meaningful and persuasive. The communication moved the receiver to action.

CATEGORIES OF APPEALS

You can appeal to the head or to the heart.

The appeals are sometimes categorized into those that appeal to the heart (striking emotional chords) and those that appeal to the head (striking rationality). Such categorizations must be treated carefully. It may be helpful to recognize such categories, but for a particular receiver, it is difficult to determine if the appeal is emotional and/or rational. Consider, for instance, "The suit will allow you to present a conservative image while simultaneously projecting a stylish and progressive outlook." Is that appeal emotional or rational? Doesn't it depend upon to whom the appeal is aimed? If targeted at a person who feels style and image are number one, then the appeal may be categorized as emotional. However, if targeted at a business person who interacts closely with top business clients, then the appeal may be simply based on a rational approach to good business practice.

Appeals serve a purpose in communications: they permit the receiver to find reasons to agree with you and to accept your conclusion. With that objective in mind, let's explore a variety of appeals.

There are various specific kinds of appeals.

Appeals to Economic Benefit

In communications about a project inside the organization or communications to a customer, economic benefit can be a persuasive appeal. The memo to your superior in which you attempt to persuade him or her to approve the purchase of a pocket dictating unit might use this appeal: "The time gained by dictating in the car coming to and going from work will amount to substantial savings—the cost of the unit will actually be recouped in less than one week." Saving time and saving money are often key appeals within the classification of economic benefit. Materials we receive urging us to purchase an automobile often use this appeal: "With your new Dodge Daytona you will increase your miles per gallon, which will result in substantial savings to you at each infrequent stop at the gas station."

There are many uses for the economic appeal.

In attempting to justify purchases, programs, and activities within the organization, the manager will often point to economics. In business, the bottom line is frequently in the forefront, so this kind of appeal is used extensively. (See Figure 11.1.)

Appeals to Pride or Reputation

For both individuals and organizations, appeals to pride or reputation are powerful motivators. The collection letter to a delinquent bill payer often uses the appeal to reputation: "Your standing among other businesses can be diminished if you do not submit your past-due payment promptly." Inside the organization, a reference to the organization's standing in the community can be a persuasive motivator: "Our downturn in sales and subsequent budget cutbacks are only temporary. Therefore, we should not disrupt long-term activities that enhance our reputation in the community. To withdraw our rather minor, but important, contribution to the Women's Center could give us a 'black eye' far worse than the cost of our contribution." (See Figure 11.2.)

Most people and organizations want to protect their reputation; therefore they respond to appeals impacting their reputations.

To gain support for nonbusiness kinds of activities from the organization (such as contributions and public services) or to motivate an image-conscious person to pay his or her bill, the appeal to pride or reputation may be the key to success.

FIGURE 11.1   Internal Memo with an Appeal to Economic Benefit

Memo

TO: Benjamin Thomas, VP Manufacturing

FROM: Cynthia Jones, Director   *Cindy*
             Manufacturing Engineering

DATE: April 8, 198_

RE: Automated Handling System

Normally, abbreviations are defined, unless, as in this case, the receiver knows the terminology (JIT, Just-in-Time).

The Status Quo
With our JIT production processes and other improvements in moving materials within a manufacturing department, we have been able to reduce personnel and increase productivity in each department. However, with our old multi-story factory, we incur substantial costs in having to use considerable amounts of personnel time to move materials from floor to floor and between departments.

The problem/situation is stated concisely.

A Concept to Consider
To complement our good manufacturing processes, it is recommended that we investigate, design, and install an automated handling system. This computer-guided robot system would, without the need for personnel, (a) deliver and pick up materials between floors, (b) deliver and pick up materials within a department, and (c) pick up and deliver materials between departments.

Besides underlining, bold facing is often an effective technique to emphasize headings.

The solution is explained simply.

The Savings
Our current slow and costly process, which involves about thirty-eight full-time employees, is out of step with our other manufacturing process. The costs of installing an automated system, assuming that the thirty-eight employees would be eliminated, would be recouped in less than three years. Beyond the wage savings, there are many other savings (e.g., no overtime or benefits to pay, plus the advantage of its ability to operate during vacation periods and strikes).

Economic benefits are emphasized in both the heading and the narrative.

Perhaps we can discuss this concept in the near future and determine if it is a project that can be included in the next capital budget.

FIGURE 11.2   Letter of Request with an Appeal to Pride and Reputation

CHAMBER OF COMMERCE
Owensboro, Kentucky   42303

March 20, 198_

Miss Mary Jane Huntley
Huntley Decorating
1717 Owensboro Road
Owensboro, KY 42303

Dear Mary Jane,

Understandably, you are certainly busy expanding your business and striving to get
established in your new location. Therefore, when extra opportunities come along, it
must be difficult to say "yes." At the same time, periodically there are beneficial
activities that are important to you personally, that are vital to the community, and that
can, in a tangential manner, enhance your business situation.

The Chamber has established a new award in our community, "The Outstanding Woman
Entrepreneur of the Year Award." The selection committee will be made up of some
current Chamber board members and augmented by one established outstanding female
entrepreneur in the community. We would like for you to be that designated person.

With your coming weeks already jammed, your first inclination may be to decline this
opportunity. However, recognize that it will put you in contact with many business
people (who now or later will be able to use your services), it will gain you newspaper
and radio-TV publicity, and it will spotlight you before the leadership of the Chamber's
board.

I know you can be a strong force on the Committee. Therefore, please consider aiding
your community and the Chamber by serving on the selection committee. I'll call you
Monday morning to discuss this with you and, I hope, receive your acceptance of this
distinguished appointment.

Sincerely,

John

John Myers
Executive Director

P.S. The article in the recent Sunday supplement about you and your business was
excellent—Congratulations!

Margin annotations:

The background situation.

The problem.

Pride—you have been selected.

Information.

Economic benefit.

Recognition/positive reputation.

Action.

Recognition/ business benefit.

Note the deductive nature of the communication—the conclusion is stated in the beginning and is then
supported with the various appeals. Pride is established at the start and a major reason to accept the
appointment would be to receive additional recognition. Also, the common reasons Mary Jane would have
for turning down the appointment are clearly stated and then dealt with.

Appeals to Team Play

In our society, the appeals to team play and team effort are legion; they tend to build on the notion of joining the crowd and contributing your fair share to the effort. Inside the organization, this appeal is used frequently to encourage loyalty to and enthusiasm for the organization: "If we can each contribute just a few extra hours after work this coming week, we will be able to have the new computer system *up* and operating perfectly in record time." The appeal to team play also is used by groups striving to attract contributors to their cause. The idea is that if everyone cooperates, the result can be accomplished without hardship on anyone: "If everyone in our neighborhood contributes to the Community Fund, we will be able to place the fund banner below the American flag at the entrance to our street; be sure you are not the one who keeps us from earning this important banner for our street!"

The appeal to team play (getting along and going along with others) influences many people. Obviously, in huge contribution campaigns, where an attempt is made to draw contributions from hundreds, thousands, or millions of people, it is hard to use the team appeal, but many organizations succeed with it. Within the organization—and particularly individual departments—the appeal to team play is common. In fact, to be labeled as a nonteam player can be a substantial blight on a person's employment record and career path (see Figure 11.3). Sales-oriented organizations often maximize the appeal: "Do your part to ensure that our region beats the goal and wins the free vacation."

Because management involves getting things done through people, and because coordinated efforts are vital to a smooth organization, the need for a team spirit and a team effort are important to an organization's success. Therefore, this appeal is widely used (perhaps sometimes abused) and can be a potent force in rallying individuals around a goal.

Appeals to Self-interest

The appeal to self-interest basically asks the individual to look out for his or her best interest and to accept an idea or product not because it is good for a group or society, but because it is good for him or her; it is in the individual's best interest.

The motivation inspired by the appeal to team effort can be strong. The motivation inspired by the appeal to take care of thyself is equally strong or stronger in many people. Inside the organization, the appeal to self-interest may sometimes be implied "if you don't do this, you will be in hot water." Fearing the unknown, or the direct or implied result, a person can be moved to action by the appeal. If you have a choice of three locations for your first assignment in a new job, self-interest can play a role in the decision you make: the head of your functional area says, "For career potential and growth in our organization, the Butte, Montana, opening is the one in your best interest."

FIGURE 11.3   Letter of Request with an Appeal to Team Play

Allis, Inc.

312 Henderson Drive
Cleveland, Ohio   44112

TO: Jackie Donovan, Accounting

FR: Bill Mahoney, Vice-President   *BILL*

RE: Smoking Policy Task Force

DT: October 25, 198_

Background. As you know, in our organization and in many others across
the nation today, smoking at work and in public places has become a
major issue. We have surveyed our employees, studied how other firms are
handling the situation, and are now creating a task force to review
these data and make recommendations on the policies and procedures for
Allis.

Your Potential Involvement. Because our fiscal year ends soon, I know
that an extra assignment for you right now would be a hardship. However,
because I need a person like you on the task force, I would like you to
seriously consider the appointment. Janice and I have spoken briefly,
and she indicated that perhaps your work load could be slightly adjusted
so you could accommodate the extra time involved in the task force activities.

In the past, whether on the blood drive, the work to set up the new departmental computer system, or aiding Junior Achievers, you have always
been one to join in, cooperate, and aid us in getting the job done on
time. The task force could use your kind of commitment in wrestling with
this controversial problem. Of course, the corporate executive committee
would welcome your involvement on this project.

Time Commitment. The group will meet initially at least twice weekly on
Monday and Thursday afternoons. At the beginning, some considerable time
will be needed to study the materials that have been accumulated. The
first meeting will be Novemeber 1, and the recommendations will be
needed on or before December 10.

If you have any questions, please call me immediately; otherwise, let's
plan to meet at my office on October 28th at 10:30 a.m. to discuss the
possibility of your appointment to the task force.

c: Janice Brockhurst, Department Head

Quickly the context
is established.

Note the you-
orientation of
getting in step with
the receiver.

It is appropriate to
follow channels;
the VP indicates
that "the boss" is in
step.

Appeal to team
play.

Recognition.

That appeal, even though you and your spouse were thinking of Chicago or San Francisco, can cause some quick re-evaluation of your immediate desires and goals. You respond, "You know, the relaxed pace, the lack of congestion, and the fresh air may be just what we need right now." Suddenly, because of the appeal and the implied consequences, you are selecting Butte!

This appeal can be used in all kinds of internal situations: "it's in your self-interest to select this option because it makes you look good." "Take the overseas assignment because it will expose you to dozens of managers throughout the organization." In internal situations, the appeal is often clothed in inconspicuous language, but it does not take much reading between the lines to understand the message and the appeal.

Appeals to Health and Safety

Because the maintenance of health and a safe environment are exceedingly important, the use of this appeal to move individuals to action is very common. Just think of the appeals of this nature you have seen in the last day or two:

Your family's safety is certainly worth $11.95—buy an Allready smoke alarm today.

Don't let a calcium deficiency cripple your later years—start today, and take a CALCAP each day.

Your employees will file fewer medical claims and reduce their absenteeism if you install Ex-O-Bikes in your rest and break areas.

There is a wide-range of safety appeals.

For ourselves, our employees, and our families, programs, products, and concepts that promote, maintain, and even increase health and safety are attractive. This appeal is used not only in selling nonprescription drugs, but in arguing for policies, like changes in the work week, employment flexibility for parents, and altering the kinds of food served in the organization's cafeteria. Of course, it is heavily used by insurance companies and many firms providing medical-related items (see Figure 11.4).

It is not easy to argue against the appeal to health and safety. Even though the appeal may be misaligned with the idea, product, or service being promoted, one can appear uncaring, unsympathetic, and selfish when attempting to negate this appeal. "By creating the in-house day-care center for employees' children, the care of the children will be enhanced, the welfare of the parent increased, and the safety of all multiplied." This is not an easy appeal to negate, and it certainly has an emotional component. Counterappeals might refer to the lack of economy, the disruption of the work flow, and the increase in liability insurance. This is an almost classic case of an argument in favor that appeals to the heart and the argument against that appeals to the head. Appeals to the heart and the head can be effective. In employing either, be certain that the appeal is fair and actually related to the topic.

FIGURE 11.4 Sales Letter with a Variety of Appeals, Including Safety

April 20, 198_

Dear Neighbor:

It is most inconvenient when the new light fixture must be wired, a sink drain cleared, or an extra cabinet installed and there is no one at home who can do it. In the past, you were forced to leaf through the Yellow Pages or seek assistance from a neighbor. The reliability of the resulting service was marginal.

Responding to your needs, we are instituting the "Call Hank" Service. For any type of minor, routine house repair, we will take the guessing out of the process. The area's top dependent plumbers, electricians, and craftspeople have been assembled by Hank. When you have a household maintenance problem, call Hank. We will have the appropriate skilled individual contact you immediately; it's safe—all personnel are certified, bonded, and have excellent performance records.

No more hours of telephoning to locate who you need—just one phone call to Hank will solve your problem. And besides being assured of top labor, you will be getting top materials; all items used by these people will come directly from Hank's Hardware and be billed to you below retail! All materials from Hank's are guaranteed against any flaw in workmanship; if any item from Hank's fails, it will be replaced at no charge.

Hank's will maintain a roster of 500 households that may use this free service.

You will want to take advantage of this immediate offer by completing and mailing the enrollment card today. To join the initial roster of "Call Hank" satisfied customers, you must enroll by May 15.

We look forward to serving you and your neighbor with this additional service.

Cordially,

Hank

Henry Henniger
Owner

Encl.: Enrollment Card

Interest is established.

Appeal to convenience.

Description.

Appeal to safety.

Proving the point.

Appeal to economics.

Appeal to joining a select group.

Appeal for action.

Friendly close.

Appeals to Sex

In promoting some products, appeals to sex are sometimes used to persuade the receiver. Just look at some of the words used to promote sales in autos, jeans, perfume, and various shaving accoutrements. It is virtually impossible to identify the product by the language: "sensuous," "exciting," and "pleasurable,"—these are provocative words for station wagons, blue jeans, and body lotions.

In mass mailings and selected other kinds of business communications, such appeals to sex may be made for particular audiences. However, in internal business communications, like memos concerning computer software programs, promoting one accounting system over another, or recommending a Big Eight firm to retain as your auditor, appeals to sex are irrelevant and will not receive positive attention nor move the reader to action. In fact, in these situations, such an appeal would probably be counterproductive.

CREDIT AND COLLECTION COMMUNICATIONS

Traditionally, business communication texts have devoted considerable space to credit and collection communications. They have an important role in our economic system. But most managers write few such communications today. Except for the small business person, the development and writing of credit and collection letters has usually been contracted to a specialty service or is handled by a specific unit within the larger organization. Nevertheless, even if you will not prepare these letters, an understanding of the appeals in effective credit and collections communications may help you in the other communications you prepare.

Credit: Appeals for Establishing a Credit Account

Attracting new customers and making it easy for them to conduct business with you is important to businesses. A common way to attract customers and make it easy for them to do business is through credit. In our economic system, credit is so basic to our way of life that many people would be lost without their plastic cards.

In seeking new credit customers, direct mail, telephone solicitations, and business letters are often used. The ability to come in, make a purchase, and do so without ready cash is attractive to many customers. Some of the common kinds of appeals that might be made are:

Status: You join a select group of individuals.

Importance: Your clout is immediately recognized.

Convenience: With this card, shopping is always easy.

Self-interest: Records of billings and interest charges make things easy for you.

Responses to credit applicants may use various appeals, but the primary purpose of this communication is to maintain contact and let the applicant know that the application is being processed. It is vital that the letter *not* suggest that credit will be granted.

Great care must be taken in communicating the decision, whether favorable or unfavorable. If the response is negative, there is still an opportunity to make a sales appeal: "You will find that our prices are always low, and we will welcome you as a cash customer." With affirmative responses, the opportunities for appeals to economic benefit, recognition, and pride are numerous.

Collections: Maximizing the Use of Appeals

When people who owe you money continually drag their heels about paying, you are going to be willing to explore a variety of ways to encourage payment. There are often several objectives you may want to accomplish in collection communications (like maintaining goodwill or retaining the customer's business), but the primary goal is to get the bill paid! Like other communications, the collection communication should be courteous and take a strong you-orientation. Like the "no" letter, this message should not lecture or harass the recipient.

The desired action is—pay the bill!

Appeals Are Basic.   The job of the communicator is to find the right appeal or sequence of appeals that will get the bill paid. A variety of appeals can be used, and if the "softer" ones don't work (like "fair play" or "pride") then it will probably be necessary to employ "harder" appeals (like "fear" or "legal action").

Collection appeals can be categorized as "hard" and "soft."

Fair Play: We played fair and provided credit; you should play fair and pay.

Customer's Credit Reputation: If payment is not received, your credit rating may suffer.

Pride: As a well-meaning person of integrity, won't you be ashamed not to meet the commitment?

Fear: You cannot threaten to put the recipient in debtor's prison, but the suggestion of courses of legal action available to the creditor may create fear in the customer.

Self-interest: Although the payment is important to the firm, it is vital to the customer's self-interest (see Figure 11.5).

Collection Agency: An appeal to avoid forcing the company to turn the account over to a collection agency may be effective. Rightly or wrongly, agencies that collect bills have a reputation for accomplishing their goal.

Suggesting that collection agencies and lawyers will become involved are appeals that move many people to action.

Legal Action: A simple statement that this is the last call before the lawyers become involved may gain action. If this decision is made and communicated, the next institution the debtor hears from should not be the creditor. It is important, from a strategic and psychological point of view, not to pull back after communicating the action to be taken.

FIGURE 11.5   Collection Letter with an Appeal to Self-interest

58 ADRIAN STREET   CHICO, CALIFORNIA   95928

October 25, 198_

Mr. Anthony Copper, Vice President
Finance Department
Conway and Copper
500 West Hunt Street
Menlo Park, CA 94025

Dear Mr. Copper,

**Clear, precise
opening statement.**

It has now been 90 days since your account for $1730 became due. Be-
cause you have always been a most cooperative customer and very concerned with your credit position, we are puzzled.

Self-interest.

In your own self-interest, this past due bill should be paid
immediately. We must insist, however, that if payment or a satisfactory explanation or offer is not received by November 5, we will have
to take steps that will prove harmful to your best interests,
including a certified report to the American Credit Association as
well as notice to the National Plastics Association.

Reputation.

Please take immediate steps to protect your credit reputation.

Sincerely yours,

James D. Andrews

James D. Andrews
President

THE SERIES

The small-business person knows that a single appeal in a single collection letter may not get the customer to pay a bill. Therefore, in bill-collecting operations, a series of communications is often used. The first communication may just be the bill with the words "Past Due" stamped on it; a second communication, a few weeks later, may make appeals to fair play and economic benefit. Later, the communications become much stronger with appeals to fear imposed through mention of collection agencies and legal action.

Once is often not enough.

The series, together with appeals, can be used by the business communicator in many more situations than just collecting money. If you wish to win people over to your viewpoint, you often must use more than one communication. It is sometimes wise, therefore, to not "spend" all your appeals in the first communication. Instead, hold some back; if the desired result is not accomplished the first time, try a second, using some other (perhaps stronger) appeal (see Figure 11.6). The following are common ways in which the series is used in business communication:

There are uses for appeals beyond collection letters.

Questionnaire Return: Getting people to return surveys is difficult—the series approach of "reminders" is often helpful.

Renewing Orders: Publications, magazines, and other journals often need to use a series of communications to get subscribers to renew. Whereas the first reminder is pleasant, "Renew and enjoy another year of . . . ," the later reminders are more urgent, "If you don't renew now, this is the last issue you will see."

Return Credit Application: The series of communications encourages people to apply for credit.

Appeals combined with the series are a potent communication approach that can be used in numerous situations. In Figure 7.2, where software was being recommended, Jane Perkins recognizes that just one good memo may not get the job done. A follow-up phone call, a conference in the hall, a meeting in the office, another memo, all can be part of a communication series to aid in getting the idea accepted.

There are many uses for appeals in business communications.

QUICK REVIEW

Whether you appeal to the head or the heart, appeals can be a substantial support in winning the audience over. Knowing the action you desire (the purpose) and then aligning the appeals for the receiver (the audience) permit you to prepare an effective communication—whether you are asking a person to speak at a civic conference or to pay a six-month-old bill! Appeals in a series of linked communications allow you to make a continuing and increasingly intense effort at achieving your goal.

FIGURE 11.6   Second Letter in a Series—To Obtain a Questionnaire Response

Pachmayer

Data   9590 Clyde Avenue

Services   Wheaton, Illinois   60188

May 2, 198_

Dr. Richard L. Owens
Heritage Building
Suite 42
Lakeland, IL 61021

Your Opinions, Dr. Owens . . .

Clear and attention-getting opening.

. . . are really needed. The ideas you can provide in the
survey you received ten days ago will be a tremendous aid to
your profession. In case you may have mislaid the original
survey, another is enclosed. Please return it no later than
May 15th.

Economic benefit.

As a small, independent professional, you can recognize the
threat that the new "fast lens" marts are creating for
established businesses. By completing the questionnaire, you
will give us ideas of how to help the independent optometrist
survive and prosper in this new sales and marketing environment.

Team play (others are doing it).

In the first week, 27 percent of your colleagues returned
their surveys; that is an excellent first-week return. But to
correctly monitor the trends in optometry, we need your
survey as well.

Self-interest (protection).

Action clearly stated.

It takes about six minutes to complete the survey; that's
going to be the best six minutes you have spent in a long
time. The data will allow us to protect your practice, so
please return the survey now—no later than May 15th.

Cordially,

Jan C. Vanderburg

Jan C. Vanderbag
Director of Research

EXECUTIVE SUMMARY

To: Business Communication Students

From: David N. Bateman and Norman B. Sigband

Subject: Motivating the Receiver to Act

The primary goal of most business communications is to encourage the receiver to act: to *accept* a viewpoint, to *implement* a recommendation, to *purchase* a product, and so on. Carefully targeted appeals can be powerful aids to reaching that goal. They can persuasively link the message to the desired action.

Appeals are sometimes thought of as either emotional or rational. But it is difficult to sort them out on this basis. Some of the major categories that have proved useful in business communication are appeals to

Economic benefit.

Pride or reputation.

Team play.

Self-interest.

Health and safety.

Sex.

Although appeals have traditionally been associated with sales and credit and collection letters, they are useful in other kinds of business communications, like convincing the boss to buy your idea, requesting contributions, or returning question-naires and offers of credit. The series of letters with appeals has proved to be especially effective.

DISCUSSION GENERATORS

1. *Appeals and Action.* Explain the relationship between appeals and action.
2. *Communication Series.* Explain the concept of *series,* and illustrate how the series of communications might use different media. Then show how appeals can be effectively used in a series of communications.
3. *Approach the Appeals.* Name the appeals noted in this chapter, and explain and illustrate each.
4. *Appeals Beyond Sales Letters.* How (and why) are appeals used in a manager's internal communications (like memos to a superior)? For your chosen profession, illustrate how this might work in a communication you would initiate.
5. *Head and Heart.* Explain and differentiate appeals that are made to the head and those that are directed toward the heart.
6. *Carrots in Business Letters?* Holding out a carrot is often used as an analogy for a way to motivate people to take a desired action. Explain how the appeals you use in a business memo to your boss could be classified as "carrots."

7. *Audience, Appeals, and Action.* Why is it that in order to obtain the desired action, it is necessary to align the appeal with the audience?

8. *It's Difficult.* Why is it difficult to reject or counter appeals to health and safety?

9. *Business and Sports.* Which of the appeals has a definite sports orientation? Why does this appeal seem to be so effective in the business organization?

10. *Business and Credit.* Why do many businesses have aggressive programs to grant credit? What are the advantages of having numerous credit customers?

11. *T.V. Credit.* The major credit cards advertise on television. Cite a card and the company's slogan or statement, and show what kind of appeal it is making to order this credit card.

12. *Positive Statement in a No-credit Letter?* What kinds of positive statements might be made to an individual or company to whom you are denying credit?

13. *Economic Benefits.* Name several different appeals to economic benefits.

14. *One vs. Group.* Explain why some appeals are related to social or interaction kinds of activities whereas others are related to the individual.

15. *Abuse.* Which appeal do the authors suggest may often be abused in the internal communications of an organization? What takes place in the organization to foster such "abuse"?

16. *Rejection Difficult.* What appeal to the heart do the authors suggest can be difficult to argue against?

17. *Internal/External.* Which appeal is rarely used in internal communications but is widely used in external communications (like sales communications)?

18. *Campus Status.* If you were developing a letter to students to interest them in purchasing your "diamond credit card," what appeals would you use?

19. *Hard vs. Soft.* Some of the appeals are labeled "soft" by the authors and others "hard." Explain what is meant, and identify the differences.

20. *Series and Eggs.* In using different appeals in a series of communications, explain what "Don't place all of your eggs in one basket" means.

APPLICATIONS FOR BUSINESS

21. *Write the Credit Letter.* John has low self-esteem and really seems to care little what other people think of him. He is very much a "loner" and doesn't interact much with people—except when absolutely necessary. John is three months behind in making payments on the Library Series of books he purchased from your book store.
    a. Identify and explain the appeals you think will motivate John to pay his bill.
    b. Implement one or more appeals in a communication to John.
    c. Show how you could use a series and indicate the appeals that would be available for the other communication(s).

22. *Appeals Aligned Inductively and Deductively.* You want to persuade your customers who purchased refrigerators to buy your three-year service contract. The appeals include self-interest, economic benefit, and convenience.

    a. Explain how induction and deduction can apply to these appeals. (Refer to Figure 11.2.)

    b. Develop a letter that uses the appeals in an inductive manner (that is, the appeals lead the reader to the conclusion to buy the maintenance agreement).

    c. Develop a letter that uses the appeals in a deductive manner (that is, the conclusion is stated and then the appeals follow and support that conclusion).

23. *Turning the Tables.* As Director of Personnel for Remington Company you want to persuade your executive committee to develop, create, and implement an on-site day-care center. You know you could make appeals to the heart, but you also know they will not work with this audience. This group will be persuaded with appeals to the head.

    a. Differentiate between the head and the heart in this situation.

    b. List appeals to the head that could be used.

    c. Develop a one-page memo that uses appeals to the head; use induction—that is, present your appeals before your conclusion and recommendation.

24. *Who's on First?* The "team player" appeal can be very strong in some organizations. As vice-president of sales for your company, you are preparing a memo for the sales personnel. The memo uses the "team player" appeal to encourage hard work to accomplish the sales goal. Using sports metaphors, list and illustrate how the "team play" appeal can be used to encourage the people to accomplish the objectives (e.g., work conscientiously—don't let your other team members down; or work hard—don't fumble the ball!).

COMMUNICATION CHECK-UPS

25. The report; it encompasses the entire project.

26. Mr. Timothy Jones, Manager
Corporate Affairs
Rex Corp.
P.O. Box 1707
Springfield, IL. 61474

27. The budget (see Appendix C) is on target.

28. Robert, Barbara and Cynthia will attend the meeting.

29. *Position Power.* This power is given to you by your position in the formal organization.

30. The advantages of excellent communication skills in an accounting department are many; both on the job and off.

31. Her coworkers joined in the tribute.

32. It is advantageous to understand the secretaries' needs and concerns.

33. Per your request, the information on the Brynson project has been sent to Bob.

34. Up the Organization is a book that will provide you with many examples you can use in your seminar presentation.

Executive
Introduction

Editorial Services
P.O. Box 1891
Tubac, Arizona 85646

William Best, Jr.

Tel: (602) 398-2322

March 3, 198_

Professor Margaret Simmonds, Director
Graduate Business Communication Studies
College of Business and Administration
Collinsville University
Collinsville, OH 45004

Dear Marg,

Good communications—in the broadest sense of the term—strongly
influence the public reputation of a company and materially affect the
quality of its relationships with its three most important audiences—
its people, its customers, and its shareholders. A factor often
overlooked in good communications is what is called "special communications." When on your campus, it will be enjoyable to share some
thoughts with your students about these matters.

Having worked with top CEOs and seeing how successful special communications aided their careers, I'll probably emphasize:

+ How thank-you letters are a requisite in business.

+ The way letters of appreciation recognize good deeds.

+ The need for congratulatory letters in the professions.

+ How the sympathy letter is very you-oriented.

Writing somewhat routine letters and memos is part of the manager's
job; special communications go beyond "the job" and differentiate the
considerate manager from others.

Looking forward to seeing you and interacting with your students.

Sincerely,

Bill

CHAPTER
12

Communicating in Special Situations

WHAT YOU CAN LEARN BY STUDYING THIS CHAPTER

In a typical day, the manager is involved in situations directly related to business as well as many "special" situations only indirectly related. Similarly, some business communications, like sales letters, are specifically about business, while others have only an indirect influence on business. These "special" communications can be very effective additions to the business communicator's repertoire of communication tools. In this chapter, you will learn about them, when to initiate them, and how to handle them appropriately.

The everyday activity of any organization involves a certain amount of communication about pressing matters: for example, calling attention to an overdue bill, placing an urgent order, indicating receipt of a credit application, or attempting to promote a sale. The messages studied in this chapter are less routine. They provide an opportunity to express your feelings about personal matters, comment on the accomplishments of another person, or simply build goodwill.

The personal message you prepare is important in modern business.

Although there are many ways to express consideration or goodwill—such as clever printed cards, or flowers—there really is no substitute for a personal message created and written specifically for the receiver. A personal message would be appropriate to thank a corporate officer for the time spent on a job interview; or to express appreciation for special assistance received or a dinner attended; or to congratulate an individual on a promotion or new job.

Some messages are very individual, written to one person for a specific reason. We will refer to these as *letters of consideration.* Others are mass-oriented, in which the message relates to a class of individuals, such as good customers, new customers, or absent customers. We will refer to these as *goodwill letters.*

LETTERS OF CONSIDERATION

Sometimes it seems that courtesy, style, and consideration are not practiced as much as they should be. We all like to be treated in a respectful manner. By writing letters of consideration, you can project your respect for others as well as your feelings of appreciation. There are a variety of situations that call for letters of consideration.

These letters are people-oriented: they are explicit expressions of your thoughtfulness to another individual or group. If business is, as one chief executive has stated, "Ninety percent people and ten percent money," the importance of these people-oriented letters of consideration becomes obvious. The basic kinds of consideration letters include letters of appreciation, thank-you letters, congratulatory messages, and letters of condolence.

It's the thought, not the length, that counts.

How long? It's the thought, not the length, that counts! You need not be bound to nor limited by 8½-by-11-inch paper. If you feel intimidated by the size of the paper ("My short message will look ridiculous on that huge sheet of paper!"), use smaller stationery or special notepaper. Figure 12.1 is an example of a note card that is used by corporate executives. These notes can be either handwritten or typed; the important thing is to express the idea.

Letters of Appreciation

The lack of expression on your part may reveal a lack of caring.

If an individual in an organization goes out of the way for you, certainly you can take a few minutes to express your appreciation. There are many situations that call for a letter of appreciation: a client rearranges her schedule so you can see her at your convenience or a sales representative puts forth considerable extra effort to move an

FIGURE 12.1   Informal Note Card

A MESSAGE
ESPECIALLY FOR YOU

Jane —

How grand that
you have been elected
to the city council —
it's excellent to see
our employees so
involved in civic work.

Ted

AB ALLEN-BRADLEY

TAKING
TIME
TO THINK
OF YOU
BECAUSE
WE CARE

The notecard can be used for both internal and external special-situation communications.

Handwriting may make a message more personal.

order rapidly through channels for you. When someone has treated you in a special way, silence on your part may reflect lack of consideration. The letter of appreciation goes beyond simply thanking the receiver for being kind; it notes the consideration, the extra effort, and the kindness extended. Figure 12.2 shows an example of an effective letter of appreciation.

When you take the time and make the effort to write a letter of appreciation, the recipient will be pleased. But you can make your gesture even more emphatic by sharing your message with others. Supervisors often take their subordinates for granted; they may not be aware of special circumstances that require extra effort. If someone has done an outstanding job that warrants attention, you can multiply your appreciation by sending a copy of your letter to that person's supervisor. (See Chapter 6 on c and bc.)

Multiplying your consideration

FIGURE 12.2   Letter of Appreciation

JASON C. GUSTAVE
Wilson Hall—203
Knox College
Galesburg, IL 61401

April 20, 198_

Dr. Francisco Petroni,
Business Department
Knox College
Galesburg, Illinois 61401

The you-oriented salutation often works well.

It was very kind of you, Dr. Petroni,

Friendly beginning.

. . . to arrange for me to meet with Jeffrey Klingberg when I recently visited Houston. The interview sessions with Oxford Oil seemed to go very well; the position they have in Industrial Marketing is fantastic and I would be pleased to be able to join an organization like Oxford's in launching my career.

Goes beyond simply thanking the receiver.

A very special part of the trip was being able to spend some time with Jeffrey. We met for dinner the evening of my arrival and he gave me a wonderful orientation to the Houston area. Since his graduation from Knox two years ago, he has moved into a responsible position with the Texas National Bank.

This letter says "thank you" without ever using those words.

Spending the time with Jeff was pleasant and it gave me background information that helped in my Oxford interviews. If Oxford offers me a position in Houston, it will be comforting to know that Jeff will be there.

Jeff specifically asked to be remembered to you and to Professeor Janice Wilson and the other members of the department. He feels very strongly that his education at Knox was responsible for his ability to adjust to business so easily.

Sincerely,

Jason

When writing in an informal manner on personal stationery, it is not necessary to type your name since it appears on the stationery.

Because of your relationship, the letter can be of an informal nature. The you-oriented salutation is pleasant. Since Jason's full name is on the stationery, signing it "Jason" is natural. Sometimes, in these more informal letters, yhou may want to sign the entire closing to the letter as the British often do; that is, besides just writing your name, also write "Sincerely" instead of having it typed.

Thank-you Letters

The thank-you letter is similar to the appreciation letter. The basic difference is that the thank-you letter relates to a more routine or typical situation for the individual being thanked: an evening of entertainment or conversation; a meeting or job interview arranged at your request (see Figure 12.3); or a reference letter written on your behalf (see Figure 12.4).

Don't overlook situations where thank-you letters are appropriate.

A thank-you letter is appropriate when you are invited to someone's home for a dinner, buffet, or other special event. If a person can go to the extra work and effort to bring you into his or her home, you surely can put forth the effort to thank that person in writing. Such a thank-you letter can be written either on your business or your personal stationery. Your own good judgment must be the guide. Figure 12.5 shows an example of an effective thank-you letter for a pleasant evening at someone's home.

The attributes of the letter of appreciation and the thank-you letter are similar. It is always in good taste to express your appreciation and thanks in writing. As illustrated in the examples, it is possible to write such letters without starting with the words "thank you," and two of the three examples never use the words—yet they are very effective, nonroutine letters of consideration that are not trite.

Congratulatory Messages

People in the professions generally are active in various business, professional, governmental, religious, political, and/or civic groups. It is not uncommon for an acquaintance, customer, or friend to assume a position of importance. It takes only a few moments to write a letter to that person. There should be a strong you-orientation in these kinds of communications; try to avoid triteness and tailor the message to reflect on the honor and what the person did to achieve it (see Figure 12.6).

Congratulatory letters should make the receiver feel good.

In the small-business situation, another more informal alternative can work. Have some folded cards printed. On the outside, have a message such as "read about your accomplishment," "saw your name in the news," or "you are in print." Insert the news clipping, and handwrite your congratulations.

Messages of Sympathy

If a professional associate dies, you should communicate with the family. To do nothing and to communicate nothing is thoughtless. If the situation involves a person with whom you have worked closely and whom you have known for many years beyond just the organizational activities of work, a personally written message is most appropriate. After expressing your sorrow, you can point to the person's accomplishments and contributions to the organization and society. If a member of an associate's immediate family dies and you know the associate well, you should express your sympathy and extend your support to him or her during the period of bereavement. Figure 12.7 shows a sample letter of sympathy. These messages are not easy to write, but they will have a supportive effect on the recipient.

Letters of sympathy should say more than you are sad.

FIGURE 12.3   Thank-you Letter Following Job Interview

On plain stationery, be sure to include the return address.

Full block letter in traditional formal style.

Friendly, positive close.

Note the relationships as reflected in the salutation and signature. Often when signing one's name, one's middle initial is not used, but it's personal preference.

1827 King Drive
San Francisco, CA 92601
June 27, 198_

Mr. Mark Alvarez, President
Mark's Food & Drug Emporiums
1777 Sutter Street, Suite 301
San Francisco, CA 92617

Dear Mr. Alvarez:

Your management group's combination of enthusiasm, competence, and flair is very impressive. I'd very much enjoy being part of this exciting team.

It was particularly helpful, Mr. Alvarez, to learn of the goals you have set for Mark's. With my seven years of retail experience, we may have a mutually beneficial match.

You and your staff were very kind in taking so much time to discuss employment opportunities at Mark's with me; the insights you provided are most appreciated. If you desire any additional information, please phone me (747-1798).

You should be very proud of the organization you have built and of the fine managers you have brought into your innovative retail business. I shall look forward to hearing from you.

Sincerely,

Nino Petroni

Nino C. Petroni

FIGURE 12.4   Thank-you Letter

1222 Westminster Drive
Des Moines, Iowa 50311
May 2, 198_

Dr. Joan L. Wallace
Department of Economics
Drake University
Des Moines, Iowa 50311

Dear Professor Wallace:

   You were very kind to take the time to write the letter of reference for me to the Graduate School at The State University of Iowa. Ms. Johnson, who conducted the personal interview with me at SUI, specifically commented on your letter. She said she sees many letters, but I was especially fortunate in having a person write who took a personal interest in students and who could provide helpful information. This is just another way in which you have been so helpful throughout my undergraduate career.

   I realize that you had to take time from your teaching, research, writing, and consulting to write the letter. Your efforts and concern are appreciated very much.

   You have been very special to me at Drake, and if I'm fortunate enough to have professors in graduate school who take just one-tenth the interest in me that you have, I'll be very lucky!

                                        Sincerely,

                                        Betty

                                        Betty Clark

c: Dean Harold Jennings

The letter reveals thought and substance.

Beware of trite statements like "your busy schedule."

Since Dr. Wallace refers to the writer as "Betty," that is the preferred way to sign.

Sending a copy of the thank-you letter to a superior is a nice touch.

Thank-you letters need not be nor appear hackneyed or trite. This letter has substance as it thanks an individual for a specific act and reflects on other contributions the individual has made.

FIGURE 12.5   Thank-you Letter

September 4, 198_

Dr. and Mrs. Randall Viera
128 Southland Road
Dallas, Texas 34723

Dear Dr. and Mrs. Viera:

After a long and hectic day of meetings and seminars at the Optometrists
Convention, it was a joy to relax and socialize in your beautiful home. It was
particularly nice to see Dr. Viero's dramatic collection of Boehm porcelain and
Mrs. Viero's unique collection of antique Wedgewood.

I especially enjoyed the opportunity to continue our discussion on strabismus,
which extended the fine paper you presented at the meeting, Dr. Viero.

As for dinner, Mrs. Viero, it was absolutely outstanding. The food was
delicious, the company excellent, and the chocolate cheesecake incredibly
sinful.

Thank you both for your hospitality and kindness.

Sincerely,

Lisa Poarch

Lisa Poarch
President

Elite Avenue
Evanston, Illinois   60201

The salutation and
closing reflect a
somewhat formal
relationship.

Be specific in
giving compli-
ments; say more
than "The meal
was nice."

When people go to the effort to invite you to their home, show you their home, and provide dinner, it is
crucial that in your communication you reflect upon the entire event and not just the meal. The you-
orientation is very important—the Vieras are interested in their collections; it is appropriate and kind to
comment on them.

FIGURE 12.6   **Letter of Congratulations**

Emerson High School
Conway, Arizona 85601

Dr. Donald Cordoni, Professor
Department of Management-Mathematics
Conway College
Conway, AZ 85601

YOUR ACHIEVEMENT IS OUTSTANDING

After your many years of work in mathematics education, it is appropriate that your devotion has been recognized with your election as
national President of the Mathematical Education Association. With our
nation's renewed focus on quantitative skills and what we can do to
improve the math skills of our students throughout the educational
system, we are all fortunate to have a person of your caliber leading
mathematic's educators.

As one who has observed your skills in the classroom, in working with
high-school teachers to hone their abilities, and in developing the innovative program at Conway College, I am particularly pleased that you
have been called upon for this leadership position. I hope that the executive personnel at Conway College recognize your accomplishments
and the recognition it will bring to the college.

Good luck throughout your two-year term; may it be exciting, invigorat-
ing, and much fun!

Hal

Harold C. Brown
Principal

c: Dr. Mary Crawford, President
    Conway College

MSL style.

Thought beyond
"Congratulations."

"Special" letters can
be substantive, they
should not be a
series of trite
statements.

The letter uses the MSL style that reduces the normal cordialities at the start and end of the letter; the
format reduces the need for tab adjustments—everything is left adjusted. Note the reflection that the writer
takes; thought preceded the writing of the letter as some history of Prof. Cordoni's accomplishment is
presented. The copy to the president is important—sometimes a person's superior may not recognize an
individual's accomplishment.

FIGURE 12.7   Letter of Sympathy

January 10, 198_

Mrs. Robert Johnson
1225 Sunset Drive
Evanston, Illinois 60201

Dear Mrs. Johnson:

Note the strong you-orientation; there is little use of the word "I."

Your loss is great, and I would like to express my sincerest sympathies to you and the other members of your family on the death of your son, Jack.

In the relatively short time Jack was employed by our firm, he gained the respect and admiration of all of his associates; he will be fondly remembered in our hearts and minds.

The letter is positive; it reflects on good memories.

As you well know, Jack rose in our organization in just two years' time to head one of our major departments. His competence in management was outstanding, and his ability to motivate others was truly unusual. All of us at Fashion Frames feel his loss very deeply.

The message has a sincere tone; it does not seem trite or routine.

Our thoughts are with you at this time. Because your family indicated a Jack Johnson Scholarship was being created at his college, Fashion Frames and its employees are pleased to make a $2,000 contribution to the fund in honor of one of our finest employees.

Cordially yours,

Lisa Poarch

Lisa Poarch
President

Elite Avenue
Evanston, Illinois   60201

LETTERS OF RECOMMENDATION

The recommendation that you write or orally relate for a colleague, subordinate, or acquaintance can be considered a special situation communication. First of all, you do not have to prepare such recommendations—and many people don't. Second, the context and content may or may not refer to business situations. Third, unless you treat people like "forms," each recommendation letter is nonroutine and will be a thoughtful presentation that reflects your insight; it has a personal tone.

Recommendations take thought and time.

Recommendations can be categorized in several ways:

Solicited vs. Unsolicited: Generally, a recommendation is solicited—either by the individual under consideration or the evaluator.

Employment and Others: Besides recommendations that refer to promotions or gaining a job, recommendations are sometimes needed for activities like civic awards, club memberships, and nominations.

Favorable vs. Unfavorable: It is beneficial to look at recommendation letters after having studied "yes" and "no" messages. Sometimes you may want to recommend the individual and at other times you may not. A "problem" in our society is that recommendation letters tend to be virtually all favorable. Often, if the message is unfavorable, the individual who has been requested to write simply does not respond. Frequently, much information is given orally, although the requirements of the recommendation do not change. However, most of us are most frank when we don't have to put our thoughts in writing. (See Figures 12.8 and 12.9.)

The recommendation letter can be a sales letter; it can be organized inductively or deductively; and it can make maximum use of headings. Like other communications, it should be substantive, and the normal triteness of recommendations should be avoided. As with all written communications, you should make the message readable; the use of an attention line (the receiver is probably getting numerous recommendations, on many people) can be very helpful.

Don't wander in your recommendation; know your logical system.

CUSTOMER GOODWILL COMMUNICATIONS

Goodwill letters may be sent to a variety of customers or clients. While letters of consideration are individually written for a specific situation, customer-related goodwill letters usually are sent to a class of people, such as good customers. The identical goodwill letter may be sent to hundreds of individuals (see Figure 12.10). However, you want to create a special identification with the recipient.

In previous examples, the concept of goodwill has been covered (see Chapters 9 and 10). In those situations, goodwill was a part of the total message; here, the entire thrust of the message is goodwill. It is the kind of message that does not absolutely

Goodwill messages tend to have a business flavor.

FIGURE 12.8   Favorable Letter of Recommendation

Whitehall University

Orange Grove, Arkansas 72201

Department of Accounting

Mr. Earl Washington, Jr., Director
Human Resources
Adams Concrete Corporation
Little Rock, Arkansas 72202

RE: Eric J. Morris

Dear Mr. Washington:

> **Attention-getting introduction; similar to a sales letter.**

It is sometimes thought that accountants are "dull pencil pushers." But, Eric is different. Besides being a most capable accountant, he has numerous other qualities that will benefit him in the corporate setting.

> **Key qualities focused in headings.**

   <u>Human Skills</u>. As an undergraduate, Eric has been active in several Business School organizations. Having observed him for over three years, I've noted that his fellow students gravitate toward him, he relates well to the faculty, and he has excellent human skills.

   <u>Communication Abilities</u>. In the College of Business, when we have needed a student representative to make presentations, we have continually called upon Eric. He is a clear and effective speaker and he also writes well.

   <u>Accounting Expertise</u>. Eric has chosen to join a corporation instead of going with one of the Big 8, although they have certainly been interested in him. There is no doubt that he will do well on the CPA exams. He understands the basics and is also excellent at conceptualizing the intricacies of accounting.

   Without any reservations, I recommend Eric to you; if for any reason you would like more information on Eric, please contact me.

Sincerely,

Gola C. Penning, Ph.D., CPA
Chairperson

The letter is basically inductive: the elements of "proof" are presented and then the conclusion is stated—Eric is highly recommended. The letter has an original start; it leads the reader. The message has a strong sales orientation, gaining attention, describing the person, providing the proof, and then recommending a specific action.

FIGURE 12.9 Unfavorable Letter of Recommendation

Whitehall University

Orange Grove, Arkansas 72201

The Reverend Basworth Kassulka
Church of the Redeemer
1818 Logan Street
Chicago, IL 61606

RE: Betty Jo Forgram

Dear Pastor Kassulka:

With the glorious new Casavant organ you have installed in your sanctuary, you are
certainly wise in seeking a bright young organist. I understand your need for an
individual who can work with the choir activities, can bring a dynamic style to your
religious service, and has a good understanding of religious music.

Betty Jo Forgram did her M.S. in Organ with me after completing her undergraduate
degree at Southern Methodist University. During her two years of study at Whitehall,
Betty Jo did not hold a church-organist position—as virtually all my students do.

During one of her two years at SIUC, Betty Jo served as my graduate assistant. She was
excellent at the various office duties associated with music and my recital schedule. Also,
she got along very well with the students and especially well with the office staff.

I hope these observations are helpful to you and the search committee; if you would like
to follow up, you should certainly not hesitate to phone me.

Again, congratulations on your new instrument. The next time I am in the Chicago area, I
hope I will have an opportunity to see it.

Sincerely,

Marianne Webb

Marianne Webb, Professor
University Organist

*You-oriented
introduction .*

*Substantive
information.*

Friendly close.

The letter indicates the qualities of the job and then lists the capabilities of the individual—they do not
match. There is nothing unfavorably stated about Betty Jo; however, she is not under consideration for the
position of office manager. The recommendation completely avoids the area of music and performance.
The unwritten message should be explicitly clear to the receiver. Yet, there is nothing litigious in the letter.

FIGURE 12.10   Goodwill Letter

Franklin's Fine Furniture

Office of the President   December 2, 198_

Mrs. Carol Melton
Preston Decorators
125 Harbon Road
Preston, Virginia 42796

Dear Mrs. Melton:

Somehow the days and months fly by and many of us forget to
say "thank you" to those who help make the time enjoyable and
worthwhile. However, we did want to stop for just a moment and let
you know how much we appreciated your cooperation, business, and
goodwill during the year.

As an expression of our thanks, we shall continue to offer you
the highest quality merchandise at the lowest possible prices.
Added to this will be an expanded advertising allowance program
for next year. And, to brighten your office this season, we are
sending you a real Maine evergreen Holiday Wreath.

We do hope you, your associates, and your family enjoy a most
happy Holiday Season, Mrs. Melton. We look forward to working with
you in the months ahead.

Cordially yours,

Carl Martin
President

2000 West Lamont
DeKalb, Illinois   60115
(815) 556-7300

Modified block style
with indented
paragraphs.

This could easily be
set up as a form
letter on a word
processor—
inserting the
appropriate inside
address as well as
the name in the last
paragraph.

have to be sent. Many organizations send messages of goodwill to customers at holiday time, in December. There are, however, other ways that may appear less mass-oriented and may not get lost in the rush of December mail, like a greeting to customers at Thanksgiving or a letter of appreciation and goodwill near the Fourth of July.

It is important that your goodwill letters be sincere in approach and tone. But remember that the purpose of the goodwill communication is not only to express a sincere idea, but also to keep your organization's name before the individual.

QUICK REVIEW

It is difficult to impart the impact and importance of special letters. For the manager who desires to get things done through people, the special communication is an important element. Although none of the communications analyzed in this chapter *has* to be sent, they all should be.

Letters of consideration are generally sent by individual managers whereas letters of goodwill are sent by organizations. Letters of recommendation are very special letters but they also meet the requirements of all special letters: they don't have to be written, they may have a business or nonbusiness orientation, and they are very human-oriented.

EXECUTIVE SUMMARY

To: Business Communication Students

From: David N. Bateman and Norman B. Sigband

Subject: Communicating in Special Situations

In the course of a manager's career, many occasions arise that may not be specifically business-oriented. In those situations, a letter may go a long way in building goodwill and friendship.

Among these "special" communications are letters of appreciation and thank-you to individuals who have extended themselves on your behalf. Congratulatory messages are often in order when you wish to simply say "well done" in writing. Although they are difficult to write, messages of sympathy are appreciated because they are personal and usually reflect a more sincere attitude than a printed card. The letter of recommendation is one most business people must occasionally write. The goodwill letter has as its purpose the building of good relations—not sales, not a favor, just good relations.

The primary attribute of all these special communications is sincerity and the personal touch that may be found in an individually composed letter.

DISCUSSION GENERATORS

1. *What Makes Special Communications Special?* The authors differentiate special letters from the others.
   a. What are the requisites that make the so-called "special" letters different?
   b. Why do the authors suggest that letters of recommendation meet these requisites?

2. *Why Write?* One reason to prepare a recommendation letter is that the individual under consideration for the job asked you to write. However, would there ever be a situation in which you would write such a letter on your own initiative—without either the person being considered asking you or the potential employer seeking your advice? List those situations.

3. *Different Size?* Why might special-situation communications be prepared on paper or stationery that is not the standard 8½ × 11?

4. *What's the Difference?* Differentiate the letter of appreciation from the thank-you letter.

5. *More Than Thanks?* What can a thank-you letter do besides "thank" the receiver for some action? How can substance and perspective be placed in such letters? Illustrate your answer by referring to the examples in this chapter.

6. *Cute $1 Cards.* The authors seem to think that spending a dollar or more for a really neat professional commercial card is "cheap" compared with creating your own thank-you communication.
   a. Are the authors correct? Why?
   b. What's the difference between the letter in Figure 12.5 and a $1.50 thank-you card designed for meals and to which the sender signs his or her name?

7. *No Thank You's.* None of the examples of thank-you letters in the text starts with "thank-you." In fact, the term "thank-you" is used only once in the three examples of thank-you letters. Why is this?

8. *C vs. BC.* In Figure 12.4, Betty placed a "c" on the letter.
   a. Was this appropriate?
   b. Would "bc" have been better?
   c. Does the writing of such letters and then adding a copy notation tend to make Betty look like she is attempting to win someone's favor?

9. *Just Congratulations?* What can a congratulatory letter do other than say, "good job"?

10. *A Report?* Reports often have attention lines and headings—but recommendation letters? Why might it often be beneficial to include them in a letter of recommendation—especially when the receiver is receiving dozens of letters?

11. *Positive, But.* Explain the strategy of writing a recommendation letter in which all the comments about the person are favorable, but the writer is actually not recommending the person.

12. *Phone vs. Write.* In all the other special situation communications but one it is suggested that writing is better than phoning. However, in the case of the recommendation communication, messages are often sent via phone. Why is this—is it just a case of speed?

13. *What Is There to Be Positive About?* The sympathy letter can be partly positive, according to the authors. What is there to be positive about when a death has occurred?

14. *MSL.* What is the Modern Simplified Letter, and
    a. what are its basic features?
    b. what does it eliminate?
    c. comment on whether you like and would use this "modern" style in your professional career.

15. *Beyond the Meal.* When someone invites you to his or her home for dinner, what can you comment on besides the meal in your thank-you letter?

16. *Signing Your Name.* In letters in special situations, does it really make any difference how you sign your name, e.g., "David Bateman" or "David"? Explain your answer.

17. *Continental.* What is the "British" style in the closing section of a special letter, and when might it be used?

18. *Not Typed?* Virtually all business correspondence is typed; under what circumstances might a special-situation letter be handwritten?

19. *Where to Place the Conclusion?* Cite different situations in which you might want to write letters of recommendation inductively and others deductively.

20. *Special Situations and Sales.* In what ways is a letter of recommendation like a sales letter?

APPLICATIONS FOR BUSINESS

21. *Good, But.* Amy Oscar is a good person for the management trainee position with Allied, Inc. However, it is going to take a whopper of a recommendation letter to obtain an interview for her. You know that the person making the interview decision has a bias against women and prefers to hire men. Amy tends to start off shy and it takes a while to discover the "real" Amy, who is most competent, analytical, and fun to work with.

    Realizing all of this, as Amy's major undergraduate professor, write a letter of recommendation that will (a) get her an interview and (b) challenge some of the preconceptions of the interviewer so he will see beyond his preconceived biases and first impressions. Give careful consideration as to whether you will write the letter from a deductive or inductive perspective; be able to justify your approach.

22. *Congrats!* As head of a local accounting firm, Andersen, Beaty and Collins, CPAs, many of your clients are local residents. Occasionally you read about these people in the local newspaper. You read, for example, that Justine Rodgers, the owner of Rodgers Word Processing Service, one of your clients, was cited as "Outstanding Business Woman of the Year" for Middlesex County. Prepare a congratulatory note to send Ms. Rodgers. Her business address is 17 Fairmont Avenue, Quincy, MA 02169.

23. *Too Brief.* The owner of a men's clothing store, Towne Shop, decided to send goodwill letters to all his charge account customers who pay their bills on time. He prepared the following communication. Critique his goodwill letter and offer him a revised version. Consider what you can offer the customers to build more goodwill.

Dear Customer:

This is to acknowledge our appreciation for your prompt payment of our bills. Customers like you help us stay in business. Visit us again soon.

---

24. *You Didn't Do It All.* As a senior at State College, you applied for a job with Plains State Bank, Milwaukee, Wisconsin. Your advisor for three years has been an economics professor, Dr. Martin Reed, who sent a letter of recommendation for you. You have just returned from a successful interview during which the bank offered you a position. Write a thank-you letter to Dr. Reed on plain stationery.

25. *A Tough Letter to Prepare.* You are Director of Training and Development for Percel Chemical Corporation, Houston, Texas. You became Director last year after your boss of fifteen years, Mrs. Linda Woodbridge, retired. You worked very closely with Mrs. Woodbridge; in fact, she recommended you for the position when she retired. Mrs. Woodbridge's husband of forty years died recently. You had met Mr. Brian Woodbridge at several social functions and enjoyed his company. Write an appropriate letter of sympathy to Mrs. Woodbridge. As directed by your instructor, prepare this letter on (a) a purchased note card, (b) plain stationery, or (c) personal stationery.

COMMUNICATION CHECK-UPS

26. Buy the cheap model because it will do a satisfactory job for us.
27. From an oral introduction: "Without further ado, let me introduce our speaker this evening—Professor Howard J. Washington."
28. In Chicago, her telephone number is 575-3332.
29. The Springfield Bank has a variety of services that many other banks in the area do not offer. For instance, the Bank provides FAX services for its customers.

30. The Association for Business Communication (ABC) has hundreds of members across the country. The ABC strives to improve the education of Business students in the area of communication.

31. The Executive Committee reached its decision in a closed session.

32. The report is all ready.

33. He is too timid to succeed in high-pressure sales.

34. On the other hand strive to maintain profitability during this period of rising costs.

35. The Personnel manager is a kind, considerate, hard-working person.

Executive Introduction

PHILLIP TRUCKENBROD CONCERT ARTISTS

A DIVISION OF TRIAD CORPORATION

15 High Street, Suite 621 • Hartford, Connecticut 06103 • (203) 728-1096

13 July 198_

Miss Donna Reynolds, President
Reynolds Dance Management
PO Box 1818
San Francisco, CA 94101

Dear Miss Reynolds:

It is good to know your business is prospering and that you are
"enjoying" the growing pains. In managing dancers, you have problems I
faced a few years ago with keyboard artists. Considering the kinds of
contacts you must make and the peculiarities of communication in our
professional circuit, it is relatively easy to pass along some hints
on setting up your office communication technologies.

<u>Computer</u>: A personal computer for billings, financial records, and
word processing is crucial. A complete software program will enable
you to generate routine promotions and create guide letters for
individualized letters.

<u>Dictation</u>: When you have a computer and a secretary, you maximize the
use of both via dictation. My machine is not only used in the office
and in the car, but also by phone for dictation of urgent messages.

<u>Telecommunications</u>: Don't forget the phone. Be sure you establish
policies, procedures, and rules for its use. Remember that when you
spend as much as $10,000.00 on a laser printer for your computer,
don't destroy the image of your company by letting staff relate to
clients and others inappropriately on the telephone.

These ideas have been exceedingly helpful to me. I hope you find them
beneficial as you set up your communication system.

Yours truly,

Phillip Truckenbrod

Phillip Truckenbrod

13

Modernizing Your Communications

WHAT YOU CAN LEARN BY STUDYING THIS CHAPTER

You have identified and may now be fluent in using various kinds of business communications, such as sales letters, inquiries, and "no" replies. You might think you are now ready to hit the pavement and start running. Probably not. In the modern organization, there are various ways in which messages can be originated, many of them involving modern technologies, and knowing the appropriate use of those techniques is another basic part of communication for the manager. When is a form letter appropriate? When should a guide letter be developed? How are computer graphics altering the creation of communications? How can dictation be used effectively? What are the hazards of using the telephone? All of these elements are part of originating communications. Although they may appear simple and obvious, you may be jumping to conclusions. Here we will review the intricacies, subtleties, and importance of the ways to originate messages.

TECHNOLOGY IS ADVANCING—ARE YOU?

Use technology to make your messages move.

There is a colorful advertisement for a dictating unit that shows the manager attempting to move into the executive suite but failing because a pencil he is holding horizontally is blocking his way. He can't get to the top by being a pencil pusher. The situation is applicable to anyone reading this book, regardless of her or his academic discipline. Communication technologies have moved far beyond pencils. If you are to survive and prosper in the modern organization, you must be up-to-date on communication technology.

Form Letters

The form letter is not new, but there are new ways to use it. The form letter is being recognized as an important management tool that can help the manager and the organization be more productive.

An old idea with new features.

A form letter is a mass-produced communication piece using a broad appeal. It is most commonly used by organizations for mass mailings and by managers responding to recurring situations.

Advertising Uses.

We have all received various kinds of sales-oriented form letters. Modern technology is giving the form letter a better image. No longer is it mimeographed; it can appear individually typed, and sometimes the letter addresses us by name, address, and some other demographic factor.

Linking data bases with form letters in advertising.

Some of the most notable of the individualized mailers are those sent by companies selling magazine subscriptions. The envelope is addressed especially to you, every paragraph contains your name, and there may even be coupons printed with your name. But it is still a form letter; the letter your next-door neighbor receives is identical to yours except for the name that is inserted at strategic points throughout the material.

The computer-assisted form letter permits targeting of markets and directing the message to a particular recipient. The computer manipulates an individual's stored data and then "talks" directly to him or her on the basis of those data. The computer-assisted letter makes possible management targeting, selection of information from data already in the computer's memory, and interpolation of that data and generation of a statement in the letter based upon them. In advertising, the form letter is used to establish contact with the receiver.

Managerial Uses.

Saving time with form letters in management.

In management the form letter is used to respond to recurring situations for which it would be inefficient, expensive, and repetitive to create a new letter each time. The form letter is commonly used by the personnel division of major corporations for responses to employment inquiries; the public affairs units of companies sending annual reports to individuals who request them, and members of Congress sending standardized letters to constituents explaining positions or votes.

Legal Advantages.   In addition to saving time, the form letter can reduce the risk of litigation. Having dozens of managers who are agents of the organization writing letters can be legally tenuous. What the agent communicates on behalf of the corporation is legally binding. One way to reduce the risk of litigation is to provide managers with form responses for recurring situations, such as turning people down for employment, refusing a request for funding from a charitable organization, or denying an employee a promotion.

Form letters can keep you out of court.

Guide Letters

Whereas the form letter is characterized by its uniformity, the guide letter loosens the reins. The manager sending the form letter does not have the option of adding sentences and inserting language. But the manager using the guide letter is given greater opportunity to insert material and thereby target the letter to a particular individual. Although recipe-like, the guide letter is less prescriptive than the rigid form letter. This kind of letter is also used for recurring situations, but ones in which there may be a need for the sender to insert some original sentences or paragraphs.

Guide letters provide basics with options to individualize.

Managerial Use of Guide Letters.   Guide letters are commonly used by customer-relations personnel responding to customer complaints, purchasing officers generating letters of inquiry, and sales representatives sending thank-you letters for clients' invitations. In these situations, there are too many peculiarities for form letters. However, the guide letter spells out the ideal response and provides a variety of options. The sender picks paragraphs that are appropriate. The guide letter might be likened to going through a cafeteria line—an abundance of options is presented, and the writer selects only those elements that meet the receiver's needs.

Master Guides.   Guide letters can be made available either in notebook form or in the computer for display on word-processing equipment. Each guide letter is appropriately titled and numbered, and each paragraph within the letter is numbered or lettered. The manager simply dictates, "Guide letter #17," indicates who is to receive it, and specifies the various paragraphs to be used. If there is a need to override the system, the manager can opt to drop one of the suggested paragraphs and add new material that is more appropriate. Figure 13.1 illustrates how the guide letter appears in the master notebook or on the word processor's display writer.

Word processing and guide letters work well together.

Specific Letter from Guide.   Dean Andrews wants to send a letter that is a bit different to Matthew Rehn. So Dean Andrews follows the guide, selecting germane paragraphs, and then overrides the system and inserts a different paragraph. Paragraph 5-A is used next, and the unique closing is dictated. The letter is quickly generated, as represented in Figure 13.2.

The guide letter, as its name suggests, is a basic map. The initiator may detour

FIGURE 13.1   Guide Letter

```
                          Guide Letter #17
                  Informing Applicant of Acceptance to MBA
                        Created March 10, 198_
                          Rev: May 20, 198_
                            Full Block

        Date

        Name (Mr., Miss, Ms., Mrs.)
        Street Address
        City, State, and Zip

        Dear Mr./Miss/Ms./Mrs.:

   1    Bentworth Graduate School of Business is pleased to inform you that
        you have been accepted into Bentworth's M.B.A. program.

  2A    All of your records are in order and you should contact the Graduate
        School Registrar within the next ____ days to make arrangements for
   or   enrolling for (Fall, Winter, Summer) semester classes.

  2B    Enough information was sent to us so that the admission decision could
        be made. However, we did not receive the Affirmative Action postcard
        from you; will you please complete the enclosed card and return it to
        us within ten days. Your admittance cannot be finished until we have
        it.

   3    You will join a class of about ____ students, this will be the largest
        group of men and women in our program since it was started.

   4    You inquired about a graduate assistantship. Now that your  admittance
        has been approved, you should complete the enclosed Graduate Assis-
        tantship forms and return them by ____.

   5    It was a pleasure to meet you when you were on campus and I look
        forward to seeing you again during the first week of classes. If you
   or   have any questions about the enrollment procedures, please contact my
        assistant, Elizabeth Polaski, or me.

  5A    I will look forward to meeting you when you are on campus during the
        first week of classes. If you have any questions about the  enrollment
        procedures, please contact my assistant, Elizabeth Polaski, or me.


        Cordially,



        Hilda C. Andrews
        Assistant Dean

        Enclosures
```

FIGURE 13.2   Letter Generated from Guide-letter Master

BENTWORTH COLLEGE
Arlington, Virginia 22204

Graduate School of Business   Hilda C. Andrews
                                                                               Assistant Dean

April 10, 198_

Mr. Matthew C. Rehn
1717 Lakewood Drive
Milwaukee, Wisconsin 53202

Dear Mr. Rehn:

The faculty of the Bentworth Graduate School of Business are pleased to inform you
that you have been accepted into Bentworth's M.B.A. program. Congratulations!

All of your records are in order and you should contact the Graduate School
Registrar within the next ten days to make arrangements for enrolling for Fall
semester classes.

You will join a class of about 135 students; this will be the largest group of men and
women in our program since it was started twenty-four years ago. We know that you
will find the program challenging and exciting.

Your father was an early and most distinguished graduate of our program, and we
look forward to welcoming you as the first member of the second generation to be
part of our fine program. Your class will be very different from your father's
class—it had only twelve students and they were all male. Nearly half of your
classmates will be women.

I will look forward to meeting you when you are on campus during the first week of
classes. If you have any questions about the enrollment procedures, please contact
my assistant, Elizabeth Polaski, or me.

If your father should visit campus during the time you are with us, several of the
faculty would enjoy meeting with him.

Cordially,

Hilda C. Andrews

Hilda C. Andrews
Assistant Dean

Basic uniform
information related
from guide.

Message individual-
ized and targeted to
particular receiver.

from the suggested route from time to time by inserting a sentence or replacing the recommended paragraph with a new one that is more appropriate. But the master guide presents the basic approach, tone, and format that the organization has found to be successful for communicating on a particular topic. The end result is a nice-looking piece of correspondence that is much less costly than a response generated from scratch for these recurring situations.

Computer Graphics

With graphics you can mix verbal and visual messages.

Not everything you write is in words; visuals are also a part of the business communication process. The next chapter describes the use of the computer in communications and Chapter 16 focuses on visuals in business communications. At this point, however, the use of computer graphics in originating the communication should be introduced. With even the simplest computer, printer, and inexpensive software, today it is easy to intermingle graphic representations with your verbal message. Intriguing charts can be inserted directly in a paragraph and attention-getting "clip art" can be placed in margins. A whole new "industry" of desk-top publishing has evolved.

Be it the simple act of making a heading "bold face" or the ingenious use of a progressive chart on each page of a several-page report, computer graphics today are part of the originating process of the communication. It is not even necessary to clip and paste; the manager can accomplish all of this from his or her keyboard and sometimes may call upon a "mouse" for assistance.

A significant advantage of computer graphics involves the rapid conversion of an enormous quantity of data (where needed) into an easy-to-comprehend visual aid. This permits managers to make rapid decisions.

Computer-assisted design and computer-assisted manufacturing (CAD/CAM) are of tremendous assistance to engineers and product designers in the development, manufacturing, and production of new items. Defense products (missiles, armaments, navigational equipment, etc.), artwork, auto and airplane configurations, clothing and furniture patterns, architectural units—almost anything can be presented graphically. These designs can be drawn and redrawn quickly with computer graphics until the desired results are achieved. They can then be fed back into the computer for the manufacture or layout of the product.

It is even possible, by using "flat screen" monitors, to take the screen with its final design, place it on a copy machine plate, and then reproduce a quantity of the computer graphic image displayed.

A further advantage in computer graphics is the ability to "animate" the design (make it move on the screen). This permits the engineer or the designer to actually see an animated portrayal of the product prior to its manufacture. In Figure 13.3 you can see four different types of computer-generated graphics.

FIGURE 13.3 Computer-generated Graphics

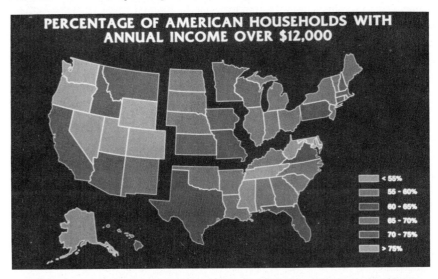

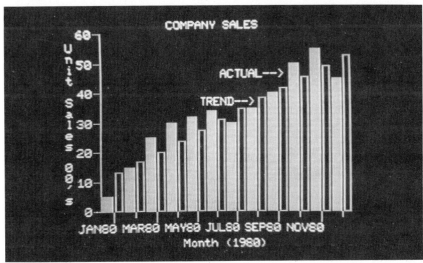

DICTATION

Letters originated in longhand are out of sync with today's communication systems, which are based on word processors, electronic mail, display writers, and laser printers. Modern managers who intend to communicate in the organization of the twenty-first century must know how to dictate, because this is the method by which

You are a slowpoke if you don't dictate.

data are input into new communication systems. It has been estimated that dictating to a machine is up to six times faster than writing a letter in longhand. Office productivity is substantially enhanced when managers dictate.

Equipment

There are many configurations in equipment, but the dictation principles don't change.

Today, most dictation is into machines, not "live" to a secretary. Therefore, our focus is on machine dictation, although the principles don't change. An advantage of dictating into a machine is that a secretary need not be immediately available to mechanically transcribe your message—you can dictate into a machine anytime, day or night. Dictation machines are very similar to cassette recorders. Some units are portable, some place you in direct contact with a central receiving center, and some may operate off your office telephone system (see Figure 13.4).

Organizing for Dictation

Good dictation involves good planning.

You must know what it is you want to communicate as well as the basic structure of the particular communication. Experienced dictators can sometimes quickly form a mental picture (an outline) of the letter. Less experienced managers will find it helpful to jot down an outline. Either way, it is essential to be organized. Have the necessary data at hand—names, addresses, and other pertinent information essential to the communication. You must also determine whether the dictation is to be prepared as a draft or as a final copy. Many managers prefer to dictate drafts. The draft is stored in the word processing system and a hard copy comes to the manager. The manager makes handwritten corrections and additions before the final copy is produced. It may seem like the work is being done twice, but it is actually very fast; it avoids mistakes and insures completeness and zero errors.

Getting Started: Apprise the Secretary

Good human relation skills will enhance your dictation.

As the communicator, you must establish the context so that the secretary can properly receive and understand the communication. In a large word-processing center, the secretary may not know you, your preferences, or just what you are attempting to accomplish with your communication. Take time to indicate (a) who you are, your department, and your telephone number; (b) whether the item is rush material; (c) what it is you are dictating (letter, memo, meeting minutes); (d) whether it is a draft or final copy; (e) the number of copies, kind of copies, and who is to receive them; (f) the format (full block or modified block), spacing, and type of stationery and envelopes.

FIGURE 13.4   Dictation Equipment: Bolstering Managerial Productivity

Dictating Hints

The dictating pros and the secretaries who listen suggest the following hints for successful dictation:

Telescoping: Recognize that the entire communication process is being telescoped. You must simultaneously envision your message, the communication process, the format, and numerous details of the content, all the while providing detailed information to the secretary.

Instructions: Provide the secretary with a clear road map. Include instructions for format, capitalization, paragraphing, and punctuation. Remember that special instructions must always precede material—the secretary will type the message in exactly the order you present it. For example: "Capital 'W' Wentworth capital 'C' Company will agree to all your capitalized OFFER. . . . " Let your tonal inflection reveal what language is for transcription and what language is passing a message to the secretary.

Voice: Use a normal conversational tone, enunciate clearly, keep an even pace, and speak spontaneously with feeling and interest.

Paper: When preparing final copy, don't assume the secretary will know what stationery to use—specify it clearly.

Format: Indicate when a new paragraph is to be started and be specific concerning any unusual formats such as special indentations, lists, columns, and double vs. single spacing.

Guides for enhancing your dictation.

Spelling: Spell out difficult words and proper names (Smith vs. Smyth).

Punctuation: Some dictators specify periods and commas and others let their tonal inflection do the job; unless you and the secretary work together regularly, it may be best to clearly specify punctuation—especially unusual punctuation like semicolons, dashes, and ellipses.

Visuals: If you must dictate tables and statistical data, it is helpful to provide the secretary with a sketch.

Closing Items: Indicate how you want the signature section to appear and whether you want enclosures listed.

Copies: Be specific concerning the number of copies and blind copies.

Bad Habits: Avoid distractions like mumbling, squeaking chairs, long pauses, eating, chewing gum, or tapping on the desk. All of the activities will come across like bomb-shells to the secretary and reduce the quality of your work.

Courtesy: Thank the secretary at the conclusion of your dictation, particularly if you have dictated some unusual or difficult material. Also, in lengthy sessions it may be appropriate to converse with the secretary for a moment. After all, the secretary may be listening to this "stuff" for hours each day. He or she may appreciate a breather.

Dictating Over the Phone

At times, you may want to phone your office to dictate material. With this type of dictation, the secretary does not have the option of going back and replaying the tape to clarify a confusing word or statement, and it will be difficult for you to know whether the secretary is keeping up with you. Therefore, you may want to

(a) stop periodically to ensure that you are both at the same point, and

(b) have the secretary read back what you have dictated; this can substitute for the draft copy you would ordinarily receive.

Practice Makes Perfect

You learn to dictate by dictating.

You may experience a type of stage fright the first few times you try dictation, but a little practical experience will help you overcome this. Try reading some copy into a

FIGURE 13.5   A Way to Practice Dictation

Read from this original copy	as if you were actually dictating.
Mrs. R. M. Smyth of Missoula, Montana has accepted our invitation to address the Annual Sales Conference on April 10 next year.	New paragraph: capital M Mrs. R. M. as in Martin capital S Smyth spelled S-m-y-t-h of capital M Missoula spelled M-i-s-s-o-u-l-a comma capital M Montana has accepted our invitation to address the captial A Annual capital S Sales capital C Conference on April arabic numeral 10 next year period, paragraph.
She will (according to her assistant) arrive on the evening of the 9th so she can attend the gala banquet-smorgasbord at the Hilton Country Stakes.	Capital S She will left paren according to her assistant right paren arrive on the evening of the arabic 9th so she can attend the gala banquet hyphen smorgasbord spelled s-m-o-r-g-a-s-b-o-r-d at the capital H Hilton spelled H-i-l-t-o-n capital C Country capital S Stakes spelled S-t-a-k-e-s.

Obviously, in actually dictating you are developing your ideas from your mind, not the printed copy of the material. But, this kind of practice introduces you to the multifaceted elements of dictation.

cassette recorder and add whatever instructions are necessary for the copy to be transcribed exactly as it appears in the original version (see Figure 13.5). With careful preparation and with consideration for the person at the other end of the machine, you can learn to dictate effectively and to access the modern communication systems of today's offices.

THE TELEPHONE

Some aspect of nearly every business transaction involves the telephone. You may want to review Chapter 1 on some of today's telephone capabilities. But whether your organization has a sophisticated system or not, the image that you and your organization present on the phone is as important as the image in written communications. Most organizations have procedures for operating the phone system. (See Chapter 14.)

Sending Calls

Check these hints for businesslike telephone use.

In business, your initial telephone contact is often with a switchboard operator, receptionist, or secretary. Generally, you do not immediately get the person you are calling. Here are some hints for effectively initiating calls:

Plan: Prepare your calls just as you would outline a letter or memo.

Identify: Immediately give your name, your organization, and your place (if long distance).

Practice: Have a friend critique your telephone voice, enunciation, and clarity. Make changes where needed.

Receiving Calls

Because there can be a direct relationship between the calls received and sales, it is important to handle incoming calls courteously and efficiently.

Promptness: Answer quickly; people don't like to wait while the phone rings or to wait long after being placed on hold.

Identify: Quickly indicate who has been reached.

Helpfulness: Strive to actually assist the individual.

Transfers: Be familiar with the equipment and expeditiously move the call to another party if appropriate.

Courtesy and Tact

Always be diplomatic and courteous with others.

Call Yourself: Beware of having a secretary place your calls—it may keep the receiving party waiting. Or it may seem pompous to the receiver.

Watch Your Language: Avoid slang, terms like "hold on" and expressions like "fer sure," "bye-bye," and "yeah." Condescending terms are also inappropriate, "honey," "sweetie," and "dear."

Protect Image: If answering for a co-worker, make him or her look good, don't say "He's late from lunch, don't know when he will be back, he didn't leave word."

Positive Pictures

Successful telephoning is often achieved when the answering party paints a positive picture of the situation with a clear, pleasant greeting and follows it up by forming a mental picture of the person at the other end of the line. In this way, it becomes easier to talk with—rather than at—that person.

KEEP PACE WITH TECHNOLOGY

Technology is clearly affecting the ways in which communications can be originated; since 1950 there have been substantial changes each decade in the ways managers can originate their messages. However, the weak link in the development is the manager who has not kept pace with the changes. Modern dictating units, sophisticated cathode-ray tubes with guide letters, and modern phones that allow you to be in contact with the world are of little value if you cannot use them efficiently and effectively. Be sure that you are not a 1950s manager as you enter the work force in the 1990s.

Make sure you are not the weak link in modern communications.

QUICK REVIEW

The form letter and the guide letter are alive and well in the organization; the modern manager knows how to use them to make her or his job easier. Dictation is becoming more vital to the modern executive. Today time is at a premium—to scratch on a legal pad is wasteful, but to dictate after work or in the auto going home enhances productivity. And today the telephone is much more than an ugly black object. However, with all of its "add ons" today, it is still important to use it pleasantly. The form and guide letter, the dictating unit, and the telephone provide you with efficient ways to originate your communication.

EXECUTIVE SUMMARY

To: Business Communication Students
From: David N. Bateman and Norman B. Sigband

Subject: Modernizing Your Communications

The ways in which business communications can be originated have been dramatically influenced by modern technologies.

Form and guide letters, for example, have been transformed from amateurish-looking results of crude mass-production techniques to products that appear to be individually prepared. Because of this improvement, the use of these efficient means of business communication has greatly increased.

Computer-generated graphics can supplement the modern business communication with professional-looking visuals. They also enable the communicator to easily manipulate masses of data and present them clearly and attractively.

Modern dictation equipment and methods enable the manager to "write" a letter six times faster than by writing longhand. But the user of dictation must fully understand the equipment and learn techniques for using it in order to achieve this level of efficiency.

Although telephone capabilities have expanded greatly in recent years, the guidelines for effective telephone behavior have remained basically the same. The business communicator must follow these guidelines if he or she hopes to take advantage of the newest telephone technologies.

DISCUSSION GENERATORS

1. *Routine?* Explain why form and guide letters are developed for routine (and not nonroutine) situations.

2. *Computers and Form Letters.* Besides making form letters look very professional, what has the computer done to enhance the effect of form letters?

3. *Form Letters Beyond Mass Mailings?* Form letters for mass mailings, as we see in various kinds of advertising campaigns, are standard. But how are form letters used in many internal business management situations?

4. *Why Guide?* If the guide letter provides the manager various opportunities to deviate from the guide, why do organizations use guide letters?

5. *Pencil Pushers.* Why might "pencil pushers" have trouble surviving in the modern organization?

6. *Efficiency.* If dictation is at least six times faster than writing out letters and memos longhand, how much time (assuming a forty-hour work week) would you save dictating rather than handwriting—in a day, a week, a month, and a year?

7. *Chit-chat.* Under what circumstances, if any, would you engage in some idle chit-chat with the secretary taking your dictation?

8. *Machine vs. "Live" Dictation.* Why is most dictation done into a machine today instead of directly to the secretary?

9. *What Telescope?* What elements in the communication process are telescoped when you dictate?

10. *Inflection or Specification.* How do you, after some practice, anticipate you will dictate?

    a. Will you specify all of the punctuation or will you let your vocal inflection tell the secretary when you are inserting a comma and period?

    b. What factors will influence your dictation style decision?

11. *Legal Advantage?* What legal advantage does an organization achieve in preparing form and guide letters for its managers?

12. *Still a Form?* Explain why a standard letter that is altered by individualizing the receiver's name and address is still a form letter.

13. *Dog on a Leash.* Using an analogy of two dogs on different leashes, differentiate between the form letter and the guide letter. Be sure to make clear which "dog" is on the longer leash (and why), and also explain why the analogy to a leash is appropriate.

14. *Cafeteria Line Stops.* The guide letter is analogous to the cafeteria line according to the authors. In actuality, however, the analogy breaks down when it comes to the writer creating and substituting paragraphs in the guide letter (that is, inserting an idea not in the guide letter). Continue the analogy to accommodate this feature (creating one's own new material) of the guide letter.

15. *Dictation Practice.* The process for practicing dictation (see Figure 13.5) will aid the neophyte in what aspects of dictation?

16. *Which Hint?* After having practiced dictating a time or two, which of the hints cited in the text proved most helpful to you and why?

17. *Identification.* In placing a telephone call to Jamie Myers at the Oster Company in New Hampshire (you are calling from Newton, Iowa), which method of identification is likely to get you through to Jamie if the secretary intercepts the call and Jamie is a bit busy, but could take a call if the secretary sees fit to put it through?

    a. "Hello, may I speak to Jamie please?"

    b. "This is David Jensen, is Jamie in?"

    c. "Good day, this is Larry Dellitt of Kathy's Temporaries calling long distance from Newton, Iowa; may I speak to Jamie Myers please?"

    Explain in some detail the "why" of your answer.

18. *Pledge, Get That Phone.* At one time, and perhaps still today, pledges in social fraternities had to make sure the phone was answered before it rang three times. For business today, is that a good idea? Why or why not?

19. *Golfing?* It is near the end of the fiscal year. A vice-president of the Plaza Department Store is phoning for Kathy Black, chief accountant, on the internal phone system. Kathy is out on the golf course with the leaders of the CPA firm that advises your organization. You answer Kathy's phone and the VP asks for Kathy. What do you say?

20. *Bad Image.* If form letters have a negative image because at one time they looked sloppy and were generally used in mass advertising, why would a manager even want to consider their use for responding to customer inquiries today?

APPLICATIONS FOR BUSINESS

21. *It's a Jungle Out There.* An amazing variety of style, sophistication, and courtesy is revealed by the manner in which organizations answer their phones and route incoming calls. For the next week, take notes on how organizations handle the phone when you call them. Prepare a one-page memo that summarizes your findings. Pay particular attention to the following elements:

—How is the phone answered? Clearly? Interestingly? Is the answering party/organization identified?

—If your call was transferred to another party, what were you told?

—If you were placed on "hold," what happened?

22. *Telescoping and Juggling.* The dictation process calls for a telescoping of a number of communication activities. When dictating, the individual is literally juggling several communication activities at one time. Carefully identify what the manager must quickly organize when preparing to dictate a letter in the following situation: You are interested in upgrading your dictation equipment; you are sending a letter of inquiry to Ms. Mary Murphy of the Tech Office Products Company, 1307 "C" Street, Fort Worth, TX 80302. Prepare a definite list of all the items that are telescoped. The list should include the type of letter, the nature of the message, and various items that the dictator must consider that the person sitting and typing the letter at the keyboard may be unaware of.

23. *Telephone Procedures at Reynolds Association Management.* You are the new lead secretary at Reynolds; you have been brought in to upgrade general secretarial services in the organization and to improve and enhance office operations. The telephone answering and transferring procedures are not a hallmark of your firm. You have appointed a four-person task force to develop a statement of procedures on telephone answering and transferring and basic telephone courtesies. You ask the task force to not look at what the firm has been doing, but to concentrate on identifying and developing procedures for the future. In small groups (probably about four), take on the role of the task force.

a. Develop a clear statement of procedures.

b. Provide explicit suggestions on achieving courtesy and pleasantness.

24. *A Fun Form.* You are the treasurer of your college alumni organization. Prepare a form letter to be sent to all alumni inviting them to homecoming and encouraging them to pay $12 each for the picnic to be held on the lawn of the alumni club at 11:00 a.m. before the game on October 23. The $12 includes champagne, hot and cold hors d'oeuvres, fried chicken, and salad. Kick-off is at 1:00 p.m.

25. *A Dictation Exchange.* Choose a partner in class for this exercise. Each of you is to take turns dictating a thank-you letter to Dr. Florence Evans, Personnel Director of your college. Thank Dr. Evans for taking the time to address your business communications class on "How to Handle the Job Interview." A third member of the class should observe your dictating and be prepared to critique each of you.

COMMUNICATION CHECK-UPS

26. Carry out this class project in a businesslike manner.

27. We hope you will not find our product unsatisfactory.

28. If you will simply read and follow the directions you will not have any trouble with your new word processor.

29. I am writing to inquire about the new Century XXI telecommunication system.

30. In your report include a description of the following items: room service; wake-up-call procedures; guest registration procedures; security configurations; convention rate discounts.

31–35. The following are all first sentences for an inquiry letter; identify and implement ways in which these messages might be improved.

31. Enclosed is a diagram of our product called Mail-Time.

32. Please allow me to introduce our company to you.

33. I am writing you to determine your interest in our new product.

34. This letter is directed to you from the ABC Company.

35. I have a product that I would like you to include in your next catalog.

Executive
Introduction

 **Airfone**

In-flight Telephone
Service

Sandra K. Goeken
Vice President
Corporate Affairs/New Business Development

GTE Airfone Incorporated
2809 Butterfield Road
Box Number 9000
Oak Brook, IL 60522-9000
312 572-1800

June 8, 198_

Miss Elizabeth Civic
Contemporary Issues Class
Bennington Senior High School
Bennington, Vermont 05201

Dear Miss Civic:

How exciting that your students are preparing to study how communications move in our modern world. Because our firm has brought the public phone to the sky, rail, and sea, we are keenly aware of how communication technologies are changing.

Personal Computers: Today's bulletin board is the electronic image on the personal computer (pc) screen.

Electronic Mail: The postal carrier is not obsolete, but many first-class messages are sent electronically today.

Telecommunications: The modern phone, with its punch key system, is also a computer and calculator.

Airfone© & Railfone™ Service: Travelers, be they on rail, plane, or boat, can keep in touch with business and personal priorities with these time-saving services. Now, some commercial U. S. aircraft are equipped with the Seatfone™ system, a seatback version of the Airfone air-to-ground telephone service. The Airfone service has saved lives by making it possible to easily reach a passenger's personal physician.

Video-Conferencing: Today firms save money by setting up video-conferences in lieu of having fifteen people each spend three days traveling.

A videotape illustrating Airfone is enclosed. This tape has been a hit around the world; your students should find it educational.

Congratulations on your creative ways of teaching; you clearly make learning enjoyable and rewarding for the students.

Sincerely,

Sandra K. Goeken

SANDRA K. GOEKEN

SKG/njp

Enclosure

14

Moving Your Communications

WHAT YOU CAN LEARN BY STUDYING THIS CHAPTER

The technologies that aid us in spreading our message to people both inside and outside the organization are continually increasing, as are their applications. About the only thing that may be slowing down business communication these days is the communicators themselves; while the technology is sprinting ahead, some managers are walking slowly or even sitting.

A key to modern communication technology for the manager is the personal computer. It has brought a powerhouse of capabilities and information to the manager's desk. With a simple keyboard, the manager today can do much to improve his or her ability to obtain data, make decisions, and communicate effectively inside and outside the organization. In this chapter, you will become familiar with terms like *uplink, Airfone, call forwarding,* and *video text.* Such terms are becoming part of the manager's communication vocabulary.

Many managers today are playing "catch-up"—attempting to get up to speed with the rapidly expanding communication technologies. As you have seen, there are many new ways of originating ideas and even more of launching communications. However, the manager must first get to the launch pad. The manager who feels that keyboarding is solely a secretarial duty is not ready to enter the world of modern communication technology.

WORD PROCESSING AND PERSONAL COMPUTERS

The Human Element

As we initiate our look at the fascinating technologies, let's not overlook the fundamental part that makes all of the communication technologies work—the human. Advanced communication systems may reduce some numbers of people in the workplace. However, the personal interactions increase and become vital in making the technologies work.

Personal Computers

PC's with professional printers permit you to really move your communications in a businesslike way.

The computers that managers and secretaries can have at their desks have revolutionized the ways data are moved and communications are handled. Because of the memory and flexibility of the small computer, today the trend is away from machinery that can just do word processing. The personal computer, on its own, is a heavyweight management tool. When the CRTs of an office are interconnected, linked to the mainframe, and can communicate to rapid and professional printers, the small computer is a powerhouse.

Developing Manuscripts

The personal computer can do many things: keep records, maintain a calendar, calculate, organize data, and word processing. Word processing has reduced the work of the typist by more than 50 percent. It is no longer necessary to retype an entire letter to correct a single mistake. The text can be read and corrected on the screen before it is printed. Even if an error is detected after printing, a single correction can be made on the storage file, and the letter can be reprinted very quickly.

Word Processing Capabilities

Word processing makes editing easier.

The basic word processing system allows blocks of text or words to be shifted around without rekeyboarding. New paragraphs or words can be added at any point, and the text will automatically rearrange itself to accommodate them, thus saving the writer time and effort. Margins can be adjusted so that the right margin will be as even as the left.

There is a continually increasing variety of options that can be added to the basic word processing system—such as an automatic dictionary to check spelling against a list of over 85,000 words or a thesaurus that provides alternative word options.

Word Processing Usage

In addition to its usefulness in preparing letters, memos, and short reports, word processing can also be helpful in situations such as the following:

- For documents such as guide letters that are used repeatedly but require minor revision from time to time.
- For sales campaigns in which identical letters must be sent to many people; each letter must appear to be an "original" copy, individually addressed.
- For data base retention. For example, a labor relations manager may need to frequently cite sections of the union contract in all types of correspondence. These sections can be stored, pulled, and inserted in any communication as needed.
- For draft documents that will undergo a series of redrafts and revisions.
- For access to the mainframe, so that data can be secured, manipulated, and printed.

The many managerial uses of word processing

Desk-top Publishing

For individuals slightly more skilled, today there is machinery and software that permits the development of professional-looking booklets, brochures, transparencies, and related items—it is called "desk-top publishing." It does what it is called; these PCs have the power, with good printers, to produce what it took a small print shop to do just a few years ago. And, for anyone who needs professional-looking print matter, the cost is substantially less than that at a print shop.

ELECTRONIC MAIL

Moving ideas in written form among geographically distant offices has become much faster and more efficient with the development of electronic mail systems. Basically, electronic mail links together each manager's CRT. Messages input by Albert at Remington's Canton office can be sent to one or more people at other offices. The advantages of electronic mail include:

The use of electronic mail is increasing rapidly.

Direct Input: The manager (or the manager's secretary) can input the "mail" (often questions or directions) directly into the system; there are no intermediary parties or delays.

Hard vs. Soft: The receiver can opt to receive the message either on the CRT screen or as hard copy from the computer's printer.

Flex-time. Messages can be sent and received at any time—the systems are "up" during nonwork hours.

Convenience: The manager can input or look at the output at his or her convenience; it is not like a regular telephone, which demands immediate attention.

Dialogue: Detailed questions or directions can be sent quickly to other parties; equally quickly, the responses can be keyed into the system and returned.

Security: For sensitive data, it is possible to key or code data so that only the appropriate party can access the CRT to obtain the information.

Electronic Mail and the Manager

Electronic mail has several effects upon the manager:

Keyboard Skills: To maximize the "dialogue" aspects of electronic mail, the manager needs keyboard skills; clearly, such skills are part of management and not cloistered in secretarial pools.

Electronic mail is affecting the manager's job.

Data Bases: Access to organizations like the *Wall Street Journal,* financial houses, and others allow dialogue and the quick retrieval of data. Having quick access to such resources increases the manager's decision-making capabilities.

Friendly Interactions: As managers interact via CRT and computer printouts, the relationships change and formalities are usually lessened. The system is user-friendly, and by interacting, two managers who may never meet face-to-face become friendly. (See Figures 14.1 and 14.2 illustrating a question/answer electronic mail exchange between two distant managers.)

Freed Time: Electronic mail is excellent for nonemergency messages; the telephone call or office drop-in is still best for emergencies. Electronic mail provides the manager flexibility to access the messages and respond to them when it is most convenient. In this way, electronic mail permits the manager to manage time more efficiently.

Mailgrams

Mailgrams bring electronic mail to the general public.

The United States Postal Service and Western Union have combined capabilities to bring an electronic system to the general public. The initiator sends a message via Western Union to a receiving station near the intended recipient; there the message is

FIGURE 14.1   Electronic Mail Dialogue—Inquiry

```
**********************  START OF MESSAGE  **************************
----------------------) HARDCOPY (--------------------------------
 DATE : 06:22:87          PAGE : 001            TIME : 15:55:20
 TO   : ELLEN             FROM  : RUTH
 POBOX : MILDBT           POBOX : MKEICTNG
 TOPIC : PRICE AND DELIVERY
------------------------------------------------------------------


 PLEASE ADVISE THE PRICE AND DELIVERY STATUS ON THE FOLLOWING
 ITEMS:  849AZOD25, 700NPTA1, 700CO2OA1, 700P1200A1.

 AWAITING YOUR REPLY.  CUSTOMER NEEDS PARTS IMMEDIATELY.




 **************************  END OF MESSAGE  **************************
```

typed on paper, placed in an envelope, and delivered to the local post office. If the message is sent before 7:00 p.m., it should be received in the following day's mail. This method of communication has the advantage of providing a written message at a relatively low cost; and it cuts the delays associated with normal postal deliveries.

TWX and Telex

When it is necessary to quickly share important text information with far-flung divisions and offices, many organizations make use of Western Union's teletypewriter and teleprinter exchange services. These systems permit direct two-way communication and provide a written record of the conversation. It is also possible to communicate with other organizations that have the telecommunication equipment.

Facsimile

Fax communication uses the telephone lines to transmit text, drawings, and photographs. This process can be useful to organizations that need to quickly exchange detailed charts, graphs, and sketches.

Fax machinery is becoming much less expensive; its popularity is increasing.

FIGURE 14.2   Electronic Mail Dialogue—Response

```
############################ START OF MESSAGE ############################
-----------------------------) ORIGINAL (-----------------------------
   DATE : 06:22:87            PAGE : 001              TIME : 16:14:59
   TO   : RUTH SEMRAD         FROM  : ELLEN DUCHROW
   POBOX : MKEICHR            POBOX : MILDBT
   TOPIC : PRICE & DELIVERY
--------------------------------------------------------------------------

   PLEASE ADVISE THE PRICE AND DELIVERY STATUS ON THE FOLLOWING
   ITEMS:  849AZOD25, 700NPTA1, 700C020A1, 700P1200A1.

   AWAITING YOUR REPLY.  CUSTOMER NEEDS PARTS IMMEDIATELY.


   ---------------------------------------------------------------------

   A-B CATALOG NUMBER      LIST PRICE EACH       DELIVERY

      849A-ZOD25              $ 128.00            STOCK
      700-NPTA1               $ 144.00            STOCK
      700-C020A1              $  84.00            STOCK
      700-P1200A1             $ 128.00            STOCK


   THIS MATERIAL MAY BE AVAILABLE FOR CUSTOMER PICK-UP OR SHIPMENT
   TOMORROW AFTER 2:00 PM PROVIDING I HAVE ORDER IN-HOUSE NO LATER
   THAN 9:00 AM TOMORROW MORNING.

   PLEASE SEND ORDER TO MY ATTENTION FOR IMMEDIATE ORDER ENTRY AND
   EXPEDITING.

   PLEASE ADVISE IF YOU SHOULD HAVE ANY FURTHER QUESTIONS IN THIS
   REGARD.

   AWAITING YOU REPLY.

   THANK YOU.

   ELLEN DUCHROW
   MILWAUKEE DISTRICT SALES OFFICE

   ########################## END OF MESSAGE ##########################
```

TELEPHONE SERVICES

The options and services of the basic telephone continue to increase. The goal is to make the manager more efficient and responsive. Many phone systems have the following features:

Hold reminder periodically returns the party to the operator/receptionist.

Call forwarding (routing) permits the manager to program the phone so that incoming calls will follow him or her via other phones; when the manager does not want to be disturbed, calls can be routed to a secretary.

Call pickup allows the answering of others' office phones without leaving one's desk.

Automatic dialers permit frequently called numbers to be reached by using shortened dialing codes.

Centrex is a computerized system that allows direct access to each manager by phone without going through a centralized switchboard.

Mobile phones (those placed in vehicles) are becoming much more common because the quality of transmission is increasing as is the number of phones that can operate.

Voice mailboxes are similar to electronic mail except they leave voice messages instead of CRT or printed messages.

To some, these innovations may seem like gadgets, but in actuality, they are electronic advancements that aid the manager in being more efficient and productive.

OTHER TELEPHONE ADVANCES

In the last decade, new phone systems have evolved (e.g., MCI, Sprint, and others) and whole new applications have been created. Airfone and Railfone are remarkable technological achievements that increase the manager's effectiveness. Until the mid-1980s, the manager was out of communication contact when flying on a commercial aircraft or traveling on a train. This is no longer true.

Airfone, an in-flight public telephone, operates on many commercial flights. It is a pay telephone that provides excellent connections to phones virtually any place in the world. Airfone works with any major credit card. The cost is $7.50 for the first three minutes on any domestic call. Considering the time that can be saved (for instance, if the flight is late) or the money that can be saved (by forwarding important information to the office), the cost is minimal. Because of its excellent engineering design, the reception is very good and transmissions go through just like any other phone call (see Figure 14.3).

Railfone has the same features as Airfone and operates on major rail systems in the United States—especially in the busy east coast corridors. Airfone and Railfone keep the manager in touch when traveling. As John Goeken, the inventor of the "fones," says in explaining his idea, "If you watch the executives getting off planes, they head either to the restroom or the phone."

Conference calls are made possible by some advanced telephone systems that enable the caller to establish at least a three-way conversation. For example, the manager at the Chicago office is talking with a sales representative in Atlanta and they decide that they need to consult their supplier in New York. With a few simple pushes of telephone buttons, the third party can be brought aboard.

Conference calls involving more than three people are usually set up through a

There are many "add-ons" for telephones today.

Clear communications at 30,000 feet

Managers no longer need to travel in a communication vacuum.

Telephonic conferences are becoming more popular.

FIGURE 14.3   Airfone In-flight Public Telephone

special conference operator at the telephone company who is notified of the location, the names of the people, and the time of the call.

As a general rule, the conference call becomes difficult when more than five or six people are involved—especially if an active exchange of ideas is involved. The following guidelines are helpful for keeping conference calls manageable:

Designate a Chief: Put one person in charge to actively direct and lead the discussion and to make sure that everyone is heard and understood.

Restrict the Agenda: Limit the agenda, preferably to just one topic. The telephone attention span—espcially when you are only listening—is rather short.

Take Turns: The discussion leader should state the topic to be discussed and then have each participant respond in turn. Although this reduces active exchange, it keeps the discussion from becoming incomprehensible with several people speaking simultaneously.

Establish Signals: If a more active exchange is desired, it is helpful to agree on a protocol for indicating when one would like to enter the discussion. In face-to-face meetings, we send one another nonverbal clues that signal we are ready to get a word in. In the conference call, the participant might say, "I'd like to respond," and the leader will know to give that individual the line.

For simple matters that need a quick turnaround or response, or for pressing situations for which a face-to-face meeting would be impractical because of time, expense, and convenience, the conference call is a medium of communication that is available to any manager and should be considered. There are added variations and the ability to bring more people into the "meeting" when speaker phones are used.

VIDEOCONFERENCING

One indication of the increasingly important role of telecommunications is the fact that many corporations are opening offices adjacent to teleports. Teleports house satellite earth stations and fiber-optics networks.

Videoconferencing: Why Now?

The technology for video conferencing has been available for some time—the videophone was introduced over twenty years ago. Why has there been such a delay in the practical implementation? What has brought about the sudden rush?

First of all, satellite capabilities today make it easy to beam messages from one place to another. Second, the oil embargoes of the 1970s, the change in air regulations, and the increased cost of travel all combined to make business travel more hectic and less reliable. When executives began to miss meetings in distant cities because of travel delays, but nevertheless incurred huge costs, they started to look for other meeting options. Third, the managerial workforce is changing—younger managers (especially parents) are often less inclined to travel; videoconferencing substantially reduces the need for long trips. Fourth, in an ironic way, the Iranian hostage crisis of 1980 played a role. At the beginning of that crisis, a relatively unknown reporter, Ted Koppel of ABC Television News, started a special late evening news program on the Iranian situation. From his Washington, D.C., studio, Koppel did live interviews with several people around the world simultaneously. Koppel used a teleconferencing approach to permit guests to exchange ideas and debate one another. Although the participants were thousands of miles apart, it seemed as though they were in the same room. Five nights a week, the American manager saw that videoconferencing worked!

The conference room is changing—video has been added.

Videoconferencing Systems

There are two types of systems—downlink and uplink, and they have different uses and capabilities. What we see on television with Koppel is an uplink full-motion video system. This means that at every location, there is the capability to instantaneously send and receive both audio and video to each of the other locations. This allows the participants to interact as if they were physically together.

For large business meetings where the goal is not to exchange ideas but to receive a message, the downlink system is used. Downlink meetings involve only one-way communication; they are very much like watching television. This system might be used by top management to report to employees in scattered locations or to introduce a new product to sales representatives and/or distributors.

Videoconferencing variations

The technology allows for many variations on the uplink system. Besides the full-motion video hookups, a less costly freeze-frame system can be employed. Freeze-frame involves a simultaneous two-way audio connection, but the picture is slow-motion video that actually is like watching a series of snapshots. Freeze-frame seems to be adequate for routine technical discussions between middle-managers. But top-level executives seem to feel that freeze-frame is too slow; they like to instantaneously see the reactions on the faces of the people at the other end.

Full-motion video can be upgraded to incorporate hard copy information such as charts, graphs, and photographs. This system utilizes two-screen live action (see Figure 14.4). Obviously, as more cameras, signals, and groups are added, the costs increase.

Videoconferencing Advantages

In addition to saving on travel costs, lost time, and lost opportunities, teleconferencing also reduces the wear and tear on people in the organization.

Another advantage is that small talk is reduced with teleconferencing compared to face-to-face meetings. Furthermore, managers seem to do a better job of preparing for teleconferencing. Of course, as teleconferencing becomes more widely used, and people become more comfortable with it, some of these initial advantages may diminish, just as they did with the telephone.

Acclimating to Teleconferencing

As might be expected, some people fear teleconferencing. Indeed, it is very different from just stepping into the conference room. The camera and the projected picture cause people to become more concerned with how they look, how they speak, and, since the sessions are often videotaped, what they say and how they say it. All of these factors influence group dynamics. Teleconferencing tends to be a bit impersonal, and it definitely seems to work best when the participants are accustomed to meeting face-to-face.

FIGURE 14.4   Uplink Videoconferencing

Both new managers and established managers are going to have to adjust to this new phenomenon; teleconferencing is here to stay. It is one more technological advancement that will help business reduce costs and increase productivity.

VIDEOTEXT

Sometimes technology is ahead of its potential uses. This seems to be the case with videotext. This technology is literally sitting on the edge of your television set waiting for someone to find a practical way to apply it in the home and in business. The concept is already in limited use in Europe, but it has barely gotten off the ground in the United States. What is this "mystery" technology? Basically, videotext connects one's television set with huge computer banks, providing access to more information than any encyclopedia could provide.

The Visionlink Company goes one step farther and is now aggressively establishing a nationwide videotext system. It features community systems and data bases that can be accessed by any subscriber in any community. Visionlink will offer individual consumers and businesses a wide range of data and permit the user to interact with those data. Under its slogan of "Connecting us one to another," the system will bring a wide variety of information and services to the home and a wealth of data to the business organization (see Figure 14.5).

Videotext is entering the office and the home.

FIGURE 14.5   Visionlink Services

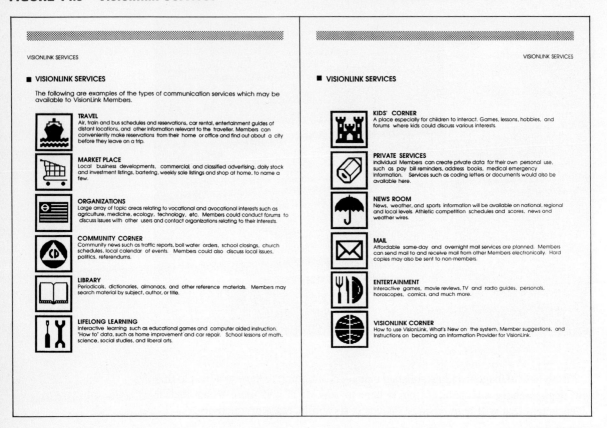

Videotext could affect communications by reducing routine letters such as inquiry letters, credit letters, and order acknowledgments. It could also speed up communications by making data more readily available.

BRIEFCASE COMPUTERS

Personal computers are nice, but you can't take one on an airplane, and the typical business conference room does not easily accommodate them. Now there is a briefcase computer (or "kangaroo") that can be a word processor, interactive terminal, electronic mailbox, or even more. The briefcase computer usually consists of a keyboard, a CRT, a telephone adapter, and some kind of small memory and/or software. All of this literally fits into a briefcase, and usually there is room to spare. Some of the uses and implications of this technology include:

In Touch with the World: When the employee's company is hooked into videotext services, the traveling executive can access, using the miniature computer and the telephone, Dow Jones stock quotes, news reports, and other information twenty-four hours a day.

Memos Away from Home. While in transit, the manager can prepare a memo by keyboarding it, displaying it on the miniature CRT, and checking it. Then the memo can be transmitted via telephone to the office for distribution.

From Meeting to Hard Copy: The manager attending a brainstorming session in a distant city can input the ideas into the briefcase computer. Later that evening, these ideas can be transmitted to the home office via telephone; when the manager returns to the office, the secretary can have a hard copy summary of the meeting prepared.

PCs on the road

Order Generation: The sales representative far from the office can speed orders quickly to the company's primary computer.

Mainframe Contact: The sales representative can, while making a sales presentation, hook into the firm's mainframe computer and generate graphs or other information that will meet the potential customer's needs. The insurance sales agent can calculate customers' various complex needs or calculate various complex premiums on the spot, rather than having to say, "I'll have to check with the home office and get back to you."

Electronic Mail: The manager with a briefcase computer need not face a stack of return call slips at the hotel desk in the evening. Instead, the computer can be plugged into the telephone and the messages projected on the screen when convenient.

QUICK REVIEW

If you are entering the job market today, be sure you know and can use the modern communication technologies—you don't want to leave the college campus driving a horse and buggy. It is not only vital to understand the communication technologies for moving information, you must know how you can make the technology work for you in making you more efficient.

Be familiar with word processing and how it makes management easier; recognize the advantages of electronic mail and use those advantages to make you more productive; understand all the "tricks" the phone can do and program it so the phone will aid your productivity; and when away from the office, recognize all the technologies that are available to keep you in direct touch.

EXECUTIVE SUMMARY

To: Business Communication Students

From: David N. Bateman and Norman B. Sigband

Subject: Moving Your Communications

Communication technology has been expanding rapidly and will doubtless continue to do so. The modern manager must keep up with procedures for transmitting communications that today's technologies make possible.

The personal computer, with its word processing and considerable other capabilities, has streamlined much of the process of written communication. Letters, memos, and reports can be quickly prepared, edited, and revised; word processing can also be used for editing, guide letters, individualized form letters, data-base retention, and manipulation of data. The personal computer has also made desk-top publishing a reality.

Electronic mail has enabled business communicators to move messages faster and more efficiently. Mailgrams, TWX, Telex, and facsimile transmittal are all accomplished electronically.

Call forwarding, call pickup, automatic dialers, centrex, mobile phones, and voice mailboxes are just some of the telephone services that businesses are utilizing to improve productivity. Other advances are airfone, railfone, and conference calling.

Satellite capabilities have combined with the need to save travel time and money to make videoconferencing—both downlink and uplink—important today. Teleconferencing is both reducing wear and tear on executives and increasing productivity.

With videotext, the technology is already here to connect the television set with huge computer data bases, but it has been little utilized.

The briefcase or "kangaroo" computer usually consists of a keyboard, a CRT, a telephone adapter, and a small memory and/or software. It may be used as a word processor, interactive terminal, electronic mailbox, and more.

DISCUSSION GENERATORS

1. *Kangaroos.* How are briefcase computers different from typical personal computers?
2. *Flexibility.* What kinds of flexibility does electronic mail provide the manager?
3. *Mailboxes.* What are the differences and similarities between the electronic and the voice mailbox?
4. *Costly?* Explain why the $7.50 cost of a three-minute Airfone call really isn't expensive for a manager in business.
5. *Differences.* Differentiate videotext from electronic mail. How are they different, and how do they affect the manager differently?
6. *Gadgets or Necessities?* Defend the authors' view that the various electronic

advances described in this chapter for moving communications are aids to productivity, not just modern executive coloring books.

7. *Keyboarding.* Why has keyboarding become a more important skill for the manager today than in the 1950s or 1960s?

8. *Powerhouse.* Explain how the relatively simple personal computer in the office can become a powerhouse, affecting the communications of the manager extensively.

9. *Justification.* Explain and illustrate justified margins.

10. *Redrafting.* Why is the word processing program on a computer so handy when it is necessary to draft, edit, and redraft a document?

11. *Software Explosion.* There are all kinds of software programs that can be purchased for the computer, such as programs to check spelling and provide synonyms. What new software programs have you discovered? How would they benefit a manager's communications?

12. *Nonemergency.* Electronic mail, according to the authors, is excellent for nonemergency information. Why is it less suitable for emergency information? After all, the information can instantaneously be sent to a number of managers.

13. *Interactions.* Over time, what does the evidence seem to indicate happens to managerial interactions via electronic mail and videoconferencing?

14. *Telex vs. Fax.* What kind of situation would call for you to use a fax system instead of a telex?

15. *Centrex.* For a busy manager, what might be a disadvantage of the centrex direct access system? What can the manager do to overcome the disadvantage?

16. *Call Forwarding.* How does automatic call forwarding save a manager's time?

17. *Airfone.* For your future profession, cite two or three examples of situations in which the Airfone technology could benefit you.

18. *Clarity.* What can you do in a conference call to keep from having all of the participants talking simultaneously?

19. *Family Life.* How has videoconferencing enhanced the family life of today's executive?

20. *Up vs. Down.* Differentiate and explain uplink and downlink videoconferencing.

APPLICATIONS FOR BUSINESS

21. *Electronic Mail Simulation.* Using personal computers (or, if they are unavailable, standard typewriters) and working in groups of four or five, simulate an electronic mail dialogue over a two- or three-day period.

    The Situation: One student is the department head and the other three or four are sales representatives in geographically distant places; everyone is interlinked with electronic mail. Electronic mail is important because the sales reps are in and out of their offices at odd times, but can regularly check their electronic mail box.

The Initial Message: Our new product—"Banana Chip Cookies"—was to be in the stores yesterday. Tomorrow, massive TV advertising will be initiated. Please keep me advised on (1) in-store product inventories, (2) customer reaction to product, and (3) store management reaction to product.

The "Electronic Communication": Carry on the dialogue; keep all records.

The Written Analysis: At the end, after at least two "electronic" exchanges, each person should summarize the "electronic mail" dialogue in a one-page memo. Also, be prepared to present your findings orally in class.

22. *Airfone Costs.* You are an assistant department head for the Oster Company; you are paid $43,000 per year plus normal benefits. Your primary duties include carefully reviewing all materials that go to the department head for signature (like formal letters, agreements, and contracts) and acting as a "trouble shooter" for Oster's operations throughout the country.

You have left Oster's headquarters in Rochester, New York, and are now on a commercial flight to Des Moines, Iowa, out of Pittsburg; your aircraft is equipped with Airfone. You have to switch planes in Chicago. For each of the following situations, determine if you would make the Airfone call from the air (they would all be put on your firm's billing card); justify your decision based on cost, convenience, and necessity.

    a. You had instructed your secretary to get an agreement out to Johnson, Inc. in the morning mail; relaxing on the aircraft at 30,000 feet reading the *Wall Street Journal,* you remember that the phrase "no later than March 10" was left out of the Johnson material; the absence of that phrase could cost Oster about $10,000.

    b. Because of traffic over O'Hare, your next flight, to Des Moines, has been substantially delayed. You are going to be 90 minutes late arriving in Des Moines, and you are not even on the ground in Chicago yet. A colleague of equal status and pay is to pick you up in Des Moines. Should you call?

    c. It's your secretary's birthday. You forgot to say anything, and you forgot to purchase a gift. It's 10:00 a.m., and you are over Ohio; you will be on the ground in Chicago for over an hour. What should you do?

23. *Videoconferencing Procedures.* Reynolds has videoconferencing, but to date it has been available for only top-level executives. It is now being made available to managers down to the department head level, people unfamiliar with the technology and the basic "how to's" of videoconferencing. On the other hand, Reynolds has an oral communication training program for all managers so they can attempt to be at ease in public speaking.

You and two other department heads are introduced to videoconferencing by the system's director. The three of you are to then prepare a handout of hints for your colleagues who will be using the system.

Take on the role of that group and prepare the handout. You should review some current nontechnical articles on videoconferencing to help you understand such systems and how the manager can adjust to this new conference technique.

24. *Holding Out for the Old Way.* As we learn about organizations and their communication technologies, we sometimes overlook one of the big bugs. Simply, old-fashioned managers (not chronologically old, but mentally old) will not adapt to nor adopt modern ways. There are thousands of managers across the nation who have PC's on their desks collecting dust; there are those who will battle traffic and sit for hours on a plane before they would walk down the hall and engage in a videoconference; there are those who will insist on dictating a message "live" to a secretary and having the secretary make a draft copy and then type it and finally send it in first-class U.S. mail rather than use the electronic mail system.

   As Director of Training for Allis, Inc., prepare (outline) a training program for "backward" managers that will attack this problem on two fronts:

   a. Overcome the mental or psychological barriers to using and becoming comfortable with modern communication technologies.

   b. Train the managers in the efficient use of the technologies, showing them how it makes them more effective and productive.

25. *First-hand Report.* To gain an appreciation of the modern technologies, conduct a study with long-term secretaries (by interviews) to determine (1) what changes have taken place in the office in the past twenty-five years, (2) how the changes have changed the job of the secretary, and (3) how the changes have changed personal relations in the organization.

   Interview at least three secretaries; use individual or group interviews. After interviewing, prepare a one-page report that answers the three questions above.

COMMUNICATION CHECK-UPS

26. Greater understanding of the basic management skills was gained from the seminar.

27. The production process known as Just-in-Time is similar to a Japanese production scheme.

28. The new service, "Rap-Mail," I believe, will decrease your telecommunication costs by 15% *and* will virtually double the transmission speed of your data.

29. It is with great pleasure that I write this report.

30. Here at Frederick's the MBO concept is used in each department.

31. More record stores are opening, thus creating a demand for our product.

32. Please consider this item—it is a winner!

33. If you have any further questions, please don't hesitate to contact the undersigned.

34. Please let me hear from you at your earliest convenience.

35. The Company does not have the expertease.

Executive
Introduction

 **Leaseway Transportation**

Charles B. Lounsbury
Senior Vice President

Leaseway Transportation Corp.
3700 Park East Drive
Cleveland, Ohio 44122
216-765-5440

Professor Albert McGregor
Department of Marketing
Seaburg University
Seattle, Washington 98122

Re: The Short Report

Dear Mr. McGregor:

It will be a privilege to prepare an article for your University's
Business Journal. The topic is one that executives will find both
timely and relevant.

In the highly competitive transportation industry, the rapid transmittal of information can provide a key marketing differentiator.
Shippers require timely and accurate reports on goods-in-transit to
meet critical "Just-in-Time" production schedules. The short report is
vital in the movement of data in today's organization.

Drawing upon the substance of business communication courses, I will
cover the following key elements in the article:

Reader Ease: The short report is meant to make access to the
data easy. Therefore, the subject statement, headings, brevity, and
use of appended materials assist the reader in accessing and digesting
information.

Psychology: Often overlooked is the psychology of the short
report. It must look short, be short, and quickly relate information
to the reader.

Kinds: Used for a variety of purposes, short reports include
abstracts of industry trends, informational pieces, progress reports,
employee evaluations, and proposals that highlight and present
specific target markets.

Short reports are critical to the success of our corporation, and
every manager prepares several weekly. If you have any suggestions,
please call me collect.

Sincerely,

Charles B Lounsbury

Charles B. Lounsbury

CBL/cf

Reporting Briefly: The Short Report

WHAT YOU CAN LEARN BY STUDYING THIS CHAPTER

Whereas the inquiry letter is the workhorse of the organization, the short report is the collector and mover of the information the manager gathers. There are many kinds of short reports. In this chapter you will learn the fundamentals of all reports, the basics of research for preparing reports, and the intricacies of the reports managers most frequently prepare—informational reports, abstracts, progress reports, employee evaluation reports, and proposal reports. Formats, logical systems, courtesies, and techniques for appending materials are clearly illustrated so that you will have a basis for preparing both short and long reports.

The what and why of business reports

As you have learned, most of the information you need to do your job can be obtained in one-page letters and memos. But after you have gathered those data, sometimes they must be combined, assembled, and reported in more depth. This is where the report comes in. Business reports can be either short (less than one page, as with some memo-reports) or very long (as with reports comprising a detailed history, analysis, and recommendation).

Short reports are exceedingly common in organizations.

If you were to review some of the earlier examples in this text (like Figure 2.4), you would discover that you have already seen many short reports. Reporting is an ongoing aspect of most organizations; most companies have rather formal reporting procedures, and some reports must be submitted on a regular basis, such as a quarterly report of expenditures or an annual report of absences.

Do not confuse the business report with a college term paper. There are substantial differences! Term papers often have no purpose other than to sharpen the investigative and writing skills of students. In business, reports are assigned to meet a definite purpose (not to meet a page-length stipulation, such as "Write a twenty-page term paper"). The business report is not busy work; *it is a crucial tool in the organization's decision-making process.* Although you may have become discouraged with term papers and jumped to the conclusion that reports are nonsense, be sure you don't reach that illogical conclusion when studying and preparing business reports.

Business reports are not term papers!

Before turning to the short report, let's look at some fundamentals that are applicable for all reports.

KEYS FOR SUCCESSFUL REPORTS

The fundamentals of communication, as presented in the first four chapters, do not change as we look at reports.

Know Your Purpose

Before starting to write a report, know *why* you are preparing it; reports can have any number of purposes, such as:

Know why you are writing the report.

- **to determine** if the L.A.-area SnakShops should return to 24-hour operations.
- **to evaluate** the potential of out-sourcing foundry operations.
- **to recommend** an individual to be the head of the marketing department.

Know Your Reader(s)

Know who will use the report.

Who the reader is will strongly influence what is contained in the report; most of the time, the busy manager does not want to be retold what he or she already knows. Look at your purpose, and focus the information on what this particular reader or readers need to know.

Know Your Terms

Much time and effort can be wasted by reports with terminology that causes confusion; do not assume your reader knows vague terms—define them in working language. Consider this statement: "To determine how to inform employees of the new automatic material handling system." What employees—exempt or nonexempt? Be sure your reader knows. In more formal and longer reports, there may be an entire section on terms. In shorter reports, terms can be defined in the text when the explanation is short.

Select your language and terminology carefully.

Know Your Procedures

How you go about obtaining the data for your report influences not only what you write, but also the conclusions you reach. Therefore, the procedures you select for obtaining data are very important. How will you obtain information to answer your questions—mail questionnaires, personal interviews, library search, observation, or computer simulation?

Carefully consider how you will obtain the information.

Know Your Limitations

Academics often have unlimited time to pursue a research question; unfortunately, business organizations generally have very limited time. So time may be one limitation on the procedure you select for obtaining information. You must consider limitations in establishing the purpose and procedures. Other important limitations might include staff assistance and money.

Be realistic in how you will accomplish the purpose.

Know Your Plan

Once the purpose, terms, procedures, and limitations are in order, you can create your plan by outlining the report. You will recall that the outline need not be neatly typed (although with PCs and word processors it is easy to create neat documents). The outline is a working document—and you should not go to work without it.

Outline before writing—it aids organization and saves time.

Know Your Sources

There are two kinds of sources of data, secondary and primary. In college term papers, students generally use secondary (library) sources—books, magazines, newspapers, reports, government documents, and the multitude of indexes that are guides to the appropriate secondary sources.

Secondary sources generally provide historical data; since the data are published, they tend to be older, but they certainly can be helpful. With the various

Data sources change from college to business.

sophisticated computer searches available today, it is often relatively simple to identify books and articles on any subject.

Primary sources are often favored by the business decision-maker. The primary source is first-hand material—such as data obtained from talking to three professional colleagues in other firms, information you derive from an employee questionnaire, or material you gather from an experiment. Conducting interviews and administering questionnaires are the most common kinds of primary research techniques used by most managers.

THE SHORT REPORT

Some have attempted to differentiate the short report from the long report by their lengths, but as we will see, that probably is not the fundamental difference. The short report is intended to quickly and concisely move information, analyses, and decisions in the organization. A strong case can be made for the one-page maxim, although some short reports may be three or four pages. The short report emphasizes:

- Quick access to information
- Rapid readability of the material
- Ease of grappling with the data

Format

The short report uses headings, is generally in memo form (although in more formal situations it can use a letter format), and has a design that facilitates the quick transfer of information.

Subject Clues: Whether the short report is in memo or letter form, let the reader know what the message of the report is. In the memo format, the subject statement provides that information. In the letter format, include a subject line. Your reporting strategy will determine whether you use a topical or informative subject statement. See Figures 15.1 and 15.2.

Sign Clues: You have already learned that headings (road signs) are helpful in moving, clarifying, and adding interest to written materials. They are virtual necessities in reports. The headings permit the reader to quickly assess, access, and re-access information in the report.

Attachments

One way you can keep the short report short is through the creative use of attachments (enclosures and appendixes). It is helpful to use "add ons" if: (1) the material is physically too large to incorporate into the report and (2) the material is supplemental and need not appear directly in the text of the report. When items are physically too

FIGURE 15.1   Short Memo Report

Remington Manufacturing

14499 Lotus Drive
Shreveport, Louisiana 71109

TO: Bill Jennings   April 20, 19__

FR: Dave Roosevelt   _DR_

RE: The Need for a New Supervisor Evaluation Form

The Need. The current form for evaluating supervisors is ten years old. When it was developed, it was excellent. The form and its implementation in performance reviews have been accepted. However, the form no longer corresponds to the kinds of qualities that are important in supervisory performance. Therefore, the form should be modified to include the Executive Committee's focus on communication.

Old vs. New. At the time the current form was created, the emphasis was on factors believed to directly affect manufacturing, such as scheduling, routing, timeliness, and quality. Today we recognize that other less direct factors, like communication, can influence manufacturing. Therefore, these factors should also be included in the evaluation scheme.

Coordination. It is important to coordinate the philosophies at the "top" of the organization with what is implemented at the "bottom," on the factory floor. If we state a principle of good communication but don't follow up on it, very little will happen. But, if the Executive Committee (1) states the importance of and its concern for effective communication and then (2) follows up with a new evaluation form incorporating that factor, then the operative personnel will know it is important and that they must address the problem.

New Form. The change is relatively easy to implement. Attachment A shows the current form, and Attachment B indicates how the evaluation form could be altered to incorporate communication skills. This can be done without lengthening the form and without increasing its complexity.

This draft is for your review and discussion with others. Will you please review it to see if it is practical and realistically implements the factor that the Executive Committee desires?

Attachments

c: Brenda Jenkins, Director
     Human Resources

Note informality in typed names; titles not used.

Quickly the history and situation are presented.

Note the deductive approach.

Attachments help keep actual report short.

FIGURE 15.2   Short Letter Report

Remington Manufacturing   14499 Lotus Drive
                                               Shreveport, Louisiana 71109

Letter format lends
formality to the
communication.

Mr. William J. Jennings   April 20, 198_
V.P. Manufacturing
Building C

Dear Mr. Jennings:

Subject statements
in letters can aid
communication.

SUBJECT: The Supervisor's Communication

The Situation. The Executive Committee's emphasis on improving internal communications is an idea many feel is vital if we are to improve our operations. About ten years
ago, we started the formal evaluation process for supervisors. Currently, the system is
working well, and at least 90 percent of the evaluators take it very seriously.

The logic is
inductive.

Evaluate What? Clearly, what is evaluated in such forms reflects what the company
feels is important. In the original form (Attachment A), it is clear that manufacturing
factors are the focus. Today we see other factors contributing directly to the process.

Coordination. The Committee has emphasized the need to improve the way supervisors
interact and communicate with their employees. There is a need to coordinate the wishes
of the Committee with the activity on the shop floor.

New Form. The Committee should consider revising the current supervisor evaluation
form to include a section on communication. It would provide explicit direction on how
to look at the complex phenomenon of communication. (See Attachment B.)

Certainly the way communication is actually articulated on the form will need
discussion and review; however, the idea that "communication" needs to be on the form
is one whose day has come. Please contact me if you wish any further explanation.

Sincerely,

David Roosevelt

David J. Roosevelt
Personnel Assistant

Note the formality
in names and
signatures.

Attachments

c: Brenda Jenkins, Director
    Human Resources

large to be included—but are crucial to the report—make sure the reader understands that they are not supplemental. To keep the text of the short report short, however, you should learn techniques for using attachments.

The Psychology of Attachments.   Readers who want to handle information quickly can become discouraged if they see a huge, thirty-two-page report. However, if three of those pages are the report and twenty-nine pages are attachments (that may or may not need to be read), the psychological effect on the reader can be positive; the report suddenly becomes much more manageable. Remember this guideline: If the data are necessary in order for the reader to understand the report, then those data must be a part of the report. On the other hand, if the data may be useful, helpful, or of interest to the reader, then they can be appended. The *reader* makes the decision about what to read.

Who reads the report influences what is appended.

Packaging Attachments. How you package your attachments also influences how your report will be received. In the case of the short report that has lengthy attachments, it is a good idea to use one of the following techniques for differentiating the three-page report from the twenty-nine pages of attachments:

Recognize the different ways to append materials.

Separate: Physically separate the attachments from the three-page report. This clearly communicates to the reader that he or she need only read the short report—not the whole package (see Figure 15.3A).

Subdivide: Similar to separate packages, the subdivided attachment is separated from the report by a title sheet or a tab that clearly shows the reader what is the report and what is supplemental (see Figure 15.3B).

Color Differentiation: If the twenty-nine pages of material are on regular typing paper and, at first glance, could appear to be part of the total report, consider placing the appended items on colored paper (see Figure 15.3C).

KINDS OF SHORT REPORTS

Short reports can be categorized in many ways, such as by their frequency—weekly, quarterly, and annual reports; by their format—memo and letter reports; or by their subject—informational, abstract, and progress reports. We will focus on the most common subjects of reports.

Informational Reports

All reports are really informational reports, but some are subcategorized because of the type of information they transmit—abstract, progress, or employee evaluation. All short informational reports analyze and quickly move data gathered by the communicator. They are often topical—that is, relating to a specific subject on which

The informational base of short reports.

FIGURE 15.3   Techniques for Differentiating Appendixes

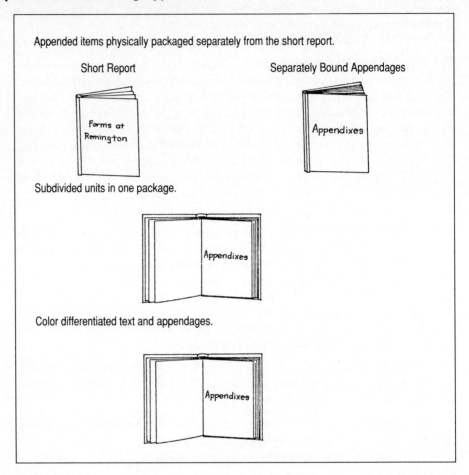

Appended items physically packaged separately from the short report.

Short Report   Separately Bound Appendages

Forms at Remington   Appendixes

Subdivided units in one package.

Appendixes

Color differentiated text and appendages.

Appendixes

the reader desires information or a recommendation: the zoning laws in East Peoria; the requirements for quality certification; how to obtain ASPA's mailing list.

The informational report can move inductively or deductively. It uses headings generously and concisely and provides all the information needed by the reader. The example in Figure 15.4 leaves the reader well informed about the research results. This report might be criticized for overusing lists, but it does transfer the information rapidly, and it allows the reader to pick out and re-access that information.

The Abstract

For situations in which it is necessary to summarize material for a superior in the organization, the abstract (or summary) is used. Although you may have learned to abstract an article as a part of a college assignment, many more kinds of communication are abstracted in business; it is common to abstract meetings, conferences, and reports. By its very nature, the abstract is short; it is generally written because (1) the person for whom it is prepared does not have time to read the entire piece but wishes to remain informed of the overall situation, or (2) the writer feels the item would be of interest to specific individuals and summarizes the material, or (3) in the case of a meeting or conference, the reader was unable to attend and needs to have a sense of the meeting.

Abstracts are written for the reader—maintain that focus.

Without fluff or any extra seasonings, the abstract quickly presents the primary ideas of the original work or activity. It is quite possible that the reader will use the information to formulate ideas or opinions and make decisions; therefore, the abstract needs to be a complete and accurate representation of the full communication.

The abstract in business is probably not like others you have done in college; those are generally done for the writer's benefit. In business, they are for the reader's benefit—the focus and purpose are substantially different.

As with any communication, the more you know about the reader and what he or she is going to do with the information, the better job you can do of formulating your purpose and providing the reader with what he or she needs. In Figure 15.5, the writer was asked to prepare an abstract of the article "The Uses of Meetings" by Norman Sigband; the abstract is needed so that the reader can implement changes in the way she conducts departmental meetings. Note how the memo is written; it meets the needs of the reader, uses headings, and concisely brings the reader up to steam on the subject. If the reader wants to see the actual article, it is attached, but the abstract can stand on its own.

Compare the abstract in Figure 15.5 to the actual article in the readings.

The Progress Report

Managers need to know the status of various projects and activities. Therefore, the progress report is common. The purpose of a progress report, as its name indicates, can be to reveal the status and schedule of an ongoing activity or to provide an evaluation of an event or project.

Certainly such reports do not contain only good news; sometimes there are problems. The progress report might include some elements of the sales communication. If the project upon which you are reporting is your responsibility, you want to look good. You have a vested interest in selling the facts in the best way possible.

The following are some of the common subjects that may be covered in progress reports:

- The current status: an overview of how matters currently stand.
- Problem areas: what are some of the problems *and* what are you doing to solve them?
- Changes: if procedures or operations have changed, be sure the reader is informed.
- Schedule: is the project on schedule? If not, what is being done to catch up?
- Costs: is the project within the budget? If over, indicate what you are doing to get costs under control.

Common elements of progress reports.

FIGURE 15.4   Short Informational Report

Tremendous amounts of information can be incorporated in a short report.

Headings highlight each important point.

MEMORANDUM

```
TO:  Joe Battoe, Vice President
     Personnel and Consumer Relations
FR:  Bill Allen  BA
     Research and Development
DATE:    March 31, 198_
SUBJ:    Improving Productivity at the Checkout Counter
```

Summary of Checkout Services Research
Last January, it was proposed that a study be conducted to determine how FoodCo could improve customer service. New scanning technology had been installed but it had not resulted in the anticipated productivity gains. The project was approved on January 10, 198_.

Methodology of the Study
The research firm Findings Incorporated was employed to complete 500 customer interviews (100 at each of our five stores). In addition, 100 employees were surveyed by mail. On February 23, the results of the survey and some recommendations were delivered to us by Findings Incorporated.

Results of the Consumer Survey
   No Greeting: Eighty percent of the consumers stated that they were not greeted at the checkout stand.
   No Sacker: Eighty-five percent stated that there was no one to sack the groceries. The customers either sacked for themselves or the checker sacked after scanning the purchases.
   No Thanks: Sixty-five percent were not thanked for their patronage.

Results of Employee Survey
   Poor Layout: Seventy percent of the employees feel that the layout of the checkout counter makes it impossible to greet and talk with the customer.
   Long Lines: Eighty percent of the employees feel that when there is a line of customers to be checked out (which is virtually all the time) they feel uncomfortable taking time to talk to the customer.
   Unfamiliarity: Fifty percent of the employees feel unfamiliar with the new scanner process and find it difficult to pay attention to anything else.

Recommendations

Based on our analysis of the data from Findings Incorporated, the following recommendations were made:

Training: Establish a training program to more thoroughly familiarize checkers with the new scanning system.

Improve Layout: Redesign the checkout counters at one of the stores so that the checker can unload the basket and have more direct contact with the customer. If successful, implement at other stores.

Emphasize Customer Relations: Develop an incentive program in which a checker will be selected as "Checker of the Month" by the store manager. The selection will be based on customer relations and productivity. The winner's picture will be prominantly posted and a $100 FoodCo gift certificate will be awarded.

Actions Taken

The recommendations were implemented as follows:

Training: The first training session on scanners was held in Store #1 on March 15; the other four stores are scheduled for training during April.

Checkout Counters: New checkout counters were installed in Store #1 on March 16.

Checker Recognition: Information concerning the "Checker of the Month" program was included with all employee checks on March 20.

Tentative Results

Training: Productivity has increased by almost 20 percent for those employees who completed the training.

Counters: At Store #1, the checkers like the new counters very much. In observing the customers and checkers it is obvious that there is more conversation between them than in the other stores—and this is accompanied with increased productivity.

Recognition: It will be one more month before the "Checker of the Month" program starts, but the checkers are already talking it up.

It is difficult to identify exactly which factor is contributing to the productivity increase, but it is obvious that this combination is working well. Training should be completed by all checkers by May 1; and the new counters will be installed in the other stores as soon as possible, but no later than April 20.

The report solves the problem and keeps the reader up to date.

FIGURE 15.5   A Short Report: The Abstract

K a t h y ' s   T e m p o r a r i e s

8765 Third Street
Denver, CO   80220

TO: Donna Wrightworth, Director
        Employment Office

FROM: Tom Henry, Office Administrator

DATE: March 28, 198_

SUBJ: Abstract of Sigband Article, "The Uses of Meetings," Nation's
       Business, February, 1987, p. 28R.

Illegitimate Uses of Meetings
Frequently these days managers call meetings not to discuss new ideas
and solve problems, but to "cover" themselves. Instead of taking
responsibility of making decisions that should be made, the manager will
call a meeting to secure consensus. Then, if the results of the decision
should turn out negatively, the manager can simply say, "The decision
was made by the meeting members and not by me."

Meetings Cost Money
Meetings are expensive communication sessions. When twelve people
assemble for two hours, the cost to the organization can easily exceed
$500. Therefore, meetings should not be called by a manager to "cover"
himself or herself, nor should they be called to decide inconsequential
items—another trend these days.

Meeting Policies Will Help
Both of the problems listed above, can be solved by having written
company policies on meetings. Such policies should include:

1. Hold only meetings for which there is a verifiable need.
2. Decide on A purpose and series of objectives for each meeting.
3. Invite only those people who can make a definite contribution.
4. Distribute an agenda and necessary handout materials to each
   invitee prior to the session.
5. Make all mechanical arrangements (room, projectors, seating,
   transparencies, etc.) ahead of time.
6. Begin and end every meeting on schedule.

Attachment: "The Uses of Meetings"

Headings assist the
abstracting process.

Key points are em-
phasized with
language and
format.

The actual article is
attached—this is
for reader's ease; it
does not mean the
article must be
read.

A good abstract will stand on its own; reference to the article abstracted would be rather unusual.

- The future: can the projected completion date be met? Do you see any unexpected problems arising?

There are routine and nonroutine status reports; when the report is routine, the organization may have a standard form on which the writer inserts the specified data and comments. In nonroutine reports, the writer starts from scratch and creates the material (see Figure 15.6).

The Employee Evaluation Report

For many managers, the most difficult periodic report is the report on the work performance of subordinates. Generally, these reports are prepared on a standardized form, with space provided for written comments. Such a report not only reflects upon the person being evaluated, it also reflects upon the evaluator. Here are some basics to consider in writing an evaluation:

Employee evaluations have language and legal ramifications.

- Be neat; your evaluation is diminished if it is sloppy.
- Be concise; generally the forms provide little space—be sure to stick to the topic at hand.
- Be consistent; the language you use to reflect your thoughts should correspond with any ratings you make on the form.
- Be clear; often the form will be seen by the individual being evaluated; don't use fuzzy language.

Most organizations today have formalized and periodic evaluation reviews. What you write and how you write it is crucial in the retention, promotion, and development of employees. Generally, a manager must draft the writing, have it approved by his or her superior, and then place it in final form before showing it to the individual being reviewed. One reason for this is to ensure that the comments do not lead to legal problems, such as discrimination on the basis of sex. Certainly what you have to say in an evaluation is important, but the evaluation process will run more smoothly if you communicate well (see Figure 15.7).

Proposal Report

Short reports can be used to propose major projects "in brief." This specialized kind of report is rather common. The proposal report explains the project and provides the reader with relevant information about the project. It proposes the project, and the reader determines if the project should then be conducted. Note that proposals, especially to government agencies, sometimes fall into the category of the long report, the subject of Chapter 16. There is often a strong relationship between the proposal report and the eventual long report that is written if the project is implemented and completed.

Proposals state what can be done; long reports do it.

FIGURE 15.6   Nonroutine Progress Report

Background data.

Substantive data.

Financial data.

Completion data.

Kathy's   Temporaries

8765 Third Street
Denver, CO   80220

May 10, 198_

TO: Brigette Bartel, Vice President
        Planning and Administrative Services

FROM: Jim Zimmerman
        Communication Coordinator

SUBJ: Progress: The "Total Information" Project

   Status and Progress. The work of the task force studying ways in
which our diverse and geographically separated employees can be better
informed has completed about one-third of its work. The group is
committed to the goal of providing wanted and needed information.

   Options for Timely Information. A major concern is how information
can be transmitted on a timely basis. Current options under review are:

   Computer Linking: Sending information to the employees' home
   computers is rapid; however, this would affect only one-third of
   our contractees.

   Overnight Mail: The next-day mails would get the information out,
   but it would not actually be received until after work on Monday.

   Saturday Regular Mail: By preparing the item on Friday and mailing
   it on Saturday, everyone would receive it on Monday, but this may
   seem impersonal.

   Telephone Call-in: The contractees would call in and receive a
   prerecorded message; it works if the employee remembers to call.

   The major items of concern are the ease in which information can
be disseminated and the timeliness of the information.

   Cost: Because it is necessary to look at these options first-hand,
the task force requests a $5,000 increase in the travel budget so that
task force personnel can observe these techniques.

   On Schedule: The group is working together exceedingly well, the
attendance at the meetings is superb, and the various subgroups are
doing their jobs. The project is on schedule and there is every antici-
pation of having the complete recommendation to you by July 1.

FIGURE 15.7   A Periodic Form Short Report: Employee Evaluation

Administrative/Professional Skills

Indicates the employee's level of performance contribution, the level of importance, and supporting facts or comMents for the following administrative/professional skills.

Skill	Perf. Rating	Level Import.	Supporting Facts or Comments
Professional Knowledge—Stays abreast of current trends and changes in the professional/ administrative areas related to the job.	OC	M	Seems to be conversational on benefit trends; rarely calls new or innovative ideas elsewhere to my attention.
Procedures and Policies—Properly interprets and applies Allen-Bradley Company and Division policies and procedures to job .	VGC	H	Must continue to reduce errors, poor interrpetation inconveniences employee— harms company.
Planning and Organizing—Established appropriate course of action to accomplish goals; makes appropriate use of resources.	OC	H	Planning and organizing crucial part of the job; like most recent college grads—needs improved planning skills.
Decisiveness—Readiness & willingness to make decisions, render judgements, initiate actions, and commit oneself to those decisions.	VGC	H	In working with employees, there is a need to be decisive; sometimes too soft spoken.
Sense of Urgency—Ability to undertake projects with an obvious desires to meet or exceed deadlines without regular reminders.	OC	H	Responds to employees with urgency, sometimes does not respond to colleagues with sense of urgency.
Coordination—Ability to work with others toward common goals & objectives.	OC	L	Job so far is very single dimensional.
Productivity Improvement—Continually aware of and recommends/implements procedures to improve productivity.	MC	M	Problem probably newness to the job and company.
Verbal Communication—Effectiveness of expression in individual and group situations.	EX	H	Vital to relate and respond to employees effectively—she does it.
Written Communication—Ability to express ideas clearly and concisely in good grammatical form.	MC	H	Reports document our work; written needs "C's"applied!
Interpersonal Skills—Ability to perceive and react to the needs of others with appropriate sensitivlty and firmness.	MC	M	Again, perhaps newness to organization, needs more interaction.

Recommendations:
•Attend coming assertiveness training seminar.
•During next 3 years take the company's written communication course and later the one on interpersonal development.

OC–Outstanding Contributor	**UC**–Unsatisfactory Contributor	**H**–High
EX–Excellent Contributor	**NE/A**–New Assign;	**M**–Medium
VGC–Very Good Contributor	New Employee, unfair to	**L**–Low
MC–Marginal Contibutor	evaluate at this time.	

The basic elements of a proposal report are as follows:

Problem: a clear statement (often a long paragraph) of the situation; this analysis puts a fence around the topic to be studied.

Purpose: a clear statement (a sentence or less) that explicitly indicates what will be done; this statement focuses on the specifics.

Definitions: the terms in the purpose are defined, ensuring understanding.

Procedures: explicitly state how the research will be conducted (library research, questionnaires, interviews, and so on).

Limitations: in this situation, the limitations of the procedures, such as allowing only people in a thirty-mile radius to be interviewed.

Time and money factors: the length of the project and the costs.

As a manager, you will prepare proposals and ask others to prepare them for you. When you are considering hiring a consultant to conduct a study "To determine the feasibility of leasing back your fifteen division offices instead of owning them," you will ask for a proposal; if you accept it, then the work will be done and eventually a long report written. In this case, you can see the relationship between the short report that proposes the research, the actual research, and the long report that analyzes the data and presents recommendations.

THE COMPUTER AND THE SHORT REPORT

PCs aid the preparation of many short reports—especially routine ones.

A writer with a storehouse of data may find a personal computer of great help in preparing the routine short report. The computer can quickly manipulate the data in numerous ways. It can also store and insert repeated chunks of text as necessary. Even though the short report is not lengthy, it can consume considerable amounts of preparation time. Any assistance the writer can get from the computer will reduce that time.

QUICK REVIEW

Short reports can be categorized by their subject, by when they are prepared, and by their format. In actuality, the categories are relatively unimportant to the manager; but it is good to know the various styles and techniques for preparing them. Regardless of the kind of short report and what the writer does to keep it short, remember that the objective is to move information in a manner that allows quick access, rapid readability, and ease of grappling with and reaccessing the data. This is all accomplished by employing the various "keys" that are applicable for any report—long or short.

EXECUTIVE SUMMARY

To: Business Communication Students

From: David N. Bateman and Norman B. Sigband

Subject: Reporting Briefly: The Short Report

The report is a crucial tool in the organization's decision-making process. To produce effective reports, short or long, business communicators must know their purpose, reader(s), terms, procedures, limitations, plans, and sources.

The most obvious difference between the short report and the long report is length, but the more fundamental difference is in purpose. The short report is intended to move information, analyses, and even decisions quickly and concisely in the organization. Often only a page long, it generally uses a memo format, although the letter format is also a possibility. Guides, like subject lines and heads, make the report easier to follow. Supplemental or supporting material can be added to the short report as attachments.

The short report can be usefully classified by subject, as informational, progress, abstract, employee evaluation, or proposal report.

DISCUSSION GENERATORS

1. *Another Hard One?* Many people feel that writing a letter of sympathy is difficult. One kind of short report was noted in this chapter as being difficult for some people to write. Which report is that, and why do you suppose it is difficult for many people?

2. *Differentiate.* Clearly differentiate between a college term paper and a short business report.

3. *Report Keys.* What are the keys for successful reports, and why are they applicable for all reports?

4. *Purpose.* Quickly state a situation, and then from that evolve a purpose statement for a short report. For example: When the campus has a three-day holiday (no classes on Monday), there is an increase in absenteeism on the preceding Friday. Purpose: To recommend a procedure that will reduce Friday absences prior to three-day weekends.

5. *Terminology.* Why is it important for the reader and writer to agree on the terms in the report? How does the writer of the short report make sure there is agreement? Cite an example of potential term confusion relating to your future profession (e.g., human resources: employees, exempt or nonexempt employees).

6. *Limitations. Limitations* are not the limitations of the person doing the short report, but of the research methods employed to gather the data. Cite an example of a research limitation, and explain it in detail.

7. *Decision-making.* In college term papers, the emphasis seems to be on drawing data from secondary sources and writing a report for the writer. In business, the data often come from primary sources and clearly the report is written to inform

other people. In your profession, cite examples of reports you would write for your boss that would help him or her in making decisions.

8. *Sources.* Differentiate and explain primary and secondary sources that can be used in short reports. Cite examples of each.

9. *Business Preferences.* What category of source, primary or secondary, does the business manager generally use and why?

10. *What Is It?* Is it the length or something else that differentiates the short report from the long report?

11. *Letter vs. Memo.* In what kind of situation might the writer use a letter format instead of the memorandum format for an internal report? Explain.

12. *Attention!* Explain the use, placement, and convenience of the subject line in the short report.

13. *Sign Clues.* What are the "sign clues" the authors note? To what are they analogous in the authors' minds?

14. *Choice.* Why does placing items in an attachment to the short report give the reader some "choice," whereas the reader has little "choice" if that same material is incorporated into the text of the report?

15. *College vs. Business.* What is the basic difference between an abstract prepared for a college course and one prepared for your boss in the organization?

16. *Progress Elements.* What are the elements included in a progress report?

17. *Employee Evaluations.* What are the basics to consider in writing employee evaluations, and why are they important?

18. *Routine and Nonroutine Short Reports.* If a short report is routine, what will the organization probably do to standardize the report? Why?

19. *In or Out?* What is the basic guideline for deciding whether some material for the short report belongs in the text of the report or appended to the report?

20. *Psychological Advantage.* If you prepare a three-page short report that has a twenty-seven-page attachment, how do you gain a psychological advantage with the reader when you package those two items separately?

APPLICATIONS FOR BUSINESS

21. *Info Needed.* Your instructor desires to become better informed about on-campus happenings. In a one-page memo report, prepare an informational piece that will (a) inform the reader of three activities and (b) indicate what students learn from each. Use an informative subject statement and vertical lists with headings.

22. *Evaluate Yourself.* In a small group, develop an employee evaluation sheet, modeling it somewhat after the one in Figure 15.7. This form is to evaluate your performance in this class. Be sure your group names the appropriate skills; then be sure your evaluation is fair, in depth, and well formatted. After you develop the form, your instructor may ask you to complete it—either evaluating your or another student's performance.

23. *PC Networking.* Your boss is considering developing a PC networking activity in

your department. Find an article that would be of interest to him or her and prepare an abstract.

24. *Progress for Parents.* Your parents have been supporting you in college. Prepare a one-page progress report for them on the progress you are making toward earning a college degree.

25. *Slides Up, Doors Closed.* You are the director of research and development for a large chemical company, Wilco Organics, in Wilmington, Delaware. This morning you met with your staff of project leaders and assigned each a specific task for the forthcoming open house. This is the time when the company opens its lab for one day for informative lectures and tours. Many of the visitors are curious about new products being developed; therefore, your department will be very busy that day and very concerned about preventing improper access to confidential proprietary information. You have planned a slide presentation to be presented by Dr. Bankowski, an introductory lecture in the auditorium given by you, demonstrations in the lab to be given by Dr. Willis and Mr. Jacobs, and a tour of your section to be led by Ms. Rosen. Prepare a brief memo report to review with these project leaders just what will be happening on Friday, June 14.

COMMUNICATION CHECK-UPS

26. With your hectic schedule you would certainly enjoy having unexpected guests arrive and simultaneously have added work dropped on you by your boss.

27. How to deal with the aforementioned dilemmas are problems for architects, lawyers, and accountants.

28. You want to determine the following: Who is the audience; What does the audience want to know; What is the current knowledge of the audience; and, What is their attitude towards the subject you are to present.

29. After the regional officers have been able to answer such questions they will be prepared to meet with you.

30. Teambuilding consists of
Letting co-workers know about each other's work experience.
Each person indicating a hobby they enjoy.
Have group sessions to discuss the departmental goals.

31. The introduction should be interesting enough to make the employees want to pay attention to the rest of the topic.

32. Avoid leading questions that could give away what the interviewer is looking for and change the answer of the applicant.

33. The structure of the organization has been changing so rapidly these last couple of weeks that it has been hard to keep up with it.

34. If you have any questions in regard to our product or the quality thereof, please contact me. Thank you for your attention to this matter. I look forward to hearing from you.

35. This device is designed to be attached to the mailbox. Enclosed you will find a sample of what the device looks like. As you can see this device is very simple.

Executive
Introduction

Firestone

November 17, 198_

Susan Mahoney
Scanlon Coordinator
Firestone
P.O. Box 7927
Wilson, NC 27893

Dear Sue:

   The Problem you described on writing productive long reports
exists in most organizations. We have faced similar problems; you may
find the following material helpful.

   The Approach was to (1) determine our problems, (2) ascertain
what was needed in long reports, and then (3) bring in an expert to
train our managers. The consultant, Dr. Norman Sigband of the University of Southern California, conducted a three-day seminar on the
basics of long reports. Enclosed is the seminar packet he designed.

   The Basics of the long report have now been applied effectively.

   The Why of the long report (why the firm needs them).
   The Who of the long report (who prepares and who reads them).
   The Purposes of the long report (why we write them).
   The Strategies of the long report (focusing on the purpose).
   The Parts of the long report (what is to be included).
   The Effectiveness of the long report (ways to have impact).

   The Results have been most beneficial. Not only do we write
better, we know how to make the long report work for us in the large
organization.

   I hope this description will help you; if there are other ways in
which we can assist you, please let me know. Organizations are often
weighted down with long reports; we know how to make them lighter so
that they can "rise" in our organization.

                                    Sincerely,

                                    Jim

                                    James E. Stirrett
                                    Personnel Manager

Enclosure: Seminar Packet

Reporting in Depth: The Long Report

WHAT YOU CAN LEARN BY STUDYING THIS CHAPTER

In this chapter you will see that virtually all of the basic elements of communication come together in the long report: the writer needs to know not only about the organization and strategies of the long report, but also about the ways to implement the message so it will be accepted by and useful to the reader. Envisioning, planning, and executing the long report are all explained in this chapter, as are the managerial ramifications of these basic steps. A variety of elements are introduced, including letters of transmittal, synopses, and internal citations.

The long report is the result of diligent research and hard work; writers must understand a number of factors before they can prepare effective long reports.

Formality

As you have observed, the business letter is somewhat formal, and the memorandum is less formal. Similarly, the long report is more formal than the short report. By its length, parts, and the elements within each part, the long report "gets all dressed up" to take its reader on a careful review of a comprehensive investigation of a subject.

Functions

The long report can serve any of a variety of functions in an organization: first, to gather data and present research that managers need to know; second, to record history; third, to project plans and future developments; and fourth, to draw conclusions and make recommendations. There is also a fifth, "unspoken" function of the long report: In some instances, the analysis and research may be more to impress and for show than for realistic actual use. Fortunately, this function is rare.

Foundation

If written and received properly, the long report provides a data base—a foundation—upon which analyses can proceed and decisions can be made.

WHO WRITES AND WHO READS LONG REPORTS?

Who writes?

In some situations, the long report may be written by one person. However, it is not uncommon today for the long report to be written by a small group, task force, or team. Various experts come together, are given a problem, and then report their results in a long report. Groups have a number of options as to how they might physically write the long report. Sections may be assigned to different individuals. Then, one person may concentrate on the whole so that the resulting report has a unified flow.

Who reads?

What makes long reports intriguing, and somewhat tricky to write, is that readers with different backgrounds often read different parts of the long report. As we look at the parts of the long report, we must keep that factor in mind. Quite often a high-level manager in the organization wants only an overview and the answer, so that person may read only the synopsis. Someone lower in the organization, and perhaps closer to the problem being studied, needs more information and reads the synopsis and the recommendations. On the other hand, individuals close to the problem and more deeply involved in the detail will be interested in the body of the report, where specific data are described and analyzed.

The point is that the entire report is important, but different parts are going to be important to different readers in the organization. So, as emphasized in the first chapter, always know the receiver(s) of your communication and tune in; in writing long reports, the "tuning" activity can be complex for the writer.

PURPOSES OF THE LONG REPORT

As with short reports, the purposes of reports can be varied; in fact, it is not unusual in a long report to have multiple purposes, such as:

Know and adhere to your purpose(s).

- to trace the history of college interns at Walt Disney World;
- to analyze the changes in the college intern today; and
- to recommend alternative training programs for college interns.

As with any communication, be sure the purpose is what the reader(s) is expecting and that you have focused it correctly. The purpose is basic; if it is off target, the whole report will be off and its recommendations invalid.

In developing the purpose, be sure you know your job. Are you just to analyze or are you also to draw conclusions? Or are you to analyze, conclude, and then make recommendations? Your purpose will indicate what you are doing and where you are stopping.

STRATEGIES

One of the more difficult aspects of the long report is understanding, and properly implementing, strategy. Your strategy is more complex than the purpose statement; by definition, the purpose is straightforward, simple, and clear. On the other hand, your strategy—exactly how you go about achieving your purpose—can be murky and much less precise—but nevertheless very important. Strategy addresses such questions as:

Purpose vs. strategy

- If I know the reader will initially disagree with my recommendation(s), how do I win him or her over?
- What logical system for presenting data can I use to accomplish the purpose?
- What appeals will work best for the reader?
- What kinds of proof should be employed and in what order?

The purpose identifies what you are going to accomplish, and the strategy indicates how you are going to get your communications through the maze. Developing and implementing strategy is hard enough in a one-page memo; in the long report—with its multiple readers, parts, and elements—the strategy takes careful thought.

Communication strategies at work

If you assume that the reader will agree with your recommendations, for example, you might use a deductive approach. The "answer" is stated up front, and then data supporting the recommendations are presented. On the other hand, if you assume that the reader will not immediately accept the recommendation, you might use an inductive approach.

As you start to look at the various elements of the long report, you must understand strategy, otherwise you are simply looking at pieces of paper without understanding their implications. Certainly your strategy determines what you say in the synopsis and the transmittal and what you include in the appendixes. Therefore, you must know your strategy before you begin to outline the long report.

Matching your strategy and report elements

PARTS OF THE LONG REPORT

We are going to look at the parts of the long report in their order in the report. Remember, however, that you will not think through nor write them in this order. In actuality, most of the first part (the front matter) is prepared last, and sometimes material in an appendix (at the end) is prepared early on in the process. Appendix C

Order of development

clearly illustrates each of the elements of the long report; it would be advantageous to study it and the figures in this chapter as you read this material.

The long report is a detailed, formal presentation, whereas the short report accomplishes its task in as little as one page of narrative. Much of the formality is evident at the very start of the report. Just as you need to know which fork to pick up first at a formal dinner, you need to know if the synopsis precedes the contents and also what each does in the long report. There are three basic parts to a long report: the front matter, the information and analysis, and the end matter.

The Front Matter: The Preliminaries

The first part of any long report is devoted to preliminary matters. Some of these are formalities that depend on company policy. Others are meant to prepare readers for the materials that follow.

Cover and Binding.   Generally, the cover is the last item prepared; however, it is an item to think about from the start. Covers need not always be bland and dull; graphics and other forms of nonverbal communication on the cover can add interest and intrigue to the long report.

As you saw in Chapter 6, a variety of techniques is available for binding the report. The amount of use, the need for others to photocopy portions of the report, and expense considerations will influence your binding decision. Figure 6.9 illustrates various binding techniques and indicates the advantages and disadvantages of each.

Title Page.   As labeled, the title page reports the title—and much more: primary reader(s) and title(s), primary author(s) and title(s), and date and place of preparation. Generally, this information is neatly spread out on the entire page and centered, unless a cover with a cut-out opening designed to show this information is used.

Do not overlook the possibility of accomplishing several objectives with the title—to stir interest, to increase inquisitiveness, and to capture the reader's imagination. They can often be accomplished through the use of alliteration, parallelism, and subtitles. Titles of business reports need not be dull.

Authorization Letter.   In some organizations, especially governmental units, the writer will have a letter authorizing the research and the report. That "charge" is included and forms the basis for the "why" of the report that follows.

Transmittal Letter.   In letter format, the transmittal literally passes the report to the reader(s). This letter should do much more than say "here is the report." For instance, it can gain the interest of the reader, thank individuals who assisted, and "sell" the receiver on reading the report and "buying" its recommendations. The letter can accomplish one or more of the following tasks:

Credibility: Establish your qualifications to conduct the research and write the report;

Purpose: State the purpose of the project briefly.

Limitations: Cite any major limitations of the report, such as interviewing few people because of vacation schedules or using a limited mail sample because of financial constraints.

Findings: Summarize the basic findings briefly and note the recommendation(s) if a synopsis is not used.

Acknowledgments: Recognize those who assisted in the preparation of the report.

The transmittal has strategic implications and the writer must plan the transmittal letter carefully. For instance, if you are presenting a recommendation that initially may be received unfavorably, you should not attempt to present and explain it in two or three sentences in the letter of transmittal. You will want the reader to get the full impact by reading more of the report and noting the logical steps that you followed to reach that recommendation. In that situation, omit the recommendation from the transmittal letter, and concentrate on such factors as the research method, basic findings, and the expression of appreciation to those who assisted you.

Know your transmittal strategy.

The transmittal takes time to prepare; too often report writers spend hours writing the report and just a few moments writing the transmittal. Most likely the transmittal letter will be the first page the reader will study carefully. As you know, first impressions are important. You can make or break your case by the way you handle the transmittal letter. (See Figure 16.1.)

Table of Contents. In the long report, reader ease—being able to access and re-access information—is vital. In the short report, headings are important in leading the reader; in the long report, the headings (the road signs) are equally important, along with the basic "map"—the table of contents. Generally, the more detailed the table of contents, the easier it will be to locate information. Again remember that not all readers are going to read the entire report. Some may want to read the synopsis and then gain added detail by jumping to particular individual pages of the report. A complete and well-formatted table of contents helps the reader locate what he or she wants to read.

The contents provide the map.

At the very least, the table of contents presents the major divisions of the report and indicates their respective pages. If the report is lengthy and has numerous subdivisions, those subdivisions can be noted, either with or without page notations. (See Figure 16.2.) Do not take the contents for granted; think how you want it to appear and how detailed it should be. Also, recognize that in the formality of the long report, different pages literally have their page numbers placed on them in different ways and perhaps in different places. See Figure 16.3 for a clear explanation of pagination.

FIGURE 16.1   Letter of Transmittal That Does Not Reveal the Recommendation

R E Y N O L D S

A S S O C I A T I O N

M A N A G E M E N T

C O M P A N Y

September 2, 198_

Formal letter format.

Mr. Toney Chevez, Director
Internship Relations and Programs
Walt Disney World
Building 17-C
Snow White Village
Orlando, FL 33101

Dear Mr. Chevez:

Positive start.

   The opportunity to return to WDW and conduct this study for you has been most rewarding. The results will be of particular interest to you as the research revealed a wealth of data about the training and internship program.

Purpose presented.

Findings.

   Some of the major findings include:
   – Multicultural. The interns enjoy the opportunity to meet, live with, and exchange ideas with individuals of different countries and cultures.
   – Responsibility. The on-the-job responsibilities and the structure of the work are seen as excellent preparation for future employment.
   – Helpful Staff. The WDW permanent staff is seen as particularly helpful in aiding the interns to understand and do their jobs.
   – WDW Attitude. The attitude that the customer is a guest and that employees are "performers" creates an approach that is transferable to one's future profession.

Acknowledgments.

Friendly closing.

   Several people were instrumental in supplying me with information and insight: Tom Jones in the employment office, Barbara Jasper, and Jerri Pullen in Information Services. It was refreshing to see the team spirit of WDW in action.
   If you have any questions or comments, please contact me.

Sincerely,

Tom Dennis

Tom Dennis
Intern

9303 Wacker Drive
Chicago, IL   60605

FIGURE 16.2 Table of Contents

TABLE OF CONTENTS

TABLE OF TABLES

iii

FIGURE 16.3   Paginating the Long Report

Pagination*	Part	Division
	Preliminaries	
Small Roman "i"**		Title page
ii**		Authorization letter
iii**		Letter of transmittal
iv		Table of contents
v		Table of charts and tables
vi		Synopsis
	Body	
Arabic numeral "1"***		Introduction
All page numbers follow in sequence		Major parts of report
	Supplements	
Arabic numerals in sequence following those of body		Bibliography or list of references
		Appendixes

*All page numbers are placed on the page centered at the top of the paper except where there is a centered heading at the top of the page. Then the number is centered at the bottom. Numbers are never set off with dashes, periods, or parentheses.

**These pages are counted in sequence, but it is inappropriate to place the actual page number on the page. Starting with "1" all page numbers will be Arabic numbers to the end of the report, through the supplements.

***Traditionally the number "1" does not appear on the first page.

Word processing software allows the option of putting a page number not only at the top or bottom of a page but also on the lefthand side, righthand side, middle, or anywhere in between. Also, if the text is to be copied on both sides and bound, the software allows you, through alternate formatting, to alternate the position of page numbers, e.g., the page number appears on the left side on one page and the right side on the opposite page.

Table of Tables.   If your report contains numerous tables and figures, a listing of tables on a separate page is necessary. Because figures and tables clearly summarize important points made in the report, it is necessary to tell the reader where these representations can be found. If your report contains only a few tables, it is acceptable to include that small listing as the last item on the table of contents page(s).

Synopsis.   Potentially the most important and probably the most read page in the long report is the synopsis (also called executive summary). It should be no longer than one page, and it can be either single- or double-spaced. It captures the essence of the entire report and usually stresses results—the findings and the recommendations.

The synopsis stresses results.

The upper-level executive who simply wants the answer and a quick look at the rationale should be able to get that information by reading only the synopsis. More than a summary, the synopsis concentrates on the results. The only time you deviate from the emphasis on results is when, as part of your strategy, you do not want to reveal the answer (the recommendation) at the beginning of the report. Then, the synopsis will summarize the findings and generally ignore the results.

The synopsis should provide a complete and clear overview of the report to the person who will read only one page. Use action verbs in writing this page and be crisp. If you must make your initial, and perhaps only, impression on one page, you must write clearly, use a format that provides plenty of white space, and use headings to guide the reader. (See Figure 16.4 for an example of a synopsis that is more summary-like because the recommendation is not being revealed up front; see the synopsis in Appendix C for a traditional results-oriented synopsis.)

The preliminaries are much more than puff and add-ons; after you prepare the analysis, you should draft the elements in the preliminaries in accordance with your presentation strategy. Remember that your goal is to make the access to the report data easy for the reader and to structure the flow of information in such a way that you will win over the reader.

Use the preliminaries effectively.

The Information and Analysis (The Body)

Regardless of the purpose of your report, the center section, traditionally referred to as the *body,* is where detailed information and the analysis are presented. Not everyone will want or need to read the detail; on the other hand, some readers must carefully comb through your analysis. So once again, careful organization and clear presentation of information are important. A variety of logical systems are possible in the body: topical, inductive, deductive, chronological, or geographical. Of course, your logic should be congruent with your strategy. You may want to refer to Chapter 2 for a review of logical arrangements and ideas.

Organize information logically.

Beyond the logical considerations, there are some recent trends that will influence how you sequence the materials in the analysis section. Traditionally, the elements flow in this order: introduction, discussion, conclusion, recommendation(s). However, some managers—for a variety of good reasons—ask writers to

FIGURE 16.4 A Summary-like Synopsis

Headings aid the focus.

The major points are emphasized.

In one page, the information is clearly presented.

SYNOPSIS

Training Perspective

No one questions the value of the training for the college interns at WDW; whereas the current interns sometimes complain that the days are too rigorous and long, the alumni state that the rigor and length were excellent in preparing them for their professional employment.

Training Emphases

Individual meetings with current interns and analysis of questionnaire results from alumni reveal congruent messages:

Guest Attitude: Treat all visitors as guests; relate to them as you would in your home. Individuals who come to WDW are not customers, but guests. This attitude, the interns relate, "rubs off" in a number of positive ways and into other business activities.

Informed: The idea that interns are to have correct information for their guests is important. Further, it aids the interns in naturally learning about the great variety of features at WDW.

Stage vs. Work: Taking a different perspective of work, envisioning it as entering onto a stage, is somewhat easy to do at WDW; however, the alumni say that this concept has aided them in their current professions and in relating to fellow workers and clients (guests).

A Philosophy: The WDW philosophy is not corny; it works. The intern learns that companies can have a philosophy and that those philosophies do have an impact on the way an individual does the job.

Training Results

The interns report that there is a direct correlation between what they learn in the training program and what they do on the job; they give the WDW training activity much higher ratings than they do their college work. But again, in college they often are unable to see the relationship between the class and work; there is no such problem at WDW.

sequence the materials with an emphasis on getting the answers (the results) up front. Figure 16.5 indicates the organizational options for sequencing the elements in this primary portion of the report. Regardless of the sequence, the purpose of the elements does not change. The report in Appendix C and the one highlighted in this chapter use the traditional organizational structure.

Options for presenting data

Introduction.   The introduction sets the stage for the analysis. Oftentimes readers already know this information and skip over it. But other readers will need to have an introduction in order to understand the what and the why of the material. You will note that much of the information included in the introduction is very similar to what is included in a short report proposal. About the only difference is that the proposal is written before the research is conducted and the introduction is written after the data are collected. So the tense changes and the substance changes depending upon the outcome of the research.

The introduction builds the report's foundation.

The introduction generally includes the following:

1. Problem: Statement of the problem.
2. Purpose: A simple statement of the research purpose.
3. Definitions: Working definitions of the terms in the purpose.
4. Research methods: A brief overview of the major secondary sources is cited. In addition, the sample size, number of interviews and/or questionnaires sent and received, plus other pertinent data are noted.
5. Limitations: Comments concerning any limitations in the research methodology(ies) used.

The introduction builds the foundation upon which the analysis can proceed; it is a very important part of the report for people who are unfamiliar with the research being reported.

Discussion.   The very heart of the report is in the discussion. The strategy you have selected will influence how you arrange the data in this section. All of the basic rules of communication and writing apply. Good format and generous use of headings are important. Visuals can add meaning and emphasis to some ideas. A clear, logical scheme for ordering the information in this section is especially important.

All the communication rules are employed in the discussion.

The documentation of ideas is honest and essential in communication, especially in the long report. You are probably familiar with traditional footnotes from writing term papers. They are fine for academic writing, but they slow down typing and the reading of the business report. Therefore, business reports are generally documented more conveniently. What to document does not change; the way the documentation is incorporated into the text changes—to internal citation.

Document your ideas carefully.

The source of either an idea or a quotation should be cited. The business report contains a bibliography that lists all sources used in the report. The internal citation method calls for assigning a number to each item in the bibliography. Then, when it is necessary to refer to that item, #17 for example, the writer simply inserts (17:3) into

Internal citations aid readability.

FIGURE 16.5   Optional Ways of Sequencing the Elements of the Discussion Section of the Long Report

<u>**Traditional**</u>
Front Matter

Information/Analysis
Introduction
Discussion
Conclusion
Recommendation(s)

End Matter

<u>**Setting, Then Answer**</u>
Front Matter

Information/Analysis
Introduction
Recommendation(s)
Conclusion
Discussion

End Matter

<u>**Answer First**</u>
Front Matter

Information/Analysis
Recommendation(s)
Conclusion
Introduction
Discussion

End Matter

In each of these organizations, the three major parts of the long report stay in order; front matter, analysis, and end matter. What can change is the sequencing of the elements in the information/analysis section. The current trend is away from putting the conclusions and recommendations at the back of the report; the newer options move the answers forward.

the text at the appropriate point. This notation indicates that the idea or quotation came from source #17, page 3 (see Figure 16.6).

Sometimes it is appropriate to use the "traditional" footnote when you want to present a critical comment, compare views of several authorities, or direct the reader to additional sources. If such a notation is very brief it can be stated parenthetically in the text. If there is only one such notation on a page, then a simple asterisk will move the reader from the text to the note at the bottom of the page. If you have very many such notes in a business report you are making the reading difficult and are slowing down the reader. (Figure 16.7 illustrates the use of the internal citation method and the "traditional" footnote method on a page; see the Bibliography in Figure 16.6 to observe how it is set up and works with the internal citations.)

Traditional footnotes are rarely used.

The use of personal pronouns should be avoided in the long report. About the only time you will use "I" is for dramatic emphasis; after all, your name is on the front of the report—everyone knows that the ideas expressed are yours!

Watch out for personal references.

The use of figures, tables, and charts is part of the communication process. When referring the reader to a visual, remember to explain before making the referral. It is the writer's responsibility to insure that the reader will understand the table. Explain the idea first in words (the narrative), then in a picture (the figure). You do yourself a disservice if you just send readers off to tables and don't explain what they are to do when they get there. The referral to a figure or table is generally done in a parenthetical statement (e.g. see Figure 2).

Explain before showing.

Internal summaries are helpful in the analysis section; they provide periodic reviews. You might view them as rest spots along the road. As you move from one major point to another, it is a good idea to summarize the point for the reader. As you will see, this will also aid you in developing the conclusion of your report.

Conclusions and Recommendations.
Every long report should have a conclusion based on the major points of the report. (Note that if the synopsis were just a summary, it would be very similar to the conclusion.) Along the way, the writer has provided the reader with internal summaries at the end of major points and sections. The conclusion then provides the overall picture, but it is summarizing, not recommending. After all, your charge may have been to investigate and analyze, not to recommend.

Conclusions and recommendations are not the same.

If you have been asked to make recommendations, then they too should be part of the information/analysis section of the report. It is generally best to separate the conclusion from the recommendation(s) to avoid confusion. In the recommendation section, the question that was proposed in the purpose is answered. Sometimes, instead of just stating the recommendations, it is helpful to quickly summarize the various options that were investigated and the pluses and minuses of each and then make the recommendations. If you have several recommendations, it is a good idea to isolate each and give each a heading. This permits the reader to distinguish each recommendation from the others.

State your recommendations clearly.

FIGURE 16.6   The Internal Citation Method for Documenting Data

Bibliography

1. Career Planning and Placement Center, Southern Illinois University, Carbondale, IL. Basic handouts and brochures for students registering with the Service.

2. Dun and Bradstreet. <u>Million Dollar Directory.</u> New York: Dun and Bradstreet, 1985.

3. Kimberly-Clark, Inc. Information Packet for Prospective Employees, 1986.

4. Lee, Robert. <u>Corporate Fitness at Tenneco Incorporated.</u> (Undated publication of the Tenneco company.)

5. Scales, Jim, Career Counselor. Interview at the Southern Illinois University Placement Service. June 3, 1986.

6. Basch, C., S. Selasko, and B. Burkholder. "An Alternative Approach for Worksite Health Promotion." <u>Health Education,</u> December/January, 1984. pp. 18-22.

7. Nelson, K. "Is Corporate Fitness Really the Career of the Future?" <u>Physical Educator,</u> May, 1984. pp. 100-103.

Sample Report Page

Careers in Fitness Program

History of the Profession
In the last century, the Pullman Company started the first recorded employee recreation program; soon after, firms like Eastman Kodak followed. (4:10-12) In 1954, the profession gained stature when the Associated Industrial Recreation Council was created. Twenty years later, the American Association for Fitnesss Directors in Business and Industry was created.

Present Status of the Profession
Today it is estimated that about 50,000 firms have some kind of formal fitness program for employees. These companies spend more than $2 million annually to maintain their programs. (6:21)

Is a Career in Fitness Safe?
There are periodically going to be shifts in the economy that can impact numerous careers. However, because of the concrete contributions fitness programs are making to corporate life, the viability of these programs is increasing (7:101). Most experts agree that the benefits of the programs include:

Decreased absenteeism
Increased quality and quantity of work
Improved quality in the people applying for work (7:103)

Fitness programs are becoming a major recruiting tool. The career possibilities for an individual trained in recreation and fitness will increase. (7:100)

Notes on internal citations:

a. The first number refers to the number item in the bibliography.

b. The second number refers to the page number; if there is no page number (in an interview, for example), then only the bibliography number appears.

c. If the citation refers to preceding sentences, it goes outside of the period. (7:15) If it refers to the single sentence, it goes inside the period (10:3).

d. When multiple pages are referenced, use (10:3-7), and if there is a break in the pages, use (10:3-7, 10-11). If there is more than one reference, a semicolon is used (7:8-10; 10:11-17).

e. When direct quotes are used, the citation follows after the quotation mark: He said, "Document carefully." (3:7)

FIGURE 16.7   A Footnote in a Report

7

<u>Is a Career in Fitness Safe?</u>

There are periodically going to be shifts in the economy that can impact numerous careers. However, because of the concrete contributions fitness programs are making to corporate life, the viability of these programs is increasing (7:101). Most experts agree that the benefits of the programs include:

<u>Decreased</u> absenteeism
<u>Increased</u> quality and quantity of work
<u>Improved</u> quality in the people applying for work (7:103)

As a result of these benefits, it is estimated that by 1990, 25 percent of all U.S. corporations will provide employee recreation and fitness programs. In addition, people are beginning to look for employers who offer more than just the traditional benefits. (3:5) Fitness programs are becoming a major recruiting tool.* In this way, the career possibilities for an individual interested in and trained in recreation and fitness will increase. (7:100)

---

*If one looks at just the growth of fitness centers in communities, it is clear that many people—especially young new recruits—feel fitness is important. Progressive firms are addressing the issue by providing the benefit at work. The literature, the comments of recruiters, and the statements made by placement professionals all confirm the growth of this new employee benefit; it is specifically aimed at the new young employee.

The End Matter

Various kinds of back-up materials may be needed for the report. They support, or back up, the body; they are placed at the end of the report and are available to the reader if they are needed. The two basic supplements are the bibliography and the appendix.

The Bibliography. Sources that were used in preparing the report are listed in the bibliography. The bibliography should list both primary and secondary sources. (See Appendix C for bibliography format.)

The bibliography reports where you obtained your information.

The Appendix. Materials that *may* be helpful to the reader are placed in an appendix. An item that is not necessary for understanding the report should be placed in the appendix, not in the text of the report.

There is really no limit to what can be placed in the appendix: a copy of the questionnaire distributed, its cover letter, a list of locations visited, photographs, the full text of a government regulation, or computer printouts, to mention only a few.

Appendixes hold items that may help the reader.

QUICK REVIEW

The long report is complex; it literally pulls together each of the aspects of communication studied in the previous fifteen chapters. Besides the research and extensiveness of many long reports, there are also a number of subtleties that make the document intriguing, such as recognizing the strategies employed in presenting the data.

Before launching a long report project, be sure that you have the basics of communication well in hand—planning, organizing, outlining, headings, logical systems, and clear expression of ideas. Each of these items is important on virtually every page of the long report. And don't overlook or downgrade the preliminaries. The synopsis, letter of transmittal, or contents page may be the item that captures the reader and sells him or her on you and your ideas.

EXECUTIVE SUMMARY

To: Business Communication Students

From: David N. Bateman and Norman B. Sigband

Subject: Reporting in Depth: The Long Report

Although the long report is similar to the short report, it is more formal, containing more parts and elements to present a comprehensive review of an investigation of a subject. It is often the foundation for analysis and decisions. Its functions in an organization can be various:

- to gather data and present research

- to record history

- to project plans and future developments

- to draw conclusions and make recommendations

The writer of the long report must know his or her purpose; the purpose is dependent on the assignment (what the writer has been asked to do) and the receivers (who will actually read the report) and what they will be looking for. To accomplish the purpose, the writer must adopt an appropriate strategy. The typical long report consists of three major parts:

Front Matter. The traditional items that precede the body of the report are, in sequence, title page, authorization letter, transmittal letter, table of contents, table of tables, and synopsis.

The Analysis (the Body). The three sections of the body of the report are:

1. Introduction—The introduction sets the stage by stating the problem, the purpose, definitions of terms, research procedure, and the scope and limitations of the research.
2. Discussion—This is generally the longest part of the report and presents the analysis, the data, and/or the interpretation.
3. Conclusions and Recommendations—Whereas the conclusion summarizes the major points of the report, the recommendation, if required, presents the possible solution to a problem.

The End Matter. The supplements to the long report might be very long. The two kinds of supplements commonly placed in the end matter are appendixes and the bibliography. The appendixes can comprise supporting data, like computer printouts, actual copies of completed questionnaires, diagrams, and architectural plans. The bibliography or reference list cites the various sources of information (both primary and secondary) that the writer used in preparing the report.

DISCUSSION GENERATORS

1. *Readership.* Why do different readers in an organization read different parts of the long report? Explain and illustrate.
2. *The Long and Short of It.* What are the differences between long and short reports?
3. *Formality.* Explain the authors' analogy in comparing the business letter with the long report and the memorandum with the short report.

4. *Road Signs and Road Maps.* Explain the authors' analogy with road signs and road maps compared to topic headings and the table of contents in the long report.

5. *Give Me the Facts without the Sauce.* What would be your response to a person who believes that readers want the facts—the hard data—and are not going to be interested in all the add-ons in the preliminaries of the long report? This person says, "When I go to the steak house, I just want a huge steak . . . forget the fancy salad; I don't want a pretty napkin; and I don't need three forks. The same applies to long reports . . . just give me the main course."

6. *Report Rudeness.* Why is it rude for the writer of a report to send the reader to a table without explaining what is to be found there?

7. *Reading Speed.* Explain how the internal citation method increases the speed by which the long report can be read.

8. *Is There a Difference?* What is the difference between a synopsis and the conclusion section of a long report?

9. *What's Moving?* What is the major trend in modern report writing? Do you agree or disagree with that trend?

10. *Footnotes.* If internal citations are used, under what circumstances would a footnote be used in a long business report?

11. *Here!* Besides simply transmitting the report (here it is), what else can the letter of transmittal achieve?

12. *Binding.* Not all bindings are binding—some can easily be unbound. If you were a manager, how would you ask that your reports be bound? Explain your rationale.

13. *Read It All.* Most readers will not read the entire long report; explain why this is the case. Is it good that some people read only a page or two?

14. *Executive Reading Patterns.* Look at different levels of management in a large organization. Explain who will read what parts of the long report in various levels of the organization.

15. *Purpose vs. Strategy.* Even if the purpose is clear and precise, why is the strategy much less clear and precise?

16. *Discussion Section.* The meat (the hard data) of the long report is presented in the discussion section. What logical arrangements can be used in presenting data in the discussion section? In what sequences can the elements of this section appear?

17. *What's Formal?* The long report is a formal document; however, what part of the report is especially formal because its parts are so heavily prescribed?

18. *Letters.* What are the two letters that might be found in the long report? Who writes them?

19. *Contents.* How does the table of contents affect the readability and the accessibility of information?

20. *Introduction.* What is the relationship between the introduction and the proposal written prior to initiating research to prepare for writing the long report?

APPLICATIONS FOR BUSINESS

21. *What's the Real Order?* The reports in Chapter 16 and in Appendix C show you the order of their elements. However, that is not the order in which the writers actually wrote the reports. Take on the role of one of the writers in the long report in Appendix C. Carefully consider the situation, and then list in sequence the parts of this long report as they would actually have been written.

22. *Limitations.* Virtually any research method you use will have some limitations. Furthermore, the situation in which you employ the method can create some problems in implementation. Here is a statement for doing some research. From it, prepare a statement on the research limitations.

    Employees will be interviewed during their 30-minute lunch hour; only employees eating in the cafeteria will be selected. Employees will be selected during each of the three lunch periods; every tenth person standing in line will be designated; the interviewer will follow that person to his or her seat and conduct the interview while the employee eats lunch.

23. *A New Plant Location.* You are Joanne Hardy, head of the physical plant for the Cornell Computer Network, Austin, Texas. You have spent six months reviewing possible new locations for your growing firm. The president of your company, Dr. John Moreno, asked you to prepare the relocation report. You have found that there are three possible sites: one in a new office park, one in an empty warehouse, and one in part of an old downtown business office building. Prepare the title page for this long report and the letter of transmittal. Here is some additional information that may be helpful to you:

    a. Moreno is in favor of moving and would prefer the downtown location, but it is the least feasible. Your study shows that the office park location is best. Moreno serves on the downtown revitalization committee for Austin.

    b. Moreno is most sensitive about being referred to formally; his doctorate in MIS is very important to him.

    c. Moreno appreciates creativity; it would be a good idea to have something other than a dull report title—or he will get bored before he gets beyond that page.

24. *Learning from Experience.* Corporate annual reports have some similarities to long reports:

    a. They are often long.

    b. They have many readers (very different kinds of readers).

    c. They present detailed analyses.

    d. If things are not going well for the firm, often that is not stated right up front in the transmittal.

    e. They are well formatted and use excellent graphics.

    There is much in well-written annual reports that we can apply in writing long reports in business. Therefore, you are to

    a. Obtain a recent corporate annual report; select one that you think is well done. (Your instructor may ask you to obtain at least three and select the best.)

    b. Study the report carefully, paying particular attention to
        (1) Letters or memos from executives
        (2) Table of contents
        (3) Format
        (4) Graphics
        (5) Internal summaries
        (6) Appended materials

    c. Write a one-page memo to your instructor in which you carefully indicate what you have learned from the annual report that you could apply to a long report you might write in a business or other type of organization.

25. *Synopsis.* The synopsis is a difficult item to prepare. There is often a vast amount of material to be presented in just one page. Therefore, any practice you can obtain in writing synopses will be useful to you.

    Read the material in Figures 16.1 and 16.4 concerning the training of interns at Walt Disney World. However, let's change some of the basic information.

    a. The data reveal that the interns want less class time; they feel they spend too much time in formal sessions.

    b. The alumni report that more time should be "structured" for social interactions—this is where "things come together."

    c. The interns feel they are underpaid and that some kind of bonus system should be created for individuals who do exceedingly well in the training program.

With this change in mind, prepare the synopsis for the "new" report.

COMMUNICATION CHECK-UPS

26. Please send information on your services, fee's and delivery procedures to my attention.

27. The following is the address:

Ms. Susan C. Donelley
Atlas Atlantic Co.
815 Broadway
Delta City, Miss 39061

28. He called the situation "A great time for profitability .."

29. Thank you in advance for considering this proposal.

30. Similarly the Denver location has problems.

31. Enclosed is the report that discusses the production options for the Denver facility.

32. The product makes it easy to know if the mail has arrived (a picture is attached.)

33. Very truely yours,

David T. Walters

34. It is appropriate for the corporation to be concerned for the pour.

35. This product has a lot of potential.

Executive
Introduction

IOWA BANKERS ASSOCIATION
430 LIBERTY BUILDING
DES MOINES, IOWA 50309
(515) 286-4300 or
1-800-532-1423 (toll-free wats)

October 8, 198_

Dr. Robert Goodman, Executive Director
Business Communication Association
University

Dear Mr. Goodman:

Because the visual is becoming a more important part of both written
and oral presentations in business and because we emphasize visuals in
all of our meetings and conferences, it will be a pleasure to prepare
the introductory comments for your special edition—"Visuals in
Business"—of The Executive Communicator.

The primary points in the introduction will be:

     I. The visual in making your conference successful.
    II. Why visuals are being used more frequently in business and
        communications today.
  III. How visuals aid moving information more clearly and rapidly.
   IV. The ways visuals can add interest and impact to "dull"
        business communications.
    V. Visuals are becoming more creative each day.
   VI. Simple techniques for making and placing visuals.

Your association is doing the profession a real service with this
special publication on visuals. It is good to see that college
students are also being exposed to this vital medium of communication.

Sincerely,

Barbara Lowe

Barbara J. Lowe
Conference Coordinator

Aiding the Receiver Through Visual Aids

WHAT YOU CAN LEARN BY READING THIS CHAPTER

Just as technological change is affecting the way you produce and move communications, it is also affecting the visual aspects of communication. For production of hard copy, for example, there are dozens of new materials for creating paste-ups, developing charts, and producing lettering. And computers are capable of producing graphics that enhance and expand the visual dimensions of business communication. Today, personal-computer programs and peripherals provide a wealth of visual options for the communicator. These technological developments can make the communicator's job easier, but the basic rules for preparing and presenting graphics have not changed. You will learn how to apply the basic rules to improve communication with your receiver. The relationship between the sender and receiver does not change—it's just that visuals aid you in achieving your purpose.

Does it seem possible that today's world is substantially more visual than the world of just a decade ago? It is! And when it comes to presenting information in the business context, it is very much more a visual world today than it was a few years ago. The "new" words in our language tell the story: "mouse," "desk-top publishing," and "CAP" (computer-aided publishing). Today, the writer sitting at the PC keyboard not only has a wealth of options to generate written text, but similarly a wealth of peripherals to quickly create materials that will represent the written word in a variety of graphics—a "mouse" that lets one draw on the CRT, "desk-top publishing" software that generates various visual images, and "CAP" that aligns the written and visual messages.

Today's world is more visual.

A decade ago, business communication texts announced that the paperless office was coming, but if you look around the office today you see *more* paper! The average office worker reads 900 pages of hard copy per month, and it is estimated that this figure is currently growing 10 to 15 percent per year. What happened? In a nutshell, the personal computer, with its word processing and its graphic capabilities, made hard copy *attractive*. In fact, the graphic elements (the visuals) are making the preparation of narrative more interesting today, and there are spinoffs throughout the organization. When desk-top generated materials look good, they set a new standard for the appearance of written documents in the organization. Report and memo writers are inspired to bring the new graphics into their communications.

Paper still dominates most offices—but today it's attractive paper.

Let's not put the cart before the horse. Before exploring the exploding world of computer-generated graphics that can be of significant benefit to the business communicator, let's make sure we clearly understand *why* the communicator needs to use something besides language to express the message. Regardless of the technological advances, the *why* has not changed. So we will first look at the reasons for using graphics and then explore the ways in which you can rather easily incorporate graphics into your writing and speaking in order to successfully communicate your ideas.

Graphics are not just gimmicks.

WHY USE VISUALS IN BUSINESS COMMUNICATIONS?

The visual aid is used to supplement, emphasize, add interest to, or clarify an idea. In business communication, visuals can contribute substantially to the total communication of an idea, but it is important to keep visuals in perspective. The visual is *not* the communication; it is but an aid to the receiver of the communication.

At one time, business writing and business presentations stood on their own narrative feet, but that is no longer the case. Today's business communications are highly visual; visual aids are not only accepted, but are expected in most organizations. The situation might be considered somewhat analogous to that of businessmen who at one time wore only white shirts. Have you looked around an office lately? There is a variety of tastefully colored shirts—including stripes and pastels. Business has changed; it has become more visual. This change shows in business communications. At the same time, taste has been maintained as the business world has become more graphic and colorful. As you become adept at using visuals in your business

Look at the color of the business shirt or blouse—today it's more visual.

communications, do not ignore the element of taste as you incorporate visuals into your narrative materials.

As we explore visuals, our approach will not be just a "show and tell" exercise. We will consider visuals through the eyes of Suzanne Settlemeyer of the Reynolds organization as she works with one of her association clients. Her visual-communication challenges are not unlike those you will face in your job. (Recall Suzanne's situation in Chapter 1.) Suzanne now has the responsibility for managing several associations and faces many communication challenges every day. One of her most difficult tasks is working with the officers, executive director, and committee chairs of the Business Communications Association, an international organization of over 2400 scholars and teachers who study and teach effective business communication. They expect excellent work from their students, so working with them calls for excellence on her part. Suzanne aids them in designing and disseminating reports for the members and preparing numerous kinds of short reports for the officers.

Supplementing and Adding Interest to the Narrative

One reason to use visuals is to supplement—that is, to provide a slightly different perspective and to add interest to the narrative. A committee chair of the BCA Research Committee has contacted Suzanne for her suggestions on how a supposedly routine subject can be made more interesting and the basic findings of a study supplemented. Sometimes it is possible to add interest and supplement ideas up front, on the cover of a report. In this case, Suzanne suggests that the attention of the receiver be quickly gained by developing a cover and placing the material in a three-ring binder; this is simple to execute because notebooks are available that permit you to insert a graphic into the vinyl cover, thereby quickly creating a report cover that adds interest to the subject and will get the readers into the report (see Figure 17.1).

Visual interest can start with the cover.

Visuals can also be used to supplement the words of the message. Computer software makes it possible to do this almost automatically. For instance, Suzanne is preparing a quarterly report for the officers of the association. She notes that because of some unusual activities of the Executive Committee, the way funds were expended this past quarter is quite different from that of the same quarter last year. Funds were expended this quarter as follows: administrative, $7,200; publications, $22,700; officer travel, $1,900; and member services, $5,300. For the same quarter last year, the breakdown was very different: administrative, $3,100; publications, $22,000; officer travel, $5,700; and member services, $5,800.

Computer graphics can aid visual impact.

Depending upon your software and printer, these kinds of comparisons of expenditures can be presented graphically in a number of interesting ways. Suzanne used the graphic in Figure 17.2, generated from a Macintosh Plus computer using a combination of software called Microsoft Chart and MacDraw and printed black and white using Apple Corporation's Laser Writer printer. Today we can incorporate the graphics with the word processing—and even have the computer graphically interpolate important data.

FIGURE 17.1   Visual Used to Add Interest—A Cover

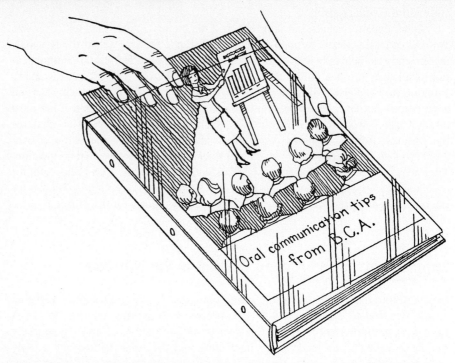

Emphasizing the Narrative

You have already learned that proofs and appeals can add emphasis to a message. Visuals can also be used to add emphasis. Through the work of Reynolds, the BCA has been most successful in increasing its membership in all categories. Certainly the numbers tell the story—student membership increased by 12 percent, two-year college faculty membership increased by 23 percent, four-year college faculty membership increased by 1 percent, and business memberships increased by a whopping 61 percent. Even though the numbers in the narrative tell the story, Suzanne found that a visual can emphasize the narrative message, providing a picture that is difficult to forget as it both delivers the message and communicates a conclusion (see Figure 17.3).

When the purpose is to emphasize, as in Figure 17.3, the communicator can sometimes take a bit of license. Rather than precise data, the overall conclusion and trend are important. For a precise representation with these data, a detailed bar chart or table would be much better. This is not to imply that a graphic used for emphasis is allowed to be misleading or not factual, but rather that the purpose is to draw attention to the trend and perhaps the conclusion.

Pictures can add power to your message.

FIGURE 17.2　Visual Used to Supplement—Computer-generated Pie Charts

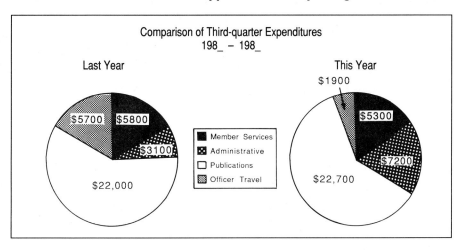

FIGURE 17.3　Visual Used to Add Emphasis—A Pictogram Bar Chart

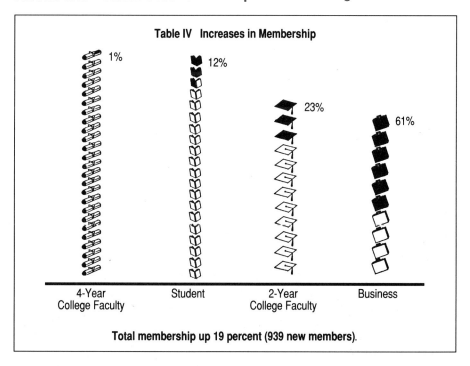

Clarifying the Narrative

Sometimes, as hard as you might try, the message you create in words is too complex. This often happens when you are forced to express numerical information concerning several different elements. It is hard to differentiate one number from another. In situations like these, you want first to do the best job you can in language and then to add clarity to your words with the use of a visual. Look at how Suzanne accomplished this by using a table to explain some aspects of BCA's membership situation (see Figure 17.4).

KINDS OF VISUALS

Whether you are working with a PC with simple graphics, a PC that has desk-top publishing capabilities, or traditional art supplies and hard copy, you have the ability to create a number of visuals to support your message. Let's look at some of them and note some pointers for their use.

Tables

Tables can be very useful (see Figure 17.4), especially if they are uncluttered, with adequate white space, and have complete titles and labels. Multiple tables should be consistently labeled and numbered. Note that the tables in this text are uniform in their format and labeling.

Photographs

Photographs can sometimes be used in a business message that is not being professionally printed. It is possible to photocopy a photograph and get an adequate (albeit faded or blurry) representation; it is also possible to paste photos to sheets that carry the narrative message. Recognize, however, that it is time-consuming and must be done neatly so that it does not turn into an amateurish job.

Clip Art

Clip art can add emphasis and interest to business communications. Art and print shops have clip art available for purchase, and today there are even clip-art software packages. Clip art, which can be pictures, symbols, and other kinds of graphics, has

FIGURE 17.4   Visual Used to Clarify the Narrative—A Table

<u>12</u>

<u>Demographic Changes</u>

With the leveling off of four-year college faculty, the availability of members from this group will decrease; within the next quarter century, the once-dominant group will change, dropping in percentage of membership by about 40 percent. If the Association wants to continue to grow, members must be drawn from other populations. Greater growth in the faculty in two-year institutions is possible because this population has not been substantially tapped. With the considerable turnover in this population, it can double as a percentage of total in the next twenty-five years. The student population continually changes. With more students taking and majoring in business communication, there is an opportunity for more than double the percentage of membership from this population group. Finally, the area for the most dramatic increase is with the business-executive population, which has the potential to increase tenfold in the percentage of total membership. Today, virtually every manager says that communications are a large and important part of his or her job, but few are members of BCA.

<u>Table III</u>

<u>Projected Percentage Increases in BCA Memberships</u>
<u>Membership Categories by Year</u>

Year	Students as Percentage of Total Membership	4-Year Faculty as Percentage of Total Membership	2-Year Faculty as Percentage of Total Membership	Business Executives as Percentage of Total Membership
1985	9%	75%	15%	1%
1988	12%	63%	20%	5%
1991	18%	47%	25%	10%
1994	19%	45%	25%	11%
1997	21%	40%	27%	12%
2001	22%	35%	30%	13%

FIGURE 17.5   Examples and Use of Clip Art

BCA Meets Many Peoples' Needs

Business Executives who spend at least 85 percent of their time communicationg not only learn how to communicate better, but more efficiently. The Journal also updates them on the latest practical research for improving communications in their organizations.

Undergraduate students have the opportunity to get a solid look at their coming professional life, to interact with top managers, and to learn (prior to launching their careeers) how to communicate effectively.

Junior-college faculty receive an excellent opportunity to publish their teaching-oriented writings in the BCMagazine and to interact with hundreds of faculty who have similar concerns and interests.

In designing a brochure that will aid the association in trying to attract members from the business, student, and junior-college faculty categories, the following narrative and clip art was developed. In final form it looks great, and it took Suzanne only a short period of time to design and implement this.

many possible uses. As with photos, noncomputer-generated clip art must be attached into your text with care. Figure 17.5 shows an example of clip art available at print shops and how Suzanne used it to add some interest and pizzazz to her narrative message.

Illustrations

Illustrations, frequently drawings of objects, are used to show the receiver the total picture. Without an illustration could you arrange a series of words to adequately describe a suspension bridge, a pencil sharpener, or even a pencil? Words accompanied by an illustration can make the job much easier.

In drawing, or having someone draw, any kind of illustration, it is important that it be drawn clearly in dark ink on white paper to allow for easy reduction, enlargement, or reproduction.

In her office, Suzanne had a rather unusual situation. Each manager was permitted an IBM or compatible PC; those who obtained traditional configurations had plenty of office furniture to accommodate their screens, keyboards, memories, and printers. Suzanne, however, selected a Compaq Portable 286. It is very convenient, but it did not fit well with normal furnishings. She needed to have a stand built, but it was difficult to describe what she needed to the office manager so he could understand and approve this unusual piece. So after explaining the situation, need, and features, she included an illustration. That made the words come to life (see Figure 17.6).

Illustrations can add clarity and emphasis.

Charts and Graphs

Charts and graphs come in a great variety, but with any chart or graph, it is important to maintain simplicity and to ensure that the data are not reported unfairly or in an exaggerated manner. Among the kinds of charts and graphs are

1. pie or circle (see Figure 17.2)
2. line (see Figure 17.7)
3. multi-line (see Figure 17.8)
4. bar (see Figures 17.3 and 17.9)
5. segmented bar (see Figure 17.10)
6. pictogram (see Figure 17.3)
7. map (see Figure 17.11)
8. flow chart (see Figure 17.12)
9. organization chart (see Figure 17.13)

FIGURE 17.6   Example and Use of Illustration

TO: Dan Jenkins, Office Manager   March 20, 198_

FR: Suzanne Settlemeyer

RE: COMPAQ PC Stand

The portable COMPAQ will work out very well for the tasks in this office and elsewhere. However, none of our standard office furnishings will satisfactorily accomodate the machine. Therefore, will you please approve the construction of a "stand" that will place the CRT at eye level and the keyboard at the standard 27" height? This custom-built stand, which can go on top of any normal typing stand or typing credenza, would contain a retractable shelf for the keyboard (the extra space would be handy for supplies and PC manuals). It would also have a moveable plastic stand that could support copy. The estimated cost, including the stain to coordinate with the office furnishings, is $97. The illustration below specifies sizes and shows how it would appear.

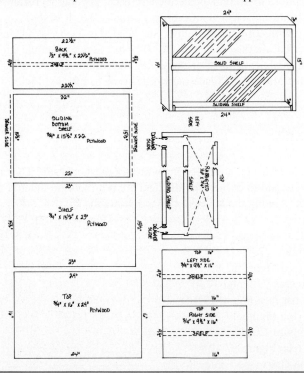

FIGURE 17.7 Examples of Line Graphs

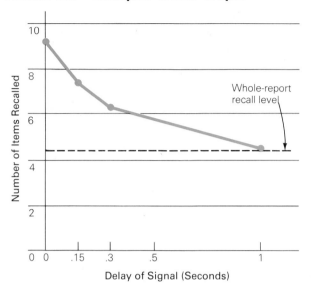

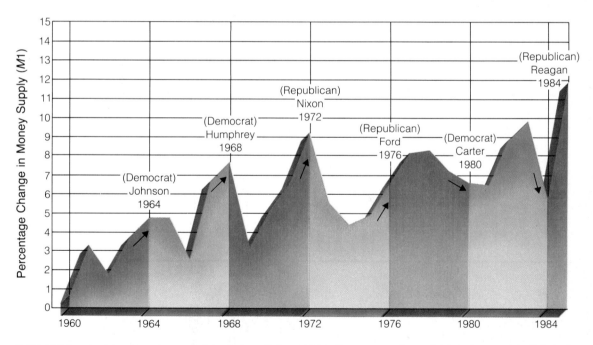

In the past two decades, monetary growth has generally been higher than average immediately before presidential elections. *Note:* The incumbent party and its candidate are shown for election years.

FIGURE 17.7   Examples of Line Graphs Continued

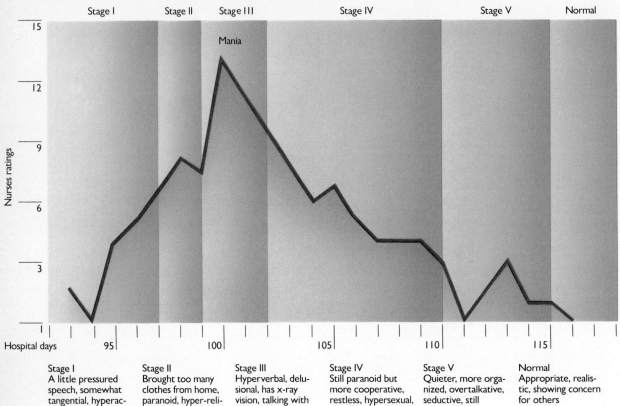

Stage I
A little pressured speech, somewhat tangential, hyperactive, happy

Stage II
Brought too many clothes from home, paranoid, hyper-religious, hyperverbal, pacing, numerous telephone calls, grandiose

Stage III
Hyperverbal, delusional, has x-ray vision, talking with dead father, panicked–afraid he might blow up, labile, suspicious, sexually preoccupied, occasionally disoriented, unable to complete a thought, very angry

Stage IV
Still paranoid but more cooperative, restless, hypersexual, manipulative, still angry, makes telephone calls

Stage V
Quieter, more organized, overtalkative, seductive, still depressed

Normal
Appropriate, realistic, showing concern for others

FIGURE 17.8   Examples of Multi-line Graphs

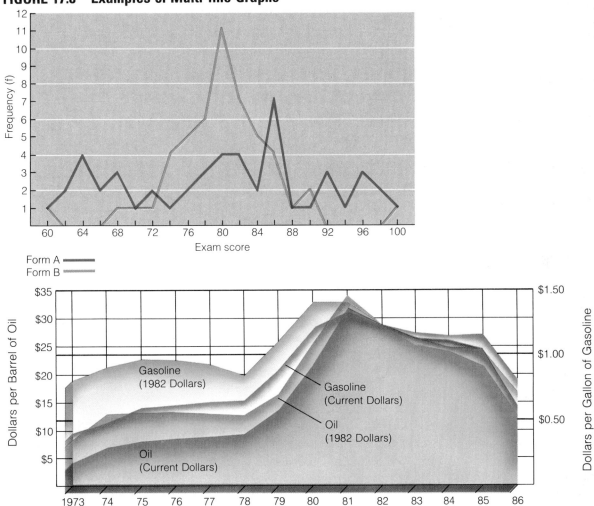

OPEC drove up the prices of oil and gasoline substantially during 1974–81. By 1986, however, conservation, the development of non-OPEC sources of energy, and the growth of cheating on limits to production by OPEC members appeared to have doomed the success of this oil cartel.

FIGURE 17.9   Examples of Bar Graphs

Major Ethnic Identities of the American People

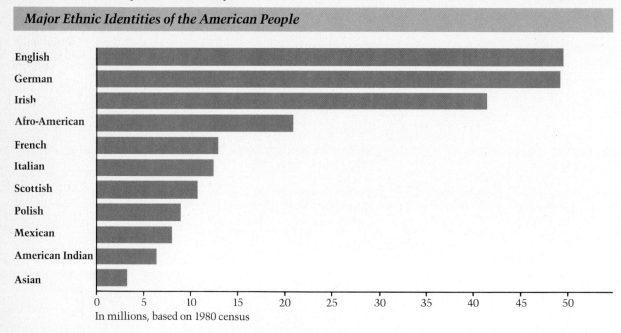

In millions, based on 1980 census

Source: U.S. Bureau of the Census

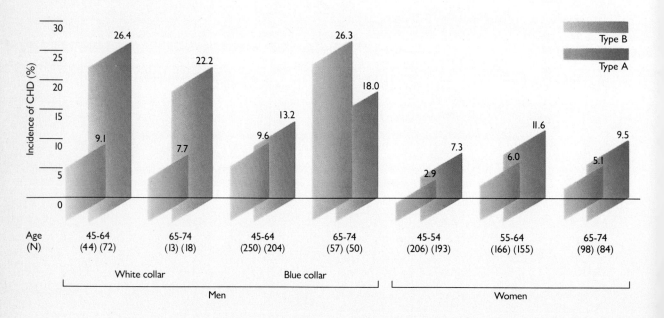

FIGURE 17.10　Example of Segmented Bar Graph

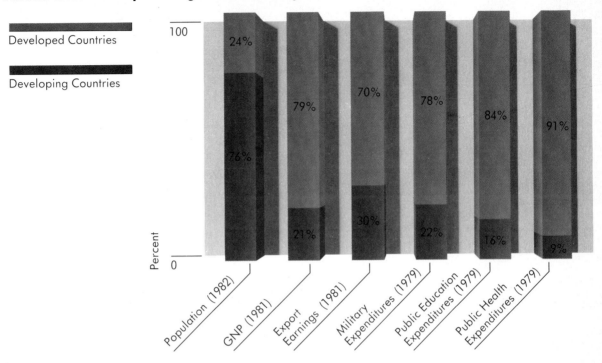

FIGURE 17.11   Example of Map Chart

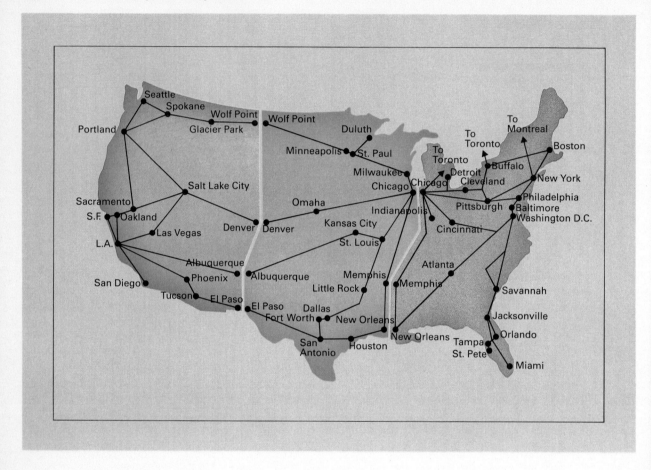

FIGURE 17.12   Examples of Flow Charts

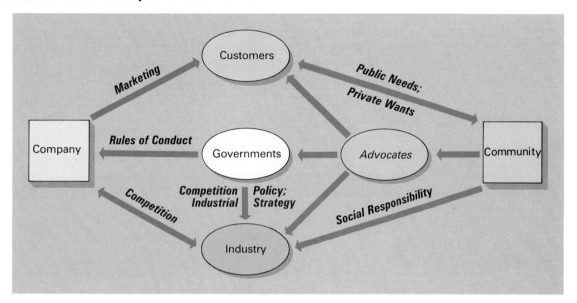

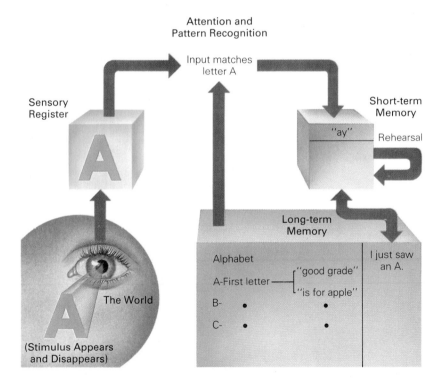

FIGURE 17.13   Examples of Organization Charts

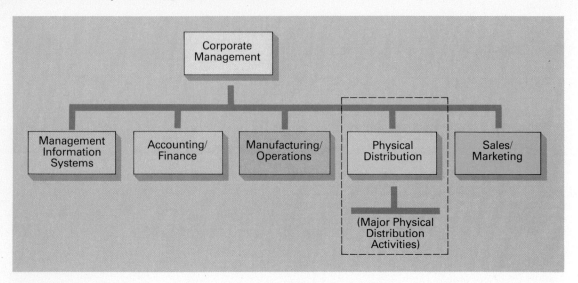

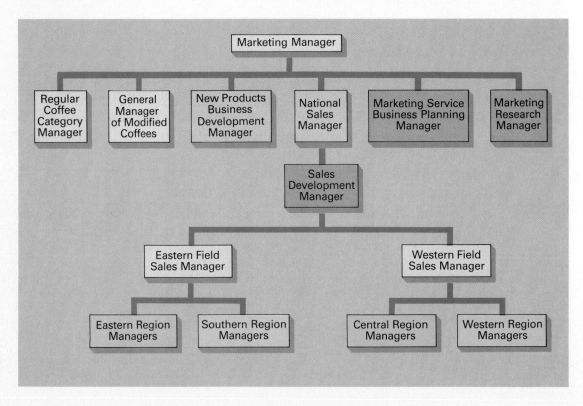

CREATIVITY AND VISUALS

Materials

The purpose of using visuals is to supplement, emphasize, add interest to, or clarify the narrative. In going to these second-dimensional items, various creative approaches are helpful. The computer allows you to be creative, as does your own ingenuity in working with hard copy. If you desire to work with traditional hard copy, it is not necessary for you to be an artist. Today, bookstores and art stores carry a variety of self-sticking materials that make it easy to design visuals. All kinds of adhesives are available for picture representations. Tapes come in a variety of widths and colors for use in bar charts and graphs. Transfer lettering and symbols are available to accomplish virtually any job.

There are various supplies that can make you an artist.

Xerography

When considering methods of creating and reproducing visuals, do not ignore xerography. This process permits you to duplicate almost anything in print (actually create your own clip art). Furthermore, some of the modern equipment lets you automatically reduce pictures, charts, and computer printouts so that they can be easily transformed into useful visuals for reports and other forms of communication. Using xerography, you can reduce a large chart so you can place it neatly on a page in your report; if you are using the chart in a talk, you can enlarge it or make a transparency or a slide.

Photocopying offers many features for the communicator.

THE EFFECTIVE PLACEMENT OF VISUALS

In written and oral communications, the general rule is first to communicate the message in words and then attempt to supplement, emphasize, or clarify with a visual. In this text, after a concept is presented in narrative form, the reader is frequently referred to an accompanying visual.

It is also important for the communicator to direct the reader or listener to the visual. As in this text, these directions are often given parenthetically, for example, (See Figure 17.x.). In an oral presentation, you can walk directly to the flip chart, move back to the screen where the transparency is projected, or move to the table where the object is sitting. Never send your readers or listeners on a wild goose chase as they try to align the visual with your message—it is your job to do the routing and to ensure that the message does not get lost!

Placc visuals appropriately to maximize your effectiveness.

A QUICK REVIEW

Visuals enable the communicator to enhance the message; there are various ways in which the sender may wish to use visuals—to supplement, to emphasize, or to clarify, for example. But in any case, the visual is a help. Whether one is using a PC or clip art and scissors, there are many materials available to assist the writer and speaker. It is helpful to know the kinds of visuals—illustration, table, photograph, chart, graph, and so on—so you can support your narrative message most effectively.

EXECUTIVE SUMMARY

To: Business Communication Students

From: David N. Bateman and Norman B. Sigband

Subject: Aiding the Receiver Through Visual Aids

Visual aids can supplement, emphasize, or clarify an idea. They can make a business document or presentation more interesting and attractive. They are no longer simply an appealing extra in business communication.

As supplements, visual aids provide a different perspective on the narrative. Just as proofs and appeals add emphasis to a message, visual aids can emphasize a message through a clear and striking image. They can clarify a message by cutting through complexities.

There are a great variety of visual aids in use in business communications today. The following are among the most helpful and common: tables, photographs, clip art (ready-made pictures, symbols, and so on), drawings, and charts and graphs. Charts and graphs take many forms. Some frequently used types are the pie or circle chart, line graph, multi-line graph, bar graph, segmented bar graph, pictogram, map, flow chart, and organization chart.

There are many options available to help you in generating effective visuals that can be created by an artist or by you, working with a personal computer or with materials readily available at art stores. Xerography affords you flexibility with your visuals: not only can you duplicate almost anything in print, you can reduce or enlarge visuals to sizes to suit your purpose.

Finally, visual aids must be strategically placed in a written or oral narrative. The general rule is to first communicate the message in words and then use the visual. It is also important to direct the receiver's attention to the visual.

DISCUSSION GENERATORS

1. *Visual Increases.* Illustrate how business people and business communications are more visually oriented than in bygone eras.
2. *Visual Language.* What are some examples of "new" words in our language that illustrate the changing influence of visuals in our communications?

3. *Visual Aids.* Explain how visuals actually *aid* the communication process.

4. *Supplementing.* If you are using a paragraph in a financial report to explain the flow of funds, what is one technique for supplementing that narrative with a visual to make it clearer?

5. *What is the Visual?* What is meant by, "the visual is *not* the communication"?

6. *Three-rings Plus.* What has been added to three-ring notebooks in order to increase the visual impact of this packaging of your presentation?

7. *Do Words Really Tell the Story?* After listing a variety of numerical figures the writer says, "These numbers tell the story." Do they? How can visuals be used to tell the story more dramatically and perhaps more quickly for the reader?

8. *License.* In what situation might the communicator take a bit of license in using visuals?

9. *What Comes First?* What should generally come first—the narrative or the visual? Why?

10. *Responsibilities.* What responsibilities does the communicator have for guiding the reader or listener to the visual? What are some of the ways a writer can direct the reader to the visual representation?

11. *Desk-top Publishing.* Briefly explain desk-top publishing.

12. *Clip Art.* Briefly explain and illustrate clip art.

13. *Labeling and Tabling.* Why is it important to be consistent in labeling tables?

14. *Photos in Writing.* What are the options for getting a photograph into the written short report?

15. *Illustrations.* Why should you, or the person preparing the items, prepare the illustrations in dark ink on white paper?

16. *Charts and Graphs.* What are three different kinds of charts or graphs?

17. *Disrupt the Flow.* Illustrate how, in written material, the visual could be so placed that it would actually disrupt instead of enhance the communication flow.

18. *Paperless Office.* What happened to the projected paperless office?

19. *PC Advantage.* With hard copy clip art, it is necessary to paste the art into the narrative. What advantages does the PC give you for incorporating clip art into the narrative?

20. *Complexity.* When you are presenting three different categories of numerical data and they are very complex, what is the most common kind of visual to aid in simplifying your message?

APPLICATIONS FOR BUSINESS

21. *The Big and Small Pictures.* Your boss is intrigued with the PC stand explained in Figure 17.6 that will accommodate the COMPAQ computer. She asks you to do two things. (1) Take just the illustration from Figure 17.6 and photographically enlarge it so you can use that illustration on an overhead transparency for a short talk. (2) To

include a representation of the illustration in the meeting agenda, reduce the illustration even more. Implement both of these procedures.

Then be prepared (in writing or orally) to inform your group of the problems encountered in accomplishing your task; what hints do you have for people faced with such tasks in the future?

22. *Clip Art Pictures.* You have completed a long report on the challenges and opportunities of dual-career families in which both parents hold professional positions and have children. The report is ninety pages long and has the following chapters:
   - Changes in the Family
   - Latch-key Children in Dual-career Families
   - Parental Stress in Dual-career Families
   - Income Differentials Between Dual-career Families and the Traditional Family
   - Implications for Our Country and Our Organizations in the 21st Century

   Develop and present the clip art that could be used on the cover, in the table of contents, and on the sheet that introduces each chapter.

23. *Visuals to Add Emphasis.* You are comptroller of the Miller Electronics Company, and you have been asked to make a seven-minute presentation to a group of investors your firm is attempting to persuade to purchase huge amounts of stock in Miller. In the written materials, the potential investors will receive very detailed and precise information. One point you want to make in your presentation is that the company has a good and growing group of skilled employees; with added investment resources, that labor pool can be maintained and enhanced. In making this point, you want to use a visual to emphasize the growth of skilled employees at Miller. Here are the raw data. Remember that in the handout the audience has a detailed precise bar chart that shows this information. How can you take the data and add emphasis?

   Data: Year one, 13 employees; year two, 28 employees; year three, 180 employees, year four, 235 employees; year five, 540 employees; year six, 701 employees; year seven, 768 employees; year eight, 845 employees; year nine, 921 employees; and year ten, 1,253 employees.

24. *Don Has Had It with Dullness.* Don Gimenez is director of finance at the Jacober Corporation. He spends about one-third of each day at meetings in which Jacober managers make presentations on various factors influencing the financial operations of the growing company. Don has had it with dullness. All he sees is transparency after transparency of laborious tables—and they are often difficult to read when projected. Don is convinced that the people making such presentations could do a much better job with their visuals to make them more interesting. You are a new college recruit who has just joined the finance department. Don literally grabs you and says: "I've had it with the dullness in these visuals—all I do is drink coffee in those meetings in an attempt to stay awake. These guys must only read financial reports—don't they ever look at things like *USA Today* to illustrate the point? By next month, I want some interest added to our meetings." Develop a list of at least three ways to add interest to financial data. Create and illustrate one of the techniques cited above.

25. *Can You Clarify That Please?* One of the chief uses of visuals is to clarify the narrative statement. For a brochure intended for entering students in your business department, here is the narrative statement; it looks intimidating, sounds confusing, and could actually drive students away from majoring in your department. After reading the statement, develop a visual that could follow the statement and add clarification.

"Entering students must have a minimum of 2.3 GPA (A = 4); then they, in their respective majors, work through several modules of courses. First there are the introductory courses (like Introduction to Business, Personal Finance, and Careers in Business), then there are the skill courses (like Statistics, Business Communications, and Business Law), then the core courses (like Business Organizations and Management, Marketing Channels, and Principles of Accounting and Finance), and finally the capstone courses (like Business Policy, Current Business Affairs, or Business in the International Marketplace)."

COMMUNICATION CHECK-UPS

26. Can you send information in regard to the standard marketing costs.
27. At this time we can not accept the order.
28. At this time we can't accept the order.
29. In todays market the old procedures will not work.
30. I have prepared some ideas for your presentation; I have outlined five market areas:
31. In writing a letter, care must be taken to put each part in its proper place.
32. Classes will be conducted in the summer in which you may enroll.
33. The profits, according to yours truly, do not reflect good management.
34. She double spaced the letter.
35. The office does not have any file folders.

Memos of Purpose

Douglas Ann Newsom

The fiscal officer of a publicly-held company called to see if he could take a writing course. The question, "Why?" had to be asked before something could be suggested.

"My correspondence just doesn't get the attention or the results that I need to be effective in my job," he said. He went through his educational experience toward a degree in accounting, certification, and previous experience at one of the large national accounting firms. "No one told me," he said, "that I would also need to be a good writer to get things done."

As a financial counselor, he was discovering the communication needs that all management advisors have, but expectations are especially high for public relations professionals. It's assumed the public relations person knows how to get results with words. That's why the public relations office is relied on to write for so many of the key officers of the organization.

As a fiscal officer, the caller's responsibility included making recommendations to top management, relaying and interpreting financial decisions to internal staff for implementation, and explaining to the corporate headquarters what the organization was doing and why, in addition to occasionally asking for decisions to be made at the corporate

offices so the local institution could make major improvements in buildings and equipment.

Most of his writing was correspondence in the form of memos, all internal. Internal, in this case, meant within the local offices of the wholly-owned subsidiary and to the corporate offices in New York.

A review of sample memos was painful reading. The grammar and spelling were perfect, but what he expected to occur as a result of his communication was a mystery. Some memos were so obscure that they defied any attempts at editing. These all were going to non-financial people, most at executive levels, no lower than manager, but a few were addressed to clerical staff. If an educator accustomed to cumbersome efforts with the language had difficulty deciphering his correspondence with careful effort, no wonder busy people who probably didn't want to hear what he had to say were not reacting. To begin with, it was difficult to determine the purpose of his memos.

Public relations memo writers have to clearly define purpose because the piece is often an effort to persuade in some way.

Memos can be sorted by purpose into six different categories: bulletin, essay, informative, action, summary, and file.

Bulletin memos have a telegraphic style, conveying the sense of urgency. Always brief, the language may even be terse. These are perfect for the electronic message centers that some companies have set up for employees.

Essay memos are of the "let's talk it over" style that encourages description. They are conversational and can be directed to anything from management philosophy to getting employees to keep the coffee room clean.

Informative memos are more detailed descriptive pieces that are fairly formal in tone because they generally document the background of a situation, action taken, its results, and projections for the future.

Action memos describe action taken or planned. When it is future action, the recipients generally are given a place on the memo to initial a section for which they will assume responsibility. There is a tone of coercion in action memos because they say, "This will happen" or "This needs to happen," so the opportunity for respondents to volunteer needs to be built-in. It's better to convey a sense of choice instead of assignment. To be effective, the writer needs to understand both persuasive tactics and the audience.

Summary memos generally are used in describing the action taken at a meeting where minutes are not kept, but where people have participated and taken some responsibilities. The memo serves as documentation for the meeting and as a reminder for duties assumed. This type of memo also is used for progress reports on projects. When it is a progress summary, some background material is included with decisions taken and actions planned. A memo of this type can be fairly long, sometimes in outline form with several headings. Its tone is usually formal.

File memos are records of occurrences or agreements that are not sent to anyone, but are used to provide organizational memory. Since these memos may be most useful long after current personnel have left, it's important to spell out names and titles and to give dates and places of action.

Just thinking about categories for memos helps focus on the purpose and keeps the message unified. The expectation, what you want to have happen, is tied to the purpose.

Getting the purpose in focus won't help, though, if the writing is obscure. Jargon is a shorthand that is often acceptable for internal correspondence, but only if the jargon is shared. A fiscal officer brings jargon from that background to new experiences and may as well be speaking a foreign language to some people. Translation to general vocabulary increases acceptance and readability of memos.

The fiscal officer's writing was not improving until he was asked to write something else, anything. He described a scene that he encountered just outside of his office that was very poignant to him. The writing was not only clear, it was eloquent. Confronted with the dramatic comparison, he said he had an idea of what business writing should be. His image of "official" correspondence was hampering a natural ability to write. Once unleashed, he found expression easier.

Public relations people are generally professional writers who put polish on their public works, but penalize their internal correspondence with memos that belie their real ability. All writing from public relations professionals should carry the hallmark of the wordsmith.

Advertisements of Their Carelessness

Joseph M. Queenan

The superfluous final comma in the ad reading, "No ifs, ands, or buts," used to bother me so much that I finally took a red pencil and corrected the poster on my commuter train. A couple of days later, someone with a different punctuation philosophy—perhaps an advertising copywriter—crossed out my correction and wrote "STET." This setback notwithstanding, I continue to wage the battle against promotional material that looks like it was written by Agthor, the Dog Boy of Cogarthanghika.

A case in point is the press kit I recently received from a West Coast celebrity-contacts broker who said that he could put my readers in contact with all the big names in sports and entertainment. If you really want to impress your clients, his brochure read, you'll want to hook up with our roster of stars, which includes such luminaries as Merl Haggard, Red Aurabauch, Julius Irving, Mohammed Ali, Sid Ceasar, Ester Rolle, Ava Gabor and Heather Lockleer, all of whose names were so misspelled. What puzzled me was: If the broker went to all the trouble to get the photos shot, the art work pasted up, the layout designed and the ad copy written, why couldn't he pay Enid Middleton, who teaches remedial reading at Pomona Junkets Middle School, to look over the text for typos? She could certainly use the work.

Errors of punctuation are especially annoying in those snooty catalogs touting upscale services for executives—and executives only. A Miami firm positing a correlation between success in the corporate world and having unsightly parts of one's body surgically renovated—or excised—recently sent me a brochure containing this delight:

"Today, men and women who experience aesthetic surgery, do so to compete more effectively in a youth oriented job market. It works like the ripple effect, increased self esteem promotes

increased achievement. Aesthetic surgery not only enhances the way you look it gives you a better feeling about yourself." Yeah, well if you guys use a scalpel the way you use a comma, you're not getting anywhere near my deviated septum.

Another time I got a haughty press release from a New York copywriting outfit offering to provide "legends in the making" to compose for clients on a per-diem basis. The five-paragraph release had seven punctuation or spelling errors, spelled the term "free lance" three different ways, and assured me that "These aren't prima donna's." I called the director of the firm to ask what kind of customer would hire an ad agency that couldn't punctuate its own press releases.

"You want to place an order?" she asked.

"No, I just thought I should warn you about the response you're likely to get to your brochure. It's a real mess."

"Let me get this straight. You didn't call me to hire a free-lancer?" (She actually said it without the hyphen; I could hear it missing.)

"No."

A pause.

"You're not being any help at all."

I never am. When I interviewed the president of a West Coast firm selling home computers Tupperware-style a couple of years ago, I couldn't help pointing out how unprofessional it seemed to have a sentence like this right there on the front page of the company's brochure:

"Within just a few years, over 70 percent of all households will own a home computer to handle a wide variety of chores, such as managing home finances, controlling energy use, educate and tutor our children, and provide many home entertainment choices."

I said that the paragraph ought to read "managing," "controlling," "educating," "tutoring" and "providing." And I suggested that grammatical errors in the first paragraph of a promotional piece touting a product's pedagogical features could make the company look kind of dumb to potential investors.

"Yeah, but you were probably an English major in college," the corporate chief said. Caught out again.

Data-Driven Report Writing

Alfred B. Hurd

You have finished interviewing, you have pored over reports, you have observed operations in the office or on the factory floor. Now you must write your report. As you look at your pile of notes and consider the modest amount of time allocated to report writing, you wonder if you can really do a good job on time—and how do you begin? Certainly, you do not want to leave out anything important; your professional pride does not permit that shortcut. Equally, you do not want to clutter the report with low-grade material. But you very much want to get on with the job.

Begin by going through your notes, every one. As you read them, circle in colored pen those ideas, insights, key statements, and central bits of evidence that you now know (having been through the whole data-gathering process) are crucial. Add remembered thoughts also in colored pen setting each sheet aside until you have addressed the whole pile.

This step may seem tedious as discussed here, but it is critical to the quality of your report. From this review of your notes—all at one sitting—you will get a sense of the dimensions of the report and how key items interact. No one can do this for you; it is a learning process. Good reports, like good computer programs, are written by authors who have the whole in their minds all the time they are writing. And you will find yourself drawn into the material, jotting ideas and follow-up queries and generally reliving the data gathering sessions with a growing sense of your ability to draw useful conclusions from a mass of detail. Even with very large amounts of data (e.g., 115 interview summaries) I have never known this process to take more than a man-day; it usually takes a morning.

Your walk through the data will have given you ideas about the kind and size of important themes. Bring them together by going back through your stack of notes and copying the circled material onto a set of 5×8 cards grouping your material by topic. Some topics will take several cards, some will have only a few entries. Don't copy every word, just key words. Use your notes for detail as you write. You can see how valuable this step is in learning your material, identifying unasked questions, and framing the report in your mind.

"Data-Driven Report Writing" by Alfred B. Hurd, *Journal of Systems Management*, April, 1985, pp. 38–39. Copyright © 1985 Association for Systems Management. Reprinted by permission.

After you have asked your follow-up questions and recorded the answers on your cards, arrange the cards by topic in order of importance. At this point, you will find this easy because you have just had two sweeps through the material and will have learned it very well. I rack my cards up in a microfiche holder to keep them in sequence as I write and so I can photocopy them, or at least their headings, if necessary (as for a table of contents).

Now start writing. Your company may have rules about report formats such as, Table of Contents, Executive Summary, Introduction, and the like. It will be practically mechanical to write these three after the rest of the report is written; the Table of Contents can be written now from your cards, if you like, and is a good guide for you while writing.

Simply spread out the first set of cards devoted to a key subject. Write from your notes until the paragraph or the section, or the chapter is done and then do the same for the second set of cards. It is important, at this point, to draft the report by writing quickly because your aim is to capture the material and not to polish each phrase—a time-consuming task. As you go, you will discover places to insert cross-references to other parts of the text previously written. Pictures, diagrams, tables, and the like (collectively called "exhibits") can be referred to from appropriate spots in the text and prepared later while your draft is being typed for the first time.

A few pieces, ideas, bit of evidence, and thoughts may not fit into your draft. Mark them on your cards with a special color, try to fit them into the report as you edit it for the first time, and discard them without regret if they do not. This technique for gathering key facts is good but not perfect; interesting but unnecessary material some-times slips through.

Think of writing the report as you would of constructing a program or set of shelves. Build it part by part and plan to edit and revise. Only freshmen imagine that they can write the final text the first time.

This method balances quality with speed by allowing you to extract what is important in your notes and group it into themes. You can move from one set of cards (theme) to the next without wondering if you have left anything out. Not having to review the material more than twice turns out to be highly productive. Also, your knowledge of your subject will inform your writing and make it more readable and therefore more useful.

Wall Street Videos

Richard Morais

Tired of annual reports thick with photographs of plant managers wearing yellow hard hats? Telerate, Inc., the $148 million (revenues) financial information firm that provides stock market quotes and the like, decided its 6,000 shareholders were tired, too. Neil Hirsch, the 38-year-old president, now sends shareholders their annual reports on videocassette. The sleeve of the cassette contains a pocket-size pamphlet packed with the numbers required by the Securities & Exchange Commission, while the video does the rest.

Thus does MTV come to Wall Street. Telerate's cassette starts with a Bach Brandenburg concerto, shots of London and New York and sophisticated graphics. Next come interviews with the customers. Even skeptical viewers are drawn to the documentary-like testimonials of Allen Sinai, chief economist at Shearson Lehman Brothers, and Masanori Kanai, the chief trader at Tokyo's Okasan Securities. These are real people talking, not obviously posed and retouched stills.

"They've turned the annual into a powerful marketing tool," says Richard Lewis, whose Corporate Annual Report in New York turns out annuals for companies like Philip Morris and Pan American. "Video is super for third-party testimonials."

Expensive? Hirsch says no. A quality printed annual costs Telerate $6 a copy. The video, including the accompanying pamphlet, costs about the same. There are some advantages, however. Hirsch needed an inventory of 25,000 paper annual reports in order to meet shareholder demand. The new videos, however, can be produced as needed.

Shareholders seem pleased so far, but not necessarily with the video. "Not one of the pages contained wasted words that I find myself wading through in other company reports," wrote one sensible shareholder. Others echoed his sentiment. Which raises an interesting point: Are annual reports, as presently constituted, really necessary?

The Unwritten Elements of Effective Business Communication

Executive Introduction

Edward D. Jones & Co.®
Members New York Stock Exchange, Inc.
Conservative Investments Since 1871 **SIPC**

Western North Carolina Offices	
Albemarle	Kernersville
Asheboro	Lenoir
Boone	Lexington
Brevard	Lincolnton
Concord	Monroe
Conover	Mooresville
Eden	Morganton
Forest City	Mt. Airy
Gastonia	Salisbury
Greensboro	Shelby
Hendersonville	Statesville
Hickory	Thomasville
High Point	Waynesville
Kannapolis	Winston-Salem

Total N.C. Offices: Over 50
Offices Nationwide: Over 1,100

January 20, 198_

Mr. Robert C. Olsson
Vice President
Sales Training
Edward D. Jones and Company
P.O. Box 97
St. Louis, MO 63166

It will be <u>fun</u>, Bob . . .

. . . to make a presentation at our annual meeting of Investment
Representatives. The tentative title is "Preparing For Success." In
our business, oral communication links directly with success; well-
planned and well-executed presentations, talks, briefings, and
speeches are important. As the title indicates, my talk will concentrate on preparing oral communications.

The equipment needed is: podium, overhead projector, and rear screen
slide projector. In the introduction and conclusion, I will use a
video. I will bring all of the materials, but will need assistance in
setting up the equipment.

The major points, as currently outlined, are:

    + Plan and Prepare for Your Presentations
    + Know the Many Kinds of Presentations in Our Business
    + Use Preparation Strategies
    + Analyze Your Audience As You Analyze Your Customer
    + Plan Each Part of Your Presentation
    + Take the Plan Off the Paper - Practice Out Loud!

Please let me know if this outline emphasizes the points you would
like to have communicated to our people; any suggestions would
certainly be welcomed. As the outline indicates, I'm already Planning,
Preparing, and Practicing!

Yours truly,

Kurt

Kurt Reid
Investment Representative

KR/rar

Preparing Oral Presentations

WHAT YOU CAN LEARN BY STUDYING THIS CHAPTER

Oral communication involves much more than just adding volume to written communications. There are nevertheless some similarities between the speaker's preparation of a briefing or a long presentation and the writer's preparation of a one-page memo or a long report. Both the writer and the speaker need to analyze the audience and strive for logical organization and clarity, while always checking to insure that the purpose of the presentation meets the needs of its receivers. One major difference, however, is that whereas the writer's feedback may not be received for days or weeks, the speaker receives some virtually instantaneous feedback. This element of the live presentation produces excitement and adds another dimension to the presentation of ideas. In this chapter, you will learn how to prepare for oral presentations so that you can approach the podium with confidence.

Oral exchanges are increasing.

In the modern organization, all you need do is look about the offices to observe two quick indicators that substantial amounts of structured oral exchange takes place. First, there are many conference rooms. Second, the conference rooms are in almost continual use; it is often necessary to reserve the rooms in advance, or you may find that space is unavailable. A major reason for the increase in oral communication is that planning calendars and product life cycles are shrinking rapidly. There is often no time to do business the old-fashioned way by preparing detailed memos and documentation. The speed of business demands more rapid exchanges via oral methods. Therefore, productive, rapid, closure-focused oral communication aids the modern organization in meeting the competitive challenges it faces.

TYPES OF ORAL PRESENTATIONS

The common oral communications used in organizations

Before moving to the specifics of preparing a talk, it is helpful to identify the types of oral communication most managers are called upon to use. Once they are identified and understood, we can determine how to plan for and be effective in those situations.

Briefings

Briefings are brief updates.

The purpose of the oral briefing is to update information for others and to put the information in an understandable context clearly and concisely. Organizations use briefings to keep busy managers current on projects that are underway at any one time. In your department's weekly or monthly meetings, you may be required to present briefings on the projects you are managing or the problems you are facing.

Informative Talks

Informative talks are intended to increase receivers' knowledge.

Somewhat longer than the briefing, informative talks are presented to groups that lack knowledge of a certain subject. For example, you may be asked to inform new personnel about company policies and benefits. In order to relate the informative presentation to the particular audience, it is important to know their understanding of the subject. A presentation on new state regulations concerning education of handicapped children to a citizen's group will be different from the presentation given to the Association of Teachers of the Handicapped. We all are annoyed when speakers do not tell us anything new or when they present data we cannot understand.

Introductions, Recognitions, and Welcomes

In giving introductions and welcomes and making recognitions, it is important to focus the listeners' attention—not on yourself, but rather on the speaker you are introducing, the award that is being presented, or the person(s) being welcomed. The keys are to know your audience and to use the you-orientation.

Don't be trite in your introductions, recognitions, and welcomes.

A creative introduction of a speaker will gain the audience's interest and provide the group with enough information to appreciate the speaker's comments. It is always polite to ask the person being introduced if there is information to include or avoid in making the introduction. Avoid the trite nonsense that is often used by inexperienced speakers: "This person needs no introduction . . . " "Without further ado . . . " "Last, but not least . . . " Remember that the listeners are there to hear the speaker, not the person making the introduction.

When presenting an award or making a recognition (employee of the month, for example), note the reason for the award, suggest why it is important to the organization, and indicate some of the attributes of the individual or group receiving the recognition. Sincerity and enthusiasm are vital in creating a positive and appreciative feeling.

If you are called upon to welcome people to your department, organization, or club, you should indicate an interest in them and communicate a sincere enthusiasm about your organization. The welcome may also convey information, such as telling people that they are not permitted to take pictures or that employees are not permitted to visit with the group during the hour.

The Long Presentation

Most organizations have dozens of studies, projects, and problems that call for longer oral reports. These presentations may last from ten minutes to an hour or more. Whereas the short presentation tends to set forth a single, definitive message for the receivers, the long presentation generally develops complex ideas in detail and provides opportunity for exchange, discussion, and debate. These discussions can lead to the resolution of problems and to reaching a consensus. Often, much information in these presentations has been written previously in memos, letters, and reports. An advantage of the oral report is that it gets involved people together in one room and provides the opportunity for the quick exchange of ideas. The effective oral presentation can permit ideas to crystallize, promote an environment for creativity, and secure interaction among interested personnel.

Longer oral presentations may involve greater interactions.

PREPARATION STRATEGIES

Preparation reduces risk—risk to you!

The planning requisites for oral communications are not substantially different from those presented in Chapter 2; however, since oral communications are live, they are potentially more volatile and more subject to the unexpected. Therefore, to reduce risk, preparation is crucial. Since all of the planning elements are captured in the long oral presentation, we will use it as our reference; remember that these planning elements are also applicable to other kinds of oral presentations, like briefings, welcomes, and introductions.

Know Your Purpose

Know and adhere to your purpose.

As you have learned, communicators in any situation must know their purpose; the purpose of long oral presentations looks strikingly similar to that of written materials:

- To inform the top management of the available options for refinancing the Brookside development.
- To persuade the divisional personnel managers to engage in an aggressive communication training program for first-line supervisors.
- To compare our marketing strategies with those of our three primary competitors.

The long oral presentation, like the long written report, may have multiple purposes. But whether the talk is long or short, know why you are making the presentation. If you don't, your audience won't understand what you are doing.

Analyze Your Audience

Tune in to your audience *before* **planning your talk.**

Just as the writer of a report analyzes the reader(s), the speaker needs to get to know the audience before ever meeting them. If you think you know your audience, take a moment to analyze them. If you don't already know your audience, take steps to get to know them. Some speakers take considerable time a few weeks before a talk to speak with the host in order to gain information and insight about the audience. If you misread your audience and carry the wrong message to them, the situation is most uncomfortable; it is somewhat similar to wearing a heavy wool suit (anticipating cold weather) and finding yourself giving a speech in a hot, crowded room. Therefore, always ask these questions:

Who will be in attendance? Knowing who and how many allows you to tailor your message and visuals for the group.

What does the audience know? If you are unfamiliar with the knowledge of your audience, you risk missing your target.

What does the audience want to know? You are not always going to be able to accommodate your audience—the audience may want you to propose budget increases when you must propose decreases. This knowledge permits you to set the tone and the logic of your talk.

PARTS OF THE PRESENTATION

The long oral presentation has three basic parts: the introduction, the body, and the conclusion. Unlike the long written report, its parts do not vary in order, nor does it have peripherals (such as an appendix or supplement). What you learn here about the long oral presentation applies to all kinds of oral communications.

The Introduction

How you introduce your subject is dependent on many factors—the length of the presentation, the subject, the audience, and the situation. Generally, the following are accomplished in an introduction. (Note that some are verbal, e.g., define terms, and some are nonverbal, e.g., establish a relationship.)

Basic to the introduction is getting along with your audience.

    Indicate Your Topic: Beware of assuming the audience really knows what you are speaking about; often you need to explain the topic.

    Establish a Relationship: Whether the talk is short or long, you want to win the audience over to *you;* in the introduction, you are striving to win acceptance for yourself. A smile or a reference to a situation or incident with which the audience is sympathetic is often helpful. Winning acceptance of your ideas comes later.

    Define Your Terms: In long presentations that involve complex subjects, define the terms for the audience. This will reduce misunderstandings.

    Gain the Audience's Confidence: Verbally and nonverbally you should gain the confidence of the audience. Some of the requisites are knowledge, preparation, and organization, as well as humility and understanding.

    Getting Started: Like the first words of a letter, the first words of a talk are difficult. Some options for opening are (1) a startling statement, (2) an unusual statement of proof, or (3) an attention-getting narrative. It is not necessary to start a speech with a joke in order to put the audience at ease. If you have a relevant humorous comment, consider using it; if not, forget it.

The Body

Like the information/analysis section of the long report, the body of the speech contains the "meat" of the talk. In developing the body, consider the following factors:

The body contains the "meat," but it need not be dull.

    Align Appeals: After analyzing your audience, align your appeals with them. Will they be moved by logic, by example, by emotional appeal, or will they be impressed with testimony from experts?

    Organization: The same organizational schemes that work for written communications can also work for the oral presentation (see Chapter 2); that is, you might present your ideas inductively, deductively, topically, chronologically, or in some other sequence.

Transitions: The use of transitions, bridges from one point to another, are vital in long talks; they are helpful in shorter ones also. In oral communication, the material is often coming to the receivers very rapidly; they need some periodic breathers. As headings in the long report give the reader an opportunity to "rest" for a moment, transitions in the oral presentation accomplish a similar objective. Some common transitions are, "Now, let's turn to another point . . . " or "However, there is another aspect that we should explore today . . . " or "With your understanding of appeals, let's look at their use in the sales letter." Without effective transitions, you are likely to leave your listeners stranded—not knowing that you have moved from one point to another.

Variety: The body of the speech is the longest portion. You do not want to exhaust your audience by being dull, repetitious, or monotonous. You can add variety to the body in a number of ways. The purpose is to keep the audience alert and also to provide the speaker with some changes of pace. All of the following options apply to shorter presentations as well. They also require some planning—they are not last minute ad libs:

Visuals.

Be sure there is variety in your talk.

Visuals can take the audience beyond the words of the speech, adding a lively variety. (Visuals are discussed in Chapter 17; how to use visuals in oral presentations is discussed in Chapter 19.)

Exemplification.

In the long presentation it is very important to change the pace as well as support ideas by providing examples. Analogies, stories, and statistics, for example, can all add variety to the presentation.

Vocal Expression.

A monotone will put the audience to sleep and kill your changes of gaining acceptance of your ideas. Practice varying your tone, loudness, and rate of delivery. Use inflection and emphasis to add interest to your statements. When your voice varies appropriately with the content, your talk is not only more understandable, but also more exciting.

Word Choice.

Vary the language you use. Synonyms, for example, can add variety to the presentation. Also, be careful of using slang. It may distract your listeners and drive them away from your point of view. Beware of such expressions as *em, un,* and *yeah.*

Participation.

Consider involving your audience by periodically asking a question or having someone contribute data. Participation should be limited, and you should always remain in control.

There is no rule about the length of the body of the presentation. Sometimes you will be given an absolute time limit for your long presenatation. The length is right if the body has adequately explained the material or concept to the audience and has helped you achieve the purpose you established for the speech.

The Conclusion

At the end of a speech, speakers often announce, "In conclusion . . . " Although we are often pleased to hear those words, the phrase "in conclusion" is overused, as is "Well, I guess that about ties it all together, unless anyone can think of anything I left out."

Plan the conclusion; it just doesn't happen.

Many members of the audience will remember your final comments. Make them memorable! Plan them; write them out. Choose key words, use personal terms; try to evoke a response—a reaction.

It is not enough to feel that if you do a good job of relating the data in the body of the speech, somehow the conclusion will fall automatically into order when you get there. In the conclusion, give the listeners something that they can take with them to add to their knowledge or to be used for decision-making. Plan your conclusion just as carefully as you plan your introduction.

Summary: Often the purpose of the conclusion, especially in an informative presentation, is to summarize the major points, or the speaker may want to re-emphasize some particular points. A summary can be more than just a rehash. Sometimes a quotation, a story, or a specific example can provide an interesting twist in summarizing the major points or leading the audience to your goal.

Recommendations/Alternatives: In the business context, the conclusion of the speech is often a presentation of recommendations. For instance, the body of the speech outlines the history of the problem and how the problem has grown within the company. The conclusion recommends solutions to the problem. At other times, your purpose is not to make a recommendation but rather to present options for solving a problem.

QUESTIONS AND ANSWERS

In oral presentations you are often expected to provide for some open exchange; it is assumed that there will be questions and that you will provide some answers. The structure of your presentation will be affected by how you handle the questions, so you will need to devote some preparation time to this portion of the talk. You should try to anticipate and list questions that might be asked and think through reasonable answers. There are three basic ways to handle questions:

Plan for questions and *your* answers.

The laissez-faire method is where you will take questions at any point in the presentation, stop where you are, and provide an answer. The advantages of this approach are that it helps to keep the audience with you, and it can provide you with the opportunity to immediately clarify misunderstandings. A disadvantage

Plan for how you will handle questions.

is that you may get waylaid by poor questions or by questions from eager beavers asking about topics that will be covered later. Or you may have to deal with someone who begins with a question but goes on to make a speech.

The question break method allows you to take breaks between major points. Summarize one section, and then ask for questions before moving to the next topic. The advantage of this approach is that it gives you some control, yet it still provides for direct audience interaction during the presentation. The major disadvantages are very similar to those noted in the laissez-faire approach—you may be sidetracked by irrelevant questions.

The end-of-speech method is traditional and works well if you are given a definite time limit. If you take questions during your presentation, you may cover only one-third of the data and spend the remainder of your time answering questions, thereby making a mess of the presentation. A disadvantage in taking all questions at the end is that sometimes people are eager to leave, and it is difficult to maintain interest during a "wind-down" question session.

Before you begin, either you or your introducer should indicate to the audience which method you will use.

In handling questions, it is very important to listen carefully to the actual question being asked. The good listener does not cut the questioner off and start answering because the actual question may be very different from the anticipated one. It is also wise for the speaker to repeat the question if he or she feels the audience has not heard it clearly or completely.

PREPARATION KEYS

We have considered kinds of talks, preliminaries to preparation, and parts of talks. Now we will look at the nuts and bolts of preparation.

Substance

Knowing how to pre-pare makes speaking easier.

Regardless of how much rhetoric is applied, if there is no meat on the bones, the talk cannot succeed. The speaker must be well-versed on his or her topic and prepared. Don't take the podium if you don't know what you are talking about. The audience will figure you out quickly. So the first step in preparation is to become informed.

Organization

Once you have the information, next work on structuring the data. The organization will depend on the audience's knowledge, your time limit, and the amount of information you desire to cover.

Preparing Notes

The preparation of notes is part of the speech planning process. In most speaking situations, especially in the long presentation, you will take some materials to the podium—an outline, detailed notes, or a manuscript. There are three basic reasons for using notes:

1. To insure that you keep to the topic and neither wander nor drop needed materials.
2. To jog your memory so that there will be a natural flow of information. You do not want to stand before the audience hemming and hawing or struggling to remember the next point.
3. To allow you to make precise statements when they are necessary.

After putting hours of preparation into a presentation, you do not want to end up at the podium fumbling with notes. You should determine how best to handle your notes, based on the type of presentation and your own preference. Among the formats you should consider are manuscript, notecards, three-ring notebook, and "hidden" notes. Whatever technique you select, be sure to practice with the very notes you will use in your talk. Gaining familiarity with your notes is vital during the prep time. Itzhak Perlman would not give a recital with a strange violin; nor should you want to give a speech with strange and unfamiliar notes. So prepare your notes and then use your preparation time to practice with them.

Determine the kind of notes you will use.

In some situations it may be necessary to present at least part of a long presentation by reading from a manuscript. If your speech is typed single-spaced on thin, lightweight paper, you will be in trouble. Use a heavy bond paper and prepare the final copy by using orator-style type. Use wide margins and double- or triple-space between lines. Indent the paragraphs substantially and leave more space between the paragraphs than between the lines of each paragraph. Even though you are working with a well-prepared manuscript, you may want to make some last-minute changes before the speech. The wide margins and other extra space will permit you to insert additional items. Also, prepare the final copy so that it will not be necessary to turn pages at crucial points in the presentation. Some speakers find it convenient to provide themselves with various cues in the manuscript: "turn the flip chart," "bring up the next slide," or "pause for a moment." In a neatly prepared manuscript, there should be plenty of room for inserting these added notes (see Figure 18.1).

Sometimes it is acceptable to use a manuscript as your notes.

Note Cards. In some situations it may be convenient to prepare the entire speech on 5-by-8-inch note cards or 8½-by-11-inch paper. In other situations, the note cards may contain only an outline, some basic notes on the major points, a quotation, or some statistical data.

Small notecards are often a hindrance.

Don't fool yourself by attempting to use small 3-by-5-inch note cards. The audience will know you have the cards, so why limit yourself to such a tiny format? The 5-by-8-inch cards permit you much more flexibility.

Whether you use typing paper or note cards, be sure to number your materials

FIGURE 18.1   Manuscript Notes with Cues

Provide substantial white space.

Insert dots, dashes, explanation points to draw attention to expressions and pauses.

Leave room in margins and between paragraphs for handwritten cues.

Use orator type to make the material easy to read.

Number pages to keep materials in the correct order.

Use heavy and sturdy paper; flimsy paper can play all kinds of tricks on you.

AND, THEREFORE, THE MANAGER MUST RECOGNIZE THAT THE "I-ORIENTATION" IS MUCH MORE THAN JUST AN ELE-MENT OF WORDS . . . IT IS A <u>CRUCIAL</u> BASIS FOR ESTAB-LISHING PROPER RELATIONSHIPS WITH PEOPLE.

THERE IS MUCH THAT THOSE OF US IN ACCOUNTING, MANUFACTURING, AND HUMAN RESOURCES CAN LEARN FROM OUR COLLEAGUES IN MARKETING AS IT RELATES TO THE ESTABLISHMENT OF POSITIVE, YOU-ORIENTED PROCE-DURES.

1. <u>THINK</u> OF THE OTHER PERSON.

2. <u>CONSIDER</u> THAT PERSON'S WANTS AND NEEDS.

3. <u>DETERMINE</u> WHAT IS IMPORTANT TO THEM.

4. <u>TARGET</u> YOUR MESSAGE EXPLICITLY TO THEM.

THE POINT IS, THE PROPER USE OF THE YOU-ORIENTATION INVOLVES MUCH MORE THAN LANGUAGE, IT INVOLVES THE WAY WE THINK AND RELATE TO OTHERS.

4

sequentially. If your cards should fall during your presentation, you do not want to have to take a great deal of time to figure out which card goes where.

Notebook.   It is sometimes useful to prepare your notes on 8½-by-11-inch paper and then place them in a three-ring notebook. The advantage of this approach is that the materials will not fall, slip out of order, or slide about on the podium as you speak. You can also insert transparencies you plan to use. In this way, you have everything that is needed for the presentation in one place and in a very orderly arrangement.

The well-organized notebook can aid in longer presentations.

The disadvantage of the notebook is that it may tend to tie you to the podium. This may inhibit your movements and deter you from using gestures and from generally interacting with the audience. The solution to this problem is to prepare the material on 8½-by-11-inch paper and then photocopy unified sections of the material and place it on 5-by-8-inch cards. The cards will exactly match the segments of the material on each notebook page. With the cards laid upon each page, you have the option of using the manuscript and/or the cards. By leaving the rings of the notebook open, it is easy to lift the materials out of the way as you speak. If you wish to move from the podium, you can take the appropriate cards with you and your mobility will not be hampered. Since the cards and the manuscript match exactly, there is no danger of getting lost in the material and not being able to find your place when you return to the notebook.

"Hidden" Notes.   There are some less obvious ways to use notes. In some situations, you may use an overhead projector throughout the presentation. If you use an overhead transparency, principal ideas can be noted by key words or an evolving outline of the speech can be projected. You can expose the outline point-by-point simply by using a piece of opaque cardboard, moving it as you proceed down your list of points. The key, of course, is that the outline or the principal ideas are also there for you, and you can elaborate on the projected information. This technique is especially helpful when you are speaking extemporaneously.

"Hidden" notes can make speaking easier.

Another type of "hidden" note is the kind that can be placed on the large flip chart along with the large print, pictures, or diagrams. In using the chart, you may want to insure that several basic points under each heading are conveyed. You can remind yourself of these points by penciling them in on the chart. These usually will not be seen by the audience; but even if they are, no harm is done. Everyone recognizes the need for notes at times. The point is that these notes are clearly visible to you as you speak, and having them on the flipchart in small letters frees you from running back and forth between your notes on the podium and the easel stand. Using this method insures that necessary information is communicated to the audience. This same idea can be used with transparencies; penciled notes that are visible to the speaker can be made on the cardboard frame that holds the transparency.

PREPARATION MEANS PRACTICE

Practice means really doing it—over and over.

The speaker has much to prepare—the substance, the visuals, and the actual delivery of the talk. After getting the materials organized, practice is in order—physically delivering the talk in isolation or to a colleague or two. Famous classical musicians are often asked "Do you still have to practice?" The questioners are often shocked to hear the answers, which range from four to six or more hours each day. The pros practice, and that practice is much more than just playing through the pieces. The pianist slowly and laboriously repeats several measures of difficult fingerings, works for several hours on the phrasing or articulation of just one passage, and then may go on to work rigorously with the metronome to get the tempos precisely correct. The speaker in business can learn much from the professional musician. If the pros have to practice, certainly the inexperienced speaker is going to have to practice. How foolhardy it is to spend weeks in developing the substance of a talk and then have it end up as a muddle because the actual delivery was not practiced and honed. And remember, real practice means actually standing up and giving the speech—not just thinking about giving the speech. As we are all "great" singers in the shower, we are also "tremendous" speakers when we practice our talks in our minds. That's the wrong way and the wrong place to practice. Instead, stand up in front of a mirror and give your speech; turn on a tape recorder, give your speech, listen, note the rough spots, and then do it again.

QUICK REVIEW

The preparation of a talk involves a variety of activities. The speaker should recognize those activities and then work through them methodically. There are several kinds of talks from briefings to lengthy presentations. The speaker must consider the purpose and audience of the speech, the parts of the speech, and factors like how to prepare for and handle questions and the appropriate kinds of notes. The speaker must also actually physically practice the speech. In preparing and organizing the substance of the talk, there are many similarities to preparing a memo or long report. However, when it comes to preparing for the physical delivery, the communication takes on many added dimensions.

EXECUTIVE SUMMARY

To: Business Communication Students

From: David N. Bateman and Norman B. Sigband

Subject: Preparing Oral Presentations

To meet the challenge of increasing efficiency and productivity, organizations are relying more and more on oral communication. Managers find themselves called upon to engage in many kinds of structured oral communication, including briefings, informative talks, introductions, recognitions, welcomes, and long presentations.

The live presentation is subject to unexpected elements. Good preparation can reduce the risks imposed by those elements. First, be certain you know your purpose and your audience. Time spent analyzing even an audience you believe you already "know" is worthwhile. Your purpose should always be related to your audience. Second, your presentation must be substantive and well organized. Third, you should use notes or even manuscript to make certain you stay on the topic, remember all your points, and make precise statements. You should practice your presentation using the notes or manuscript. Try practicing in front of a mirror and recording your talk.

Like the written report, the oral presentation has three major parts—the introduction, the body, and the conclusion. Do not assume once you have the body of the speech that you will somehow get started and that the speech will end when you run out of information. Effective speeches have introductions and conclusions as thoughtfully prepared as the body of the presentation.

Presentations are often used to provide an open exchange of information. In the long presentation especially, it is assumed that there will be questions and that the speaker will respond to them. You must not only anticipate questions, you must also indicate to the audience how you intend to handle questions—at any point in the presentation, during periodic breaks, or at the end of the presentation.

DISCUSSION GENERATORS

1. *Planning.* Why is it just as important to plan your conclusion as it is to plan your introduction?
2. *Variety.* What are four ways you can add variety to a speech?
3. *Bridges.* What are *bridges* in a speech? Cite an example of one—an example other than one from the text.
4. *Vocal Expression.* Name three kinds of vocal expressions, and illustrate each.
5. *Confidence.* Why is it so important for the speaker to gain the audience's confidence in the introduction? What may happen if the audience loses confidence in the speaker?
6. *Audience Wants and Needs.* Explain the difference between analyzing what the audience wants to know and what the audience needs to know. Cite a specific example of how this might work in your chosen profession.
7. *Parts.* What are the parts of the long speech, and how do these parts differ from the parts of the long report?
8. *Briefing and Informing.* What are the similarities and the differences between a briefing and a speech to inform?
9. *Introductions.* What are two key factors to keep in mind when you are called upon to make an introduction?
10. *Oral Increases.* According to the authors, why is there more oral exchange in the organization today compared with a few years ago?
11. *It's Just a Joke.* What's wrong with starting your speech with a joke?
12. *Extraneous Words.* What are extraneous words in a speech? After listening to

yourself, what are some extraneous words that enter into your speech? What can you do to eliminate these?

13. *"In Conclusion."* What is wrong with using the phrase "In conclusion..." as a transition from the body of your speech to the summary section?

14. *"Hidden" Notes.* Explain the two kinds of hidden notes, and indicate how they can be used in the speech.

15. *It's Clear in My Mind.* What is wrong with practicing your speech in your mind instead of standing up and practicing it in front of a mirror?

16. *Running Through a Speech.* Considering the analogy of the professional musician practicing, why do you think the wise speaker who is preparing a long talk should not practice by running through the speech several times? Illustrate what he or she should do instead.

17. *Notes.* For what purposes will a speaker use notes?

18. *Old Notes.* Why is it important for the speaker to use the notes he or she has practiced with instead of preparing new notes for the actual presentation?

19. *Questions Please?* What are the three ways the speaker can opt to take questions? What are the advantages and disadvantages of each?

20. *Sales.* What might be done in an introduction of a speech that is similar to what might be attempted in the first sentence of a sales letter?

APPLICATIONS FOR BUSINESS

21. *Tuning in to the Audience.* Sophia Goldwater of Sophisticated Bikercise, Ltd., has accepted the invitation to speak at a banquet in Silver City, N.M. (see Figure 9.1). It is not Sophia's *modus operandi* to walk into speech situations ill-informed. She insists on having information about the audience. Take on the role of Sophia and prepare a more detailed inquiry letter to Ms. Murphy that will produce information about the exact nature of the audience she will be facing. You want to prepare a letter that will produce valuable data so that not only will the talk be germane, it will be right on target for this audience.

22. *Stamping Out Triteness.* As Director of Communications for the Oyster Organization, you have just sat through a week of presentations where various department managers gave talks to dealers. You were impressed with the substance that was presented and with the enthusiasm. However, good managers used trite phrases introducing their talks: "It is a pleasure to be here today"; as a final transition in a series: "Last but not least"; and as a lead-in for a summary: "in conclusion."

You want to help these managers. There were many positive features of the conference, but the overuse of trite phrases, you feel, tended to diminish the worth of the messages. The triteness trivialized the ideas being delivered.

In a kind, positive tone, prepare a memo for general circulation to Oyster managers that highlights at least ten overused phrases (try to avoid those already cited in the text), and suggest what speakers might use in their place.

23. *How to Practice.* A major portion of preparation is actually practicing the speech. As the writer proofreads and rewrites, the speaker speaks, hones the talk, and

speaks again before ever appearing in front of an audience. Prepare directions on how to practice the following techniques:

- Clear and precise transitions
- Preparing notes
- Inflection and emphasis

24. *International Audience.* Today, business schools are emphasizing international studies. It is one thing to study the culture and people of a country, but it is a much different thing to learn their language. As president of the student advisory board in the Department of Business at your college, you have had the opportunity to meet with many executives, and you are familiar with the Department's curriculum. The way international business is currently taught is by faculty periodically injecting some "international flavor" into their courses.

   There is a proposal before the Department's curriculum committee to require all business students to take at least two semesters of a foreign language. You are in favor of this proposal, and you are going to need to make two presentations covering basically the same material—but the audiences will be very different.

   One audience, the faculty on the curriculum committee, will be sympathetic; they favor the proposition. They are not averse to increasing the hours to graduate to accomplish the task, and they really won't be directly involved, since the language courses will be taught outside of the Department.

   The other audience, the student advisory board, has many concerns. It will lengthen the degree program, it will be difficult work for many students, and further, many students do not see the benefit.

   The conclusion to both speeches will be the same, but how you get there and the arguments you use will change. Outline both speeches, and highlight and explain where the differences, because of the audiences, will appear.

25. *Anticipating Questions.* Besides preparing the speech, the prepared speaker also thinks through how to respond to questions. In the preceding situation, you would certainly be asked many questions by students, such as, "What other universities are doing this for their students?" Prepare a list of at least fifteen questions you think you might be asked if you were to deliver this talk.

COMMUNICATION CHECK-UPS

26. He seen the operation first-hand.
27. Me, John, and the other colleagues enjoyed the tour of the facilities.
28. Irregardless of the profits, that is not the kind of business to pursue.
29. Surly they will not buy that!
30. Useing her skills well, she rose quickly in the organization.
31. From the beginning she new the deal was sour.
32. He recieved the message graciously.
33. The official, governor Wilson, will be at the presentation.
34. Generally, the company should expand toward the West.
35. This however is a very different situation.

Executive Introduction

July 10, 198_

Mr. Jeffrey Rowland
Account Representative
Wang Laboratories
1703 5th Avenue
New York, NY 10029

Dear Jeff,

It was <u>great</u> to hear from you and especially kind of you to comment on the various speeches I made when we were in college together. Your position with Wang sounds fantastic, and I'm sure you will have a rewarding career.

Concerning your questions on the delivery of oral presentations, I've found the following practices most helpful:

o   Consider the audience—their needs and interests.

o   Plan and practice the presentation.

o   In practicing and in actually delivering the oral presenta
    tion, pay particular attention to:

    + Establishing eye contact with the audience.
    + Gaining and maintaining audience interest.
    + Varying your voice to create different expressions.
    + Having simple notes to aid the extemporaneous style.
    + Checking posture and appearance.
    + Using visuals creatively and effectively.
    + Familiarizing yourself with the surroundings.

I hope this letter doesn't sound like an old college lecture! But each week I conduct staff meetings and find these keys helpful.

Have a great time and challenging business experiences in New York; keep in contact, and let me know how these hints work for you.

Cordially,

Amy

Amy Meyer
Group Sales Manager

FOLEY'S

Delivering Oral Presentations

WHAT YOU CAN LEARN BY STUDYING THIS CHAPTER

It is difficult to practice speaking if you do not know the many elements that can be practiced and polished before you ever get to the podium. This chapter covers those elements, specifically indicates *how* to practice, and integrates materials on visuals (Chapter 17) into the speech context. Guidelines for actually presenting a speech are explained and the modes of delivery are discussed in a business context. As good writing involves good editing, good speaking involves good revision and practice. For numerous situations, you are provided with hints on practice so that your eventual presentation will be effective.

Preparation and practice for presentation

The actual presentation of a talk is the culmination of pulling together the substance, organizing the materials for the audience, and then practicing the physical delivery of the talk. It is presentation that concerns many people so much that it keeps them from ever moving to the podium. That is unfortunate considering the importance of oral communication in today's organizations. In this chapter, we concentrate on literally how to deliver ideas orally. The chapter is based on the assumption that the speaker is knowledgeable and well-prepared to handle the substance. If he or she is not, it is virtually impossible to consider delivery options or to work to overcome some of the initial uneasiness we all face when we move to the podium.

GUIDELINES FOR PRESENTING YOUR SPEECH

Look at Your Audience

Practice establishing visual contact with your audience.

"Look at your audience" does not mean periodically glancing at the group; it means communicating with them visually. We have all been in situations in which someone presented a speech while looking at the podium or over our heads. We felt that the speaker was leaving us out. Look directly at individuals in the audience. Be alert to audience feedback, and make adjustments as necessary. Maintaining good eye contact permits you to relate information *to* them instead of *at* them. Practice by either giving your talk in front of a mirror or video camera. Watch where you focus your eyes. If that focus is not on the area where the people will be, you will tune out your audience.

Vary Your Volume and Speed

Listen and practice your vocal volume and speed.

Inexperienced speakers often do not speak loudly enough. It is important to speak up! Let your voice bounce off the back wall. The audience cannot believe what it cannot hear. Some ideas need to be stated rather forcefully; others should be noted softly, respectfully, or sympathetically. Like a good piece of music that is alternately slow, fast, high, low, loud, or soft, a speech should reflect such changes to match the content of the ideas. How boring and monotonous is a piece of music or a speech that goes on and on at one volume and one speed! Practice by audiotaping your talk to discover where emphasis needs to be placed; make some marks in your notes and then retape your talk.

Speak Clearly

State words correctly.

As you practice, listen to yourself and consider having someone else listen. Do you hear yourself saying "comin'," "goin'," "don'tcha"? Enunciate every necessary sound in every word. It is just as easy to do it correctly as to drop a syllable here and there. Check the pronunciation of words; are you placing the correct emphasis on the correct syllables? Practice by audiotaping your talk and also by listening carefully to your normal conversation. If you leave the "g's" off words in conversation, you will do the same in a more formal talk. Become conscious of your failings, and then concentrate on listening to yourself and correcting them.

Use Appropriate Gestures

A broad smile, a clenched hand, a fist hitting the rostrum, hands on hips, all can communicate very specific information to the audience. In preparing your speech, analyze the ideas and the feelings you want to express. Then determine what gestures will help in communicating the idea to the audience. Standing before a group with both hands in your pockets while reading a speech is not making the best use of the oral situation.

Your hands, face, and arms are part of your speech.

Gestures can be used in many ways:

- to aid in picturing the speaker's words—"The economy has been like a roller coaster." (the speaker moves a hand and arm in a waving motion)
- to add emphasis to a point—"We should clearly understand . . . " (the speaker strikes the podium)
- to help the audience know that a new piece of information is going to be introduced—"Second, let us turn to the foreign market implications," (speaker holds up two fingers and makes a turning motion to the audience).

Ideally, gestures should come naturally. But many effective speakers plan carefully and practice diligently to incorporate them into the speech. Regardless of how the gestures get into the speech, whether as natural expressions or as calculations to provide special emphasis, they are an important element in oral communication. In the elocutionary period of rhetoric, at the turn of the century, much emphasis was placed on how to stand and how different positions of the hand communicated different ideas (see Figure 19.1). Work to see that your gestures are not rushed—you do not want to appear to be swatting flies. Practice the gestures you want to make, and then practice in front of a mirror, observing how you actually carry out the gestures as you give the talk.

Check Your Posture and Appearance

Obviously a speaker should dress and stand in a manner appropriate for the presentation. Just as the sales letter is typed neatly on company stationery, the sales speech is presented by a neatly dressed representative of the organization. However, there is another important aspect of appearance—distracting gestures.

As noted earlier, when used appropriately to supplement the spoken words, gestures can add substantially to the presentation. At the same time, watch out for and eliminate unnecessary and distracting gestures. Continually putting a hand into your

Recognize the various aspects of appearance.

FIGURE 19.1   An Analysis of Gestures

Although you will not be asked to get this detailed in analyzing your gestures, note the way gestures can be categorized as represented in this 1893 book; clearly, much more than just standing straight and not wiggling is involved in using gestures to aid you in communicating your ideas.

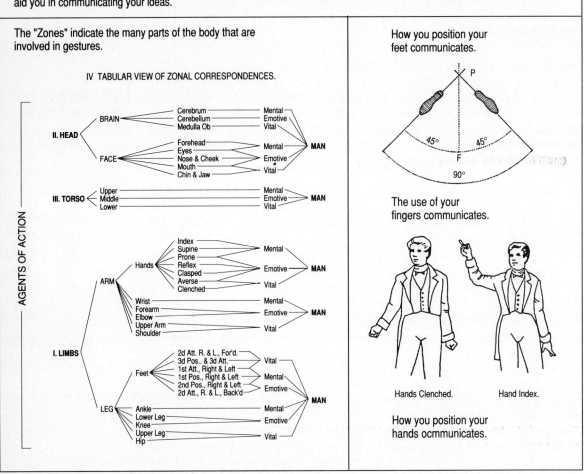

From Fulton, Robert and Trueblood, Thomas. Practical Elements of Elocution. NY: Ginn and Co., 1893.

coat pocket or jingling coins or keys can prove distracting. Don't let your appearance, posture, or distracting gestures override your message. It is important for you to dress properly, stand correctly, and focus the attention of the audience on your message. Practice by thinking ahead about your clothing; ask someone to observe you practice and note any distracting gestures. Unnecessary gestures (standing on twisted feet, placing a finger in your ear, making an unnecessary fist) are often so much a part of our "speech style" that we are not going to recognize these bad habits until someone points them out to us.

Be Knowledgeable and Be Prepared

Your research should extend to areas related to your topic as well as ideas that oppose your own. This will prepare you to handle questions, objections, and rebuttals with confidence. You must be able to substantiate facts and justify your recommendations.

Have information beyond just what you intend to say.

Watch and Listen for Feedback

Regardless of how much you plan and practice, the actual presentation will be different from practicing the speech. The alert speaker looks for feedback. If the audience looks confused on a particular point, you can assist by interjecting a statement like, "Let me repeat that . . . " or "Perhaps I can state this another way." Besides helping the audience to understand the message, these statements indicate that the speaker is paying attention to the audience. Also, if the audience laughs longer than expected at a humorous comment, the speaker who is tuned in to feedback does not just plow ahead; instead, the speaker pauses and permits the audience to catch up. The oral presentation allows you to actually interact with the audience. By looking at the people in the audience and interpreting their feedback, you can keep the message on target. If you do not react to the audience's feedback, the speech might as well have been presented on tape.

Let feedback work for you as you speak.

Successful interaction with the audience is, to a large extent, the element that makes your listeners glad they have come to hear you. It is the element that is missing when they listen at home on television to even the most polished and charming of speakers.

MODES OF DELIVERY

There are four basic ways to present a speech: memorization, impromptu, reading, and extemporaneously. You may prefer to use a combination of modes in one presentation. For example, you may present the speech extemporaneously, but read some specific figures, memorize a relevant quotation, and respond to questions with an impromptu answer.

Memorization in Speech

Potentially the most dangerous and deadly mode is the memorized talk. First of all, it takes time to memorize. It may be okay to memorize Lincoln's Gettysburg Address for a public-speaking class, but why memorize welcoming comments to a group of high-school seniors or an introductory statement for the department conference? Second, the act of memorization may pull the speaker away from interaction with the audience. When presenting a memorized speech, the speaker may be saying, "I

Memorization can be useful in small doses.

figured out exactly what I'm going to say, and regardless of the blank looks on your faces, I'm forging ahead."

There is another danger in memorizing—what happens if you forget what to say next? People have a tendency to memorize words, not ideas. If a word is forgotten, where does that leave you? Although memorizing an entire speech is not recommended, the memorized statement can be very effective. For example, inserting a memorized poem or quotation in a speech may serve to unshackle the speaker from the notes and the podium and allow an idea to be presented in a very special manner.

Impromptu

Impromptu means applying all speech techniques quickly.

When the speaker is given little or no time to prepare, the approach is called impromptu. On the spur of the moment, the individual must quickly develop a presentation and begin. The impromptu speech is frequently used in conference situations; an issue may emerge in the discussion that you will be called upon to present immediately. Perhaps you will have a few moments to jot down some notes and make a rough outline, and then you will be on your feet and talking. Never begin speaking without at least determining the order in which you will present your points.

Reading

The read speech calls for considerable practice.

Unfortunately, many business speeches are read. If all the presenter does is stand up and read from a manuscript, we have to ask: "Why wasn't the speech just duplicated and sent to us?"

There are times when it may be appropriate to read, for instance, when the statements, statistics, and policies presented are so vital that they must be absolutely accurate. Heads of state usually read their speeches. What they say often has tremendous impact; an unfortunate slip of the tongue could be subject to gross misinterpretation and could lead to domestic or international problems.

A speech that is read can be very effective if it is written in a conversational manner and delivered informally. The speech should be typed in large print. (Very large-sized type—referred to by typewriter manufacturers as "orator-style"—is available; see Figure 18.1.) It is also a good idea to leave plenty of space on the paper between lines and paragraphs. Key ideas can be underlined in red to remind the speaker to give those points emphasis. Green marks can be inserted in the margins to remind the speaker to look up and at the audience. At appropriate places, the marginal note "smile" may be written. It is most important to go over and over the pages so that you can read with force and clarity, knowing precisely what comment and idea is coming up next. These techniques can aid in making the read speech acceptable communication.

Extemporaneously

The extemporaneous mode is the generally preferred way of delivery. *Extemporaneous* means that the speaker has given careful thought to the presentation, has outlined what is going to be said, but is not going to read it or memorize it. The key word used to explain the extemporaneous mode is *conversational.* The speaker presents the speech in a way that achieves close interaction with the audience. Not all of the language is precisely established beforehand, but the speaker knows the basic ideas to be presented, knows the order in which topics will be treated, and has developed a clear introduction and a meaningful conclusion.

The extemporaneous speech allows you to adjust the presentation to the situation. Audience feedback tells you whether to expand or eliminate a subject, tell the joke, shorten or lengthen the talk, or poke fun at the guest of honor. It is all spontaneous, but thoughtfully so. Extemporaneous does not mean "spur of the moment," "off the cuff," or "winging it." The extemporaneous speech is a well-prepared presentation.

The extemporaneous style conforms to the conversational style of U.S. business communications.

USING VISUAL AIDS

The use of visuals has been discussed at various points in the text. Visuals can be an integral part of the oral presentation, just as they are for the written report. It is difficult for a speaker to hold an audience's attention for forty-five minutes on the pros and cons of establishing new production techniques; but the effective use of visuals can help clarify the material and can add enough variety to the presentation to maintain the audience's interest. It is not possible to absolutely prescribe what visuals should be used in each situation, but by becoming familiar with the types available, recognizing the pitfalls and advantages of each, and knowing the audience, you can make decisions on how to use them.

The physical layout of the room where the presentation will be made definitely influences what visuals should be selected. Carefully consider such factors as room size, electrical outlets, availability of projection screen or chalkboard, and the ability of the speaker to easily control and dim the lights. Let's look at various types of visuals that can assist in communicating ideas in speech settings.

Visuals can aid the talk in many ways.

Handouts

Placing materials literally in the hands of the audience can help them to better understand the presentation—for example, charts, tables, diagrams, or financial data.

If several handouts are used, it may be helpful to print them on different colors of paper. This permits keeping everyone with you, "look at the pie chart on the yellow

There are ways to coordinate your handout with your talk.

paper." Everyone is actually looking at the pie chart on the yellow paper and not the bar chart on the blue paper.

Do not let the handouts distract the audience. Determine in advance how they can be distributed. It is usually best to have someone distribute the handouts at the precise time you will refer to them; if they are distributed at the beginning of the speech, some members of the audience will begin to study them rather than listen to you.

If you use a handout and slide at the same time, be sure that the item projected matches exactly what the people in the audience have in their hands. If the two items differ, you will get numerous questions and comments about the difference. This breaks the continuity of the presentation and detracts from your credibility.

Reports

Focus the audience's attention when a report is used as a visual.

Sometimes the audience will have received a written report or a detailed summary of your data prior to the presentation. In this case, it is assumed that the audience will be informed and that the oral presentation will consist of more than just reading from materials previously provided.

If the written report contains tables, charts, or other visuals, you can have the audience turn to these items as they are explained in the context of the oral report. However, if twenty people all have a fifty-page report in their hands, it will be very difficult to get all of them to look at the same page at the same time. People are naturally curious, and while you are attempting to direct their attention to a point you are making with the aid of the overhead projector, some will be flipping through their reports to see how some idea relates to an interesting table in the written report.

In a courteous manner ("Let's all look at the vital statistics on page 12"), attempt to keep the audience's attention on the relevant material. Also beware of reading too much material from the report; it is best to speak extemporaneously about materials in the report and to look directly at the audience.

Chalkboards

Some conference rooms have white chalkboards that may also be used as projection screens. A visual such as a balance sheet or a form can be projected on the white chalkboard and the speaker, using colored chalk, can insert data as needed. Some white boards can be written on with felt-tip markers.

Try to "hold" or cover material on the board until needed.

If there is a series of boards, each on its own track, it is possible to prepare materials in advance, keep the boards covered, and then slide out the appropriate board when needed. The chalkboard also may be helpful during the question-and-answer period when it is necessary to quickly illustrate a point.

Sometimes working with a chalkboard and different colors of chalk can become messy. In addition, if the chalkboard cannot be covered, the speaker is forced either to place the information on the board before the presentation and let everyone look at it before it is presented or to stop the speech to write on the board. Both of these options are distracting. Another disadvantage of chalkboards is that usually the boards are placed at a height convenient to the speaker rather than the audience. If there is a relatively large group, it may be difficult for some of them to see the material on the board.

Slides

Colorful photographic slides can be prepared on almost any subject. They can project photos of products, typewritten lists or charts, or even collages that help to summarize several points. Slides make it possible to represent complex ideas pictorially and may provide just the dynamic boost your presentation needs.

There is a tendency sometimes to let the slides become too overpowering in making the presentation. Be sure that they do not detract from the major points. When using slides, give careful consideration to when you will switch from one to another. The audience will find it very distracting to be looking at a picture concerning product use in snowy Wisconsin while you are speaking about the use of products in balmy Florida. Slides often call for dimming the lights, so if you are presenting material that will require the audience to take notes, slides may be inappropriate.

Slides can be great, but call for consider- able practice.

Practice with the slides and be sure that they are in the correct order. Insert blank slides when you prefer to project nothing. The blank slide that reveals a subtle color is not distracting and won't be as visually upsetting to the audience as glaring white light.

It is generally best to use a projector that allows you to adjust the focus and movement of the slides. Take time to learn how to work the controls. If someone else is going to run the machine, try to work with him or her in advance, and make sure the individual knows when to change pictures. Work out a system or unobtrusive signal with this person. It is distracting to have to repeatedly say, "Next slide please."

Large Flip Charts

One of the oldest and yet most practical means of handling visual information is the flip chart. The charts are portable; they can be prepared in advance, or they can be used during the meeting to jot down ideas or questions from the audience. There are many state-of-the-art visual techniques available today, but for useful and practical on-the-job business communications, you will find yourself using flip charts fre- quently.

The flip chart consists of large sheets of paper, usually about 3 by 2 feet, fastened together and hinged on a tripod in such a manner that each page can be flipped over and out of the way, thereby exposing the next page. The pads of paper can be purchased, and the sheets are thrown away after use.

Don't overlook the con- venience and ease of using the flip chart.

The flip chart can be useful in providing a list, an outline, a basic graph, or a diagram, or in developing a progression of ideas—one page to the next. The material placed on the flip chart is drawn or printed by hand. Using felt-tipped markers, you can present the material in different colors to highlight specific items. Compared to fancy overlays and slides that can take days or weeks to prepare, the flip chart does not call for much lead time. To prepare charts, you need only a few minutes, the pad, and several colored markers.

A major advantage of the flip chart is that it gives you so much control. It is easy to alter the sequence of materials or to refer to items previously cited (see Figure 19.2).

Table Flip Charts

For a small group seated close to the speaker or around a table, the table flip chart is a convenient way to present visual material. Much smaller than the large flip chart, the table model can be placed on a conference table and is very easy to flip; it also makes a compact, easily portable package. The table flip chart is suitable for presenting charts and graphics that have been prepared in advance, but it is not a handy device to attempt to draw on during a speech.

The most common use of the table flip chart probably is in sales presentations. If a sales representative is going to make a similar presentation a number of times in a number of different places to small groups, the table flip chart can be very handy.

Table-top flip charts are great for very small groups.

The major limitation of the table flip chart is its size. It is not appropriate for a group that is larger than six to eight people, and it should not be used in a situation in which individuals will be seated more than ten or twelve feet from the chart. The table flip chart is excellent for indicating a progression of ideas or thoughts. However, be sure that those ideas progress correctly on the chart and that they match identically the context of the spoken material.

Overhead Projectors

One of the most versatile pieces of visual equipment is the overhead projector. It can project images of items the speaker writes on the spur of the moment, and it can project drawings, tables, charts, and other visuals that have been prepared in advance. The advantage of the overhead projector is that it can be used in a well-lit room; you can stand next to the machine and introduce transparencies when you want. The overhead is becoming even more popular today because a speaker can produce large print and graphics with the PC printer and, using xerography, quickly have a professional-looking transparency.

Most conference rooms have overheads—use them to aid your talks.

The overhead can be used in several ways:

1. **Acetate Roll.** Some overheads have rolls of acetate attached; this makes it possible to draw anything on the roll with a grease pencil or a transparency pen and project it.
2. **Transparencies.** Printed and typed materials or drawings can be reproduced

FIGURE 19.2   Flip Charts: Ideal Visuals for Speech Situations

Advantages of the Large Flip Chart

•Easy to prepare in advance
•Can be used during the talk
•Very portable
•Permits "covering up" points until time to reveal them

Advantages of Table Flip Chart

•Very portable
•Requires no special lighting or electricty
•Can be used repeatedly

onto single pieces of acetate with a copy machine that has this capability. This technique is handy when you wish to prepare material in advance; it is a good idea to type the material using orator-style type so the print will be large enough for everyone in the audience to see. Of course, there are machines available that print large-size letters, numbers, and symbols specifically for use on transparencies; it is also possible to prepare the original copy, enlarge it with xerography, and then make the transparency (see Figure 19.3).

3. **Overlays.** You may wish to develop an idea in a series of related steps, and it may be distracting to keep switching individual transparencies. In this situation, the overlay, which is a series of hinged transparencies, is useful. For example, if letter format is being explained, the first transparency shows the piece of stationery, the second transparency is laid over the first to show where to place the date, the third shows the salutation, the fourth adds the body of the letter, and so on. The overlay permits you to develop an idea in steps by adding material in sequence.

In any of these three techniques, there are two ways of pointing to the material being

FIGURE 19.3   How Amateur Speakers Can Make Their Own Professional-looking Transparencies

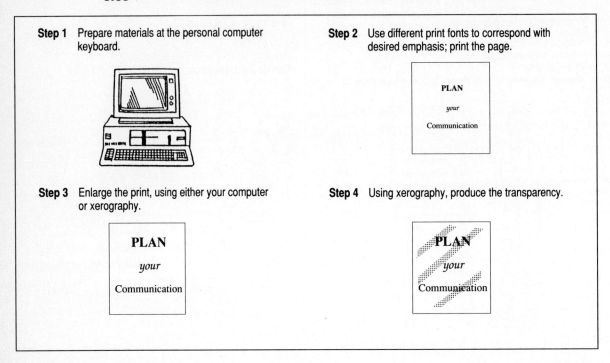

Step 1   Prepare materials at the personal computer keyboard.

Step 2   Use different print fonts to correspond with desired emphasis; print the page.

PLAN

your

Communication

Step 3   Enlarge the print, using either your computer or xerography.

Step 4   Using xerography, produce the transparency.

PLAN

your

Communication

PLAN

your

Communication

projected. You may use a pencil and point to the material on the transparency or acetate, which will cause the shadow of the pencil to be projected. Or you may go to the screen and point to the material.

Other Visuals

There are many technologies to aid your oral communications.

Visuals can bring an interesting dimension to the oral presentation and can help to add variety. Besides the techniques noted, there are other forms of visual and audio media. These include motion pictures, film strips, opaque projectors, audio tapes, and videotapes. There is even a new board (like a moveable chalkboard) upon which you can write and draw. Then, if desired, you push a button and a photocopy is created and transmitted to a photocopy machine, which can provide a hard copy for each person in your audience. If you were to use any of these forms, your organization would probably provide experts to assist you in preparing the presentation.

Today, with the increasing ease of videotaping, this medium is becoming widely used. You may use videotape to present product demonstrations, new production procedures, or even testimonials from individuals who cannot be present for the speech.

Practice with Your Visuals

It is important to practice with your visuals. Never go into a speech situation having practiced only the oral aspects without practicing the integration of visuals. What a waste to have taken time to prepare transparencies, and then to stand in front of the projector and block the visual. Do not assume that the visuals will just work in to your speech naturally. Practice your movement involved in using the flip chart; practice the advancing of slides; practice advancing the acetate on the overhead. Many speakers have a tough enough time giving a speech when all they have to do is stand at a podium and gesture. You are adding more dimensions when visuals enter your speech— practice and walk through the presentation and become comfortable with your materials, your notes, and your visuals.

Practice *with* your visuals.

The Power of Oral and Visual Communication

Good visual aids that supplement and emphasize your oral comments add a powerful dimension to your presentation. You actually are communicating on two levels with your audience; the listeners hear your message and simultaneously see your key points. Presenting your speech in this manner assures you of delivering a "knock-out, one-two punch."

Combining visual and oral impact

THE LAST DETAILS

Usually you will be in familiar surroundings when you speak and you will have ample time to examine the room. It is your responsibility to check the podium, the lighting, and any other details. There are all kinds of things that can go wrong. By checking out the arrangements in advance, you can head off such problems as the following.

Check these items out—avoid items that can ruin your talk.

1. You will have to turn down the lights for the presentation of your twelve slides. Where are the light switches?
2. The offices have soft music playing constantly. Is there a switch in the conference room that will turn the music off?
3. Your flip chart sheets do not match the stand in the conference room. What do you do?
4. You practiced your presentation in a well-lit room at a podium with a light. You are provided a room that is relatively dark and the podium has no light.
5. The overhead projector works fine but goes out during the talk. Do you know where a replacement bulb is?

Although these may seem like small problems, they can make you uncomfortable, cause you to lose concentration, and interfere with the effectiveness of the presentation—so they are major considerations. A little forethought and five minutes spent in the conference room prior to the presentation can help to avoid such problems.

QUICK REVIEW

There are numerous details involved in successfully presenting the oral talk. As noted, for each of the basics there are specific ways you can practice in advance so that the actual speech can succeed. Also, there are specific details you can check in advance (e.g., podium height) so that you are not tossed any unexpected "curve balls." Although many people concentrate only on presentation factors at the time of the presentation, there is much that can be done in advance to aid in giving a good talk—know your mode of delivery, practice it, and work on your voice, gestures, and speech rate.

EXECUTIVE SUMMARY

To: Business Communication Students

From: David N. Bateman and Norman B. Sigband

Subject: Delivering Oral Presentations

The first prerequisite of an effective oral presentation is, of course, well-planned, well-prepared material. However, the best material can be sabotaged by poor delivery.

It may require a great deal of practice to produce a poised and confident delivery. Some helpful guidelines are: (1) look at your audience; (2) vary your volume and speed; (3) speak clearly; (4) use appropriate gestures; (5) check your posture and appearance; (6) be knowledgeable and be prepared; and (7) watch and listen for feedback.

You will have to decide whether to memorize your speech, present it impromptu, read it, or present it extemporaneously. In some situations, a combination of these modes may be most effective.

Visuals can add variety to your presentation and help to maintain interest. However, you must take special care to ensure that the visuals do not become disruptive to the flow of information. Some of the factors that will influence the type of visuals you should use (slides, flip chart, handouts) are the physical layout of the room, the size of the audience, and the availability of electrical outlets.

Practice with your visuals: if possible, practice in the room where your presentation will be given. This will give you an opportunity to check on the lighting, the podium, and any other details.

Preparation is the key—preparation of the speech, of notes, of visuals, of key ideas, of the concluding statements, of the conference room equipment, of everything!

DISCUSSION GENERATORS

1. *The Look Advantage.* Why is it advantageous for the speaker to really look at (have visual interaction with) the audience? In preparing your response, indicate why it would be a poor practice to pick out a few spots on the back wall and look at them instead of establishing actual visual contact with the group.

2. *Music and Speech, Speed and Volume.* Explain the authors' analogy of a good speech and a good piece of music.

3. *Dangers.* For each of the modes of delivery, identify a potential danger in delivering a speech using this mode:
   memorization
   impromptu delivery
   reading
   extraporaneous speaking

4. *Interactions.* Explain how feedback to the speaker can enhance the "dialogue" between the speaker and the listeners.

5. *Just Comes Naturally.* Why is it desirable for most speakers, especially inexperienced speakers, to practice gestures? Shouldn't the gestures just evolve naturally?

6. *Clothing.* What is wrong with a man wearing a tie that is not coordinated with his suit when he is called upon to give a speech?

7. *Practice.* Why is practice much more than just working through the speech from start to finish? Cite explicit activities the speaker should carry through when practicing a speech.

8. *Extemporaneous Practice.* Is it possible to practice the extemporaneous speech? Explain your response in some detail.

9. *Telescope.* When called upon to give an impromptu speech, the speaker must quickly "telescope" the speech elements and then begin to talk. Briefly explain what would be involved in this telescoping process.

10. *Listen to Yourself.* If you are going to give a speech next week, why is it important to listen to yourself in normal conversation this week?

11. *Practice Visual.* Explain how the speaker should practice using a flip chart and an overhead (using acetate). Be very specific in describing why the person should practice and how the practice should be accomplished.

12. *Manuscript Read Speech.* What kinds of notes might a speaker make in a manuscript speech to be presented to the Chamber of Commerce this evening? Cite a specific example and explain.

13. *One Word.* What is the key word used to describe the extemporaneous mode of delivery? Why is it advantageous to speak in this manner in most situations when giving a talk in the United States?

14. *Color Coding.* If you have three handouts for the audience and you are going to refer to them at different points throughout your talk, why is it advantageous to print them on different color paper? Explain your answer in terms of feedback.

15. *Feedback.* When giving a talk, you will receive feedback. List at least four different kinds of feedback you may receive, and for each, indicate what you are to do in response to that feedback.

16. *Chalk Board Disadvantage.* If you are giving a talk for which you will use a chalkboard that has no sliding panels, what are the disadvantages of using this visual if you want to prepare your visual in advance? In this situation, what would be the advantages of a flip chart?

17. *Glaring Lights.* Why is it disruptive to project a white light with a slide projector? What can you do to avoid creating this kind of distraction?

18. *PCs and Transparencies.* How have PCs enhanced the use of transparencies for today's speech-maker?

19. *More Details.* The text lists five last-minute details that the experienced speaker will check before giving a speech. What are three additional items for the experienced speaker to check so that he or she is not surprised upon arriving at the podium?

20. *Read Dangers.* A primary danger with inexperienced speakers reading a speech is that they will not look at the audience and will read in a monotone. What are four specific suggestions for practicing the read speech so these problems will not evolve?

APPLICATIONS FOR BUSINESS

21. *Transparency.* As a manager in the Oyster Organization, you are to make a presentation on one of the following subjects. Prepare a transparency that will aid you in communicating your subject.
    - Tuition Refund Plan
    - In-house Education Program
    - On-the-job Training

22. *Misinterpreted Gestures.* Gestures are supposedly used to aid and promote the communication process. However, that may not always be the case. It is possible for gestures to disrupt and in fact disgust the audience.
    a. List three or four gestures in the context of a talk, and indicate how they might be misinterpreted.
    b. List two or three gestures that would be acceptable in this country, but would have another meaning in another country.
       Be prepared to discuss these issues.

23. *Campus Critique.* Unfortunately, it is easier to critique and make suggestions on how other speakers can improve than it is to apply those standards to our own presentations. At the same time, the insightful observer can note positive and negative attributes of a speaker and then strive to add and eliminate such elements from his or her own speech patterns.

    Premised upon the various oral communication elements you have studied in this chapter, locate a guest speaker on campus. Attend the presentation, and then in a one-page memo to your instructor, critique the speech.

24. *Speaker Detail.* The Reynolds Organization, as part of their recent remodeling, have completely redone their conference rooms. They have a variety of new features including:

   - Incandescent and fluorescent lights that dim.
   - Moveable and automatic rising podiums; podiums that are equipped with lights and timers.
   - White chalk boards with green chalk boards on tracks in front of the white panels.
   - Cork walls upon which completed flip sheets can be posted for later reference.

   With all of these physical improvements, the vice president has asked you to prepare a brief handout for each manager that, in an interesting and insightful manner, indicates all of the elements that the thinking speaker will check prior to giving a talk in one of these rooms.

25. *Building an Overlay.* An overlay is a series of attached transparencies. Each individual sheet of acetate contains some information (or sketch), and as one is overlaid the other, "the story builds." You are giving a talk to fellow managers at the Reynolds organization on one of the following topics. Build an overlay for this talk that contains at least three different sheets.

   - The block format for a letter.
   - The different parts of a memo, e.g., TO, FR, SUBJ; Attachments; Headings.
   - Successful steps in practicing a speech.
   - Additions to a well-prepared manuscript talk.

COMMUNICATION CHECK-UPS

26. George Atworth will cover the booth and Betty Rathy will run the computer operation at the convention.

27. This was a good year to hire more staff however, our budget would not permit the expansion.

28. The Ajax bonds, which were issued in 1955, paid 5%, the municipal bonds, which came out in 1960 paid 6%, and the Bronson Company stock, purchased in 1977, paid 12%.

29. You should consider visiting the following facilities Portland, Montgomery, Milwaukee, Peoria, Springfield, Los Angeles, Greensboro, and Hillsdale.

30. Both of the computers, he purchased an Apple and a Compaq, were specially painted a bright yellow.

31. John felt that he should immigrate from South Africa to the United States.

32. In large operations, stationary is always expensive.

33. There were fewer good candidates from the first college than from the second.

34. His stated coarse of action is on target.

35. Mary and Ann can always be counted on to provide you with excellent council.

Executive Introduction

FOOD MARKETING INSTITUTE

1750 K STREET, N.W.
WASHINGTON, D.C. 20006
202/452-8444
TELEX: 892722 FMI USA WSH
FAX: 202/429-4519

August 3, 198_

Mr. Bruce J. Konklin
Northridge College Council
Northridge College
Northridge, MN 55055

Dear Mr. Konklin:

As you assume the responsibilities for leading the Northridge
College Council for the coming academic year, you will find yourself
involved in a great many administrative duties. Leading meetings and
conferences and holding interviews will take up a great deal of your
time. However, all managers, whether in the public or private sector,
find this time.

Such sessions—whether meetings or interviews—can prove costly to
an organization if improperly conducted. And when one considers how
many meetings take place in almost every organization in just one
month, the cost can be staggering. It is for that reason that every
step should be taken to insure that every meeting and conference held
not only reaches its objectives, but that it be conducted as efficiently as possible.

The enclosed material makes suggestions on effective leadership
and participation. In addition, it sets standards for conducting
various types of interviews such as those labeled informational,
appraisal, counseling, technical exchange, and others.

As Chair of the Student Council, you will find these suggestions
valuable in achieving your goals. You will also find that there are
specific techniques for "meeting" with success. These will prove both
cost effective and vital to you in your capacity as a group leader.

Good luck in your responsible, new assignment.

Cordially yours,

Ted C. File
Vice President
Education

TCF:tls

Conducting and Participating in Meetings, Conferences, and Interviews

WHAT YOU CAN LEARN BY STUDYING THIS CHAPTER

As a future manager, you have a tremendous challenge ahead of you. Many managers spend well over half of their working lives in meetings, conferences, and interviews—and they waste a large portion of that time. In the United States, we have somehow developed a tolerance for slipshod meetings. In the competitive worldwide marketplace we now face, however, that attitude must change. Your challenge is to reshape the way American managers view and participate in meetings, conferences, and interviews. In this chapter, you are provided with ways to accomplish the task. You will learn how to identify meeting policies, establish agenda, distribute minutes, and set up conferences. You will review many of the kinds of interviews managers must conduct. Of course, it is much easier to outline the ideal meeting on paper than to actually implement and conduct one, but if you learn the basics here, you will have established a solid foundation upon which to build your meeting strategies for the future.

The role of oral inter-actions in organiza-tions

In order to be efficient, organizations today find it necessary to rely more heavily on direct and live interactions than on written exchanges, with their slower feedback. Unfortunately, the techniques for improving these oral interactions are mastered slowly. This chapter highlights the basics of successful interaction for the meeting leader, the meeting participant, the conference leader, and the interviewer. The importance of correctly applying these concepts cannot be overemphasized for the manager who desires to be productive and efficient in the modern organizational setting.

MEETINGS

Effective meetings don't just happen—they are planned and organized. Before we look at procedures for arranging meetings, two issues of overriding concern must be explored—time and costs.

Time Considerations

Reducing meeting waste is as important as reducing factory waste.

Saving time is always important to managers. Efficient communication is an impor-tant key to reducing waste, increasing productivity, and saving time. A single manager at his or her desk daydreaming is wasting time, but at least it's only one person's time. On the other hand, eight to ten people waiting for a meeting to start is a huge waste of time. Remember that the wastefulness of a meeting must be multiplied by the number of people in attendance.

Cost Considerations

Meetings are costly.

Most managers spend about 75 percent of their time in some kind of meeting activity each day—formal meetings, informal/unscheduled meetings, and telephone con-versations. Managers' salaries are high, and when they are calculated on a per-minute basis, dozens of dollars are involved. Therefore, wasting minutes in meetings is a costly expenditure that is never recouped.

Needed: Meeting Policies

Organizations often have many policies—but none for meetings.

Organizations have policies for almost everything; amazingly, most don't have policies for the activity in which most of their managers spend most of their time: meetings. Some basic guidelines for all leaders and participants would increase efficiency in an organization almost overnight. Here are some examples of some rather simple, but effective, policies:

Meeting policies can be stated simply.

Invite selectively: Include only those who can make a contribution to the objectives; protocol, politics, and historical precedent should not dictate who attends.

Create an agenda: Prepare and distribute the agenda in advance or, in the case of meetings called on short notice, post it at the beginning of the meeting. The agenda sets the tone and substance for the meeting and helps to eliminate costly digressions.

Distribute minutes: Within twenty-four hours after the meeting, minutes should be distributed. Besides recapping the session, the minutes should indicate who is responsible for various items requiring action.

Start/stop on time: Begin and end the meeting precisely at the stipulated time. Don't wait for latecomers.

Other policies might concern such details as who is to take minutes, how people are to be seated, or whether substitutes can be sent in place of invitees who can't attend. Like other activities in the organization, policies and procedures that are developed carefully and used consistently can enhance the quality and productivity of meetings.

THE PARTS OF THE MEETING

The meeting has three distinct parts: the premeeting, the meeting, and the postmeeting. If the manager views the meeting as a three-stage process, it will be possible to eliminate unnecessary meetings, conduct effective sessions, and maintain good records.

Meetings have a three-stage process.

The Premeeting

Planning is one of the key ingredients in organizing a successful meeting. Premeeting planning activities include a number of steps.

Establish Need.   Does the meeting actually have to be held? Is a face-to-face session necessary? Will a conference call or videoconference be acceptable?

Define Purpose.   Why is the meeting being called—to gain consensus, to define a problem, to hear varying opinions, to provide necessary information, to answer questions, to exchange technical data, to make a decision, or to make a recommendation? In writing a report, the purpose influences what the report is called and who receives it; in the meeting, the purpose influences who attends and what is included in the agenda.

Don't overlook pre-meeting activities.

Establish Type.   Once the purpose is known, the type of meeting can be determined—informational, problem-solving, training, technical exchange, general discussion, or decision-making. It is possible to combine the types; for example, the group may first exchange information and then try to reach a consensus on an action to be taken.

Determine Invitees and Leader.   Individuals should be invited based on their ability to contribute to the topic. The leader selected should be articulate, patient, and impartial.

Identify Topics.   After the purpose is established, the topics to be discussed should start to fall into order; they will become the basis for the agenda.

Prepare and Distribute Agenda.   Besides listing the topics to be discussed, the agenda includes:

1. Date, time, and place of the meeting.
2. Topics and subtopics for discussion.
3. List of participants.
4. Materials for the meeting (if needed).

Tact and courtesy are involved in agenda construction.

There are many elements of protocol and courtesy involved in the agenda. Everyone should know who will be in attendance and what will be discussed. It is unfair to surprise attendees by having the executive vice-president attend or by suddenly bringing up topics that people did not have an opportunity to investigate in advance. Figure 20.1 shows an agenda with the distribution listed. The agenda should be distributed so that people have time to prepare and will know who will be attending.

When meetings are called on short notice, it is not always possible to distribute the agenda in advance. In such cases, a secretary can phone the agenda to participants or the agenda can be placed on a flip chart or chalkboard in the meeting room prior to the session.

The agenda serves several purposes. It tells the participants what will be discussed, and it provides the meeting leader with a "baton" and a "stop watch" to keep the meeting on target and on time: "that's a good point, Joe, but right now let's get back to item three on the agenda." It also encourages the meeting leader and the participants to plan and prepare.

Make Physical Arrangements.   Many organizations provide checklists for physically arranging meetings. Some of the details to consider are seating, equipment for visual presentations, provision of note pads, and refreshments.

The Meeting

Dynamics of the actual meeting

As we have seen, an effective meeting does not just happen; it must be planned and organized. But it is one thing to plan the meeting on paper and quite another to make the meeting click when the people gather. First let's concentrate on the role most of us will assume at most meetings: participant.

FIGURE 20.1   Meeting Agenda

Remington Manufacturing

14499 Lotus Drive
Shreveport, Louisiana 71109

DATE: March 10, 198_

TO: L. Jameson, Facilities Manager

FROM: S. Wilkerson, Vice President   *Sue*

SUBJECT: Meeting, March 17, 198_
            Conference Room C — 1:30 - 3:00 p.m.
            Review of Space Administration

Major Topic for Discussion

> Acquisition of additional manufacturing area for the new
> product: Multipurpose cabinets, #202

Specific Items for Discussion

> 1. Advantages and disadvantages of acquiring additional space
> (approximately 25,000 square feet) at an off-plant site vs.
> add-on to Plant #3 (L. Jameson).
>
> 2. Cost analysis of space required in three off-plant sites
> (L. Kelly).
>
> 3. Personnel staffing needs and availability (A. Chui).
>
> 4. Capital investment considerations (new site vs. in-plant)
> (L. Kelly).
>
> 5. Review of pros and cons of acquisition off-site vs. plant
> add-on.
>
> 6. Other business.

Distribution

L. Jameson, Facilities Manager   R. T. Weston, Exec. Vice Pres.
R. T. Burton, Production Manager   L. Kelly, Financial V. P.
M. M. Watson, Mfg. Manager   S. Wilkerson, Vice Pres.
L. M. Cruz, New Products Manager   A. Chui, Human Resources V. P.

Participant.   In the United States, most articles written about meetings concern how to lead one. But each of us is more often a participant than a leader. There are some keys to being an effective meeting participant; learn and follow these keys appropriately, and you are on the road to becoming an effective manager.

Keys for being an effective participant

Arrive on time, in fact a bit early. First, you will not be disruptive, and second, by arriving early you will have added moments to size up the situation.

Do your homework and be prepared to contribute to the meeting at appropriate times. Work conscientiously to not monopolize the discussion; strive to be clear and succinct in your comments.

Be courteous and generally nonabrasive to other meeting members; you will probably be working with these people again, so don't wear out your goodwill.

Strive to summarize and determine if the group is reaching a consensus; in this way you can help the group reach closure instead of taking them down another path.

Each person cannot always get his or her way in meetings. Try to find areas of agreement, and avoid being a disruptive force, although this does not mean you must cave in on matters of principles. A good meeting participant will strive to participate and to not be disruptive to the meeting process.

Leader.   The leader should have the ability to involve all participants, keep the meeting on course, help reach a consensus, and promote goodwill. The meeting leader should always:

There is an art to leading a meeting effectively and harmoniously.

1. encourage participation;
2. move through the agenda;
3. begin and end on time;
4. secure decisions when needed; and
5. thank the participants for their preparation, participation, and attendance.

The primary role of the meeting leader is to serve as a catalyst. The leader should not dominate but rather should encourage discussion, bring a variety of views together from the participants, encourage analysis, and seek possible solutions.

Note the nonverbal communications of the meeting leader.

The leader's choice of seating position is significant. Sitting alone may indicate that the leader will be in charge. It may be wiser for the leader to sit among the participants. It is important to be sensitive to the climate and to have everyone relaxed.

The meeting leader should appoint someone to take the minutes; a participant can often take minutes more effectively than an "outside" secretary. Although minutes can be recorded on a pad of paper, the trend today is to have the "secretary" use a flip chart. In this way, the participants can check the notes and make corrections (by voicing their opinions) immediately.

As the time approaches for the meeting cut-off, the leader may wish to take a vote or gain a consensus on key issues, establish action items, and designate who will carry them through (or secure volunteers), and finally, offer a summary of the key areas discussed and the decisions reached.

Postmeeting Activities

Almost invariably, new problems surface during the meeting, new opportunities are recognized, and old issues continue. All of this requires follow-up. The session is not over when the meeting has adjourned and the participants have dispersed. The decisions that have been reached must be acted upon, the action items must be implemented, and the follow-up steps initiated. (See Figure 20.2.) The advantages of preparing and distributing the minutes promptly are:

Postmeeting: Generally the meeting isn't over when it's over.

1. **Consistency.** All of the attendees receive the same view of what took place. If the minutes are distributed soon after the meeting, they can be quickly corrected, if necessary. Corrections become more difficult after a delay because it is difficult a month later to recall the details of what actually transpired.
2. **Follow-up.** Items are investigated, researched, evaluated, or secured; action items are clearly noted in the minutes along with the name of the individual who is responsible for completing the task. This helps avoid the problem, "But I didn't know I was supposed to obtain that information."
3. **Accurate Record.** The minutes become a matter of record. They may be used for review by those who attended the meeting, for study by those who were absent, and for reference by those who may need the information months or years later.

CONFERENCES

The terms "seminar," "workshop," "convention," and "conference" are often used interchangeably, but there is general agreement that whereas "meeting" often refers to a small gathering, "conference" usually suggests a larger group. Active two-way interchange of information may not be a goal of the conference. For example, conferences in business are frequently used when the organization wants to inform employees, dealers, or agents about some particular topic. The communication is predominantly one-way, and audience participation may be limited or not even sought at all. Today, meetings and conferences can be conducted in person and via video.

What is a conference?

Planning

Many large corporations have specialized departments that plan conferences. Independent consulting firms also provide conference planning services.

Many factors are involved in organizing a conference, depending on the size, site, and nature of the gathering. Just some factors to be considered are meeting rooms, registration, lodging, entertainment, speakers, timing, logistics, and publicity.

FIGURE 20.2   Meeting Minutes

Remington Manufacturing

14499 Lotus Drive
Shreveport, Louisiana 71109

DATE: March 17, 198_

TO: L. Jameson

FROM: S. Wilkerson   *gw*

SUBJECT: Minutes of meeting, March 17, 198_

Present

L. Jameson	R. T. Weston
R. T. Burton	L. Kelly
M. M. Watson	S. Wilkerson
L. M. Cruz	

Absent

A. Chui

Summary of Topics Discussed

1. Review of cost figures was presented for acquisition of new space and conversion cost of existing facilities (see Appendix #1 for data). L.Jameson and L. Kelly

2. Review of capital investment required for going into production (see Appendix #2 for data). R. Burton

3. Personnel (not covered; A. Chui absent)

4. Discussion of pros and cons of acquisition vs. conversion

Decisions Reached

1. A tentative offer of $.60 per sq. ft. to be made for Site #2

2. No discussion to be held at this time with union bargaining unit

3. Target date for initial production: Dec. 1, 198_

Action Items

Item No.	Topic	Responsibility	Due Date
1.	Breakdown on all personnel needs for Site #2	A. Chui	April 10, 198_
2.	Tax implications for Site #2, Maywood, CA	L. Kelly	April 10, 198_
3.	Financing cost: Bank loan of $500,000	L. Kelly	April 20, 198_

Attachments

Sessions

The traditional view of a conference is of a large meeting at which everyone convenes at one location; for example, Caterpillar tractor dealers meet in Peoria, Illinois, at the corporation's headquarters, to see the new line of earth-moving equipment. Since dealers are brought together from all over the world, the company organizes a variety of sessions for them, including panels and presentations on corporate strategies, parts promotion, competition, market penetration, inventory control, collecting receivables, and so on. With the advent of videoconferencing, however, the format and geography of conferences are changing.

Note the orchestration of a conference compared to the give-and-take of a meeting.

Personnel

In contrast with meetings, conferences often include professional presentations. Scripts are prepared, leaders are selected with care, and the topic (the introduction of new equipment, for example) is approached with both fanfare and finesse. When the audience will do more listening than interacting, it is important to select conference personnel who can relate well to those assembled and maintain their interest and enthusiasm.

INTERVIEWS

As a manager or employee, you will frequently assume the role of interviewer or interviewee. As a job seeker, you will be an interviewee; as a manager looking for competent employees to fill an opening, you will be the interviewer. Whether as a buyer or seller, a husband or wife, a parent or child, you will be in one position or the other. What all this means is simply this: understanding the interview process and being competent as an interviewer or interviewee can be extremely important to both your business and personal life.

Interview interactions are a major factor in our lives.

We usually think of the interview as a situation involving two people—one asking questions and the other answering. It is that, but it is also much more. The interview is an exchange of thoughts, feelings, and attitudes in which ideas, goodwill, and understanding can grow as a result of the efforts of the individuals involved. Each person must receive (listen) as well as send (talk) in the exchange.

The interview is an effective communication method for sending and receiving information and for gaining understanding and acceptance of ideas. The interview is also an excellent device for developing and changing attitudes and behavior and for motivating individuals to work toward common goals.

Steps in the Interview Process

Regardless of the type of interview, there are some basic steps for each kind of interview.

Preparing for the Interview.

Few activities can be conducted successfully without preparation, and the interview is no exception. It is a good idea not only to prepare, but to actually write out key items such as background data, objectives to be achieved, critical questions, and possible courses of action.

Review the following checklist before the interview to be sure you have done all the necessary preparation:

Obtain the necessary background information to successfully conduct the interview.

Establish goals or objectives for the interview.

Design or formulate critical questions or points for discussion.

Consider, to the best of your ability, the interviewee's needs and personality, and make provisions to adapt to them.

Determine possible solutions, courses of action, and appropriate reactions to specific proposals or alternatives.

Select a satisfactory interview site.

Conducting the Interview.

Your goal in the interview is to gain the information you need. The following guidelines should help ensure your success in achieving that goal.

Establish a congenial climate by choosing a satisfactory and comfortable meeting place for the interview. Begin at the time scheduled, cordially greet the interviewee, and provide handouts, reference materials, and/or refreshments if appropriate.

Listen effectively to gain active participation.

Supply relevant information.

Ask key questions.

Note when crucial periods arise; these may be signals for closure, new directions, agreements, or compromise.

Observe, evaluate, and note the interviewee's comments, nonverbal communications, and reactions.

Identify key items for action (commonly called action items) and a schedule to follow-up.

Close the interview in a thoughtful, appreciative way.

Don't permit a phone call or some other interruption to cause a disruption.

Following Up on the Interview.   The interview has been prepared for and held; however, the circle has not yet been closed. It is now necessary to follow up to make sure that the agreements reached and the decisions made are completed. Be sure you have a list of items you are to follow up as a result of the interview.

Interviews generally call for some follow-up.

The interview can be the vehicle for problem solving, goal setting, information exchange, and building goodwill. Because people are involved—and people never react according to a formula—every interview will be different. Nevertheless, it is an activity in which you should be proficient.

Types of Interviews

There are many types of interviews. They can be distinguished by their goals and the strategies needed to make them succeed.

Different types of interviews have different goals.

Employment Interview.   In the employment interview, the interviewer wishes to obtain information on the prospective employee's qualifications, personality, and attitudes, and the job seeker wants to learn as much as possible about the organization. This obviously means that both must go into the interview with a list of specific questions and goals to be achieved. (Employment interviews are covered in more detail in Chapter 23.)

It is wise to write out the questions and test them before the interview so that a carelessly chosen word does not derail the interview. For example, the job seeker should inquire about promotion, but to ask, "When do I get promoted?" is aggressive and premature. "What is your firm's policy on promotion?" is much more appropriate.

One should select language carefully in an employment interview.

Careful preparation of questions is also important for the interviewer. There is a further consideration for the interviewer, however. With the Fair Employment Practices legislation, Equal Employment Opportunity regulations, and other laws, there is a whole series of personal questions concerning age, marital or parental status, race, and religion that if asked, could be cause for legal action.

Appraisal Interview.   Most organizations require that managers at all levels periodically review subordinates. The reviews generally occur quarterly, semiannually, or annually. The purpose of these appraisals is to mutually review performance in such areas as production, efficiency, responsibility, creativity, initiative, and judgment. This interview should also review how well previously established goals have been met and should establish new objectives for the interviewee.

Some managers find conducting the appraisal interview difficult.

In almost every instance, a form is completed that both parties sign or initial. This is done to indicate that the meeting was held and the information was discussed. (See Figure 15.7.)

Counseling/Coaching Interview.

Coaching is increasing in the manager's job.

Supervisors are often called upon to offer suggestions and advice to subordinates; today, the supervisor is sometimes viewed as a coach who meets with employees to literally "coach" them in areas where improvements can be made and to recognize areas that meet or exceed standards. In an interview situation, the manager may wish to counsel a worker on various methods of motivating others, arranging a production operation, mediating a problem, setting goals, dealing with suppliers, increasing production, and so on. At other times, it may be appropriate for a supervisor to counsel a subordinate on personal problems such as finances, participation in overtime, or health care plans.

It is important to recognize, however, that most managers are not professionally equipped for counseling in depth or in areas such as alcoholism, marital problems, and drug abuse. Some firms have a professional psychologist on the staff or on a retainer basis for such cases.

Disciplinary Interview.

Discipline—don't avoid the problem and don't use accusatory language.

In the disciplinary interview, it is important to retain the goodwill of the interviewee while pointing out the problem. This can be accomplished by avoiding accusatory language that is likely to arouse antagonism. Rather than saying "You failed to . . . ," it is better to say, "When you do it this way, you will achieve. . . . " Instead of saying, "I was disappointed that you, . . . " it is better to say, "I learned that you. . . ." This is never an easy interview to hold, but problems don't go away by themselves. A well-conducted interview brings problems into focus and permits solutions to be reached while maintaining goodwill.

Exit Interview.

Exit interviews should result in useful data for the organization.

Much can be learned from employees who voluntarily or involuntarily leave the firm. Such information may help future operations. To be successful, however, this interview must be structured carefully. If it is not, it may become a gripe session in which disgruntled employees disparage the actions of their former bosses or fellow workers in an effort to relieve their guilt or make themselves heroes.

Normally, the interview should be conducted by an objective individual from the personnel department. Discussion of personalities should be avoided, if at all possible. The focus should be on the office process or on the methods of production, sales, distribution, transportation, or other areas. What specific actions were followed? What should be done? How could it be done? What recommendations does the interviewee have?

Other Types of Interviews.

There are several other types of interviews not listed and discussed above: Technical exchange, informational, and persuasive. However, the basic principles are the same for all to achieve success: careful planning and preparation.

KEEP THE LINES OPEN

Meetings, conferences, and interviews are different in size, form, and format, but each is an extremely valuable communication vehicle, and they all have elements in common. Each contributes to participatory management, and each can open and keep open the lines of communication in complex organizations.

QUICK REVIEW

In meetings, conferences, and interviews, the basic planning devices studied in Chapter 2 continue to apply. Before writing a one-page memo, it is important to know your purpose. In considering a meeting, conference, or interview, it is vital to know your purpose before proceeding. Organizations can improve their meetings if they establish and follow some meeting policies. Besides just looking at the requisites for being a successful meeting leader, don't overlook the requisites for being a successful meeting participant. Probably the most important recurring theme throughout the discussions of meetings, conferences, and interviews is that they do not just happen. Careful planning and organization must take place.

EXECUTIVE SUMMARY

To: Business Communication Students

From: David N. Bateman and Norman B. Sigband

Subject: Conducting and Participating in Meetings, Conferences, and Interviews

In today's business world, more and more meetings, conferences, and interviews are being held. These sessions usually accomplish goals more quickly than written exchanges among several people and also permit participative interaction.

All small-group sessions use time, and when too much time is used or when it is used inefficiently, costs increase. Because many managers spend up to 75 percent of their time in sessions where two or more people are involved, it is vital that time be expended efficiently.

This chapter suggests a systems approach to meetings and interviews and includes specific actions that should be taken before, during, and after these sessions. There are several different types of meetings as well as different types of interviews. Conferences are different from meetings.

The manager should keep in mind that good meetings, interviews, and conferences don't just happen; they are the result of careful preparation and planning.

DISCUSSION GENERATORS

1. *Meeting Policies.* The text suggests a few meeting policies; what are two additional examples of policies for meetings that most organizations should establish?

2. *Waste Multiplication.* Explain how the potential waste of time multiplies in a meeting in contrast with an individual manager's working at her or his own desk.

3. *Premeeting Activities.* Compare and explain the similarities (or differences) between premeeting activities and the steps involved in planning for a long report.

4. *Agenda Items.* Name and explain the elements that should be included in an agenda.

5. *Not Enough Time.* Typed agenda take some time to prepare and distribute to meeting attendees. What can the person calling the meeting do if there is not enough time to type and distribute an agenda?

6. *Leader/Participant.* Looking at the attributes of a good meeting leader and a good meeting participant, identify the elements that are common to both.

7. *"Insider."* Why should an "insider," a person who regularly attends and participates in the meetings, take minutes instead of an "outside" secretary?

8. *Minutes Distribution.* How does the taking and quick distribution of meeting minutes to meeting participants aid in saving time at a future meeting of the group?

9. *Meeting vs. Conference.* Meetings as described by the authors are clearly two-way participative activities. Conferences, on the other hand, are described as being more one-way. Explain the difference.

10. *Conference Leadership.* Why are poise and rhetorical ability probably more important in conference leadership roles than in everyday meeting activities?

11. *Employment Interview.* Give an example of a question it would be illegal to ask a job applicant.

12. *Coach.* When it comes to many supervisory activities, including counseling, why is the supervisor considered a coach today? Illustrate one activity in which the supervisor could successfully coach an employee.

13. *Write Out Questions.* Is it a good idea for the job applicant to write out questions to ask the interviewer? Should the individual take written questions into the interview and periodically select one from the sheet?

14. *Seating.* Should the leader of the meeting always sit at the head of the table? Explain and defend your answer.

15. *Action Items.* What are action items and what should the group leader do to insure action is taken on these items?

16. *Meeting Time.* About how much time, on the average, will a future manager spend in meetings, according to the authors? How do you think that amount of time fluctuates with one's level in the organization?

17. *Stop Sign.* How does the agenda aid the group leader in accomplishing the goals of the meeting and stopping on time?

18. *Meeting Parts.* Name and explain the three parts of a meeting. Why is it important to recognize all three parts and not just the "meeting" part?

19. *Who's Coming.* As a participant in a meeting, why will you be interested in knowing who else is coming to the meeting? Why don't you want to be surprised by going to the meeting and discovering some unannounced people are present and will participate?

20. *Closure.* Why is reaching closure so important in meetings?

APPLICATIONS FOR BUSINESS

21. *Premeeting Physical Arrangements.* The dean of your college or school is hosting a meeting of the institution's executive advisory board. This board meets three times a year. The dean uses these meetings to act as a "laboratory" for students to learn the ins and outs of successful management.

    The board is meeting in one month, and the dean has asked you to handle the premeeting arrangements. It is crucial that the meeting take place without any problem. Before you implement your plan, the dean has asked you to prepare a memo in which you indicate what you will do and when you will do it.
    Some facts about the meeting are:
    • Eleven executives are on the board.
    • The executives come from throughout the nation.
    • The meeting starts on Wednesday morning at 8:15 a.m.
    • The out-of-town members will arrive the previous evening.
    • Besides the dean, the dean's staff of three will attend the meeting.
    • There will be refreshment breaks at 9:30 and 10:45 a.m. and 2:30 p.m.
    • Lunch will be served from 12:00 to 1:30 p.m. at the student center.
    • The meeting must end at (or before) 3:45 p.m. because many board members must catch late afternoon flights.

22. *Agenda.* Suzanne Settlemeyer of the Reynolds organization has one of her two annual meetings with the executive director of the association she manages. To insure efficient interactions and that all of the necessary work gets done, she prepares an agenda six weeks in advance. She and the executive director discuss and revise it and reach consensus on what will be discussed four weeks prior to the meeting.

    Relying on the information presented in Chapter 17 concerning Suzanne's relationship with BCA, prepare the memo and the draft agenda that Suzanne could send to the executive director six weeks prior to the meeting.

23. *Meeting Time.* Most managers work longer than eight hours each day. In your chosen profession, you may put in much longer days. But even if you work eight hours per day, if you spend 75 percent of your time in meetings, that would mean

six hours each day is involved in some kind of group interaction. Gather information and carefully analyze the job you plan to have and the meetings you will be
called upon to attend. In order to accomplish this task it will be necessary for you
to talk with several people who hold similar jobs today.

Provide a detailed outline of an "average" day. Show when your work day
starts and how it progresses. Clearly mark the meetings and indicate the types of
meetings in which you would be participating each day. Show the percentage of
your time you spend on each activity.

24. *What Does It Cost?* In Chapter 1, there is the meeting in which Jane O'Mayer, a
vice-president, and a manager similar to Suzanne are involved in a videoconference. Excluding the cost of the video, very carefully determine the personnel
cost of that meeting for the two people in this meeting. Going to sources like the
Occupational Outlook Handbook and *The American Almanac of Jobs and Salaries,* estimate the salaries for the individuals. Then, cost out the meeting. Be very
detailed, and carefully specify where and how you obtained the salary data.

25. *Meeting Policies.* Most organizations in the United States tend to run their
meetings in a slipshod manner. Recognizing how much time is spent in meetings,
this is most unfortunate. Dan Peterson of the Bikercize organization has had it.
Dan is VP for administration, and he feels it is his duty to aid the company in
shaping up its meetings.

Taking on Dan's role, send a memo to all department heads in which you (a)
state the need for meeting policies, (b) point to the advantages of being productive in meetings, and (c) outline meeting policies that are to be followed in the
future at Bikercize.

COMMUNICATION CHECK-UPS

26. Please refer back to the data presented in the July memorandum.

27. I am writing to accept your invitation to attend the meeting on April 10, 19—.

28. Belmont Company is pleased to inform you that your name was drawn and you
win the free dinner at the Chason Club.

29. This device can be used to alert the resident that the mail has arrived; further, the
device is easy to install, and the device has been approved by the postmaster
general for use.

30. The word questionnaire is often mispelled.

31. In our case, here at Belmont, the accounts receivable are monitored weekly.

32. The following is the actual top portion of a final copy of a memo; is it ready to
send? Assume that the date and name of the organization are cited elsewhere on
the memo form.

TO: Bob James, Director
Product Training

FR: Kathleen O'Hare, Assistant Director
Product Training

RE: Potential New Markets for Term-Line

33. 5,000 copies of the book Economics Today must be destroyed.
34. The following is the inside address and salutation in a letter.

The Helen Gallagher-Foster House
6523 North Galena Road
Peoria, illinois 60611

Dear Sirs:

35. Per the Tax Reform Act of 1986, all employees must complete a new W-4 form.

ALLEN-BRADLEY
A Rockwell International Company

INDUSTRIAL CONTROL GROUP
1201 South Second Street
Milwaukee, WI 53204 USA
Telephone 414/382-2000
Telex 026 699 & 431 1016
Fax 414/382 4444

November 22, 198_

Miss Janet Brookmeyer, President
ASPA Student Chapter
School of Business
University of Wisconsin - Whitewater
Whitewater, WI 53190

Dear Janet:

Your recent letter about my meetings in Whitewater was delightful; your comments concerning my presentation made my day!

You have had an excellent education in business and specifically
in the human resource speciality. When you ask about what the human
resource professional should do to "stay on top of things," two areas
come to mind immediately: listening and reading.

<u>**Listening**</u>. An individual involved in any aspect of personnel who
does not listen is in trouble. This means listening well to both your
superiors and your colleagues; you must listen equally effectively
when discussing issues with employees, unions, and many others to get
their reaction and feedback. Listening in the classroom is very
different from listening at the workplace, with its numerous distractions, massive amounts of data, and frequently high stakes. You must
listen keenly and sort out the real messages.

<u>**Reading**</u>. College students feel (and I did too when I was in
college) they read a substantial amount. Generally, the reading and
the time-pressures on reading are much more substantial in business
than in college. While you are still in college, read beyond your
texts (keep up on current affairs and related business activities).
All of the top executives I know are exceedingly well-read.

Effective listening and reading — these are basic requisites for
success in business, particularly in human resource management.

Sincerely,

Ted A. Hutton

Ted A. Hutton, Director
Human Resources
Industrial Control Group

TAH/jp

CHAPTER 21

Keeping Your Communications on Track: Effective Listening and Reading

WHAT YOU CAN LEARN BY STUDYING THIS CHAPTER

Since we "listen" and "read" all the time, it is generally difficult to get people to recognize the need for improvement in these areas. When listening and reading are part of the production-oriented environment of business, however, the need for improvement becomes obvious. Enhancing your listening and reading skills is not particularly difficult. You must know what can be done and then conscientiously practice. So far, this text has emphasized the sending side of the communication process. In the next few pages, the receiving side is emphasized. By understanding and employing these elements, you will have completed the communication process. You will find that you do not have to entirely change your behavior in order to improve your listening and reading. Success depends on your attitude and your ability to get organized.

Completing the communication process

So far, the emphasis in this text has been primarily on writing. In addition, the preparation and delivery of the oral message has been reviewed and analyzed. If we divide communication into sending and receiving, the focus has certainly been on the sending aspects. In this chapter, we focus on receiving the messages that bombard us.

There is nothing automatic about listening or reading.

There are two dominant ways to receive messages—listening and reading—and the manager must be proficient at both. These are skills that must be learned; it is foolish to assume that we are automatically good listeners and readers.

Business and management place such an emphasis on objectivity and obtaining facts that sometimes it appears as though we educate our future managers to ignore everything else. If that is so, then we are training managers to be insensitive listeners because we all communicate facts *and* feelings; if our boss receives and responds to only the facts, then he or she is missing huge amounts of communication and, further, frustrating us with partial responses to our *total* communications.

For the manager, it is crucial to tune into the total message. This can be accomplished by removing the barriers to effective listening and then listening carefully for the facts and the feelings the sender is attempting to get through to us.

BARRIERS TO EFFECTIVE LISTENING

We are poor listeners for several reasons. Some of the barriers to effective listening are imposed by external factors and others we erect ourselves. But, in any case, as managers whose job it is to get things done through people, it is our responsibility to remove the barriers.

Competition

Competition is all over the place—not just in the marketplace.

Look at the competition for the manager's attention in most offices: stacks of reports, ringing telephones, discussions at adjoining desks, plus all the "hidden" competitors—the manager's concern about being prepared for the meeting he or she chairs in ninety minutes and worry about his or her daughter's driving home on ice-slick highways, for example. If you want to talk to that manager, he or she may mean to listen, but the competition for attention is so intense that your transmission may lose out to one of the other competitors.

Concentration

Listening involves concentrating and focusing.

There is a built-in bias against effective listening in our internal communication system. People talk at about 150 words per minute, and we are capable of listening at a rate of 600 words per minute. If listeners do not concentrate on listening, they will fill in the voids with other matters.

Emotions

The sender's choice of words, appearance, or perhaps unusual voice may cause us to make a snap judgment—"what does this person know?" Once we do that, we have tuned out and, although physically present, are mentally on a different agenda. If we really want to listen, we need to train ourselves to keep our emotional reactions in control.

Don't let your emotions cloud the sender's message.

Work

Most of us don't work hard enough at listening—and it is work. We over-relax, don't force ourselves to concentrate, and refuse to review what we just heard. If we really want to listen, we are going to have to really work at developing our listening skills and habits.

Listening involves *work*.

Of course, there are other barriers that inhibit effective listening: bias, a society that trains us *not* to listen (TV), and the dozens of distractions that constantly impinge on us as we try to listen.

LISTENING FOR FACTS

Managers need facts in order to function and make decisions. As you have already learned, organizations today rely heavily on the quick oral transmission of data. If listeners do not receive the facts or if the facts become scrambled or convoluted, problems will arise. Here are some relatively simple steps you can take to improve your listening for facts.

Catalog Key Terms

Even though the speaker may not organize well, the listener can organize what is being said by labeling the primary ideas with key terms and retaining those terms. Those key terms will be your reminder of the major subjects and ideas addressed by the speaker.

Suggestions for listening for facts

Review Key Ideas

You have the ability to listen faster than speakers can talk. Use that extra time to concentrate and review the key ideas the speaker is sending. As you do this, differentiate between those ideas that are key and those that are secondary or less important.

Be Open and Flexible

Listen to ideas and expand your knowledge. Your first job as a listener is to obtain the data, not to determine if you agree or disagree with it.

Evaluate, but Don't Tune Out

Too often when we hear ideas with which we disagree, we stop listening. Certainly you need to evaluate (filter) the information, but don't shut off your ears as you do—listen and evaluate simultaneously.

Resist Distractions

Rarely will you receive messages in perfect soundproof rooms where there are no distractions. You have the power to focus your attention where you desire to focus it; good listeners focus their attention on the person sending the message.

Work at Listening

Sit up straight, consciously listen, and review key ideas. Be alert mentally and physically. All facets of effective communications require concentrated attention; listening is no exception.

The ability to listen better for facts is extremely valuable. For students, it can add to their assimilation of information and therefore help their grades. For people at work, it can make a major contribution to their effectiveness and their advancement in the organization.

LISTENING FOR FEELINGS

Be prepared to tune into the sender's feelings.

Listening for feelings is rigorous work because we live in a society that often inhibits us from saying what is in our hearts; many of us will work in organizations that downplay feelings, that ask us to "stick to business." But all of us at various times will have strong or subtle feelings to communicate. The perceptive manager will receive those messages and probably react to them.

Let's look at a few situations in which the keen listener, tuned into the total communication, would be able to get both the facts and the feelings, and respond meaningfully. Remember all of the forces that are at work: some people have difficulty voicing feelings, some organizations basically say "stick to business," and some listeners are looking only for facts. Look at Dave in the following situation:

Boy, oh boy! This was some job you asked me to complete by 10:00 a.m. today! I was here Thursday night and Friday night and spent most of my Saturday here. Digging out all the data on inventories for the last four years was murder. But I've got it all—and one hour ahead of schedule. If you never give me another job like that, I'll be happy!

If Dave's boss, Vern, should now reply, "Great, now what about the sales figures for the same period?" communication will certainly break down.

What was Dave really saying with his deeply expressed comments on "Thursday night and Friday night and most of Saturday"? What was the hidden message in what he was saying?

"Give me a pat on the back"?
"You're unreasonable in your assignments"?
"How about overtime pay"?
"Don't give me another job like that"?

It could have been any one of these four messages or others. But we do know that Dave was saying more than what he was actually saying. How do we know what the unspoken message is? If he is praised but was looking for overtime pay, communication between Dave and Vern will still break down.

Certainly Vern can't say, "What are you really saying, Dave?" If he could, Dave probably would have told Vern in the first place! The answer probably lies in knowing Dave. If we really listen *with* people, we can determine what feelings they are expressing even when they don't actually voice them. Knowing our children, our friends, and our fellow workers tells us enough about them that we can understand what they feel in what they say. Of course, we may not always be correct, but one factor we do know about Dave's message is that he was feeling more than he was saying!

Don't forget to listen to the nonverbal messages.

Because Maurice knows Louise, he knows what she really is saying when she walks into the house, slumps into a chair, and says, "Boy, another killer day." And he responds correctly. "That boss of yours never lets up, does he?"

Louise in turn knows what Maurice really is saying when he asks, "How do you like the new tie I'm wearing to the Donalds' party tonight?" She replies, "You'll be the handsomest man there." Interestingly enough, neither one replied to the facts in the statements, but both did respond to the feelings.

How to Listen for Feelings

As our examples suggest, some people are not going to catch the feelings unless they are hit by the proverbial Mack truck; all of us—including those who are less sensitive—could benefit from applying the following suggestions for improving our abilities to listen for feelings:

If you don't listen to feelings, you probably miss most of the message.

Listen with the speaker: Appreciate the speaker's values, perceptions, cultural background, expectations, hopes, and desires. It isn't necessary to agree or accept those values or desires, but it is necessary to understand them.

Understand the connotations: What does the speaker mean by words he or she is using, such as "inexpensive," "unreasonable," or "early"?

Hints for tuning into feelings

Note the nonverbal communication: Do hands, eyes, facial expressions, tapping heels, and drumming fingers indicate agreement or disagreement with the message that is being voiced?

Listen and respond to what isn't said in what is: What is he or she thinking when he or she says, "I really don't mind not going to the game after all," or when he or she says, "Well, it really wasn't such a great return; I just happened to get back, and the ball dropped in the right spot"? Responding to what a speaker thinks is often more important than responding to what is said!

Listen attentively: Even if you don't hear the speaker's feelings, the fact that you obviously are trying to hear those feelings may well be all that is necessary to maintain the flow of communication.

Guidelines for Total Listening

The person credited with highlighting our lack of listening and who worked with many corporations in attempting to get their managers to listen better was Dr. Ralph G. Nichols. Even today, his article, "Listening is a 10-Part Skill,"* is an excellent primer for reviewing and honing our abilities to listen:

1. **Find an area of interest.** Look for an idea or concept that is interesting and focus on it.
2. **Judge content, not delivery.** Don't judge the speaker's appearance or voice. What can you derive from the content?
3. **Hold your fire.** Don't evaluate so quickly that you don't really listen to the entire message.
4. **Listen for ideas.** Listen for total concepts. Don't focus on a few facts and lose others or the central ideas.
5. **Be flexible.** Because speakers organize differently, we must be flexible in our listening and note-taking. Be able to move from one method of listening and note-taking to another according to the situation.
6. **Work at listening.** Sit up straight, establish eye contact, concentrate, and review. Good listening is hard work and requires the expenditure of energy.

---

*From *Successful Management* by Ralph G. Nichols. In *Nation's Business.* The Chamber of Commerce of the United States, 1957.

7. **Resist distractions.** Fight noise and other distractions.
8. **Exercise your mind.** Work at listening to difficult, technical, expository material.
9. **Keep your mind open.** Don't let emotional ideas or words cause you to suddenly close your mind. This is especially important when those words or ideas disagree with your ideas. Listen, and don't "tune out."
10. **Capitalize on thought speed.** Use the difference in listening speed and speaking speed to review the ideas you've heard, to recapitulate the comments made, and to hear "between the lines."

These suggestions for effective listening are easier to offer than to carry through. In striving to implement them, recall the you-orientation; in all communications—including listening—focusing on the other person seems to enhance the opportunities for understanding and for a meeting of the minds.

Total listening involves the you-orientation.

LISTENING: ADVANTAGES FOR THE RECEIVER

There is an old saying that you can get a reputation for being a wonderful conversationalist if you are an effective listener. Beyond the basic truth of that statement, we also gain other advantages:

Information that helps us in our tasks.

Ideas that will advance us on the job, in class, and in our interpersonal relationships with others.

Understanding of people: He needs stroking, she doesn't. He is an introvert, she is an extrovert. He is terribly angry inside, she is confused. Such understanding may well assist in communication.

Cooperation. When the other person feels you have really listened and understood, he or she will listen to you—not in every instance, of course, but most of the time.

Better management and human interactions through better listening

No one ever said effective listening for facts and feelings is easy. It requires sensitivity to others, hard work, and a deep desire to communicate effectively with those around us, whether we agree or disagree with them. But the rewards are worth the effort. Nothing contributes to effective communication as much as sensitive and efficient listening.

In a world in which more and more people are shouting to be heard, effective listeners are not easily found. But when they are, they are not only effective decision-makers, but respected spouses, friends, parents, teachers, coworkers, and managers as well.

GETTING ORGANIZED TO READ EFFECTIVELY

Your in-basket is always full.

Each month the average manager has at least 900 pages of reading material coming across the desk. If you assume twenty working days per month, that works out to about forty-five pages of reading per day! Little wonder managers are exhausted at the end of a day. You spend 75 percent of your day in meetings, you have many communications to initiate, but then there is continually a huge stack of reading. And it is getting worse—the manager's reading "in" box grows 10 to 15 percent each year. But there are some steps you can take to improve the situations.

Reading Skill

Suggestions for enhancing your reading

As a first step, you should read well, comprehend quickly, and retain important information (being able to differentiate the unimportant from the important). If you are rusty on any of these basics you should take a reading course—they are readily available for adults in evening programs, and many employers offer them. There is no stigma involved. As some people join Toastmasters to work on their speaking skills, others take reading courses to hone their reading skills. There is much more to successful reading than just increasing reading and comprehension rates, however.

Segregating the Input

There is no way one can manage effectively by reading thoroughly each of the 900 pages per month. The manager must quickly differentiate among the incoming materials. Some items need to be read and perhaps reread thoroughly; others need only a quick scanning. How you differentiate among and then read the materials will make it possible to handle today's forty-five pages.

There are four basic reading strategies, and you apply a different strategy depending upon the nature of the reading. How you categorize the reading determines your reading strategy and amount of time devoted to it:

Know what to read carefully and what to scan.

Type of Material	Reading Strategy	Estimated Words per Minute
Items of importance	Careful	50–350 wpm
Seeking picture; obtain main points	Rapid	300–600 wpm
Looking for general overview	Skimming	1,500 + wpm
Only a "snap shot" is needed	Scanning	3,000 + wpm

The point is that one of the essential elements in successful reading is knowing what is important. This will permit you to focus your time and then align your reading strategy.

Hints for Improving Reading

There really are no patent medicines or easy ways to improve one's reading, but there are some useful suggestions that are good to review; check to see how you apply these on a regular basis:

Time: Know what times of the day you are most alert; select those times for reading. Everybody's body clock is different—know yours and do your reading when the clock is "on."

Break Up: It is generally a good idea, especially for concentrated reading, to break it up. To attempt to read difficult materials in one long session is often counterproductive.

Comfort: Be comfortable when you read. Make sure you are sitting properly and that the temperature is appropriate and ventilation adequate.

Lighting: Speed of reading is markedly influenced by the light; proper nonglare lighting is crucial to rapid reading.

Materials: Be sure you have the proper materials needed for effective reading— a pencil, paper, a dictionary, and a thesaurus are often helpful.

Quiet: If you are really interested in comprehension and retention, reading needs your undivided attention. Background noises and stereo headphones are not conducive to reading and achieving any satisfactory level of assimilation.

More than speed is involved in effective managerial reading. As you outline and get organized to write a short report, note the organizational aspects of reading. By applying these organizing concepts, you can improve the effectiveness of your reading.

Simple suggestions for improving your reading

QUICK REVIEW

Receiving messages correctly and quickly is an important aspect of being an effective manager. By listening and reading more effectively, it is possible to increase the effectiveness of your management style. Although business tends to emphasize the facts, remember that good managers also listen for the feelings. In reading, learn to differentiate the stacks of incoming materials—categorize them and then use the appropriate reading strategy for each different material. Remember, every piece of paper need not be, and should not be, read carefully. Often a quick skim or scan will be most appropriate.

EXECUTIVE SUMMARY

To: Business Communication Students

From: David N. Bateman and Norman B. Sigband

Subject: Keeping Your Communications on Track: Effective Listening and Reading

This chapter introduces you to the receiving side of the communication process: listening and reading. Listening is the communication skill that, as a manager, you will probably use more than any other communication technique, and it is also the one that, as a student, you will have studied the least. And although you may have studied reading, probably a long time ago, you will need to prepare for the avalanche of reading you will face as a manager.

As students, we become rather proficient at obtaining and remembering facts; we tend to listen for them. As managers, we will also have to learn to listen for feelings.

In listening for facts, you should try to (a) catalog key words, (b) review key ideas, (c) be open and flexible, (d) evaluate, but don't tune out, and (e) resist distractions.

In listening for feelings, try to (a) listen *with* the speaker, (b) understand the words as used, (c) note the nonverbal connotations, (d) respond to what isn't said in what is, and (e) listen attentively.

In listening for feelings and facts, one of the primary reasons we are often inefficient and ineffective is that we permit outside factors to interfere. These factors include: distractions, emotions, evaluating, and laziness.

Some specific actions you can take to become a more effective listener are:

- Find an interest area
- Judge content, not delivery
- Hold your fire
- Listen for ideas
- Be flexible
- Work at it
- Resist distractions
- Exercise your mind
- Keep your mind open
- Use your listening speed

Not only is it polite and courteous to listen and to listen well, but there are also some direct advantages to you. These bonuses might include gaining more information, picking up more ideas, bettering your understanding of people, and gaining cooperation as listeners recognize that you are *really* listening.

In order to become more efficient at reading, you should brush up on your reading skills, classify your reading tasks according to the amount of time and attention they merit, and control the conditions under which you read to guarantee optimum use of your reading time.

DISCUSSION GENERATORS

1. *Systems Problem.* Explain the built-in system defect in human communications that inhibits the ability to listen well.

2. *External Forces.* List at least six external distractions today that are seeking your attention and that can disrupt your intention to listen to others.

3. *Barriers.* List and exemplify in an interesting way the barriers to effective listening. For each, explain if someone else or you erected the barrier.

4. *Educational Review.* For a moment, review your education. Have you been taught to listen for facts or for feelings? How will this influence your behavior as a manager?

5. *Concentration.* Why do you suppose many managers find it difficult to concentrate on the oral messages being sent to them?

6. *Competition.* In the classroom where this class meets, what are examples of things that compete with the instructor for the student's attention?

7. *Emotions.* Whose emotions get in the way of effective listening—the emotions of the sender or of the receiver?

8. *Openness.* In being open, why is it important to not determine if you agree or disagree with the point the speaker is making?

9. *Women and Feelings.* What effect do you suppose the advent of women in management has had on the communication of feelings in business communications?

10. *Connotations.* Why is it important to receive the speaker's connotations—not just the dictionary definitions of his or her words?

11. *Listen to What is Not Said?* Explain the idea of listening and responding to what isn't said in what is. How does this work? Cite an example.

12. *Nonverbal Signals.* As an attentive listener, what are you to do if Joan greets you by saying, "Nice to see you," but does so with a huge frown on her face?

13. *Capitalize on Thought Speed.* Explain the idea of taking advantage of your thinking-receiving speed and the rate at which the communication is coming at you.

14. *Listening Benefits.* List and explain, in a managerial context, the advantages the receiver gains from being a better and more alert listener.

15. *Reading Speed.* Successful readers employ much more than just speed. Name and explain the other aspects of effective and efficient reading.

16. *Categorizing Your Incoming Paper.* For your future job, identify the kinds of material that will make up your 900 pages per month. Then, clearly indicate how those items will be categorized relative to the reading strategies.

17. *Time.* What is the best time of day for you to read? What is the worst time of day for you to read? How will this influence your management style and the way you function in an office?

18. *Materials.* What are the materials, besides the actual reading, that you will need in order to read productively? Explain your use of these ancillary items.

19. *Comfort.* Are there mixed signals concerning the issue of comfort and reading? Would it be possible to get so comfortable that you may just doze off while reading? Explain.

20. *Beyond the Office.* The authors make the point that good listening will not only benefit your management style in the office—it will help elsewhere. Cite an example of how the advantages of listening can help you beyond the office.

APPLICATIONS FOR BUSINESS

21. *Stamp Out the Competition.* In the United States, there are laws and regulations prohibiting companies from literally stamping out the competition. However, when it comes to reducing the competition (distractions) for listening, you have no laws or regulations to slow your attack.

    Jane of the Dana Company just returned from a special management seminar on listening. Now she notices the many things around the office that seem designed to reduce listening, even though the company keeps saying that it wants employees to be more productive. Jane feels that a good place to start is by reducing the barriers (competitors) to effective listening. Jane is going to make a presentation to her boss on that issue, but right now she is constructing a detailed list of the barriers. Using virtually any office as your referent, take on Jane's role, and (1) construct a list of listening barriers in the office, and (2) establish procedures for stamping out those barriers.

22. *Stick It in Your Ear!* It is other people's business if they want to listen to portable radios and tape players with headphones. It is a private matter. However, some employers feel that background music is soothing. You find background music in the office most disruptive and irritating, especially when you're wading through forty-five pages of reading daily and trying to accomplish simple listening. You even think that companies that play music while you "hold" on the phone are slowing you down—if you didn't have to listen to that music you could read or write a draft of an important memo. In fact, sometimes you are forced to listen to "rock" in the office and Bach on the phone—it's no wonder productivity in America is declining!

    In a thoughtful, and perhaps humorous, letter to the editor of your firm's company magazine, address this issue and propose a solution.

23. *Maximizing Reading Time.* You and five other senior students have been asked to pick a study-hint subject and address the entering class. You each will take a different subject and explain how the students can succeed by following your suggestions. You select *reading.* Employing the "Hints for Improving Reading," develop your five-minute speech. Strive to be interesting, relate directly to the students, and speak in a convincing manner so that the students can take full advantage of your suggestions.

24. *Executive Secretary.* Take on the role of executive secretary to Sophia Goldwater of Bikercise, Ltd. In this job, you do much more than just handle Ms. Goldwater's outgoing correspondence. You are actively involved in determining who gets to see Ms. Goldwater and what pieces of paper reach her desk.

    Even Ms. Goldwater will need to read some things carefully and others only at a glance. You have been asked to give a talk to the speed-readers group at Bikercise. You want to emphasize that more than speed is necessary in successful reading. Getting organized and developing a strategy is vital. Prepare a brief memo of suggestions on how to read more effectively. The memo will be distributed to the speed-readers group.

25. *Listening vs. Acceptance.* At first reading, some of the suggestions for effective listening might be interpreted as automatically accepting what the speaker is saying. Clearly, that is not the case. Citing a specific example, illustrate how the following listening hints do not mean acceptance, but simply listening strategy:

    - Hold your fire
    - Be flexible
    - Keep your mind open

    Place your comments in a business context because many business people would find it difficult to not want to immediately refute ideas that are contrary to the ones they hold. Present your comments in a memo or in a brief oral presentation (as indicated by your instructor).

COMMUNICATION CHECK-UPS

26. Attached are two insurance forms that give you a quick reference of the medical insurance coverage.

27. I have listed below five potential new applications and markets for our small computer terminal.

28. The most exciting market I believe is the new discount chains.

29. Hardware stores, which have thousands of inventorial items.

30. 2 thousand copies of the book was received incorrectly bound.

31. The following is the first sentence of an inquiry letter: I am inquiring if you would be interested in marketing our new product.

32. All but review copies for sales representatives have, thus, been returned for rebinding.

33. (A drawing is attached for your information.)

34. People can tell, without necessitating a walk to the box, that the mail has arrived.

35. Keep your memos brief—generally one page will do.

Private Preparations for Public Speaking

Mary Miles

Few public speakers feel completely at ease. As important a communications medium as the formal presentation has become in today's corporate world, chances are you'll be called upon from time to time to have your say, solo, in front of an audience. Good preparation is the only way to thwart failure, but preparation doesn't pertain to words alone.

A persuasive speech is analogous to an effective musical rendition. It isn't enough for a musician to tune his or her instrument, or to be aware that pitch, timing, and dynamics are the essentials of artistry. An audience has to be enticed. To do so requires knowing an audience and knowing where, when, and under what conditions the rendition will be performed. The organizational scheme of a performance should be aimed at sending the audience away satisfied, humming the right tune. To this end, a program needs an arresting opening, followed by a unified and suspenseful message. The closing should be timed so that listeners are on the edges of their seats, ready to applaud—a sure sign that the performance will be remembered.

More often than not, however, speakers—not speeches—are remembered for how boring they are. Most speeches are boring, according to Jonathan Price in his book *Put That in Writing* (Penguin Books, $5.95). They are apt to be too long, unfocused, not relevant to the audience, repetitious, and too complex or technical. If there is a message, it has little chance of getting across.

Many speeches are unsuccessful because of the speaker's fear, poor organization, and inadequate preparation. Knowing your subject will diminish your fears, but strong knowledge doesn't equal strong delivery. "You may know your material in a technical sense," says Sybil Tonkonogy, a senior consultant at Speech Improvement Co., a Brookline, MA-based communications consultancy. "But unless you can organize and communicate it in a way that is clear to those who will be listening, you'll lose them." A speaker's confidence and the audience's confidence in the speaker depends on how well the speaker puts together the program.

For starters, it helps to recognize that listeners are a unique entity. Speakers must keep in mind the audience's knowledge and needs, says Sybil Tonkonogy. Are they likely to have strong feelings about the topic? Does the audience have a vested interest? Are they part of the audience because they want to be or because they have to be? Are they apt to be active or passive listeners? Will they be more attuned to statistics or to chatty personal examples?

Ask not only what the audience wants from you but what you want from the audience. Are you seeking votes? Selling? Explaining how something works? Teaching? "Your job is to get remembered," writes Price. Prepare your speech with a certainty of what you want your listeners to do and think after you're through.

Only after you've done your homework and know your material are you ready to construct the speech. Here, the analogy to a musical performance is especially apt. Both the musical and the spoken program have a distinct shape. A good singer, for example, tries to begin the concert with an attention-grabber and sequence the rest of the pieces in a unified fashion—to make sense, sustain interest, pique curiosity, inform, give satisfaction, call forth recognition and enthusiasm, and provide a touch of drama.

The introduction. The functions of the introduction are twofold, says Anita Taylor and her associates in *Communicating* (Prentice-Hall, 1977). First, a good introduction grabs the attention of an audience. Second, it points listeners in the desired direction. Taylor counsels that an introduction shouldn't be carved in stone until after the body of the speech has been refined, and for good reason. The first words of a speech can make or break an entire performance, and what you have learned from refining the speech will have refined your opinions.

"Make your listeners like you—or admit they don't," Jonathan Price advises. "Give them half a dozen reasons why they should bother to listen."

Exactly how a speaker grabs an audience's attention will depend on many factors, not the least of which is personal style. Humor may be a good way to open. "But any humor you use must relate to your subject," warns Tonkonogy. "You don't want to tell so many funny stories that when you proceed to your main topic, the listeners will be so relaxed as to be distracted or so amused that they'd rather you continue with the jokes."

Some speakers begin by asking a question: "Who cares about artificial intelligence?" Stating the thesis outright can be effective, too. But it can be daring, because it requires the audience's complete attention. If part of the audience is still unseated or fussing with briefcases and coats, the opening line may be lost.

However you choose to begin, reckon with your nervousness. Breathe deeply. Even secure and seasoned speakers choose introductions that relax them and their audience, giving both a chance to get their bearings. The first sentence is the hardest. Although volumes have been written about clever and effective introductions, two cardinal rules are essential: Speak clearly and stand up straight.

The main body. When planning the main part of a speech, too many speakers assume an audience shares their knowledge. To say, "We all remember the Gilfobey Law" risks alienating those who don't. If a thesis starts at D and proceeds to Z, assuming that the audience already knows A, B, and C, the speaker risks provoking irritation or inattention.

Many speakers try to cover too much ground. Jonathan Price advises developing a central idea, which "offers the audience a way of organizing what it hears, anticipating what you will say, and spotting the intelligence behind the flow of facts and phrases."

Much as the solo musician attends to props and accompaniment, supporting devices and materials can round out a program and help drive home a point. A speech can be buttressed by charts, films, handouts, microphones, and the speaker's appearance, including dress, stance, movement, and gestures. Verbal effects include the use of examples, statistics, and such rhetorical devices as comparisons and contrasts, repetitions and restatements.

The close. Everyone has had the experience of lingering uncomfortably at the front door with a guest who repeatedly says goodbye but doesn't leave. In *Communicating,* Taylor advises speakers to let the audience know that the speech is concluding and to wind up as quickly as possible. A concise and graceful summary will leave an audience with a feeling of closure.

"This is where they sign on the dotted line," Taylor writes. Make sure they'll remember your speech positively. As Emily Post puts it, "Remember, the speech that charms is the one that ends to its listeners' regret."

Presentations With Punch

G.A. (Andy) Marken

Just a few hours after Governor Mario Cuomo of New York completed his opening remarks at the 1984 Democratic National Convention, people were wondering if the wrong person was being nominated. It was an excellent speech. Focusing on his audience's wants and needs, the speech was full of action. It made use of every word and pause, and had the impact of moving an entire country to think.

While this is an extreme example of the power of persuasion, such influence is not reserved for the political podium. Just about everyone has a specialty or a topic that he or she could speak on. For instance, a manager with expertise in office automation, marketing, or another area could expand his or her organization's sales and influence by giving persuasive speeches and presentations.

This may even be the best opportunity for influence, because for 30 minutes to an hour the manager has a semicaptive audience who has come to hear what she or he has to say.

OPPORTUNITIES

Every city, country, and region has numerous opportunities for speakers on business topics. These include community groups, management associations, lawyers' councils, medical associations, teachers' associations, engineering or manufacturing groups, or any of a hundred other professional and paraprofessional organizations.

There are certain generic guidelines a person can follow to give powerful and persuasive speeches and presentations. Perfection, however, only comes with practice. With each speaking engagement, the manager will see steady improvement.

Good speakers research new trends and the problems that interest people most. Using experience working with customers in a variety of areas, the speaker can determine what new ideas and hints

to offer. The information that managers learn from their customers can be of considerable interest and assistance to others.

Of even greater importance is the research on the audience. Governor Cuomo's speech probably wouldn't have half the influence if given to the American Management Association or to the Republican National Convention. But he had done an excellent job of researching the demographics of his audience. He knew the mixture of sexes, the age range, their interests, as well as their wants and needs.

Other speakers can do the same. By reading the trade, business, and daily press, they can draw on information to make for contemporary speeches. People who have become committed spokespersons for their organizations will find themselves keeping files of facts, figures, and ideas to use at future speaking engagements.

The most difficult part of giving a speech is to make the audience remember it. The problem with most speeches and presentations is that the speaker has so many things to say that he or she fails to tell the audience anything.

So, rather than do a data dump on the audience, the speaker should pick one central idea he or she wants them to retain. Once that idea is clearly established, the speaker can start building the speech by gathering data and information which supports the theme. Then the speaker should write down a simple outline listing the points to be covered in the presentation.

A good speech is nothing more than a few statements backed up with and reinforced by examples. Following are the basic elements of a good speech: 1) an arusing and interesting opening; 2) body of the speech; 3) climax of the presentation; and 4) dynamic summary.

DOs And DON'Ts Of Speechmaking

► Don't memorize words. Your speech's objectives should be to present ideas convincingly and forcefully.

► Don't glance over the audience. You need to make eye contact throughout your audience. Pick a face here and there in the audience, and talk to that individual. Make a point, and then move to someone else in the audience to make another point.

► Don't talk too fast. Make your points deliberately. Develop a sense of timing, and give your ideas a chance to be absorbed and understood.

► Don't use irrelevant material or stray from your main idea.

► Don't be long-winded or use long words or sentences that don't help make your points quickly.

► Don't end abruptly. Warn your audience that you are coming to a conclusion.

► Do use inflection for emphasis. Silence at just the right time can be more effective than anything you might say.

► Do be yourself. Some speakers insist on becoming overly dramatic and in pontificating the minute they step up to the podium. The audience can sense a phony in a few minutes and will quickly lose interest.

► Do be enthusiastic. For those few short, precious minutes that the audience is in front of you, it is yours to educate, entertain and inform.

► Do get the audience's attention immediately.

► Do summarize what you are going to present in key points, emphasize those key points, and end by summarizing the points presented.

► Do use the present tense whenever possible. Keep your audience involved by showing that you are involved.

► Do keep your presentation simple and to the point.

FAMILIAR WORDS

Speakers should develop the speech and presentation in their own words. Anything that wouldn't be said in an ordinary conversation shouldn't be used in a speech. If the terminology isn't common, the speaker will probably forget it when giving the speech. Or worse yet, the speaker will fumble over the word, phrase or thought.

Speeches should be written in detail, covering the central theme and the supporting facts and how they relate to the audience. The audience must constantly be told why the topic is important to them. The speech should be read and reread. Changes should be made where necessary to make certain that it flows properly. The speaker should almost be able to present it from memory.

Some people are most comfortable reading their speech. Others prefer to give it from an outline, using index cards. Still others will stand up and make their presentations virtually from memory, using only a minimum of notes. The latter approach usually develops the best speaker and audience involvement.

The one thing that is important in any type of presentation is eye contact. The same things used in a person-to-person discussion or selling situation are needed when presenting a speech to 20 or 2,000 people. Unfortunately, there's no fast, easy way to develop these qualities. The only method is practice, which comes by making speech after speech, and presentation after presentation.

Before the speech is presented, however, it can be practiced. This can be done aloud and in front of a mirror. Or, it can be practiced in front of a live, friendly audience. Another method is using videotape for a self-critique.

The speaker should tape and keep every second or third rehearsal. In this way, the speaker can analyze his or her speech, mannerisms, animation, and delivery. This also allows the speaker to see improvements more dramatically as well as to pick out those areas which really need work. Just a single evening of going through this exercise can improve a speaker's performance greatly.

Everyone who has attended a seminar, an association or professional meeting, or a civic event has his or her ideas as to what they like or dislike about speakers. Good speakers soon learn how to concentrate on the delivery and the intensity of the delivery. The accompanying sidebar offers some tips on speechmaking.

All too often, people are content to make a presentation before a professional, technical, trade, or consumer group. Many don't realize, however, that the speech provides an excellent opportunity to gain additional coverage and exposure in the local and national press.

Before the speech, the speaker should send the press an announcement stating that she or he will be speaking before a particular group, where the presentation will be made, the date and the subject of his or her speech, and a summary.

The speaker should contact not only the local radio, television, and newspaper press, but also pertinent local offices of the business, financial, and trade press. To verify information about a specific publication, check the masthead or call the managing editor's office.

The day of the event, the speaker should send a summary release of the presentation to all of the appropriate editors and publications. At the end of the release, offer a complete copy of the speech and the visuals used.

When giving the speech, the speaker should have copies of the summary release as well as copies of the complete presentation for members of the press who might be in attendance.

A person's first speech can be a pleasant experience or it can be a disaster. It really all depends how carefully the person has prepared, how well the person has researched the subject, and how well the person has developed and refined the presentation.

The speaker should keep in mind that he or she was invited to speak before the group to help them gain some new information or a new perspective. Whether the assemblage is 20 or 2,000, it is made up of individuals. And managers, by definition, have had to be successful in speaking to individuals.

Each member of the audience came at this time, to this place to enjoy the speech. Therefore, the speaker has before him or her a very positive group of individuals who honestly want to hear the presentation. The speaker should express gratitude by being as prepared and as enthusiastic as possible.

And don't be worried about being nervous. Speakers who say they aren't nervous before a speech are either lying or really don't care about the audience. Direct that nervous energy into a positive image, an enthusiastic manner and delivery. The speaker will be a resounding success by making certain that she or he doesn't let the audience down.

The Uses Of Meetings

Norman B. Sigband

"I hold more meetings than ever before. It's because I really believe in participative management."

These pious words certainly seem to reflect the new manager—who respects and listens to his or her people and wants to give them a piece of the action.

But all too often, what the words reflect is insincerity.

More and more these days, managers are calling meetings not to find ideas and solve problems, but simply to cover themselves. A manager who should be making decisions on his own is not. Instead he calls 10 or 12 colleagues and subordinates together, secures a consensus and announces the decision. If the decision turns out to be poor, he can always say: "Don't blame me. That is what the participants to our August 23 meeting wanted. It was their idea, not mine."

On the other hand, if the decision was good, the same manager will not hesitate to point out "how carefully I led the August 23 meeting."

I learned not long ago of a meeting at a small plastics manufacturing firm. Present were a division manager, six department heads and the heads of three sections. The topic: Should a replacement be hired for a recently injured secretary, or should a typist be secured from a temporaries service and kept on a week-to-week basis?

It took 50 minutes to reach a consensus on that question. Actually, the decision should have been made privately by the division manager or by the manager of the one office involved.

What was decided is not important. The effect of such meetings on the company is. Because of the length of the discussion about the secretarial replacement, time ran out before a second topic could be considered. A decision on it was not reached until another meeting weeks later. The topic: Should a new fluorescent lighting system for the plant be installed? Involved were not just one office but four departments—not to mention a $28,000 investment.

It should not be that way. First of all, meetings are expensive. When 12 people, each paid $15 to $25 per hour, meet for two or three hours, the cost for one session may easily exceed $500. Such a price is justified when it is necessary to bring representatives from engineering, production, finance and marketing together to solve a legitimate problem. But when the session is held to get a consensus on whether coffee breaks should be taken at 10 a.m. and not at 10:30, or whether the copying machine should be moved 50 feet, blowing $500 worth of time on a meeting is unconscionable.

Second, when a manager calls meetings to decide on items that are inconsequential or that he should handle himself for other reasons, the importance of future meetings is diluted. People will find reasons not to attend whenever they can— a pity, because there will be some vital meetings that require input from everyone invited.

And third, when meetings are called by a manager who wishes to spread responsibility, a signal is given to his subordinates: "This is a policy you may wish to follow when you become a manager. Always cover yourself."

These situations tend to reduce initiative and harden the organizational arteries.

How can they be eliminated? For starters, by changing the company climate. This is almost totally dependent on the chief executive officer and his staff. They must make it clear that a decision that does not work out does not automatically mean decision makers will have their heads chewed off— that it is acceptable to fail, provided the decision was based on careful analysis.

Another important step is policy setting. Companies have written policies on all sorts of subjects: finance, production, construction, personnel, marketing, employee benefits, quality control and on and on.

Why not policies on meetings?

Such policies should be aimed not only at cutting down on unnecessary gatherings called by managers who are reluctant to make decisions, but also at ensuring that every meeting is as productive as possible. Specific requirements:

1. Hold only meetings for which there is a verifiable need.
2. Decide on an overall purpose and series of objectives each time.
3. Invite only people who can make a definite contribution.
4. Distribute an agenda and necessary handout materials to each invitee prior to the session.
5. Make all mechanical arrangements ahead of time (room, projectors, seating, transparencies, etc.).
6. Begin and end every meeting on schedule.

"The Uses of Meetings" by Norman B. Sigband, Nation's Business, February 1987. Copyright © 1987 Chamber of Commerce of the U.S. Reprinted by permission.

If you consider the losses in both morale and dollars when people are made to sit through unnecessary meetings, such as those to make decisions a manager should have made on his or her own, it is obvious that a list like this should be distributed to all managers and that they should be made to stick to it.

Learning to Listen

Stephen D. Boyd

"It took me ten years to learn how to listen," says the president of a communications company. "More important than technology is the ear—learn how to listen."

Listening skills, according to a research team at Loyola University of Chicago, are the most important attributes a manager can have. In the study, the most common positive response received from thousands of workers was, "I like my boss; she listens to me," or "I can talk to him."

Without effective listening, communication cannot take place, and right decisions cannot be made. Every day, 45 percent of our communication time is spent listening.

Yet we do not always listen well. Poor listening costs us in human relations. It causes wasted time to correct the problems caused by poor listening, and sometimes poor listening costs us in tragic ways. Reports from a nightclub fire said an attendant took the microphone from two comedians on stage, told the audience there was a fire, explained where the exits were, and told the people to leave immediately. It took the audience a full minute to respond. Many thought he was part of the act. People lost lives because of a listening problem.

Making sense. There are four factors which make effective listening especially difficult. First is the misconception about what listening is. Most of us do not perceive a difference between hearing and listening. Hearing is the physiological process involved in picking up sounds. But listening is making sense of those sounds. We may hear a person, and never listen to the message he or she is communicating to us.

The second factor is the meaning of the message. The speaker's real meaning may not be comprehended by the listener. Sometimes the speaker assumes the listener understands the message when that is not the case at all. As a result, the listener may entirely miss the point that the speaker is making. Both the speaker and the listener must be aware of this meaning factor.

A third factor is the difference between speaking and thinking time. While the average person speaks at a rate of 140 to 150 words per minute, the listener thinks about four or five times that fast. Consequently, the listener has thinking time left to daydream, or think about personal problems, or what he or she is going to have for lunch. This makes it hard to concentrate.

A fourth factor is that most people don't realize that effective listening is hard work. The heartbeat rate increases and blood pressure rises when a person is really listening. After an hour, you may feel weary after listening well. Listening well takes work and practice.

Easy talking. The following are ways to improve your listening and increase your managerial effectiveness. First, place a high value on listening when you are talking to someone. Close the door to your office, hold phone calls, and avoid playing with a pen or doodling when the other person is talking. You might want to have a listening chair in your office to get away from your desk. This tells the person that you are going to give your undivided attention.

Second, make it easy for the other person to talk. Make the talker comfortable by smiling, making eye contact, and providing comfortable seating. Be pleasant in your responses, and allow pauses in the conversation.

When the person stops talking, don't immediately begin speaking. A short pause may encourage the speaker to provide more information. A tested formula for listening to people is the following: 1) Listen to the other person's story; 2) Listen to the other person's full story; and 3) Listen to the other person's full story first.

A third way to increase your listening skills is to use feedback techniques that ensure understanding. Knowing that you are going to give specific feedback will make you listen better. Feedback techniques encourage the other person to give you more information, thus increasing the odds that you will understand. Responses like "Oh," "I see," "Really," and "I understand," said with vocal emphasis on the end of the phrase, will often provide you with more information.

Ask questions that will help you keep up with the speaker, and increase the possibilities for understanding. The following questions will help keep you on track: 1) Open-ended questions such as How do you feel about . . . ; 2) Seeking information questions such as Can you give me an example . . . ; 3) Paraphrasing questions such as Are you saying that . . . ' and 4) Clarification questions such as What do you mean by the word or phrase. . . .

A fourth way to improve your skills is to listen for ideas. As you listen, ask yourself, "What is the point the person is trying to make?" Before ending the conversation, paraphrase what the other person has said.

Too often managers get only bits and pieces of information, instead of a specific message. Don't be selective in your listening. Instead, try to understand the main idea of the person talking to you. One of the ways to use your leftover thinking time is to compile the information you are hearing to ascertain a main point.

The fifth way to improve your listening is to empathize with the speaker. Try to put yourself in the speaker's place so you can see her or his point of view. Try to find out as much as possible about the person to whom you are talking.

The keys to effective listening can be summarized with the EAR acronym: *E*nthusiasm for listening—make listening important to your managerial style; *A*ttention to the speaker—concentrate on what he or she is saying; and *R*einforcement by feedback—always listen by providing feedback. When we listen well, we have more information with which to make good decisions, and we tell the speaker that what he or she is saying is important to us.

Communication Strategies for Employment

Machinery Systems, Inc.

614 E. State Parkway • Schaumburg, Illinois 60173 • (312) 882-8085 • TLX: 206842

February 5, 198_

Mrs. Georgia C. Benson, Director
Placement Services
Antworth College
Billings, MT 59102

Dear Mrs. Benson:

Students often ask, "How do I find a job?" It is unfortunate that
after years of education they are willing to settle for anything
instead of THE position for which they should be uniquely qualified. I
advise student groups across the country to develop employment
strategies. Here are the key aspects of the process:

Strategy, Then Resume: Generally, students get the cart before the
horse. They want an instant resume before carefully developing the
"what" they can do and "where" they can go.

Unknown Person: Who is this person? Before thinking about a job, get
to know yourself; the employment process permits you to look carefully—and honestly—at yourself.

The Last Step: In preparing for the employment exploration, one of the
last steps is the development of the resume.

This process is explained in Chapter 22 of **Communicating in Business**,
by Bateman and Sigband. Your students may benefit from reviewing this
material as they plan their employment strategies.

Thank you for your inquiry; we are pleased to be of assistance to you.

Cordially,

Rory Clark

Rory Clark
Director
Recruiting and Training Division

Reaching Potential Employers: Developing Your Resumé

WHAT YOU CAN LEARN BY STUDYING THIS CHAPTER

Some people feel that a resumé is a passport to employment that can be quickly tossed together at the print shop. Actually, the resumé itself may be a relatively minor part of finding *the* job you want, but the process of evolving the appropriate strategy and developing the resumé prepares you for the job hunt and eventual employment. This chapter thoroughly explores that process and explains, in detail, each of the elements—analyzing yourself, analyzing the job, identifying the employment strategy, and then presenting this on a sheet or two of paper, that is, preparing the resumé. After working through the various background steps, the preparation of the resumé is relatively simple because you have the information and you know where you are going.

The resumé is not a passport to a job; it just gets you to the starting line. Like the thoroughbred that has been carefully groomed for the big race, you too should manage each of the elements of your employment strategy well so that you can use the resumé to move yourself effectively out of the starting gate and achieve your desired professional goal.

IN PURSUIT OF HAPPINESS

Personal and profes-sional concerns

The United States Constitution is unique among all such documents in guaranteeing to each citizen the right to pursue happiness. Unfortunately, when it comes to seeking employment, too many people set aside that precious right. Most managers will spend more time on the job than they will spend with their friends or family. Yet too many people are in the wrong jobs and are unhappy. And most people who are in the wrong jobs have no one to blame but themselves.

Therefore, in pursuing your personal and professional happiness, in exercising your right to pursue the kind of employment you want, investigation and planning well will help you find rewarding and satisfactory employment.

This chapter is primarily about resumés. Some people who pick up this book will immediately turn to the resumé examples and copy various features to construct their own resumé. That is like signing up for a marathon and then taking a shortcut through the woods and collecting the T-shirt at the finish line. You got the "documentation" at the end, but you certainly did not perspire or dodge any potholes to get to the end result, nor did you really win a prize.

Perspiration

Developing the resumé calls for some perspiration; there are actually no short-cuts. Therefore, we will look at the preliminaries and strategies that should help you develop an effective resumé.

EMPLOYMENT STRATEGIES

Without a strategy, your resumé will be strange.

Resumés are not passports. They are more like targeted missiles directed toward rather specific employment opportunities. You evolve a strategy to attract the attention of a particular employer; the resumé is simply the culmination. Too often people first print a resumé and then look for a job. Instead, know the employment you want, evolve your strategy, and *then* create the resumé that can lift you off the launch pad to an interview.

Think Strategically

Focus on and support your career goals.

There are a number of factors to consider in developing, rethinking, and implement-ing your employment strategy; the resumé is the *last* step. As we look at the various elements, think clearly and perceptively; be realistic, but remember that you are limited only by your own capabilities. Identify your career goal(s) and then present information that supports your ability to do that job. You evolve the strategy and make the case. You cannot simply lay out a smorgasbord of data on a sheet of paper and expect the potential employer to create a nine-course meal. (See Figure 22.1—note the clear strategy based upon work experience and skills for the vocation.)

In conceiving your resumé strategy, consider your employment objective and determine what it is that will convince a potential employer to "buy" it. You bring your talents and experiences into the equation and then strategically blend them. The strategy depends on you. For the same sales representative job, one person may evolve a strategy based on an understanding of the marketplace, the use of computer technology in marketing, and summer work experience in market research. That is what the person has to "sell," and she methodically builds the case. Another individual, less conceptually oriented, is more tuned in to people; he emphasizes his social fraternity, his summer job on the golf course, and his sales awards in various college jobs. He builds his case as a get-with-it, people-oriented person who can sell!

Kinds of Strategies

There are all kinds of strategies. Know your employment objective, know the kinds of skills and attributes it takes to achieve that objective, and then pull forth the data strategically in the resumé to bring closure. The strategy builds upon your strengths, such as

Identify a strategy that will work for you.

- Applied work experience
- Excellent academic preparation
- Superb human-relations skills
- Solid, well-rounded experiences
- Goal- or achievement-orientation

GETTING TO KNOW YOU

Most of us think we know ourselves fairly well, but generally we are not terribly perceptive. Therefore, in developing your employment strategy, it is crucial that you ascertain your own likes, dislikes, interests, and preferences. If you don't, you could be the square peg trying to fit into an employer's round hole.

A good first step, even if you think you know and understand yourself, is to prepare a personal data sheet; it is an inventory of all the kinds of facts, interests, likes, attributes, and traits you can muster. Another person should be able to look at it and know what is "in" you. The inventory is for your eyes only; it will contain favorable and unfavorable information about you. Value-free items are included, too. For instance, one person wants to work in a metropolitan area, another in a rural setting; one wants employment in a small organization, another in a large one; some people want to live in a cottage in the woods, others like the excitement of a mid-town condo. It is your job to align your values with the types of employment available. These

Take time to prepare a personal inventory.

FIGURE 22.1   Topical/Chronological Resumé

LYNN C. O'HARE

College Address
College Court # 1
Metro Community College
Tampa, FL 33606   813/676-1993

Home Address
101 Sea Drive
Kennington, FL 33501
813/681-0225

Employment Objective

Applying excellent office administration skills with an ability to effectively coordinate people and activities, desire to start as an executive
secretary and eventually become an office manager.

Skills for the Career

- Type 70 w.p.m.   - Desk-top publishing skills
- Proficient dictation transcriber   - Competent with major
- Good human supervisory skills   word processing software programs

Education

- A.A. Metro Community College (M.C.C.), with honors, May 1988.
- Apple's 3-Day Desk-Top Publishing Conference, January 1988.
- Dictaphone's Skill Building Seminar, October 1987.

Work Experience

- Part-time Special Secretary to Director of Metro College's 25th Anniversary
  Celebration. November, 1987 - May, 1988.
- Student typist, Music Department, M.C.C. Academic Yr. 1987-88.
- Temporary Office Worker, Tampa Temporaries, Summer, 1986.
- Part-time Clerk-Typist; Dye's CPAs, 1983-86.

Extracurricular Activities

- Member, Secretarial Society of Central Florida.
- Member, Volleyball Intramurals.
- Secretary, M.C.C. Professional Secretarial Club, 1987.

References

Mrs. Carol Dye, Senior Partner
Dye's CPAs
P.O. Box 187
Kennington, FL 33500   813/681-2535

Dr. George Mason, Chairman
Department of Office Administration
Metro Community College
Tampa, FL 33606   813/676-2101

Professor Donna C. Wright, Chair.
M.C.C. 25th Anniversary Celebration
Metro Community College
Tampa, FL 33606   813/676-2101

Provide complete address information.

Indicate what you can do for the employer.

Don't hesitate to identify skills.

Generally list education and jobs in reverse chronological order.

Employment can stress work history and/or job responsibilities.

Activities can cite added responsibilities.

Provide complete data on references; cite formal names with titles of respect.

preferences reflect values. There are no rights or wrongs. But you are wrong if you want to live in a cottage in the midwest and a firm says they will place you in the heart of San Francisco—and you agree!

In constructing your inventory, you first need to identify categories into which you can place the details. Remember, you are not creating a resumé. An inventory does not look like a resumé—it is a several-page list of all kinds of specific data organized into categories. The categories may include, but are not limited to:

Interests	Skills	Daily routine
Education	Traits	Potential references
Travel	Intelligence	Previous employment
Lifestyle	Working style	Extracurricular activities
Location preference	Health	Grade point averages
Security/risk preference	Career objectives	Desire to stay in one place
Company size	Income needs	Types of people interaction
Dress preferences	Commuting time	
Weekend work		

Evolve and fill in the categories for your personal inventory.

The inventory is very detailed, and there will generally be a number of detailed pieces under each category. For instance, under *previous employment* you would list the places you have worked and include the job, address, and the name and title of each of your employers; under *potential references* you would list name, title, firm, address, and phone; under *traits* you would list both favorable ("like detail work") and unfavorable ("rarely get work done on time").

The inventory is used only by you and can serve multiple purposes. Incidentally, because of the length, detail, and continual change and updating, it is an excellent item to complete and maintain on a word processor. First, when it comes time to prepare the resumé, virtually all the information you will need about yourself is available on the data sheet. Actually, in preparing the resumé, you will be selecting data from your inventory, organizing and presenting it to support your employment objective. Second, the pros and cons on the data sheet aid you in evaluating what kind of position you really want to secure. For instance, if the data reveal that you want to live in a rural area, have a family with three children, spend huge amounts of time with your spouse and children, work in isolation versus interacting continually with people, and don't want to travel, you would be miserable taking a job in downtown L.A. as a sales rep for an office machinery company—a job that calls for work every weekend plus frequent travel. There is nothing wrong with L.A., there is nothing wrong with sales, and there is nothing wrong with office machinery *except* that they do not correspond with *you*—your interests, your desires, your abilities, and your skills. If you are going to pursue professional happiness, you must make the inventory/job happiness match!

Construct the inventory fairly—the only person you will fool will be you.

YOUR EMPLOYMENT AUDIT

It's your job to know what you want to do.

It is your task to determine what kinds of employment opportunities are available and the kinds of jobs you can do for a potential employer. After all, the case is relatively simple. Who would you hire: Jane, who responds to the employment interviewer's question with, "Gosh, I think I'm looking for something in marketing," or Dan, who responds, "With the sales experience I've gained working through college, the courses in engineering, and an ability to interact well with people, entering your sales representative training program, and probably aiming toward a position in industrial sales, would be great." Who is the interviewer going to be able to have a mutually beneficial conversation with? Remember, the interviewer's job is to find people to fill slots the firm has open, not to counsel the "Janes" of the world about where they might find themselves in the world of employment.

Job Titles

Know the name of what you want to do.

A good first step is to name your job. This seems to get more difficult as more new jobs are added and firms change the titles. There are some quick ways to learn about the names of jobs: look in the classified ads of major newspapers; talk to professionals, professors, and campus guest speakers about job titles and activities; and look at sources like the *Dictionary of Occupational Titles*. Once you know the title and description of the job, you can move quickly to determine how your skills, traits, and interests correspond.

Employment Trends

Know what's up—is there really a career where you are looking?

Although the trends may shift rapidly, it is beneficial to know what kinds of skills are currently prized, what industries are flourishing, and where the experts say the jobs can be found during the next few years. College placement offices generally have a variety of brochures and articles that address these issues.

SOURCES OF EMPLOYMENT INFORMATION

Informal sources can provide you with current insight.

As you review your employment options, do not overlook informal sources of job information such as talking with your instructors, meeting with employers, and calling former students who have secured jobs. It is vital in using informal sources that you gain specific information and that you carefully differentiate the chaff from the wheat. Beware of accepting "sophomore dorm talk" as perceptive employment advice. On the other hand, comments from a former student who has a job similar to what you want can be very helpful.

Newspapers, professional trade journals, employment agencies, college placement services, and various books can provide information about employment. There are reports like Northwestern University's annual Endicott report that identify trends and salaries and there are generally one or two best-selling softbound books that provide useful information. For instance, in the early 1980s, Tom Jackson's *Guerrilla Tactics in the Job Market* (Bantam Books, 1978) was popular. Other sources include:

Formal sources can provide a breadth of information.

National Business Employment Weekly. Published each Sunday by *The Wall Street Journal,* this tabloid contains career-advancement positions in organizations throughout the nation. The jobs listed in the weekly are not available in any regional edition or single issue of *WSJ.* The publication is available by subscription or on newstands.

Occupational Outlook for College Graduates. Published periodically by the Government Printing Office, this item contains employment information on jobs for which some education beyond high school is needed.

The Encyclopedia of Associations. Available in most libraries, this book lists trade associations and organizations. These groups can provide up-to-date information on the job outlook in their fields.

College Placement Annual. Produced annually, the directory contains career information supplied by about a thousand employers. The annual is published by the College Placement Council and is generally available free of charge at all college placement offices.

THE RESUMÉ

Picturing the Resumé

Knowing details about yourself and understanding the kind of employment you desire, you are now ready to construct the resumé—and it is definitely a construction project. The "materials" you are going to need are:

- A statement of your employment objective (or career summary).
- The specific data from the inventory that supports your objective.
- An organizational strategy that presents your information efficiently, attractively, and persuasively in conjunction with your employment objective. (See Figure 22.2 for an example of a resumé with a strategy of emphasizing employment history.)

What you need to develop a workable resumé

The resumé is a detailed statement that neatly, precisely, and clearly provides a potential employer with a quick, convenient, and favorable overview of your employment qualifications. In a limited amount of space, you attempt to represent yourself in the way that you want the receiver to see you. The resumé represents a very important

FIGURE 22.2   Topical/Chronological Resumé in Narrative Format

Topical/chronological resume in narrative format employing a strategy emphasizing employment history.

Names of previous places of employment are highlighted; responsibilities noted.

It is not always necessary to place education at the top of the resume.

Complete information makes it easy to contact these references.

ANTHONY C. RODRIGUEZ

Campus Address
Dillard University, Collard Hall-213
Philadelphia, PA 19123
215/767-1903

                                       Home Address
                                       1703 W. 32nd St.
                                       Maynord, PA 19207
                                       215/332-2254

Employment Objective

To apply six years of restaurant experience plus a Management major to aid a lodging facility to revitalize its food and beverage operations.

Qualifications and Skills

With a strong record of performance in restaurants and front desk management, and a Management degree, can aid the operation—know computer operations, good typist, short-order cooking skills, banquet service coordination abilities.

Work Experience

Green Gables Inn, Philadelphia, PA   1987 - present
Night Manager with direct supervision of all personnel; responsible for all financial and operational matters during the shift.

Dillard University Food Services, Philadelphia, PA   1986 - present
Special banquet part-time aid in ordering and preparing food; planning and coordinating service and clean-up.

Windsor Hotel, Mansford, PA   1985 - 1987
Waited in coffee shop, filled in at front-desk; aided in maintenance; assisted comptroller in maintaining and preparing daily statistics.

Four Seasons Motel, Philadelphia, PA   1984 - 1985
Starting as a bell-boy, was provided chance to gain skills in the restaurant, recreation, housekeeping, and customer relations areas.

Education Background

B.S. in Management, School of Business. Dillard University, June, 1988
+ Worked continually to earn educational expenses.
+ Gained classroom knowledge while applying it in hotel/restaurant industry.

References

Miss Sandra Washington   Mrs. Barbara Turkington   Mr. Gary M. Sanchez
Director, Food Services   Owner, Four Seasons Motel   Green Gables Inn
Dillard University   1032 Airport Road   P.O. Box 7676
Philadelphia, PA 19123   Philadelphia, PA 19172   Philadelphia, PA 19126
215/767-2932   215/623-2323   215/832-2000

commodity—you. In one or two neatly typewritten or printed pages, it presents a well-organized statement of your abilities, qualities, accomplishments, and job aspirations. The subject—you—is complex, but you must boil the information down to represent yourself in the best light possible.

Using the Resumé

You can read many articles suggesting that resumés rarely lead to employment. Recognizing the odds, it is very important to not place all your hopes on a resumé. However, the resumé serves a variety of purposes for you:

- The resumé process forces you to crystallize your employment thinking and summarize it in a page or two.
- Resumés don't get jobs, but they are excellent in aiding you to obtain employment interviews and serve as reference points during an interview.
- In any employment situation, it is generally a good idea to be able to provide the potential employer with your resumé. Remember, it has been carefully constructed to promote and highlight your best features. Therefore, even though you filled out an employment application, try to have the interviewer look at your resumé.
- Finally, resumés are just part of the manager's toolbox—you are expected to have one.

Make your resumé work for you.

Mirroring Society

Resumés tend to reflect attributes and expectations of our society. Therefore, what is to be included in a resumé—or excluded—changes from time to time. For instance, prior to the antidiscrimination legislation of the 1960s and 1970s, the first item generally addressed in a resumé was one's personal data. Today, it is generally recommended that the personal items be left off completely. In the late 1980s, the trend seems to be to (1) emphasize the applicant's career objective and factual qualifications for the job; (2) place little or no emphasis on personal characteristics (height, weight, physical condition, sex, health, marital status); (3) identify specific short-term and perhaps long-term employment objectives; and (4) highlight for the potential employer exact skills that the candidate has for the identified job.

Be current on the ins and outs of resumé contents.

Formatting the Resumé

Various formats can be used to present your information. The resumés shown in Figures 22.1 through 22.6 are examples of some of the many options available. Note that the resumé in Figure 22.3 presents the information from Figure 22.2 in an

How you format your resumé influences its acceptability.

FIGURE 22.3   Topical/Chronological Resumé with "Bulleted" Points

Topical/chronologi-
cal resume with
"bulleted"
information;
employment history
is emphasized.

Strive for action
words in
describing
experience.

Note jobs in
reverse order—
increasing respon-
sibilities over time.

Reference informa-
tion allows caller to
know who they are
talking to.

ANTHONY C. RODRIGUEZ

Campus Address
Dillard University, Collard Hall 213
Philadelphia, PA 19123
215/767-1903

Home Address
1703 W. 32nd St.
Maynord, PA 19207
215/332-2254

Employment Objective

To apply six years of restaurant experience plus a Management major to
aid a lodging facility in revitalizing its food and beverage operations.

Qualifications and Skills

* Six years in the industry
* Banquet coordination and front-desk skills
* Knowledge of computer software

Work Experience

Green Gables Inn, Philadelphia, PA   1987 - present
* Supervised employees and shift finances
* Experience in all operations
* Recognized for customer relations

Dillard University Food Service, Philadelphia, PA   1987 - present
* Prepared food and planned banquet activities
* Coordinated preparation, service, and clean-up
* Worked on clean-up crews

Windsor Hotel, Mansford, PA   1985 - 1987
* Gained financial experience
* Simplified front-desk operations

Four Seasons Motel, Philadelphia, PA   1984 - 1985
* Gained housekeeping experience
* Waited tables and operated recreation room

Educational Background

B.S. in Management, School of Business. Dillard University, June 1988.
* Worked continually to pay educational expenses.
* Gained both classroom and applied knowledge of hotel/motel industry.

References

Miss Sandra Washington	Mrs. Barbara Turkington	Mr. Gary M. Sanchez
Director, Food Services	Owner, Four Seasons Motel	Green Gables Inn
Dillard University	1032 Airport Road	P.O. Box 7676
Philadelphia, PA 19123	Philadelphia, PA 19172	Philadelphia, PA 19126
215/767-2932	215/623-2323	215/832-2000

alternative format. Use the format that represents you best, fits your employment strategy, and presents a favorable image, with plenty of white space.

For college students, a one-page (8½ × 11 inch, typewritten) resumé is almost always adequate. In some situations, however, it may be necessary to make the resumé longer. It is a good idea to make your resumé as compact as possible.

You have spent thousands of dollars on your education, so don't be overly frugal in preparing your resumé. If you are pursuing two different types of employment, why not prepare two different resumés? One way to make your resumé a flexible, "living" document is to put it on a word processor. For example, the employment objectives and skills required for a position in industrial marketing are different from the skills required for a position in retail marketing. If you would like to pursue employment options in both fields, use of a word processor will make it easy to tailor your resumé to the specific interests of potential employers.

Word processors can aid resumé construction and retention.

TYPES OF RESUMÉS

There are two basic types of resumés that seem to be acceptable to employers today, the topical/chronological and the functional/skills. The former is still the most common, but you must be guided by personal preference and which of the types best fits your information.

Functional/Skills

The skills needed for the job are emphasized and supported in the functional skills resumé. Be sure you understand the logic and strategy of this approach. The career objective states what you want to do; then the skills or functions should automatically support the conclusion that you can do the job. The remaining narrative adds proof and support (see Figures 22.4 and 22.6).

Select the type of resumé that best reveals your qualities.

Topical/Chronological

The topical/chronological type of resumé identifies the job and then summarizes the qualifications, placing them in somewhat standard types of groupings—education, employment, extracurricular activities, and so on. Here the approach is to state the employment objective and then gain the receiver's interest by showing different topical areas where you are strong. The chronology enters in because generally the specific listings within groupings are presented in reverse chronological order (see Figures 22.2 and 22.3).

FIGURE 22.4   Functional/Skills Resumé

MATTHEW G. WOEBLER
517 W. Bowlingreen Drive
Montclair, NJ 07070
201/562-1931

Employment Objective

To apply work experience in marketing and a broad education in health care to aid a large hospital's marketing activities.

Relevant Marketing Experience	* <u>Headed</u> campus blood donation campaign; set New Jersey record, 1987.
	* <u>Supervised</u> sales staff for University's paper; directed work of seventeen sales reps, 1985 - 1987.
	* <u>Worked</u> as a "gopher" in the Marketing Services Department of Fairfax Mfg. Co., Summer, 1986.
Excellent Health Care Knowledge	* <u>Major</u>: Health Care Administration; New Jersey State University, 1984-1987.
	* <u>Marketing</u>: Took six additional Marketing courses.
	* <u>Special Study</u>: Completed under Prof. M. C. Detomasi an independent study, "Modern Trends in Hospital Marketing."
Good Human Skills	* <u>Vice-president</u>: New Jersey State University, Health Care Club, 1987.
	* <u>Executive Committee</u>: Wesley Foundation, 1987.
	* <u>Dorm Council</u>: Dorm coordinating group, 1986.
Relevant References	* Mr. Jayson Waymann, Asst. Dir. of Administration Montclair County Hospital 1717 Main Street Montclair, NJ 07072 201/673-4343
	* Dr. Marilyn C. Detomasi, Assistant Professor Health Care Administration Department New Jersey State University Montclair, NJ 07070 201/562-2176
	* Mr. James C. Preston, Manager Marketing Services Department Fairfax Manufacturing Co. P.O. Box 1776 Bedford, NJ 07083 201/867-2000

Note how skill categories support employment objective.

Work experience (including volunteer activities) and education blend to indicate Matthew can do the job.

Note the logic:
• The desired job.
• The relevant skill categories.
• The specific qualities of Matthew.

Note the different look of this resume compared to the normal topical type.

COMMON SECTIONS OF THE RESUMÉ

We will focus on the topical/chronological type in our consideration of the sections of the resumé. Similar sections appear in the functional/skills type, although the format would be different.

The Career Objective

The statement of what you can do for the potential employer is probably the most important item in the resumé; it sets the stage. The remainder of the employment strategy is built around this statement. You select the skills, previous employment, and references based on the career objective.

The career objective is a strong you-oriented statement.

There are several guidelines to keep in mind as you struggle to write a sentence that captures your years of experience and your employment aspirations.

- State the career objective in terms of what you can do for the potential employer; it is trite to state the objective as "To obtain employment . . . " or "To secure a position. . . ." Everyone knows you want a job—the important question the employer has is, what can you do for me?
- Career objectives tend to be rather specific; therefore, if you are interviewing in two or three different job categories, prepare two or three different resumés.
- Beware of relying too much on your education (e.g., "four years of accounting courses to lead to a position with a Big-Eight firm"). There are thousands of educated people, and you do not necessarily differentiate yourself by saying education makes the employment match.

Strive to make your career objective you-oriented; attempt to be humble and not overstate your case. But at the same time, indicate that you are ready to get to work and enter the organization with both feet on the ground. The single sentence career objective generally works well for students graduating from college. On occasion, besides the immediate objective, some people indicate a long-term objective, for example, "Using positive interpersonal skills and three years of accounting experience to enter the auditing department of a Big Eight firm; to strive for a partnership position by age 35."

The Career Summary

As noted, the career objective is important for the first job; you are targeting rather specifically and attempting to launch your career. Later, after you have some practical work under your belt and a variety of worthwhile experiences, a specific, simple sentence employment objective may work to your disadvantage. This is where the

If you have a career to summarize, the career summary can lead the thinking of the reader.

longer and less directed career summary statement may work well. In two to four sentences it captures the progress of your career and paints a positive future-oriented outlook. It does not state exactly what you can do; it summarizes what you have done and permits the reader to say, "I think this person 'fits' what we are looking for" (see Figure 22.5).

Here are some guidelines for writing the career summary:

- Strive to lead the reader, allowing the reader to fill in the last step (the conclusion)—"This person has the background for our position."
- Capture your experience in short phrases, and use action-oriented words; remember, you are not writing a dull history; you are preparing a future-directed plan.

Skills

In today's market, if you don't have skills to sell, you will find it difficult to find a buyer.

Today, many employers are placing a premium on identifiable and usable skills, especially for entry-level positions. In other words, to just say you attended college may not pull much weight; many employers want to know specifically what skills you possess that you can implement on your first day on the job. In listing skills, be precise, not general. In other words, don't say "good communicator"; say instead, "Can write crisp one-page memos." This section can also incorporate important human relations skills, like

- Meet and interact well with people
- Effective speaker
- Motivate people easily

For each section of the resumé, consider two things. One, what are the attributes, skills, experience, or background that will support the career objective or career summary? Two, use appropriate material from your data sheet to support the career objective—attempt to direct the reader to a conclusion that he or she should talk to you.

Education

Don't just stick education in the resumé; make it part of your strategy—emphasized or deemphasized.

How much education is emphasized depends on your school experience and your employment strategy. If you were a "C" student, you may want to downplay education; if you were a top-achiever and the recipient of various scholarships, you may want to emphasize it. Some kinds of employment call for strong academic backgrounds and others don't. All of these factors will influence how you approach this

FIGURE 22.5 Resumé with a General Employment Summary

ROBERT J. JENSEN

1703 Magnolia Court   home: 213/612-2309
Long Beach, CA 90802   business: 213/543-1700

Background Summary

   Sales experiences seem inborn—won national Junior Achievement sales award
and sold delivery services during junior high; following college joined an
office products firm as a Sales Representative where gained grassroots
knowledge—became a group leader. Joined a "mini-bell" and applied office
knowledge to telecommunications industry; now have over five years experience
with ever-increasing responsibilities in marketing, sales-strategy, and new
product/service development.

General employment summary used instead of the specific job objective.

Sales/Marketing Accomplishments

   * Established "Sales Rep Handbook" for office products sales reps.

   * Instituted economical follow-up procedures for sales calls.

   * Broke region's sales records for three consecutive quarters.

   * Lead a group of ten sales reps in developing coordinated team approach.

   * Organized sales-marketing task force promoting videoconferencing.

   * Streamlined reporting procedures for sales calls.

   * Designed strategy for selling "call holding" to businesses.

Business record of accomplishments highlighted.

Education

   B.A.   Chico State College, Marketing.   1975
   M.B.A.   University of Southern California.   1984

Professional Activities (Selected)

   President: Southern California Sales Rep Association, 1984 - 1985.
   Director: American Marketing Association College Outreach Program, 1987.
   Board Member: Community Hospital of Long Beach, 1985 - present.
   Chairman: Fund for the Arts, Long Beach, 1984 - 1986.
   Member: Long Beach Yacht Club, since 1986.

Activities— interactions— beyond work clearly noted.

Personal

   Married, two sons; excellent health.

Personal data almost perfunctory.

Action-oriented Language for Resumés

PERSONALITY TRAITS		WORK EXPERIENCE	
Active	Imaginative	Adapted	Guided
Adaptable	Persistent	Completed	Organized
Articulate	Persuasive	Conceived	Revised
Competent	Realistic	Created	Simplified
Dependable	Self-starter	Designed	Streamlined
Determined	Tactful	Developed	Structured
Enthusiastic		Directed	
		Established	

category. Generally, high school work is not included unless there was something unusual. Also, be careful of listing courses; this should only be done if they are crucial in emphasizing your career objective.

Work Experience

Whereas some people have a strong suit in education, others have it in work experience. Since an employer is hiring you to work, it is often a good idea to let him or her know that work is not new to you.

Describe your work and responsibilities using action words.

There are various ways to format the work experience section of the resumé. Generally, you want to name the job, the employer, perhaps some responsibilities and accomplishments, and the dates of employment. In describing your work as well as your traits, try to use action-oriented language.

Extracurricular Activities and Interests

Activities beyond those of work and study can reveal much about you.

Most resumés will list awards, achievements, scholarships, and activities. Some people think it beneficial to indicate some nonwork interests in an attempt to reveal well-roundedness. Awards and achievements can build the case that you are an achiever; extracurricular activities can indicate that you pursue activities that are not required. Often these activities can reveal management, motivational, and communication attributes you possess.

Personal Data

Factors that are not work-related are marital status, health, age, physical size, and other such items. Today these are generally downplayed or not included in resumés. You would interject them only if they uniquely support your career objective. It is legal for you to include these items; however, it is illegal for the employer to ask you questions concerning most personal matters. (See Figure 22.6 for a resumé with more personal data, references not included.)

If you include personal data, know why you are doing it.

References

For jobs right out of college, references are often not checked. On the other hand, to list references as an element of proof, "Look who can vouch for me," might be a good persuasive technique. Your strategy will determine what you do. If you are emphasizing your personality and work experience in qualifying you for a sales position, then previous employers who can directly address these subjects may be important to you. However, regardless of whether you place the references on the resumé, be sure you have some people on call to serve you in case you ever need them.

References, whether checked or not, can provide your resumé with an excellent form of "proof."

References are generally categorized as educational, work-related, or personal/character references. If you list references, be sure to obtain the permission of the references. On the resumé, give the person's full formal name (e.g., Dr. Janice E. Dye), title, organization, specific address, and telephone number.

Other Items

You are a unique individual; you may have characteristics or experiences that don't fit the normal mold. Keep in mind that you are evolving a strategy to entice a potential employer to seek you out. You are including data that support the employment objective and steer the reader to say, "She can do that job!" There are many additional questions. Here are twenty common questions people ask about resumés.

Question	*Response*
1. Should grade points appear?	1. Generally not unless it builds your strategy. If you include GPA, be sure to indicate the grade scale (e.g., 3.4 when A = 4).
2. Should salary needs be stated?	2. No—it's too early.

FIGURE 22.6   Functional/Skills Resumé Without References

JESSICA C. ABALONI

Present Address
604 W. Gaylord
Bloomington, IL 61703
309/838-1602

Permanent Address
6616 Dunham Road
Des Moines, IA 50314
515/729-8271

Career Goal

To apply work experience and knowledge of exercise science as a Fitness Coordinator in a private, industrial, or public organization.

Note how adjectives in skill categories relate to exercise and fitness.

Coordinated Work Experience
- Coordinator and recruiter for Lassie League Youth Softball; much interaction with coaches & parents; Downers Grove Park District, summer, 1988.

- Coach and fitness coordinator; summer basketball program for boys and girls; Downers Grove Park District, summer, 1987.
- Fitness manager internship, Kimberly-Clark Inc. Neenah, Wisc., Fall, 1987.

Specific qualities are noted within each skill area.

Developed Skills
- Certified in CPR.
- Cardiac rehabilitation experience.
- Fitness testing abilities.
- Good cooperation and interpersonal skills.

Strong Academic Record
- Double major in Industrial Recreation and Exercise Science; Illinois State University, May 1988.
- Recognized as an All-Illinois Scholar-Athlete.
- Extra courses in Business—including Business Communications.

Exercise Vitality
- Varsity basketball letter winner, four years.
- Member: Industrial Recreational Association.
- Participant and leader in intramural sports.

For this type of employment, it may be logical to cite more personal data.

Active Interests
- Jog and swim daily.
- Willing to travel and relocate.
- Enjoy all sporting activities and encouraging others to participate.
- Excellent health; single.

References are not listed.

References
- Available from Placement Service, Illinois State University, Normal, IL 61761; 309/627-0321.

3. What about including a photo?

3. Photos are not "in" today.

4. I'm a member of a minority race; should that be highlighted?

4. Don't highlight it, but consider including it subtly; perhaps a group membership will suggest it.

5. My work experience is not in the field I'm entering. Should it be listed?

5. If it's all you've got, list it; right out of college it is important to indicate you have worked!

6. I'm getting married before I'll ever take the job. How would that be addressed?

6. Skip it; those are issues or concerns that can emerge in second interviews if you want to pursue them (unless it builds your strategy of maturity and responsibility).

7. What about the statement, "References available upon request"?

7. Rarely will anyone call for them; a better approach is to indicate their availability from a third source, such as your placement service.

8. I didn't get along on one job; I'd prefer that a potential employer not call. How do I accomplish this?

8. A workable technique is to list "selected work experience," then you carefully select who you list and don't list.

9. I want to list personal data; where should it go in the resumé?

9. The entire sequencing of information categories is up to you. But today it probably should go at or near the end.

10. My work experience is nil because until my father's death this year, I spent my time at home taking care of him. What do I do?

10. Always play to your strengths; you can evolve a long list of attributes from this experience: patience, devotion, and organization are just a few.

11. I have high blood pressure that is well-controlled with medication. Need this be listed on the resumé?

11. No, there may be some medical concerns you would want to bring up in later interviews, but don't bring them up before round one.

12. My name is Raymond C. Sittlington. I don't like the name "Raymond" and everyone calls me "Chip." What goes on the resumé?

12. Make it easy for the reader if they have the opportunity to ever talk with you; cite your name as Raymond "Chip" Sittlington.

13. For ten years I've worked in my parent's grocery store so they know my work best. Can I list them in the references?

13. No, but there are other options: perhaps a nonrelative manager in the store or a wholesaler or other party who can comment on your work experience.

14. My work experience was in the Army where my skill was peeling potatoes. How does that relate to my career in banking?

14. Build on what you gained—discipline, devotion to duty, long hours, and perhaps special awards. If you got an award for peeling potatoes, the sky is the limit!

15. My spouse and I insist on both securing professional jobs in the same city. Should that be included?

15. No, the resumé is no place to make demands or erect potential barriers—that issue can wait.

16. I'm twenty, married with one child, and will graduate soon. I have worked through college and am responsible. Should this personal data be included?

16. Maybe yes. If your strategy is built on the responsibility issue, this kind of personal data may work to your advantage.

17. Offset printing looks nice. What about having the resumé printed?

17. Be careful. You are locked into the printed resumé at some considerable expense. Consider good and flexible word processing combined with good photocopying.

18. What about stationery color—is white still the color preferred?

18. Today there are various colors that are considered businesslike, but there is nothing wrong with white. Some individuals prefer beiges and light grays.

19. My work experience is skimpy, but I've successfully held several leadership positions in student organizations.

19. If you can organize, motivate, and manage in volunteer organizations, you will do well in business—emphasize these activities in the way you would stress on-the-job work experience.

20. I'd like to eventually attain an executive position. How do I list that without sounding overly positive?

20. There is nothing wrong with stating (in the Career Objective section, for example), "Applying skills in quantitative methods and computer operations and building on the sales experience, to aid a Marketing Department as a junior researcher and to eventually become a Marketing Director."

QUICK REVIEW

Developing a resumé is a process that is best implemented with a strategy. Develop your employment strategy, and then develop the resumé to accomplish your objective. Do not go to a print shop and pick and choose a "fill-in-the-blank" resumé and then see where it might lead you. A tremendous advantage of preparing the resumé conscientiously is that it aids you in facing and answering so many of the fundamental questions concerning employment. With those personal and professional elements understood, maximum time can be spent finding the job you want.

EXECUTIVE SUMMARY

To: Business Communication Students

From: David N. Bateman and Norman B. Sigband

Subject: Reaching Potential Employers: Developing Your Resumé

Before you can create an effective resumé, you must know yourself and the kind of employment you want and its requirements. You must develop a strategy that will attract the attention of the right potential employers.

A personal inventory of your interests, attributes, habits, education, and skills can take you a long way toward knowing yourself, and an employment audit can inform you about jobs that you are qualified for and that are available. Matching the results of the personal inventory and the employment audit should enable you to prepare a well-targeted resumé.

In one or two well-organized and well-formated pages, your resumé should represent you as you wish the receiver to see you. Achieving that goal requires choices and decisions. What should your statement of a career objective be? Should you organize the resumé functionally or chronologically? How can you state your skills specifically? How should you format the parts of your resumé? If you have honestly and thoroughly developed your employment strategy, the answers to these questions should not be difficult to find.

DISCUSSION GENERATORS

1. *Last Step?* Explain why the authors suggest that the resumé is the last step in the employment strategy process. Don't most people think the first thing you do is write a resumé?

2. *Informal Sources.* What are the advantages and disadvantages of using informal sources for employment information?

3. *Formal Sources.* What are the advantages and disadvantages of using formal sources?

4. *Word Processing.* How can preparing the resumé on a word processor make the document more flexible for you?

5. *Societal Change.* Explain what the authors mean when they suggest the importance of revising the resumé to keep "in step" with the changes in society.

6. *Uses.* Beyond employment, what other uses are there for a resumé?

7. *I Want a Job.* Why do the authors suggest that employment objectives that state "To secure a position as . . . " are I-oriented?

8. *Objective vs. Summary.* Clearly differentiate the career objective and the career summary.

9. *When.* Explain the situations in which you would use a career objective and the situations in which you would use a career summary.

10. *Resumé Types.* Name and explain the two types of resumés illustrated in the chapter.

11. *Happiness.* Why is happiness such a big factor—isn't just getting a job a primary concern?

12. *Action.* Why is action-oriented language beneficial for a resumé—especially a resumé going to a business organization?

13. *References.* What are the categories of references and how might the selection of references relate to your employment strategy?

14. *Height, Weight, Age.* Why has the listing of personal data on the resumé diminished in recent years?

15. *Education.* Why should some people downplay education in their resumés?

16. *Offset Printing.* What is the disadvantage to having your resumé printed with an offset press?

17. *Skills.* Why are employers today looking for specific skills that potential employees possess?

18. *Nickname?* If you are not called by and do not like your given name, how can you handle this on your resumé?

19. *Whoops.* You are listing references on your resumé. What is wrong and potentially confusing about the following listing?

Lynn Trapp
1701 Brook Lane
Murfressboro, TN

20. *References.* Reviewing the kinds of proof presented earlier in this book, what kind of proof can references provide for the resumé?

APPLICATIONS FOR BUSINESS

21. *Job Search.* Within a particular employment category (e.g., retail, personnel, or production), identify six specific job titles that look interesting to you. For each, give the following:
a. The characteristics you possess that align with the job
b. Traits or characteristics you have that are not congruent with the job
c. Whether the job is a "dead end" job or one from which you can grow and move
d. Name the sources of your job information

22. *Junk.* There is really a huge amount of trash in resumés. Without revealing names (so the guilty can be protected), find an example of a poor resumé. There are various sources of "junk." Look at what some friends have done; go to the print shop and look at their examples; look into those books of resumés that some college groups assemble.

 Either in a memo or in a three-to-five-minute talk, display the resumé and
a. Indicate its weak points
b. Indicate its strongest points
c. Cite the employment strategy
d. Give the resumé a grade it would receive in your course
e. List and explain some simple improvements that would raise the grade at least one letter.

23. *Operation Update.* You are an officer of a student organization, and you see that many of the seniors in your organization do all kinds of "old fashioned" things in their resumés. They tell everyone how current and "with it" they are, but their resumés (the categories, style, and language) look like the '50s.

 There is something ironic about a college senior who dresses in the most modern clothing being over a quarter of a century behind with the resumé. Therefore, you and three or four others decide you will conduct a brief seminar on the resumé—"Coming Out of the Dark Ages."
a. List some "old fashioned" resumé techniques.
b. Show the modern approach for each technique listed in "a."
c. Illustrate how they could use word processing to modernize the approach to resumé construction.

24. *Happiness.* As a manager in a personnel department, it becomes obvious to you that a large percentage of people are not happy with their lives (or life-styles) and that this affects their work habits; other people find themselves in wrong jobs, and this certainly influences the way they approach work and the people around their work.

You decide that a series of voluntary seminars for all employees would be helpful. The seminars would include individuals who would make presentations and panels of people who would present current thinking on the relevant issues.

You see the connection between appropriate job selection and happiness on the job and at home. You need to do the following in organizing and then "selling" the idea of the seminars.

   a. In some detail, list and explain the subjects that would be addressed in the several seminars.
   b. Name individuals who could be brought in to present the needed information.
   c. Indicate the cost of each person and then a total budget for the project.
   d. Take the above "raw" information, and prepare a proposal report for the vice-president. In the proposal, make sure the VP understands the concept and how employees will be benefitted by attending such programs.

25. *Who Is Responsible?* It often seems that the employer is responsible for virtually everything. It is the employer's responsibility to motivate the employee to work, to place the employee in the right job so he or she will be happy, and so on. With the employer accepting so many responsibilities, what is the employee responsible for in the modern organization?

Prepare a one-page editorial that could appear in a coming edition of your company's magazine. The theme of your piece is that employees must assume responsibility for selecting the right job and then doing it well. Write your piece carefully, and strive to be very practical.

COMMUNICATION CHECK-UPS

26. You are cordially invited to the Scholars' Reception on Sunday, August 24, 198—, at 2:00 p.m..

27. Your secretarys telephone manner with people is outstanding.

28. The Workshop is a manufacturing agency and do not have the facilities or abilities to handle the marketing function.

29. The modern bookstore would be a viable market for our products.

30. Inside Address and Salutation

Bruce Bolind Co.
Boulder, CO 80302

Dear Sir or Madam:

31. First, establish the goal; secondly, evolve the procedures; and three, determine the rules.

32. He ended his speech most appropriately with a meaningful quotation from the bible.

33. By instituting the new manufacturing processes here at Bellmount Corp. we were able to reduce scrap by over 20 percent.

34. This would be a good year to make the purchase, however, the budget will not permit the expense.

35. The company—it was started in Rhode Island—is growing rapidly in Missouri today.

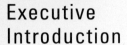

Executive
Introduction

DRAKE BEAM MORIN, INC.

January 28, 198_

Professor K. John Benton, Ph.D.
Department of Management
Virginia Regional University
Richmond, Virginia 23284-2100

Dear Mr. Benton:

Your inquiry about our work and how it relates to business students is fascinating. DBM provides many services to corporations, and currently a dominant one is our "outplacement" counseling. We work with executives to find new employment when they have been displaced. Our activities are very similar to what you and others teach in business communications courses. Some illustrations:

<u>Self-Analysis</u>: Carefully analyze your abilities, and then be able to summarize and present them in employment letters and resumes.

<u>Persistence</u>: Everyone is busy; a single contact may not get this job done. Knowing when and how to follow up is basic.

<u>Obtaining Interviews</u>: Learn techniques for making personal contact with potential employers.

<u>Interviewing</u>: Get smart! Do the best you can, in advance, to understand the culture of the firm interviewing you. As the old Holiday Inn advertisement said, "The best surprise is NO surprise."

These are some of the techniques we present to experienced executives so they can find satisfactory employment. It is good to know that the literature of your discipline deals with this vital topic. The better you do your job, the easier you make our job; in fact, if you are inordinately successful, you will put us out of business!

Sincerely,

William J. Morin

William J. Morin

WJM:ms

CHAPTER 23

Persuading the Employer to Consider You: Letters and Interviews

WHAT YOU CAN LEARN BY STUDYING THIS CHAPTER

Effective employment letters have many of the characteristics of effective sales letters: they *arouse interest, describe* qualifications, *prove* statements, and *request* an interview, for example. In this chapter, you will learn how a letter with these qualities can work for you in your employment search. The employment interview generally follows such a letter, unless the interview was arranged by a third party, such as a placement service. The interviewer who has read your employment letter already knows something about you. You will see, however, that good preparation for the interview—by gathering information about the organization, for example—is another way to attract and hold the attention of the organization you hope to work for. The letter and the interview, together with various follow-up communications, are your first contacts with your potential employer. If you don't want them to be your last, you should implement these communications with care and sensitivity.

How to contact a potential employer

Now that you have done your "homework"—analyzed your capabilities, the employment market, and job requirements—and have prepared an effective resume, you need to establish meaningful contact with potential employers.

We know that salespeople often have tough jobs—people say they are not home, won't answer the door, and tell them to go fly a kite. In searching for a job, you are attempting to sell yourself, and even though you have a good product, it is not always easy to make the contact, and it is even harder to make the sale. As any good sales rep will tell you, don't get discouraged; periodically review your approach, and keep moving ahead. The same applies to the job search. There are a variety of ways to attempt to make the initial contact:

Walk In: Walk into the organization and ask for an interview.

Fee Paid Employment Service: Go to an employment agency, and ask them to find you a job (the fee may be paid by you or by the hiring organization).

Employment Service: Use a free employment service (state agency or college placement service) to put you in contact with potential employers.

Orally Announce: Make your employment desires known to teachers, friends, and associates so they might call your attention to job openings.

Mail Campaign: Start a mail campaign in which you send your qualifications to potential employers even though they did not seek your services.

The Classifieds: Monitor and respond to the help wanted advertisements in the local or regional newspapers; read advertisements in trade and professional journals of your occupational choice.

You may find it beneficial to use a combination of several of these methods to make contact with someone who can offer you the job you want.

EMPLOYMENT LETTERS

Employment letters may be routine for the receiver, but not for the writer.

You only need look at the classified ads in the newspaper to note that employers seek employment letters as a device for obtaining new employees. The newspapers of major cities carry hundreds of advertisements asking individuals to reply by letter to indicate their interest in filling specific positions. Companies also are accustomed to receiving letters from persons who are not replying to an advertisement but are simply prospecting to determine if a specific company has an opening. The importance of these letters cannot be overemphasized; they make the first impression, and you do not want to come across as dull or trite.

The Cover Letter

Cover letters are very similar to sales letters, and they literally cover the resumé. Like the sales letter (see Chapter 7), these letters should accomplish four main purposes.

1. Arouse Interest.

Without being cute or pushy, you must arouse the interest of the potential employer. Avoid leading off with a dull statement that may convince the reader you also are dull. Do not start with a statement that reflects concern for only your interests rather than the reader's. The following I-oriented statements will turn your reader off:

I will get my A.A. degree this month and I will be ready to take a job.

This letter is in reply to your ad which recently appeared in the *News.* I think I would be interested in the job you listed.

Up, up, and away! I'm "Sky King" and I'm ready to put my piloting skills to work for Airgot Airlines. Call me today and I'll fly for you tomorrow.

After four years of hard work and intensive effort, I'm ready to take a position with your firm.

Instead, provide the reader with a brief statement of your qualifications. Immediately address the issue of how the organization might benefit from your abilities. At the same time, remember that you are not going to save the organization. Start your letter with the you-attitude instead of the I-attitude illustrated in the examples above.

Two years of part-time experience as a bookkeeper, a college degree with a major in accounting, and a desire to work hard are the qualities that I can bring to the position you advertised.

Your employment announcement calls for an individual with an engineering-technical background and business experience; this description matches the qualifications I possess.

Work experience as a part-time private security officer, an associate's degree in law enforcement, and an ability to work with others are probably the attributes you seek in the "Security Deputy" for which you advertised.

These approaches to introducing yourself are fresh and attempt to indicate how your abilities can help the organization. Note that the introductory sentence can provide a summary of your selling points: education, special abilities, training, and experience.

2. Describe Your Abilities.

As best you can, attempt to match requirements of the job with your experience and abilities. If a particular technical skill is required and you have it, emphasize this point in your letter. Your letter should do much more than just say "Here is my resumé." It should emphasize your abilities, your experience, and your accomplishments. Interpret and go beyond what is on the resumé; do not restate the resumé materials.

3. Prove Your Statements.

Provide the potential employer with evidence of your abilities. There are various kinds of evidence: references (former employers, teachers, service organization sponsors) course work, previous employment (indicating your duties and responsibilities), and leadership positions in religious, school, and civic organizations.

Recognize the similarities between the cover letter and the sales letter.

The I-orientation is overwhelming.

The triteness is boring.

You can be too cute!

Don't be pushy—the receiver will decide if you are qualified.

Qualifications can often catch an employer's attention.

Attempt to correlate your abilities with the employer's needs.

Strive to immediately provide some interesting and relevant data for the receiver.

Interpret what is listed in the resumé.

Attempt to support the data presented.

Don't forget the purpose of your letter—to obtain an interview!

4. Request an Interview.

The purpose of writing the letter is to get a job. To get the job, you will need to be interviewed. Therefore, your letter must get you the interview. Move the reader to action. Your request for an interview should not be fuzzy or hesitant. Suggest in your request that you have told only a part of your story. The interview will give you an opportunity to tell the prospective employer about the additional attributes you possess. In the last paragraph, a statement such as the following is helpful:

> On Tuesday morning, April 10, I'll phone your office to discuss with you the possibility of setting up an interview.

> On Thursday afternoon, July 10, at about 2:00 p.m. I'll contact your office to insure you have received these materials and to discuss with you the possibility of scheduling an interview in the near future.

> In order to discuss my qualifications and desire to make an advancement in my career, I'll phone you at 10:00 a.m. on Wednesday, March 3.

Do not force your reader to call you; if you know who the receiver of the letter is, tell him or her you will make contact shortly to discuss your employment qualifications.

Two Kinds of Cover Letters

Cover letters may be either solicited or unsolicited. Solicited cover letters are those that are sent in response to an advertisement in a newspaper or trade journal, an announcement on the school's placement office bulletin board, or a personal request. The unsolicited employment letter is sent out "cold" to a firm for which you would like to work.

The Solicited Cover Letter.

The solicited cover letter is sent when an employer has requested material. You may be responding to an advertisement or to an oral request for a resumé. In these cases, you know that the employer has an opening and is expecting to receive resumés.

If you are responding to an individual who asked you to send a resumé, you will obviously be able to address that person by name and title (see Figure 23.1). Sometimes an advertisement seeking resumés will identify the potential employer and give the name of the personnel coordinator.

Frequently, however, firms that advertise employment opportunities do not identify themselves. Their ads are known as blind advertisements. You are required to respond to a newspaper's box number, not to an individual. Traditionally, blind employment letters have been addressed, "Dear Sir" or "Dear Sirs." However, the male gender cannot be assumed and you risk offending female recipients. Some

Even though expected, the solicited cover letter can say much more than "here is my resumé."

FIGURE 23.1   Solicited Cover Letter

517 W. Bowlingreen Drive
Montclair, NJ 07070
April 5, 198_

Mrs. Martha J. Hanover
Marketing Director
Holy Cross Hospital
East Orange, NJ 07019

Dear Mrs. Hanover:

"Years of compassion combined with the latest scientific applications"—the Holy Cross motto—aptly describes your organization. Your commitment to the organization and work in relating this message to others create a positive work environment. Thank you for requesting additional information after our meeting at the Campus Career Fair.

The ways you strive to let people know of your facilities and competent personnel are fascinating. There are several dimensions of my background that seem to match nicely with your efforts as you seek a Coordinator of Public Affairs.

The marketing of health-related services became most real when I headed the successful campus blood campaign; a record number of students and several hundred townspeople came to donate blood.

The modern trends of hospital marketing, and how it differs from retail and industrial marketing, were heightened through special study; an article from that work will appear in a coming issue of The Hospital Administrator.

The ability to lead and work with people was honed when serving as supervisor of sales; in the hospital, the qualities of compatability and cooperation are even more crucial.

A discussion of the possibility of joining your staff would be ideal; on Tuesday, April 16, I'll phone your office at 10:00 a.m. to see if we might set up a time to discuss the opening in your department.

It was good of you to come to campus; you not only made a positive impression on me, but on several other students majoring in the health care area, who commented specifically about how you related positively to them.

Sincerely,

Matthew Woebler

Matthew G. Woebler

Attachment: Resume

This letter "covers" the resume in Figure 22.4.

Often these letters are prepared on plain stationery.

Consider relating to the receiver and the organization before addressing your qualities.

Don't repeat resume information—interpret and relate it to the position you want.

Consider headings to make your key points jump out.

Never say, "contact me at your convenience."

Close in a friendly manner—strive to establish goodwill.

Don't forget to note what is enclosed.

people start the letter with "To Whom It May Concern," "Dear Personnel Manager," or "Dear Sir or Madam," but this kind of all-inclusive terminology may seem awkward or condescending.

Don't be trite in a response to a blind ad: "Dear Sirs" is out!

Another technique that is growing in popularity is to make the salutation a short you-oriented phrase that greets the recipient and states the reason for writing or an attention-getting statement that attracts interest using the Modern Simplified Letter format (see Figure 23.2). Use the form and format that is most comfortable for you, but try to avoid the stereotyped "Dear Sir." Another option is to place the cover message for the blind response in memo form; it may differentiate your message, avoid sexism, and get an "attention-gaining" statement up front:

TO: Firm Looking for Computer Programmers

FROM: Daniel O. Pinkham

SUBJ: Here is a Good Match

The Unsolicited Letter.   The requirements of the unsolicited cover letter are the same as for the solicited letter, but your task is more difficult. Because you are writing to a potential employer who has not asked to be contacted, it may be much harder to secure the individual's attention and sell yourself. The unsolicited letter should emphasize your interest in the firm and show that you are familiar with the organization. Your qualifications to perform a specific job should be stated clearly.

In unsolicited letters, you must gain the reader's attention before your letter heads for the waste can.

Send the unsolicited letter to a specific person.

Never send an unsolicited letter to just an organization or an office. Sending an unsolicited letter "To Whom It May Concern" is an exercise in futility. Take the time to find out the name (correct spelling is important) and title of the individual responsible for employment. A phone call to the firm's switchboard operator is usually all that is needed.

There can be any number of reasons why you would be interested in working for an organization for which you have not seen an employment notice. For example, (1) the company is in the industry in which you would like to work, or (2) you want to live in a specific geographic region or metropolitan area, perhaps because your spouse has accepted employment in the area, and you also desire employment.

Clearly state why you are writing; try to avoid appearing as if you are on a "fishing trip."

It is wise to say why you are writing when the firm has not asked to be contacted. With employee turnover and potential expansion, you may very well be the kind of person the employer is seeking. Also, many firms will retain your materials for several months just in case an opening occurs. Therefore, do not hesitate to send the unsolicited letter, but understand that it must incorporate all the requisites of a positive sales letter. Your unsolicited employment letter is just like the unsolicited letter you may have received today from Visa encouraging you to apply for one of their credit cards. Visa wants to get your attention, acquaint you with their attributes, and get you to take positive action. That is exactly what you want your employment letter to accomplish for you when it lands on the desk of a potential employer (see Figure 23.3).

FIGURE 23.2   Solicited Cover Letter Using Modern Simplified Letter Format

517 W. Bowlingreen Dr.
Montclair, NJ 07070
March 3, 198_
201/562-1931

New York _Times_
Times Square
NYT #17
New York, NY 10035

EXPERIENCE, KNOWLEDGE, INTEREST . . .

. . . along with a solid education in marketing and health care are
some of the attributes that you may be seeking in a Marketing
Assistant in your hospital. Hospital marketing is a relatively new
field, and it has been possible for me to obtain an excellent
education in this developing area while simultaneously gaining a
considerable amount of real-world experience.

Beyond the classes and textbooks, the work heading up the blood campaign taught me how to relate health-care matters to others. Super-
vising the sales staff exposed me to the intricacies of human
interactions and how to motivate individuals to meet organizational
objectives. There has been no doubt in my mind for several years
concerning my career choice. Therefore, it has been possible to
tailor my studies and my work toward gaining experience that will aid
me in hospital marketing.

The experience, knowledge, and interest in the new area of hospital
marketing are real, and I'm ready to put them to work in an organization. Please phone me (201/562-1931) so that we might arrange a time
to discuss this position and how my qualifications fit with your expectations.

Matthew Woebler

Matthew G. Woebler

Encl. Resume

This letter "covers" the resume in Figure 22.4.

The modern simplified format works well for blind ad responses.

Even though the phone number is in the narrative and on the resume, it is acceptable to place it in date area—make it easy for the reader to communicate with you.

When you don't know the receiver's name, the modern simplified letter format is ideal.

Note how resume information is interpreted and "sold."

The actual color of the stationery may be white or another pleasant, conservative light color—tan or gray, for instance.

FIGURE 23.3   Unsolicited Cover Letter

This letter "covers" the resume in Figure 22.1.

The receiver (the organization) is recognized early.

"Why" I'm writing.

Modified block format with right adjusted indented paragraphs incorporates right adjusted "boxes" with headings.

The attributes of the writer are highlighted with headings.

The closing is positive and action-oriented.

College Court #1
Metro Community College
Tampa, FL 33606
August 24, 198_

Mr. Harris C. Snodgrass, Jr.
Employment Coordinator
CNN
P.O. Box 10
Atlanta, GA 30320

Dear Mr. Snodgrass:

CNN news is modern, quick, receiver-oriented, and professional. Similar qualities are needed by an excellent secretary. In my work and education, supervisors have continually complimented me on my modern skills, quick mechanical and thinking processes, people skills, and handling of situations in a businesslike manner.

CNN is familiar to me through its innovative news programming, and during college I prepared two term papers on the network. Now that I will be relocating in Atlanta, I would like to explore the opportunities for a secretarial position with CNN.

    Productivity. In today's office, the secretary is more than just a typist and organizer; the secretary aids office productivity by doing more in less time. This lesson was impressed upon me during my work with Tampa Temporaries.

    Beyond Word Processing. Seminars conducted by Apple added to my skills in desk-top publishing, which aids in preparing office documents and a variety of internal communications.

    Supervisory Experience. Although I would not start in a supervisory position, supervisory experience has taught me to be a team member and to contribute to department goals.

If you have a need for an energetic executive secretary with these kinds of experiences and skills, I hope we can meet when I'm in Atlanta the week of September 10; you can expect a call from me on Monday, September 3, at 10:00 a.m. so that we might discuss the possibilities of meeting.

          Cordially,

          Lynn O'Hare

          Lynn O'Hare

Attachment: Resume

The two-part approach (the cover letter and resumé) is traditional. In developing your package, strive to avoid triteness and to indicate a sincere interest in the potential employer. Look at the two-part approach as a package—the resumé (the sales literature) highlighting your capabilities and virtues and the cover letter (the sales letter) gaining the attention, interest, and action of the receiver.

One-part Employment Letters

Sometimes an application letter is sent without a resumé. The one-part letter combines the features of both the cover letter and the resumé. It is preferred when you want to make the maximum impression in a minimum amount of space.

Much of the basic information that would appear in a resumé is included in the application letter. However, the format is substantially different, and many of the specific details are not included (see Figure 23.4). In writing to firms that have not asked to be contacted, you may find that the one-part application letter (in this case unsolicited) has several advantages:

The one-part approach combines the features of the cover letter and the resumé.

1. It establishes interest and, in summary form, highlights your abilities.
2. It interests the receiver without the need to provide details relative to your references, educational background, or personal data.
3. It provides the employer with the opportunity to contact you to obtain more detail; this can be a good gauge of how your job search is progressing.

The employment letter, the vehicle often used to make your initial contact with an organization, is probably one of the most important communications you will ever prepare. Whatever type of employment letter you use, be sure it gains the attention of the reader and presents you in a positive way.

EMPLOYMENT INTERVIEWS

The purpose of the application process is to get an interview. To some degree, the letter and resumé are one-way communications. The employment interview, on the other hand, is very much a two-way communication process. In preparing your cover letter and resumé, you were able to draft and rewrite your presentation. In the interview situation, there is no such thing as a redraft. You must respond to questions and show that you have a pleasant personality, can communicate effectively, have knowledge of the job and organization, and are familiar with topics of professional, socioeconomic, and cultural interest.

Interviewing—changing from a one-way to a two-way process

FIGURE 23.4   One-part Employment Letter

Collard Hall - 213
Dillard University
Philadelphia, PA 19123
March 27, 198_

Mrs. Gerri C. Green, Director
Catering and Food Services
The Newcastle Hotel and Resort
Atlantic City, NJ 08404

Dear Mrs. Green:

The Newcastle's new ownership and new team seem determined to bring revitalization to this once grand establishment; working with a rebuilding team to bring new vitality and profitability to the food, beverage, and catering services of a lodging establishment is an immediate goal.

As a team member, I would be more of a "utility player" than a person who could bring but one specialty to your efforts; my established abilities include:

Banquet Management Experience that has taught me how to work effectively under pressure.

Behind-the-scenes Budgeting Experience that has shown me that people in the office also have a job to do—it is better to work with them than against them.

Front-line Customer Experience as a bell hop and as a front-desk clerk taught me to appreciate and respond to customer needs . . . quickly!

Basic Housekeeping Experience where I got my hands dirty and my sights set on the kind of position I want in the lodging industry.

With a record starting at the bottom and growing, I desire to work as an assistant in a new operation where it will be possible to apply that background, work with a talented team, and continue to grow in applying my knowledge and experience.

Because I will be in Atlantic City between April 12 and 14, it would be possible to meet with you. Can we arrange for a meeting during that time?

Yours truly,

Anthony C. Rodriguez
215/676-8202

Although no resume goes with the one-part letter, this letter corresponds with the resume in Figures 22.2 and 22.3.

Experience is quickly summarized and highlighted.

Without a resume, it is important to highlight qualities you can bring to a job.

Note parallel headings.

The letter strives to "tickle" the interest of the receiver—to want to gain more information.

Note this closing; if a response is not received in about ten days, it is most appropriate to follow up with a phone call.

Preparing for the Interview

In gaining knowledge of the job and the organization, and by preparing the employment letter and resumé, you have some basic bits of information needed for an interview. However, the interview can be considerably less structured than your resumé. Therefore, perhaps one of the best ways to prepare for the interview is to do what is often done in preparation for an oral examination. List the questions that might be asked. Carefully think through how you would answer each one. The possible categories of questions are your background, your personal interests, your knowledge of the organization, your previous employers, people with whom you have worked, civic activities, your personal and professional goals, and your attitudes on leadership.

Get informed about yourself and about the organization.

You have a responsibility to be well-informed about the organization that has asked to interview you. Do your homework. If the organization is a local concern, you can gain information by talking to employees, picking up literature at the company, or by reviewing the files at your college placement office. If you are interviewing with a large regional or national firm, you can obtain information from some of the following sources:

The firm's annual report. Many libraries have annual reports of major organizations. The modern annual report, besides providing basic financial data, presents detailed statements concerning the markets, the emphasis, and the direction of the company. Today many libraries have the current report on microfiche.

Dun & Bradstreet Million Dollar Directory. This publication lists over 30,000 companies that each have a net worth in excess of $1 million. Information includes addresses, product lines, and names of top company officials.

Sources for obtaining information on potential employers

Dun & Bradstreet Middle Market Directory. Similar to the Million Dollar Directory, this publication provides information on over 33,000 companies whose worth is estimated to be between $500,000 and $1 million. Both Dun & Bradstreet publications are handy because they provide names of people, addresses, and telephone numbers. .

Fortune. This magazine annually lists rankings of U.S. and foreign firms. The listings provide information on sales, profits, number of employees, and gains or losses compared to the previous year. (The May issue covers the 500 largest U.S. corporations; the June issue, the second 500 largest U.S. corporations; the July issue, the 50 largest companies in insurance, utilities, banking, services, and others; and the August issue, the 300 largest corporations outside the U.S.)

Dun & Bradstreet. Dun's *Employment Opportunities Directory* gives a detailed description of 5,000 leading employers, indicating what they want and what they offer.

The 100 Best Companies to Work for in America, by Robert Leving, Milton Moskowitz, and Michael Katz. Each firm is charted, indicating its pay, benefits, job security, ambience, and chances for advancement.

College Placement Annual. Published annually by the College Placement Bureau, it contains basic information about job opportunities in hundreds of companies and organizations.

Making a Good Impression

Often the first sixty seconds are crucial.

First impressions are significant in most situations—especially in the interview setting. Through your mode of dress, conversation, courteousness, alertness, and enthusiasm, you will provide the interviewer with ample verbal and nonverbal cues about your ability to fit the employment position.

The first impression is a lasting impression, and it may color the interviewer's interpretations of everything you say. There are numerous studies dealing with how to dress and act for success. Some studies suggest that many interviewers make an initial judgment in the first sixty seconds or less. Strive to get to first base quickly and safely. If you stumble initially, it is much more difficult to get to home base, which, in this case, is generally moving on to a second interview. A few suggestions:

- Shake hands firmly
- Smile; be pleasant
- Be confident, but not cocky
- Look at the interviewer
- Have substantive comments
- Indicate that you know where you are going
- Be current on the organization

You, the interviewee, can have a definite effect on the verbal and nonverbal interview setting. Obviously you should sit up straight, maintain good eye contact, watch your enunciation, and be aware of other details. You know, of course, that you should not slouch, drum on the desk top, or wear a T-shirt in an interview. You can influence the nature of the interview and obviously the end result—getting the job.

Know your responsibilities in the interview.

Generally, interviewees should remember that they have a responsibility to provide the interviewer with information about themselves and to aid the interviewer in obtaining the necessary information in a comfortable manner.

In addition, you should do your homework on the organization before the interview. Acquaint yourself with the firm's background; be familiar with its products and services; read the annual report. Being able to speak of the organization with some degree of knowledge will reflect your interest in it and your desire to become part of it.

Many people find it helpful to prepare three or four intelligent questions to ask the interviewer. Such questions might touch on the firm's future directions, its diversification policy, its benefit package, its policies on promotion, and the like.

OTHER EMPLOYMENT COMMUNICATIONS

You probably will find it beneficial to initiate other kinds of communications in addition to the basic employment communications we have already discussed.

Inquiries

If you wait a reasonable period of time after sending an organization your resumé and you get no response, it is acceptable to write an inquiry letter. It could be that your materials have been misplaced. Certainly you would not want to miss the chance for an interview through no fault of your own. Your letter, which basically inquires about the status of your materials and the potential of getting an interview, should follow the basics for inquiry communications (see Chapter 8).

One approach is to send a short letter to a person (not an office) in the personnel department or to the person you originally contacted. Simply state that you previously wrote (cite the date) about potential employment and that you are interested in the organization and are concerned that you have had no response.

Another way to establish contact is to send a copy of the original materials. Include a note indicating that you are still interested in the organization and that you are concerned about not having received a response.

Perhaps you would like to be hired by Company Y, but before you have a chance to interview with them, you receive an offer from Company X. It is acceptable to contact Y and inform them of your situation. Be straightforward. Indicate that you would like an interview with them before making an employment decision if they are interested in talking with you. You may want to either phone or write Company Y, depending on the time limits you are facing.

> Don't be too hesitant to follow-up to an unanswered employment letter.

> Keep your options open—don't unnecessarily close employment doors.

The Follow-up Letter

After an employment interview, a follow-up thank-you communication is always appropriate. This type of letter thanks the interviewer for the time, briefly reviews your qualifications, and indicates your serious interest in the position. The letter can be especially effective if it refers to some high point in the interview or an area of common interest between you and the interviewer. It should be mailed the same day or the day following the interview (see Figure 23.5). Do not overlook the sales emphasis in this kind of communication (see Chapter 7).

> Thank-you communications can quickly differentiate you from others.

Accepting a Job Offer

If you are offered a position, you should accept the position in writing. If the job offer is extended orally, your letter of acceptance should restate such important facts as the name of the job you are accepting, the salary, and any special benefits or perks that are included, along with when and where you plan to report to work (see Figure 23.6).

> There are several benefits in accepting employment in writing.

FIGURE 23.5 Thank-you Letter Following Interview

You have "met" Matthew previously in Figures 22.4 and 23.1.

Full block format.

The you-oriented salutation focuses on the receiver in a positive manner.

Besides complimenting the interviewer, and/or the organization, it is possible to reemphasize a positive point or two of your own.

End in a positive manner; it is okay to say "call if you have any questions," but that is generally understood.

Note how Matthew's signature changed as he became better acquainted with the receiver.

517 W. Bowlingreen Dr.
Montclair, NJ 07070
April 23, 198_

Mrs. Martha J. Hanover
Marketing Director
Holy Cross Hospital
East Orange, NJ 07019

You were most kind, Mrs. Hanover . . .

. . . to meet with me concerning professional opportunities in the Marketing Department at Holy Cross Hospital. Throughout our communications, you have been most considerate and prompt—obviously qualities that influence your successful career at Holy Cross.

After seeing your organization and meeting some of your staff and observing their teamwork, it is clear that launching one's career at Holy Cross would be ideal. With my experiences and background in health-care marketing, I think I could quickly become a contributing member of your team.

Thank you for the excellent introduction to Holy Cross and its marketing efforts; I hope to hear from you soon.

Sincerely,

Matt

Matthew G. Woebler

FIGURE 23.6   Letter of Acceptance

604 W. Gaylord
Bloomington, IL 61703
March 9, 198_

Mrs. Margorie Lingle, Director
Corporate Fitness
Kimberly-Clark, Inc.
Neenah, Wisconsin 54956

It will be great, Mrs. Lingle . . .

. . . to join you and the members of your staff as a Fitness Coordinator. Your call offering the position was a delight—these are just the kinds of responsibilities and the type of organization I am seeking!

As you requested, on April 15, 198_, at 8:00 a.m., I will be at your headquarters facility to begin orientation week. All of the terms you reviewed in our telephone discussion are most satisfactory—a beginning salary of $19,500, full benefits, and a two-week vacation period after one year of service.

As you know, your organization and the members of your team made a most favorable impression. The goals and plans of your department are most progressive, and I look forward to aiding you in achieving them.

It will be personally and professionally rewarding to make contributions to the Fitness Program as we strive to improve the fitness of the Kimberly-Clark employees.

Cordially,

Jessica

Jessica A. Abaloni

This letter relates to the resume in Figure 22.6.

The you-oriented salutation has a friendly and fresh approach.

This "yes" letter adheres to the "yes" process.

The tone is positive and "up."

The basic numbers are stated to avoid potential misunderstandings.

This letter need not be long—but it should make the receiver fell good.

FIGURE 23.7   Letter of Rejection

This letter relates to the resume in Figure 22.5.

> ROBERT J. JENSEN
> 1703 Magnolia Ct.
> Long Beach, CA 90802
> April 4, 198_
>
> Mr. Reingold C. Bentenhausen
> Vice President - Sales
> The ICI Corporation
> ICI Square
> Portland, OR 97202
>
> Dear Casey:
>
> It was delightful to receive such a favorable response to our discussion concerning the regional sales opportunity with ICI. As you know, this is the kind of position that seems to be in step with my career ladder.
>
> There would be several benefits in joining ICI—a major one would be a reporting relationship with you. However, because of another offer that is currently more satisfactory to my family and to my professional goals, I must decline your generous offer at this time.
>
> Thank you for discussing the possibilities with me, explaining the fascinating operations of ICI, and for being so gracious in inviting me to your home for dinner. Your wife Joan deserves a special medal.
>
> Am certainly looking forward to keeping in contact with you and to having the opportunity to converse with you in the future. Thank you very much for the employment offer and the tremendous confidence you showed in me.
>
> *Sincerest regards,*
>
> *Bob*

This "no" letter adheres to the "no" process.

The letter says "no" but does not close the door on future discussions.

On personal stationery, it is sometimes acceptable to add a more personal tone by penning the entire closing section.

Declining a Job Offer

If an organization is kind enough to offer you a job and you cannot accept the position, you should be courteous enough to respond in writing. This brief letter can thank the organization for the offer, point to the attributes of the organization, and state why you are declining the offer. Be positive and polite. At a future date, you may want to be considered by the organization for another position (see Figure 23.7).

Communicate to get the job you want.

COMMUNICATING FOR REAL ACTION AND RESULTS

Throughout this text we have emphasized various strategies for selling, moving receivers to action, and gaining the result you desire. When it comes to employment communications, it is no longer theory. It is an important and applied activity. By planning, organizing, and practicing the elements of communication, you should be well prepared to initiate successful communications concerning employment.

QUICK REVIEW

Preparing an employment letter and participating in the employment interview are rigorous activities. It is possible to understand them intellectually on these pages and still have problems implementing them appropriately. With thorough preparation and experimentation, you can get your employment strategy and employment communications in order. The cover letter is difficult because it cannot be ego centered, yet you need to express your thoughts and "position yourself" favorably. The interview is challenging because every interviewer and interview will be different. Therefore, know the basics and be prepared to adjust to these opportunities.

EXECUTIVE SUMMARY

To: Business Communication Students

From: David N. Bateman and Norman B. Sigband

Subject: Persuading the Employer to Consider You: Letters and Interviews

Although many job seekers view the resumé as the ultimate employment document, it is really only the foundation for a series of communications in the successful job hunt.

There are a variety of ways to contact employers: walking in cold, using an employment agency, interviewing at a college placement service, making contact through friends, initiating a mail campaign, or responding to an advertisement. Each of these requires a resumé.

Whereas the resumé is basically a listing of qualities, history, and traits, the cover letter must be a narrative that arouses interest, describes your abilities, proves your claims, and then moves the reader to action—to interview the writer.

Making contact with potential employers and getting your qualifications before the appropriate person in an organization can be difficult. There are three kinds of letters that might be used—the solicited cover letter with resumé, the unsolicited cover letter with resumé, and the one-part employment letter.

The considerable amount of time and effort spent in preparing the resumé should be redoubled in preparing for the interview. Instead of just concentrating on yourself, the interview calls for you to focus on the employer.

Other employment communications of importance are the inquiry letter, the follow-up letter, the job acceptance, and the job refusal.

Employment and communication go hand-in-hand; the ability to implement appropriate communications in a timely, efficient, and courteous manner can certainly enhance your opportunity to gain desired employment.

DISCUSSION GENERATORS

1. *Sales Similarities.* What are the similarities between the sales letter and the cover letter?

2. *One-part.* What are the advantages of the one-part employment letter, and when might you use it instead of the two-piece cover letter and resumé?

3. *Cover Purpose.* In the two-piece package, if the resumé lists your attributes and experience, what does the cover letter do?

4. *Action.* The sales letter moves the reader to action—"buy this product." What kind of action does the cover letter attempt to achieve?

5. *Kinds of Covers.* The authors identify two kinds of cover letters; what are these letters and what are the basic differences?

6. *Nontrite Blind Responses.* The salutation for letters can sometimes be trite, especially when responding to a blind ad. What suggestions do you have for an alternate approach?

7. *A Memo?* For what situation might a cover message be placed in memo form? What are the advantages?

8. *Name Three.* What are three things wrong with using the salutation "To Whom It May Concern" in an unsolicited cover letter?

9. *Receptionist/Switchboard Operator.* How can an organization's receptionist or switchboard operator be of assistance when you are preparing a cover letter?

10. *Contact.* List, explain, and cite the advantages of the various ways that can be used to contact potential employers.

11. *Communication Techniques.* What are the ways in which you can attempt to establish contact with a potential employer? What are the advantages and disadvantages of each?

12. *Who Moves?* Why is it probably best for you to indicate in your cover letter that

you will call the potential employer rather than that you look forward to hearing from him or her?

13. *One-way/Two-way.* Explain the notion of one-way and two-way communications in different stages of the employment process.

14. *Redraft.* You can redraft your cover letter; can you redraft an interview? Why?

15. *Sixty seconds.* Why are the first sixty seconds so crucial in the employment interview?

16. *A Subtle Little Difference.* In interviewing, explain the difference between being confident and being cocky.

17. *Limp Wrist.* When greeting an interviewer, should a woman shake hands strongly?

18. *Sales Orientation.* For various kinds of employment follow-ups, explain and give an example of the subtle sales aspects.

19. *No Thank You.* Why is it in your best interest to decline a job offer in writing?

20. *Interview Aids.* What kinds of things can the interviewee do to aid the interviewer during the interview?

APPLICATIONS FOR BUSINESS

21. *Changing the Roles.* Assume you are on campus to interview graduating students for positions with the Reynolds Organization. As part of your interview strategy, you want to initiate the interview with a positive statement or question.
    a. List five such statements.
    b. Explain the rationale of each.
    c. Be prepared to role play these situations.

22. *Inquiry Communications.* You have not heard from an organization to which you sent your resumé three weeks ago. You are going to follow up, but via phone instead of a letter. In conjunction with another student, role play this telephone situation in front of the class. Before starting, explain the context and set the stage meticulously.

23. *Name vs. No Name.* Today, generic products are common in grocery stores. Some people seem to live on these "no-name" products, whereas others will buy only brand names.

    As personnel director at Bikercise Co., you are getting ready to place an advertisement for a market researcher. The position has been approved and you know the qualities the person should possess. You must decide whether you should submit a blind ad or an ad in which you name the company, having the applicants send materials directly to you.

    List the advantages and disadvantages of both, and then make your decision; be prepared to defend your decision and cite your pros and cons.

24. *What's First?* First impressions are important in almost everything. They are especially important in the employment interview. They are even important in less formal exchanges. Sometimes students say unusual things to faculty, such as,

"Are you doing anything important in class tomorrow—I'll be out of town?" What sort of impression will that question make on a professor?

Make two lists (of at least four statements each) of opening statements *not* to make. One list is of statements not to make to professors; the other list is of statements not to make to interviewers seeing college students for potential employment.

25. *Follow-up Thank You.* To follow up an interview with a thank-you letter is a good idea. However, it appears that many of these letters are cut with the same cookie cutter. They share the same trite words and sentiments. Write a thank-you letter, but avoid using the following expressions:
    - Thank You
    - For your valuable time
    - Interesting
    - Pleasure
    - Pleased
    - Thank you in advance
    - Exciting

COMMUNICATION CHECK-UPS

26. The price quoted for the car is $18,078.00 FOB Detroit.
27. A large amount of people walked into the room.
28. Please altar the report before submitting it to the Vice President.
29. Its' vital that the project be completed on time.
30. "The information was related . . . and the process was initiated."
31. "The situation will be stabilized soon [the reporter stated from the scene] and the plant will again be in operation."
32. "Her language is full of slang, such as a lot."
33. When meeting with clients, it is vital to maintain report.
34. She is a well known tax expert.
35. Janet is a woman whom will do well in marketing.

Sell Yourself With a Good Letter of Application

St. Louis Post-Dispatch

When you're looking for a job, suddenly it seems that everyone else is, too. How do you stand out from the crowd? In an excerpt from her book, "Martin's Magic Formula For Getting The Right Job," job counseling expert Phyllis Martin offers special insights on how to fill out application forms.

By all accounts, the letter of application is the best way to obtain an interview. You must remember this above all else: You're asking for an *interview,* not a job. That comes later.

You'll want to start with an attention-getter, something that will catch the eye and interest of the person with the power to hire you. Ask yourself, "What attracted me to this company or field of work?" An outstanding story on the business pages? A remark by a friend? A speech I heard by one of its officers? A recruitment ad in the newspaper?

Whatever it is, use it.

The guiding principle is this: be specific. Your letter should be so specific that no one else could possibly have written it. Your letter should be so specific that it could go to no other person, save the one addressed.

Let the follow-up be with you, the seller. After all, you are selling yourself, remember? You retain control over suggesting and setting up an appointment time.

Learn the correct name of the company and of the company representative. Spell those names correctly. Elementary? Yes. Generally observed? No.

Write to a specific person, not just to a company. Your letter should be neatly typed on a standard 8½-by-11-inch white or light paper.

Have someone you trust look over your letter to point out any errors in spelling or grammar. Put your name and address on the letter and on the envelope.

The prospective employer expects an original letter from you. It is not good practice to send a form letter of application. You might just get a form letter or rejection in reply.

Here's an example of a letter of application. It won an interview—and ultimately a job—for the sender.

"My attendance at the 75th anniversary celebration of your company last month was in response to the casual invitation of a friend. But there is nothing casual about this letter.

The remarks you made on that occasion so intrigued me that I made a point of learning more about Foster Chemicals. I'd like to learn still more.

I'm confident you would find a personal

"Sell Yourself With a Good Letter of Application" from *St. Louis Post-Dispatch*, June 2, 1986.

*meeting interesting; it could prove mutually profita-
ble as well. I say this because some of my
experience in the chemical marketing research field
relates to what you are doing and apparently plan
to do at Foster Chemicals.*

*I will telephone your secretary in a few days to
arrange an interview or brief talk at your convenience."*

Now, what about your resume? A resume is a
condensed career autobiography. It's you on one

white or light 8½-by-11-inch piece of paper (at
most, two pieces).

There are two basic designs:

1. *The chronological resume.* This is a factual
   record of the jobs you've held and the schools
   you've attended, all in chronological order.
2. *The functional resume.* This design lets you
   tell not only where you worked, but what you
   did there—your accomplishments.

Job Hunt?

Business Week Careers

If you want a new job as soon as possible, try
following these 11 tips from James Challenger,
president and founder of Challenger, Gray &
Christmas, the Chicago outplacement firm. Challenger has counseled more than 20,000 displaced
executives in the techniques of job hunting.

1. Consider your search a full-time job. It's
important to put in 8 to 10 hours a day, 5 days a week.
"Don't wait," says Challenger. "Go out and fight for a
job. Attack the market."

2. See at least 10 potential employers a week.
Get interviews with the people you want to work for.
Don't see personnel people unless you have to. The
more interviews you go on, the better your chance of
getting hired. See people even if they say they have no
openings.

3. See your friends and ask them to help. Don't
phone; if you confront the person, they are more
likely to do something. Some people would say that
this is cashing in. It is, and you have to do it.

4. Prepare a resume, but keep it only for people
who insist on seeing it. Resumes lose more jobs than
they gain. If your resume doesn't have on it exactly

what the employer wants to see, he or she assumes
that you're not the person for the job. Instead, talk
with the employer and try to sense what he or she
wants to hear. With that in mind, talk about yourself.

Remember That You're a Seller in a Buyer's Market

5. Keep in mind that the employer is always
right. Don't say that a qualification for the job is not
important, or that it is less important than another. As
a job-seeker, you are a seller in a buyer's market. The
employer is buying what he or she wants for the
company. Don't insist he or she should want something different.

6. Know where the interview is and allow yourself extra time to get there. Even if a tardy bus is the
cause of your lateness, the message that gets through
is that you do not care enough. Someone else will be
hired.

Dress Up, Smile, and Tell Them How Good You Are

7. Dress up. Look good, but conservative. It tells the employer that you think enough of the company to make the effort.

8. Don't knock yourself. Humility is fine most of the time, but not in a job interview. If you don't tell the employer how good you are, who will?

9. Don't knock your former employers, either.

10. Avoid asking about vacations, holidays, and benefits. The employer will conclude that you are not interested in the work, only in yourself.

11. Smile. Happy people get jobs. People would rather work with people who have pleasant dispositions. And as Challenger says, "If you have been looking for a job for three months with no success, it may be hard to smile, but make yourself do it. It works."

Blueprint for Your Resume

Tom Jackson

Here is a step-by-step process to assist you in designing a hard-hitting, forward-looking resume.

1. Identifying your qualities and skills. Before starting your resume, it's important to take stock of the underlying qualities and skills from which to build the marketable capabilities you will use in the resume, targeted to a specific job. In this instance, a quality is a specific intrinsic personal attribute or value (such as integrity, perseverance, loyalty, assertiveness, responsibility, imagination, and creativity) that can be important in achieving effective results.

A skill is something you know how to do well. How well? At least well enough to put the skill to work profitably for someone else. There are basic skills: writing, organizing, communicating, designing, and drawing, and there are specific, or applied, skills: writing financial reports, organizing lab experiments, delivering speeches, and designing floor plans.

2. Including your interests. Your personal interests and values play a big part in determining the kind of work you will enjoy taking on and do

well. Unfortunately, many people tend to overlook their interests in career planning. This is a mistake. Surveys have shown that people who enjoy what they are doing do better and go further.

3. Selecting your job targets. A job target is a work direction that combines at least one component of interest and one or more specific skills or qualities. A good job target seriously motivates you by including your interests and directs you practically by using your strong marketable capabilities. If you have specific career directions in mind, the resume and job search are much easier to focus. With more than one major job target area, you may want to have more than one kind of resume.

4. Choosing the correct resume style. There are several resume formats or styles to choose from, depending on how your specific background and experience relates to your job targets.

Chronological. If you have had a strong continuing

Abridgement of "Blueprint For Your Resumé" by Tom Jackson, *The Plymouth Guide to Building a Resumé.* Reprinted by permission of the Plymouth Division of Chrysler Motors Corporation.

work history directly related to the career direction you now wish to pursue, the chronological format is for you. You will organize your experience by date, from the most recent work backward to the earliest experience, giving attention to the continuity through time.

Functional. This format is appropriate when you have had a variety of jobs or assignments not directly related to your career targets (a job in the school cafeteria, for example), but which included relevant functions or responsibilities ("Supervised 6 people; managed a budget"). In the functional resume format, you headline the main paragraphs by type of function performed (supervision, planning, research, budgeting) and include under this heading any accomplishments associated with it. Functional paragraphs are presented in order of importance to your future goals, not chronologically.

Either of these two resume formats could be right for you. They are both popular and, where appropriate to your needs, useful. You can get additional information about each of these formats from your career planning office or from the many books written about resumes.

A resume for the future. One of the characteristics of both of the above resume formats is that they are based on what you have done, rather than what you can do. We think that with our swiftly moving technology and economic base, it is necessary to consider a new format.

The primary distinction for the future-looking approach we recommend is in its emphasis on your capabilities (things which you know you can do, even if you haven't yet had the opportunity to prove it formally). By starting with your capabilities related to your job target, you demonstrate to the employer that you can probably make an immediate contribution to a real need. You are not leaving it to the resume reader to try to figure out what you can do for the firm. The capabilities section is followed by a section covering your experience,

stressing those accomplishments in past work or nonwork activities that demonstrate you know precisely what you mean when you talk about your capabilities.

5. Exploring your capabilities. The first rule to follow in selecting and developing the short list of capabilities to use on this resume is to know your job target subject well. For example, you may be an English major with a business minor. If your general job target is to be an editorial assistant or something similar (copy editor, reviewer), the first thing to do is to find out exactly what an editorial assistant does day-to-day on the job. Pick up the phone and carefully question people in publishing; read material on the subject. Find out what makes a good editorial assistant promotable and hireable? With good information about the job, you can stress the capabilities you have that are most relevant.

6. Your experience. In detailing your experience, you should include past accomplishments that are most relevant to your intended future. Be sure that the accomplishments listed will support the capabilities you have asserted in the first part of the resume. The heading is Experience, and under it you will list six to eight specific things you have accomplished in past work and nonwork activities: To be most powerful, these statements should start with action verbs. (See box below for sample statements.)

7. Education. As a student, your top information element is education. (Five years out, we move the category to the bottom.) Play it simple and straight. No need to include details on high school unless they are additive. Show honors if you have them. List degrees and majors but not minors or courses unless they add scope to your target.

8. Names, dates, places. Remember, before you get hired anywhere, you will have to fill out an application form. That is the place to record most of the data about addresses of prior employers, references, exact months and days of employment, social security number, height, and weight. Limit your resume to the essentials. When preparing any resume, have it proofread and edited. Use a good typewriter, and have it printed by a pro.

The custom cover letter. The cover letter that accompanies your printed resume can transform it from a simple form into a customized communication to a specific person. To do it right takes a bit more research—one or two calls to get the name of the person in the company who is in charge of the area you are going for.

Cover Letter Guidelines

1. Write to the specific person in the company responsible for that work area: use name and title.
2. Communicate how your specific abilities might be put to use in the firm.
3. State that you will be calling to set up a meeting (interview) to explore future possibilities. And make that follow-up call.

Appendices

BRIAN McCARTHY

A Brief Guide to English Usage

In preparing a speech, writing a report, or composing a letter, all of us, from time to time, have to stop and check on the correct use of a punctuation mark, the spelling of a word, or the grammar of a sentence. Should it be *continual* or *continuous? Farther* or *further?* Do semicolons go inside or outside quotation marks? Should it be *who* or *whom?*

The sections that follow may be used as a quick reference guide to answer these and other common questions. There are English-usage manuals and handbooks available that offer a more comprehensive discussion of the following areas of diction and grammar should you need more information pertaining to standard English usage.

PUNCTUATION

Use a COMMA

1. To set off an introductory word, phrase, or subordinate clause from an independent statement.

Examples
a. Meanwhile, I am reading my History 101 assignment. (introductory word)
b. While waiting for a train, James Johnson read the editorial section of the morning newspaper. (introductory phrase)
c. Since we have no job openings now, we are not accepting applications for summer work. (introductory subordinate clause)

2. Before coordinating conjunctions (*for, and, nor, but, or, yet*) joining two independent clauses. If the independent clauses are very short, omit the comma.

Examples
   a. Mary dictated the letter and John typed it. (no comma needed)
   b. Barry shouted and Carlota turned. (no comma needed)
   c. My parents had hoped that their three children would enter the family furniture business, but my two sisters and I decided to open a small boutique in Greenwich Village.
   d. Key management personnel in the organization should be carefully selected, and all managers should be informed of their responsibilities.

3. To set off nonrestrictive (nonessential) phrases or clauses.

Examples
   a. The new procedure, as we mentioned in our telephone conversation, will begin the first of next month. (nonrestrictive)
   b. That new procedure we discussed yesterday will begin on Monday. (restrictive, so no commas are needed)
   c. Dr. John Kelly, who taught philosophy for twenty-five years, received frequent commendations from students and faculty. (nonrestrictive)
   d. A professor who taught philosophy for twenty-five years is speaking to our class this Friday. (restrictive, so no commas are needed)

4. To set off phrases or words in apposition.

Examples
   a. My new graduate student, Manuela Ortega, is interested in doing an independent study on "Women in Management."
   b. Mrs. Spear, fashion director for Century Clothes, was elected president of the Designers' Association.
   c. Our first customer, a man about sixty-five years old, bought two sleeping bags and a knapsack.
   d. His sister Marijean teaches in a community college. (Marijean is essential to complete the message—he has more than one sister—so commas are omitted.)

5. To set off a name directly addressed.

Examples
   a. Mr. Barclay, write me at your earliest convenience so I may arrange a tour for your group. (name at the beginning)
   b. Write me at your earliest convenience, Mr. Barclay, so I may arrange a tour for your group. (name in the middle)
   c. Write me at your earliest convenience so I may arrange a tour for your group, Mr. Barclay. (name at the end)

6. To set off a mild interjection.

Examples
   a. Oh, I didn't want you to purchase a new one.
   b. Well, well, so we finally finished that project.

7. When two or more adjectives separately modify a noun, and a conjunction is omitted.

    Examples
    a. Our minister is a kind, considerate, hard-working person.
    b. I have a dark blue suit. (omit comma as *dark* explains blue, not the suit)
    c. My nephew is a tall, thin teenager.

8. To separate the elements of a series. When the last two elements in a series are joined by a conjunction, a comma is also used before the conjunction.

    Examples
    a. The very contemporary design had lines and patterns of red, green, blue, yellow, violet, and white. (series of words)
    b. The sofa was clean and uncluttered, inexpensive but not cheap, and colorful but not gaudy. (series of phrases)
    c. Typewriting I, Shorthand I, and Business Communications I are required courses for first-semester secretarial science students. (series of words)
    d. Will the conferences be held in Spokane, in New Orleans, or in Philadelphia? (series of phrases)

    Note—Do not use a comma to separate the parts of one measurement or one weight.
    It took him 1 hour 35 minutes 15 seconds to jog around the park.
    The measurement you requested is 1 yard 2 feet 7 inches.

9. To set off the term *etc.*; however, use of this term in running text is discouraged.

    Examples
    a. An accounting student should be familiar with working papers, profit and loss statements, balance sheets, etc.
    b. A personnel interviewer judges skills, personality, work experience, etc., when offering employment to a job applicant.

10. To set off a quotation from the reference source in a sentence.

    Examples
    a. "I shall arrive in Los Angeles before midnight," said Mrs. Kelly.
    b. Mr. Fujikawa said, "I will be unavailable for Saturday meetings."
    c. The memorandum read, "Our sales representative will send you a mailgram when the contract is signed."

11. To indicate the omission of a word or words that are understood.

    Examples
    a. Buckingham Way has been renamed Washington Street; Devonshire Place, Adams Avenue; and Kavenaugh Way, Jefferson Street.
    b. Binswanger Realtors sold our home; Cross Realtors, our office building; and Johnson Realty Company, our apartment building.

12. To offset a parenthetical (nonessential) word or phrase.

Examples
a. The most important item on the agenda, I believe, is the discussion of word-processing equipment.
b. I understand, however, that the management consultant disagrees with the comptroller of your company.
c. Let me say, at the very start, that you will find this lecture series to be very helpful when taking your graduate examinations.

Use a SEMICOLON

1. Between coordinate, independent clauses not joined by a coordinating conjunction (*for, and, nor, but, or, yet*).

Examples
a. Ms. Sigowitz submitted her monthly report to the board; it was accepted without comment.
b. Some of our secretaries take dictation from the executives; other secretaries use transcribing machines.
c. The full-time faculty asked for the advanced classes; the part-time faculty settled for the freshman classes.

2. Before a conjunctive adverb (*nevertheless, moreover, therefore, however*) joining two coordinate clauses.

Examples
a. I thought his report was much too long; therefore, I read only his summary of findings.
b. The girls enjoyed their vacation; however, their funds were badly depleted by the end of the second week and they had to return home.
c. My cousin graduated first in his law school class; moreover, he has enrolled for the fall term in Jefferson Medical College.

3. Before a coordinating conjunction joining two independent clauses if the clauses are very long or have commas in them.

Examples
a. When the race, which has been held every year since 1955, was scheduled, we had twenty-two contestants; but five additional entrants paid their fees to the official registrar, who immediately issued a qualifying certificate.
b. After studying business communications, John realized that effective written and oral communications are necessary for a successful business; and the mastery of the skills needed to write acceptable letters and memos will assist all business persons.

4. To separate a series if any of the items in the series already contain commas.

Example
Attending the ABCA international conference were Florence Walks, executive director; Louis Fineman, president; Reginald Bankenshire, first vice-president; and Gary Dunkins, journal editor.

Use a COLON

1. To introduce a list, a statement, a question, a series of statements, a long quotation, and in some cases a word.

Examples
  a. Each person should bring the following equipment: one sleeping bag, hiking boots, rainwear, a small shovel, and heavy outdoor clothes.
  b. The needlecraft skills that are necessary for this job are these: crewel stitchery, knitting, needlepoint, and crocheting.
  c. The following suggestions are important when typing a title page for a report:
    1. Center each line.
    2. Type the title of the report in capital letters and all the other lines in initial capitals.
    3. Include the name of the writer, the date, the course, and the title of the report.
  d. Dr. Lindquist said: "My medical conference is in Chicago on May 19. I will attend that first, and then I will travel to Los Angeles to deliver my speech at the medical college."

2. Before or after a specific illustration of a general statement.

Examples
  a. In the first week he broke a turning rod, dropped a glass test kit, and tore a rubber protection sheet: he was an extremely negligent worker.
  b. Winter arrived with a sudden fury: the temperature dropped to fifteen degrees below zero, six inches of snow fell, and the wind howled.
  c. The vacation you describe sounds very inviting: the cost is low, the accommodations are comfortable, the mountain scenery is beautiful, and the fishing is the best in the Southeast.

3. Following the salutation in a business letter.

Examples
  a. Ladies and Gentlemen:
  b. Dear Mr. Jamison:
  c. Dear Sir or Madam:

Use a DASH

1. To set off and emphasize parenthetical (nonessential) material.

Examples

a. James Rolsted—you know he worked for us since 1955—retired in June this year.
b. We plan to see that our faculty—some of whom have been with us since our college opened—receive cost-of-living raises in the next contract.

2. To indicate when the idea in a sentence has been broken off sharply.

Examples

a. Do you believe that—
b. Here is an excellent textbook—economical, too!

3. To indicate a sudden change in thought within a sentence.

Examples

a. Do you believe that—no, I'm sure you would never accept it!
b. The spring meeting is at Indiana University in Bloomington, Indiana—or is it at Indiana State University in Pennsylvania?

4. To precede a summarizing statement at the end of a sentence.

Example

Magazines were everywhere, the record player was on, clothes were tossed helter-skelter, food disappeared like magic, laughter filled the air—the girls were home for the weekend.

Use PARENTHESES

1. To enclose ideas not directly related to the main thought of the sentence.

Examples

a. The politician heard from only a few (three) of his many followers.
b. I received a letter from Loretta Lawn (formerly Loretta Lyman) last week.
c. Zorniatti's periodic reports (following the format recommended by the National Trade Council) were submitted by all department managers to the general superintendent.

2. To enclose a numerical designation of a verbal statement—sometimes found in legal documentation.

Example

The deposit of five hundred dollars ($500.00) will not be refunded except through court order.

3. To set off references and directions.

Examples

a. The information appears in the appendix (see pages 181–183).

b. Because of the present renovations to our hospital (see the enclosed news letter), we must postpone using your window-washing service until next spring.

Use BRACKETS

1. To enclose an explanatory comment within a quotation or to insert a correction into quoted material.

Examples

a. In her article on political upsets, Sarah stated, "Martin was defeated in the election of 1966 [he was defeated in 1962] and this marked the end of thirty-six years of Democratic treasurers in Wade County."

b. The newscaster stated, "The hostages are all safe [the local newspaper questioned the location of one hostage] according to the diplomats."

Use QUOTATION MARKS

1. To enclose direct quotations.

Examples

a. Sally said, "People don't change; their basic characteristics remain the same throughout their lives."

b. "I don't agree," said Frank.

2. To enclose slang words or expressions.

Examples

a. The wild-eyed professor was going absolutely "bonkers."

b. He may or may not know the facts, but I notice he just "ain't sayin' nothin'."

3. To enclose a quotation within a quotation. The initial quotation is enclosed in double quotation marks; the quotation within that in single; and a quote within that in double.

Examples

a. Stevenson said, "If we are to live in peace, we must, as the Israeli representative has indicated, 'Appreciate the dignity of all people at all times.' "

b. "Men's cologne and other cosmetics are 'in' for 'today's man.' "

c. The professor said, "All groups of people have the same pleasure values, although Johnson disagrees with this when he says, 'Entertainment values are not the same for all age groups; a "trip" to some is attractive; to others, repulsive.' "

4. To enclose titles of articles, chapters or sections of a book, lectures, essays, sermons, paintings, poems, and sculptures.

Examples
  a. Picasso's "Guernica" will be shipped from the Museum of Modern Art to a museum in Madrid.
  b. Thomas Carton wrote the article, "The Problems of International Finance," which recently appeared in *The Financial Quarterly.*
  c. The poet saw his finished work, "The Light-Hearted Lass," in the *Ladies Home Journal.*

5. To define terms.

Examples
  a. A "television addict" is someone who turns on the set on waking and leaves it on until he or she goes to sleep.
  b. A "principal" is the head of a school while a "principle" is a rule or precept.

6. Other punctuation marks are used with quotation marks in the following ways:

  a. Question marks and exclamation points are placed inside the quotation marks if they refer to the quoted material and outside the quotation marks if they refer to the statement as a whole.

    Examples
    1. Dr. Martinez asked, "Isn't that their usual performance?"
    2. Did Dr. Martinez ask, "Is that your usual performance"?
    3. A voice exclaimed, "Stand up!"
    4. What a disgraceful example of "goofing off "!

  b. Commas and periods are placed inside quotation marks.

    Examples
    1. I just read Shirley Jackson's famous story, "The Lottery."
    2. "I will see you on Saturday," he said.

  c. Colons and semicolons are placed outside quotation marks.

    Examples
    1. When I saw her, she said, "I will arrive at 10 P.M. on Tuesday"; however, she is still not here.
    2. Take the following books from the box marked "History 321": *Ancient Civilization, The Old World,* and *Egypt Versus Greece.*

Use a HYPHEN

1. To divide a word at the end of a line between syllables. Divide hyphenated words (*self-assurance*) only at the hyphen. Do not divide the last word of a paragraph or page.

2. To form compound nouns, verbs, and adjectives.

Examples
   a. Mrs. Lubichek was my mother-in-law. (compound noun)
   b. He was angry when he saw that I had double-spaced the letter. (compound verb)
   c. He is not a well-known artist. (compound adjective)

Use an ELLIPSIS

1. To indicate the omission of a part of a sentence from a direct quote. Use three dots if the omission is within the sentence. If the omission is at the end of the sentence, use a period followed by three dots.

Examples
   a. "The transaction was completed . . . and provided for Garson to receive the car plus miscellaneous items. . . ."
   b. "Is anyone able to explain why? . . . What were they planning?"

Use an EXCLAMATION POINT

1. After interjections of very strong or sudden emotion.

Examples
   a. "I will not!" he shouted.
   b. Be quiet!
   c. No! It isn't true!
   d. Hush! Hush! She is asleep.
2. See also the section on quotation marks.

Use a QUESTION MARK

1. After a direct question.

Examples
   a. Have you completed your analysis of the Compton Company case?
   b. He asked if we were coming. (indirect question—omit question mark)
   c. The client asked, "Is my case ready for suit yet?"
2. In a series of questions.

Examples
   a. Are you opening a branch office in Newark? in Albany? in Princeton?
   b. Who is making the speech—the president? the dean? the manager?
3. See also the section on quotation marks.

Use a PERIOD

1. After a complete declarative or imperative sentence.

Examples
a. Your merchandise will be delivered tomorrow. (declarative)
b. Return the defective iron to us. (imperative)

2. After a request phrased as a question.

Examples
a. May we hear from you within two weeks.
b. Will you please call us tomorrow.

3. To indicate an abbreviation.

Examples
a. He worked for Kingston, Inc., for over ten years.
b. Dr. George Krishnamurti lives at 1346 Landview Drive.

Use an UNDERLINE or ITALICS

1. To indicate a foreign expression that is not part of the English language if it is likely to be unfamiliar to the reader.

Example
There was a true spirit of gemütlichkeit at the family reunion.

2. To indicate titles of complete works that are published as separate items, such as books, pamphlets, magazines, newspapers, films, and plays.

Examples
a. Every typist will find the handbook Typing in Business a necessary reference book.
b. The Philadelphia Inquirer has a very large classified section.

Use an APOSTROPHE

1. To indicate the omission of one or more letters in a contraction or one or more digits in a numeral.

Examples
a. He hasn't been home since he graduated in '70.
b. Our motto is "Don't call us; we'll call you."

2. To form the possessive case of nouns.

Examples
a. The three boys' jackets were red.
b. He purchased a dollar's worth of candy.

c. That was my aunt's coat.
d. The men's tools were left behind.

Note—If the word in question already ends in *s* (plural), add only an apostrophe; if it does not end in *s* (singular), add apostrophe *s* ('s).
> The girl's coat was green. (singular possessive)
> The girls' coats were green. (plural possessive)

Note—It is best to avoid the use of possessives with inanimate objects; e.g., sink's top, lamp's cord, or chair's leg. Sink top, lamp cord, and chair leg are standard usage.

Additional Uses of the APOSTROPHE to Indicate Possession

1. If two or more persons or objects own one item, possession is indicated on the last-named only. If the writer wishes to indicate individual possession, an apostrophe is used with each name or object.

Examples
a. Robin and Shelley's car (Robin and Shelley own one car in partnership)
b. Robin and Shelley's cars (Robin and Shelley own more than one car in partnership)
c. Robin's and Shelley's cars (Robin and Shelley each own one or more cars individually)

2. In compound words, an apostrophe is added to the second or last word to indicate possession.

Examples
a. My brother-in-law's car was damaged. (singular possessive)
b. My brothers-in-law's cars were all parked in front. (plural possessive)
c. You are using somebody else's dictionary. (singular possessive)

3. Certain phrases involving time that seem to express possession use the apostrophe.

Examples
a. A month's pay was granted.
b. Three hours' time is not adequate for the job.
c. His dream was to take four weeks' vacation in Hawaii.

4. The apostrophe is used to indicate possession with indefinite pronouns.

Examples
a. One's thoughts are sometimes private.
b. Anybody's ideas are acceptable in this brainstorming session.

5. Possession is indicated on the *Jr., Sr.,* or *Esq.*

Examples
a. Martin Kelly, Jr.'s coat was a plaid.
b. Thomas Fonveille, Sr.'s store was sold.
c. Lawrence McDonald, Esq.'s briefcase was stolen.

6. To indicate possession. For names ending in *s,* practice varies. Either *'s* or simply an apostrophe can be added, according to which stylebook you follow. Whichever style you adopt, be consistent.

Examples
a. Mr. Jones's car
b. Mr. Williams' car

7. Where an appositive is used, possession is indicated on the appositive, rather than the preceding noun.

Examples
a. That is Mr. Carson, the maintenance man's, responsibility.
b. This was Marie Locke, our ex-employee's, personnel file.

Note—Pronouns in the possessive case do not use the apostrophe to indicate ownership; such words are already possessive.
The radio is ours.
The chair is yours but the radio is ours.
Its surface was scratched, but it's (contraction of *it is*) really of no great importance.

SENTENCE CONSTRUCTION

1. Avoid pieces of sentences or fragments by using a subject and a predicate in each sentence.

Examples
a. In the mail she found a check. Which came as a complete surprise. (fragment)
b. In the mail she found a check, which came as a complete surprise. (sentence)
c. On the train I met a neighbor. Also a friend of mine. (fragment)
d. On the train I met a neighbor who is a friend of mine. (sentence)

2. Avoid run-on sentences. (two independent clauses merged together)

Examples
a. Warren was the lawyer's son he was an accountant. (incorrect)
b. Warren, the lawyer's son, was an accountant. (correct)
c. Warren was the lawyer's son; he was an accountant. (correct)
d. Those two books are on the shelf the other two are on the chair. (incorrect)
e. Those two books are on the shelf; the other two are on the chair. (correct)
f. Those two books are on the shelf, but the other two are on the chair. (correct)

3. Avoid comma splices. (two independent clauses separated by a comma without a conjunction)

Examples
   a. Suzanne graduates from nursing school now, John will graduate next year. (incorrect)
   b. Suzanne graduates from nursing school now, and John will graduate next year. (correct)
   c. Suzanne graduates from nursing school now; John will graduate next year. (correct)

Subject-verb Agreement

1. A predicate (verb) must agree in number and person with the subject.

Examples
   a. The typists who work in our office *have* excellent skills.
   b. Behind the chairs *was* the trunk to be sent to the children's camp.
   c. Walter and Nancy *are* students at the Sorbonne.
   d. There *is* a speaker on the platform.
   e. There *are* speakers on the platform.
   f. The house, together with the furnishings, *is* very desirable.

2. If the subject is a word that means a part of something *(some, half, one-third),* the number of the predicate is determined by asking, "Part of what?"

Examples
   a. Some of the report *is* well written.
   b. Some of the reports *are* well written.

3. The words *each, every, neither, either, somebody,* and *anybody* are singular in meaning and require a singular predicate.

Examples
   a. Each of us *has* his or her own closet.
   b. Everybody on the stage at the graduation ceremony *has* to wear a cap and gown.
   c. Neither of the proposed suggestions *is* acceptable to us.

4. When a compound subject has words joined by *or* or *nor,* match the predicate with the word preceding (closest to) the verb.

Examples
   a. Neither the student nor her professors *were* satisfied with her academic performance.
   b. Neither Jane's professors nor Jane *was* satisfied with her academic performance.
   c. Either Marvin or the auditors *were* asked to revise the balance sheet.
   d. Either the auditors or Marvin *was* asked to revise the balance sheet.

Pronouns

Pronouns take the place of nouns and permit us to avoid constant repetition.

1. A basic rule for the use of pronouns is that they agree in person, number, and gender with the word to which they refer (antecedent).

Examples

a. *Joan* gave *her* **coat** to the WAITER, and HE took **it** to the check stand.

b. The *boys* ran to the oak tree, and then *they* cut across the field.

c. *Cecilia* got *her* car from the parking lot attendant right away; the other **girls** had to wait for **theirs.**

2. Use a singular pronoun for antecedents connected by *or* or *nor.* The pronoun refers to one or the other antecedent singly, not to both collectively.

Examples

a. Shelley or Claudine will give you *her* key if you arrive before noon.

b. A rake or a hoe will serve no purpose if *its* handle is broken.

c. Neither Mr. Carleton nor Mr. Frankenheimer will give you *his* advice without an assurance of confidence.

3. The pronoun should be plural if the antecedents are connected by *and.*

Examples

a. The car and the train blew *their* horns simultaneously.

b. My cousin and I visited *our* grandparents.

4. When two antecedents are simply different names for the same person, the pronoun is singular.

Examples

a. The professor and conference leader received a scroll for *his* efforts.

b. I missed my dog and best friend when *he was* placed in a kennel.

5. When two antecedents refer to different persons, the pronoun is plural.

Examples

a. The professor and the conference leader received scrolls for *their* excellent contributions.

b. I missed my dog and my best friend when *they* went to the park together.

6. When two or more antecedents are closely associated by usage or practice, a singular pronoun is used.

Examples

a. Tea and toast has *its* place in a convalescent's diet.

b. Pie and ice cream is delicious. *It* is my favorite dessert for dinner.

7. Antecedent nouns take either a singular or plural pronoun, according to the sense of the sentence or the idea to be conveyed.

Examples

a. The jury reached *its* verdict. (one verdict coming from one jury)

b. The jury put on *their* hats and coats and left for home. (the members of the jury are considered to be acting separately)

8. The following words, when used as antecedents, should take singular pronouns:

anybody	everybody	nobody
neither	someone	any
either	everyone	one
each	somebody	another

Examples

a. Neither of the men paid *his* bill.

b. Everybody in the room has *his* own opinion.

Note. Neither one of the men. Every one in the room.

Personal Pronouns

The choice between *I* and *me, she* and *her, they* and *them* sometimes causes confusion. Each explanation that follows includes the standard grammar rule as well as a short-cut method. Here is a review of the pronouns in the objective and nominative cases:

	Singular	*Plural*
Nominative	I, you, he, she, it	we, you, they
Objective	me, you, him, her, it	us, you, them

Nominative Case

1. A pronoun takes the nominative case when it serves as the subject of a sentence or a clause.

Examples

a. Betty, Dorothy, and *I* (not *me*) have made arrangements for the party.
   Short-cut method: Would you say "*I* have made arrangements" or "*Me* have made arrangements"? You would choose the former. Therefore the sentence must be "Betty, Dorothy, and *I* have. . . ."

b. Mr. Kelly and *I* (not *me*) were selected.
   Short-cut method: Would you say, "*I* was selected," or "*Me* was selected"? Certainly you would choose "*I* was selected." Therefore the sentence must be "Mr. Kelly and *I* were selected."

2. A pronoun following a connective verb or predicate complement (*am, is, are, was, were, be, been,* or *will be*) should be in the nominative case.

Examples
  a. It was *he* who was selected.
  b. I believe it is *she* who should receive the award.

3. When the pronoun is the subject of an implied verb, the nominative case should be used.

Examples
  a. He is quicker than *I*. (not *me*)
    Short-cut method: Would you say, "He is quicker than *me* am quick," or "He is quicker than *I* am quick"?
  b. He did more for the Church than *they*. (not *them*)
    Short-cut method: Would you say "He did more for the Church than *they* did for the Church" or "He did more for the Church than *them* did for the Church"?

Objective Case

A pronoun in the objective case is chosen when it is the object of a verb or a preposition or when it serves as an indirect object.

Examples
a. He mailed the books to Bob, John, and *me*. (not *I*)
  Short-cut method: Would you say, "He mailed the books to *I*" or "He mailed the books to *me*"? Certainly it is the second; therefore, the sentence must be "He mailed the books to Bob, John, and *me*."
b. He called Miss Johnson, Miss Short, and *me*. (not *I*)
  Short-cut method: Would you say, "He called *I*" or "He called *me*"? Obviously, the second sounds better; therefore, the sentence must be "He called Miss Johnson, Miss Short, and *me*."

Relative Pronouns

Some of the more frequently used relative pronouns are *who, whom, which, what,* and *that.* The two that are often confused are *who* and *whom.*

Nominative—WHO

Who, like personal pronouns in the nominative case, is used as the subject of a sentence or a clause.

Example
Miss Costello is a girl *who* (not *whom*) I am sure will do well.

Short-cut method: Would you say, "I am sure *she* will do well" or "I am sure *her* will do well"? Certainly "*she* will do well" sounds better than "*her* will do well." Inasmuch as *she* and *who* are both in the nominative case, the sentence must be "Miss Costello is a girl *who* I am sure will do well."

Objective—WHOM

Whom, like the personal pronouns in the objective case, is used as the object of the verb or preposition or an indirect object.

Examples
a. The soldier *whom* (not *who*) she loved has been sent overseas.
   Short-cut method: Would you say, "She loved *he*" or "She loved *him*"? Obviously "She loved *him*" sounds better than "she loved *he.*" Because *whom* and *him* are both in the objective case, the sentence must be "The soldier *whom* she loved has been sent overseas."
b. Miss Colgate is the girl to *whom* (not *who*) we gave the award.
   Short-cut method: Would you say, "We gave the award to *she*" or "we gave the award to *her*"? The second choice is preferable and because *her* and *whom* are both in the objective case, the sentence must be "Miss Colgate is the girl to *whom* we gave the award."

WHOEVER and WHOMEVER

Whoever is the nominative case and *whomever* is the objective case. Their use follows the same principles as for *who* and *whom.*

Examples
a. The company will award contracts to *whomever* (not *whoever*) they find acceptable.
   Short-cut method: Would you prefer "They find *they* acceptable" or "They find *them* acceptable"? The second choice is better and because *them* and *whomever* are in the objective case, the sentence must be "The company will award contracts to *whomever* they find acceptable."
b. Mrs. Taylor, Miss Weinberg, and *whoever* (not *whomever*) else is selected will vacation in England.
   Short-cut method: Would you say, "*She* is selected" or "*her* is selected"? You would say, "*she* is selected" and because *she* and *whoever* are in the nominative case, the sentence must be "Mrs. Taylor, Miss Weinberg, and *whoever* else is selected will vacation in England."

CAPITALIZATION

1. Capitalize the first letter in the opening word in a sentence, a direct quotation, or each line of verse.

Examples
a. He was an outstanding student.
b. Mr. Boynton said, "Effective communication is the executive's primary management tool."
c. My heart leaps up when I behold
    A rainbow in the sky:
So was it when my life began;
So is it now I am a man:
So be it when I shall grow old,
    Or let me die!
The Child is father of the Man;
And I could wish my days to be
Bound each to each by natural piety.

2. Titles associated with proper names are capitalized.

Examples
a. Senator Birmingham
b. President Adams
c. Aunt Anna
d. Commissioner Baxter

3. Names of national groups, races, languages, religions, or similar designations are capitalized.

Examples
a. Blacks or Afro-Americans
b. French
c. Israelis
d. Canadians
e. Americans

4. Names of holidays, days of the week, holy days, and months of the year begin with a capital letter.

Examples
a. Veterans' Day
b. Wednesday
c. Good Friday
d. Rosh Hashanah
e. June

5. Capitalize the first letter in words that designate names of historical periods, treaties, documents, laws, government departments, conferences, commissions, and so on.

Examples
a. Renaissance
b. the Monroe Doctrine
c. Clayton Act
d. United States Supreme Court
e. Bill of Rights

6. Capitalize the first letter in words that refer to names, national or international organizations, or documents.

Examples
a. House of Representatives
b. Drug Council of the International Medical Association
c. World Council of Churches

7. Capitalize the first letter of a word referring to a deity, a Bible, or other religious reference sources.

Examples
a. the Bible, the Koran, and the Torah
b. Allah
c. God, Lord, and Almighty
d. the Congregation of the Missions

8. The first letter of each important word is capitalized in titles of magazines, books, essays, plays, and so on. Short prepositions, articles, and conjunctions in such titles are not, except for the first and last words.

Examples
a. *Journal of Business Communication*
b. *An Analysis of Government Taxation*
c. *The Taming of the Shrew*
d. *The Decline and Fall of the Roman Empire*
e. *My Fair Lady*

9. Capitalize a general term that is part of a name: Santa Fe Railroad.

Examples
a. Southern College of Arts and Sciences
b. Baptist Church
c. New Horizons Psychedelic Temple
d. Green Street
e. Temple University

10. Although words that refer to directions are not capitalized, words that are derived from directional terms are. Names of specific geographical areas or directional

terms that have reference to parts of a state, a nation, or the world are also capitalized.

Examples
   a. A path directly northwest of the tower.
   b. He lives in the Northwest.
   c. Far East
   d. Wild West
   e. Orient
   f. a Southerner

EXPRESSING NUMBERS

Should numbers be expressed in figures or words in written communication? To help solve this question, a number of general rules have been established.

1. When several numbers are used in one sentence and they are all above ten, use figures. If they are below ten, write them out. If a sentence begins with a number, write it out. If the number beginning a sentence is long when written out, it is usually wiser to revise the sentence.

   Examples
      a. We shipped 75 chairs, 90 tables, 32 lamps, and 32 pictures.
      b. You have requested two rugs, three TV sets, and eight area rugs.
      c. Seventy-five chairs, 90 tables, 32 lamps, and 32 pictures were shipped on December 3. (see below for improved sentence)
      d. On December 3, we shipped 75 chairs, 90 tables, 32 lamps, and 32 pictures.

2. When numbers are below ten, write them out; when they are above, use numerals. When some above and some below are used in one sentence, follow one pattern for consistency. Round numbers over ten are usually written out.

   Examples
      a. He owned three shares of AT&T, seven shares of Sears, and fifty-five shares of Zenith.
      b. The scouts consumed 8 pies, 7 chickens, 8 quarts of milk, and 32 bottles of soda.
      c. He made two great throws, one of sixty feet and the other of fifty-five.

3. When one number immediately follows another, spell out the first number unless the second number would make a significantly shorter word.

   Examples
      a. He purchased five 59-cent notebooks for use in his spring-quarter classes.
      b. Please get me 65 fifteen-cent stamps.
      c. I ordered 36 eleven-foot boards for the building project.

4. Place a comma between two unrelated numbers when they immediately follow each other.

Examples
a. On March 12, 32 new policemen were hired in New York.
b. In 1975, 96 supersonic aircraft should be available for commercial use.

Dates

1. Write out the month when expressing a date.

Examples
a. June 27, 1984
b. 27 June 1984
Note—It is recommended that numerals for both month and day not be used. Although North American custom is to place the month first and then the day, the reverse is true in many countries of the world. Confusion in interpretation can thus easily result.
1-4-84—Preferred: January 4, 1984 or 4 January 1984
3/7/84—Preferred: March 7, 1984 or 7 March 1984

2. Only use *d, st,* or *th* with the day of the month when that day precedes the month or stands by itself.

Examples
a. She became engaged on the 4th of January.
b. In your order of the 2d, you did not list the colors desired.
c. Your shipment of the 1st was lost in transit.
d. Please mail your check by March 28.

3. Well-known years in history and reference to class graduation years may appear in abbreviated form.

Examples
a. The class of '51 was honored.
b. The blizzard of '88 was the worst storm of the century.

Addresses

1. House numbers should always be expressed as numerals except *one,* which should be written out.

Examples
a. One East Wilshire
b. 10 North Roscomare Road
c. 215 South Kansas Street
d. 2157 South Topeka Avenue

2. Use words for streets from one to ten inclusive; use numerals for streets after eleven. The letters *d, st,* or *th* may be used with numerals.

Examples
a. 2115 West Fifth Avenue
b. 1115 West Tenth Street
c. 210 North 19th Street
d. 400 East 121st Avenue
Note—The latest practice is to omit the *th* and *st* in examples such as (c) and (d) above.

3. When a number is used as a street name, use a dash to separate it from the street number only if a street direction is not included.

Examples
a. 210—10th Street
b. 2100—7th Avenue
c. 2111 West 45 Street
d. 206 North 41 Street

Amounts of Money

1. All sums of money, domestic or foreign, should be presented in figures.

Examples
a. Johnson paid $155.60 for the merchandise.
b. It is difficult for me to convert £275 into dollars.

2. For sums of less than a dollar, follow the figure with the word *cents.*

Examples
a. It cost 25 cents.
b. It wasn't worth 65 cents.

3. In a sentence with a series of amounts, to be consistent use the dollar sign with a decimal point to indicate cents.

Examples
Tom paid $.75 for the sponge ball, $5.00 for the baseball bat, and $14.95 for the baseball glove at the discount store.

4. The symbol ¢ for cents is used in price quotations and in technical communications.

Examples
a. 150 slats at 99¢
b. 5 bags of cement at 98¢

5. When expressing round sums of money, do not use the decimal and zeros.

Example
His payment was $275.

6. In legal statements the numerals should be enclosed by parentheses and the sum written out.

   Example
   A firm offer for the car of seven hundred forty dollars ($740) is hereby made.

7. Money in round amounts of a million or a billion may be expressed partially in words.

   Examples
   a. The school board's budget increased by $2 million.
   b. The youngster could not understand how the government could allocate $5 billion.

Decimals and Fractions

1. When a decimal begins with a zero, do not place a zero before the decimal. If the decimal begins with a number other than zero, precede the decimal with a zero.

   Examples
   a. .04683
   b. 0.1746 (The zero prevents the reader from overlooking the decimal point.)

2. Simple fractions are written out. When whole numbers and fractions make up one unit, a decimal may or may not be used.

   Examples
   a. It took him one-half hour.
   b. I gave him three-quarters of my allowance.
   c. It was 25.5 feet long.
   d. It was 25½ feet long.

3. Spell out a mixed number only if it begins a sentence.

   Example
   Three and one-half of the five boxes were used.

Miscellaneous Quantities, Units, and Measurements

1. Distance: Use numbers unless the amount is less than a mile.

   Examples
   a. We were one-third of a mile from the house.
   b. It is 9 miles to Kingston and 350 miles from there to Prampton.

2. Financial quotations: Use numbers.

Example
American Telephone and Telegraph hit 56⅞ this afternoon.

3. Arithmetical expressions: Use numerals.

Example
Multiply 70 by 44 and you will have the area of the house in square feet.

4. Measurement: Use numerals.

Examples
a. The land produced approximately 95 bushels per acre.
b. He quickly found that 15 kilometers did not equal 16 yards.

5. Specific numbers: Use numerals.

Examples
a. The engine number was 4638147.
b. Write for Training Manual 255.

6. Time: Use numerals with A.M. or P.M. Use words with o'clock. When expressing time on the hour without A.M., P.M., or o'clock spell out the hour.

Examples
a. The plane leaves at 7:17 P.M.
b. We leave for work at 8:30 A.M.
c. He is due to arrive at ten o'clock.
d. They prefer having dinner at seven. (not 7)

7. Dimensions: Use numerals with either $\times$ or *by*.

Examples
a. The room measured 10 $\times$ 15 ft.
b. The trim size of the annual report was 8½ by 11 inches.

8. Age: Use numerals except where approximations are used.

Examples
a. She became 21 and got engaged on the same day.
b. I would say that he's about seventy years old.
c. For your information, Bob is exactly 3 years and 6 months old today.

9. Government units: Write out such expressions as congressional units or districts.

Examples
a. He served in the Eighty-seventh Congress and represented the Tenth Congressional District of the state.
b. James Jones represents the twenty-third ward.

10. Book or magazine references: Major units or divisions are indicated by Roman numerals; minor units by Arabic numbers.

Examples
a. He found the reference in Volume XX, number 4.
b. You will find Figure 4 next to Table 7 on page 83 of Section 4.

100 FREQUENTLY MISSPELLED WORDS

accommodate	calendar	discrepancy	fourth	occurrence	procedure	stationery
acquaintance	canceled	eligible	government	omission	proceed	strictly
advertise	chief	embarrass	grammar	omitted	professor	tomorrow
✱aggressive	committee	endeavor	grateful	opportunity	quantity	too
all right	✱confident	envelope	guarantee	original	questionnaire	transferring
already	conscientious	equipped	incidentally	paid	receipt	truly
analysis	conscious	especially	inconvenience	pamphlet	receive	unnecessary
analyze	convenient	exceed	its	personnel	recommend	until
apologize	criticism	existence	laboratory	possession	reference	using
appearance	deceive	✱experience	legible	practically	referred	Wednesday
attendance	deferred	extension	loose	precede	repetition	
beginning	definite	familiarity	necessary	preferred	schedule	
believe	develop	February	ninth	prejudice	separate	
benefited	difference	foreign	occasion	privilege	similar	
business	disappoint	forty	occurred	probably	sincerely	

WORDS FREQUENTLY CONFUSED

Accent: to stress or emphasize; a regional manner of speaking.
Ascent: a rising or going up.
Assent: to agree; agreement.

Accept: to receive, to give an affirmative answer.
Except: to exclude; to leave out; to omit.

Access: admittance or admission.
Excess: surplus or more than necessary.

Accidentally:
Incidentally: In both these cases, the *-ly* ending is added to the adjective forms, *accidental* and *incidental,* and not the noun forms, *accident* and *incident.*

Ad: abbreviation for *advertisement.*
Add: to join; to unite; to sum.

Adapt: to accustom oneself to a situation.
Adept: proficient or competent in performing a task.
Adopt: to take by choice; to put into practice.

Advice: counsel; a recommendation (noun).
Advise: to suggest; to recommend (verb).

Affect: to influence (verb).
Effect: result or consequence (noun).
Effect: to bring about (verb).

Aggravate: to increase; to intensify; to make more severe.
Irritate: to exasperate or bother.

All ready: prepared.
Already: previously.

All right: completely right.
Alright: an incorrect usage of *all right.*

Allusion: a reference to something familiar.
Illusion: an *image* of an object; a false impression.
Delusion: a false belief.

Almost: nearly; only a little less than.
Most: an informal use of *almost;* correctly, it means greatest in quantity or the majority of.

Altar: a place to worship or pray.
Alter: to change.

Altogether: completely or thoroughly.
All together: in a group; in unison.

Alumnus (sing.): male graduate.
Alumni (pl.)
Alumna (sing.): female graduate.
Alumnae (pl.)

Amount: quantity without reference to individual units.
Number: a total of counted units.

Anxious: upset; concerned about a serious occurrence.
Eager: very desirous; anticipating a favorable event.

Anyone: any person in general.
Any one: a specific person or item.

Balance: as an accounting term, an amount owed or a difference between debit and credit sums.
Remainder: that which is left over; a surplus.

Being as, being that: should not be used for *since* or *because.*

Beside: by the side of.
Besides: in addition to.

Biannually: two times a year.
Biennially: every two years.

Borne: past participle of *bear* (to carry, to produce).
Born: brought into existence.

Can: refers to ability or capability.
May: refers to permission.

Cannon: large gun.
Canon: a law; church official.

Canvas: a coarse type of cloth.
Canvass: to solicit; survey.

Capital: a seat of government; money invested; a form of a letter.
Capitol: a government building.

Carat: unit of weight generally applied to gem stones.
Caret: mark showing omission.
Carrot: vegetable.
Karat: unit for measuring the purity of gold.

Cease: to halt or stop.
Seize: to grasp or take possession.

Censor: a critic.
Censer: an incense pot.
Sensor: an electronic device.
Censure: to find fault with or to blame.

Cereal: any grain.
Serial: arranged in successive order.

Cite: to quote from a source.
Sight: act of seeing; object or scene observed.
Site: a place, such as "building site."

Coarse: composed of large particles; unrefined.
Course: a direction of progress or a series of studies.

Collision: a clashing of objects.
Collusion: a conspiracy or fraud.

Command: to direct or order; an order.
Commend: to praise or laud.

Complacent: satisfied, smug.
Complaisant: obliging.

Complement: that which completes or supplements.
Compliment: flattery or praise.

Confidant: one who may be confided in.
Confident: positive or sure.

Consensus of opinion: redundant; *consensus* means "general opinion."

Continual: taking place in close succession; frequently repeated.
Continuous: no break or letup.

Core: a center.
Corps: a body of troops; a group of persons in association.
Corpse: a dead body.

Council: an assembly of persons.
Counsel: to advise; advice; an attorney.
Consul: a resident representative of a foreign state.

Councillor: a member of a council.
Counselor: a lawyer or adviser.

Credible: believable or acceptable.
Creditable: praiseworthy or meritorious.
Credulous: gullible.

Critic: one who evaluates.
Critique: an analytical examination of.

Currant: fruit.
Current: timely; motion of air or water.

Deceased: dead.
Diseased: infected.

Decent: correct; proper.
Descent: going from high to low.
Dissent: disagreement.

Decree: a proclamation of law.
Degree: difference in grade; an academic award.

Defer: to delay or put off.
Differ: to disagree.

Deference: respect.
Difference: unlikeness.

Deprecate: to express disapproval of.
Depreciate: to lessen in value because of use and/or time; to belittle.

Desert: to abandon.
Desert: a barren geographical area.
Dessert: a course at the end of a meal.

Differ from: to stand apart because of unlikeness.
Differ with: to disagree.

Disapprove: not to accept.
Disprove: to prove wrong.

Disburse: to make payments; to allot.
Disperse: to scatter.

Discreet: prudent; good judgment in conduct.
Discrete: separate entity; individual.

Disinterested: neutral; not biased.
Uninterested: lacking interest; not concerned with.

Disorganized: disordered.
Unorganized: not organized or planned.

Dual: double or two.
Duel: a contest between two antagonists.

Dying: in the process of losing life or function.
Dyeing: changing the color of.

Each other: refers to two.
One another: refers to more than two.

Either:
Neither: refers to one or the other of two. With *either* use *or;* with *neither* use *nor.*

Elicit: to draw forth, usually a comment.
Illicit: unlawful; illegal.

Eligible: acceptable; approved.
Illegible: impossible to read or decipher.

Elusive: difficult to catch.
Illusive: deceptive.

Emerge: to come out.
Immerge: to plunge into; immerse.

Emigrate: to travel out of one country to live in another.
Immigrate: to come into a country.
Migrate: to travel from place to place periodically.

Eminent: outstanding; prominent.
Imminent: impending, very near, or threatening.
Immanent: inherent.

Envelope: container for communication.
Envelop: to surround; cover over or enfold.

Exceptional: much better than average; superior.
Exceptionable: likely to cause objection; objectionable.

Expansive: capable of extension or expansion.
Expensive: costly.

Extant: living or in existence.
Extent: an area or a measure.

Extinct: no longer living or existing.
Distinct: clear, sharply defined.

Facet: a small surface of a cut gem stone; aspect of an object or situation.
Faucet: a spigot.

Facilitate: to make easier.
Felicitate: to greet or congratulate.

Faint: to lose consciousness (verb); feeble, weak (adjective).
Feint: to pretend or simulate; a deceptive movement.

Farther: refers to geographical or linear distance.
Further: more; in addition to.

Fate: destiny.
Fête: to honor or celebrate (verb); a party (noun).
Feat: an act of unusual skill.

Flair: natural ability.
Flare: a signal rocket; a blazing up of a fire.

Formally: according to convention.
Formerly: previously.

Genius: unusual and outstanding ability.
Genus: a grouping or classification, usually on a biological basis.

Healthful: giving or contributing to health.
Healthy: having health.

Hoard: to collect and keep; a hidden supply.
Horde: a huge crowd.

Holey: having perforations or holes.
Holy: sacred; saintly.
Wholly: entirely; completely.

Human: pertaining to mankind.
Humane: kindly, considerate.

Imply: to hint at or allude to in speaking or writing.
Infer: to draw a conclusion from what has been said or written.

In: indicates location within.
Into: indicates movement to a location within.

Incite: to stir up.
Insight: keen understanding; intuition.

Incredible: extraordinary; unbelievable.
Incredulous: skeptical; not believing.

Indignant: angry.
Indigenous: native to an area or country.
Indigent: needy; poor.

Ingenious: clever, resourceful.
Ingenuous: frank, honest, free from guile.

Inside of: informal use for *within* as "inside of five minutes."
Outside of: informal use for *except* or *besides* as "outside of those three members. . . ."

Its: a possessive singular pronoun.
It's: a contraction for *it is.*

Later: refers to time; the comparative form of *late.*
Latter: refers to the second named of two.

Learn: to acquire knowledge.
Teach: to impart knowledge.

Less: smaller quantity than, without reference to units.
Fewer: a smaller total of units.

Let: to permit.
Leave: to go away from; to abandon.

Likely: probable.
Liable: legally responsible.
Apt: quick to learn; inclined; relevant.

Load: a burden; a pack.
Lode: a vein of ore.

Loath: reluctant; unwilling.
Loathe: to hate; to despise; to detest.

Lose: to cease having.
Loose: not fastened or attached; to set free.

Magnate: a tycoon; important official.
Magnet: a device that attracts metal.

Marital: used in reference to marriage.
Marshal: an official; to arrange.
Martial: pertaining to military affairs.

Maybe: perhaps (adverb).
May be: indicates possibility (verb).

Medal: a badge of honor.
Metal: a mineral substance.
Meddle: to interfere.

Miner: an underground laborer or worker.
Minor: one who has not attained legal age; of little importance.

Moral: a principle, maxim, or lesson (noun); ethical (adjective).
Morale: a state of mind or psychological outlook (noun).

Notable: distinguished.
Notorious: unfavorably known.

Observance: following or respecting a custom or regulation.
Observation: act of seeing; casual remark.

Oral: by word of mouth.
Verbal: communication in words whether oral or written.

Ordinance: a local law.
Ordnance: military weapons; munitions.

Peak: top of a hill or mountain; topmost point.
Peek: a quick look through a small opening.

Peal: sound of a bell.
Peel: to strip off.

Percent: should be used after a numeral *(20 percent).*
Percentage: for quantity or where numerals are not used (a larger *percentage*).

Persecute: to subject to harsh or unjust treatment.
Prosecute: to bring legal action against.

Personal: private; not public or general.
Personnel: the staff of an organization.

Plaintiff: the complaining party in a lawsuit.
Plaintive: sorrowful; mournful.

Plane: to make smooth; a tool; a surface.
Plain: area of level or treeless country; obvious, undecorated.

Practical: not theoretical; useful, pragmatic.
Practicable: can be put into practice (not used in reference to people).

Precedence: priority.
Precedents: cases that have already occurred.

Principal: of primary importance (adjective); head of a school; original sum; chief or official.
Principle: a fundamental truth.

Proceed: to begin; to move; to advance.
Precede: to go before.

Provided: on condition; supplied.
Providing: supplying.

Quite: almost; entirely; positively.
Quiet: without noise.

Recent: newly created or developed; near past in time.
Resent: to feel indignant.

Respectfully: with respect or deference.
Respectively: in order named.

Resume: to begin again.
Resumé or résumé: a summing up.

Rise: to move upward; to ascend (rise, rose, risen).
Raise: to elevate; pick up (raise, raised, raised).

Sit: to be seated (sit, sat, sat).
Set: to put in position (set, set, set).

Sometime: at one time or another.
Sometimes: occasionally.

Stationary: not moving; fixed.
Stationery: writing paper or writing materials.

Statue: a carved or molded three-dimensional reproduction.
Stature: height of a person; reputation.
Statute: a law.

Straight: direct; uninterrupted; not crooked.
Strait: narrow strip connecting two bodies of water; a distressing situation.

Than: used in comparison (conjunction): "Joe is taller than Tom."
Then: relating to time (adverb): "First he ran; then he jumped."

Their: belonging to them (possessive of *they*).
There: in that place (adverb).
They're: a contraction of the two words *they are*.

To: preposition: "to the store."
Too: adverb: "too cold."
Two: number: "two apples."

Toward:
Towards: identical in meaning and used interchangeably; *toward* is preferred.

Vice: wickedness.
Vise: a clamp.

Waive: to give up; relinquish.
Wave: swell of water; a gesture.

Weather: climate or atmosphere.
Whether: an alternative.

Who's: a contraction of the two words *who is*.
Whose: possessive of *who*.

Your: a pronoun.
You're: a contraction of the two words *you are*.

Style, Format, and Mechanics of Business Letters

There really is no correct or incorrect set of letter mechanics. However, each piece of correspondence—regardless of the style selected—should provide key information that permits accurate processing.

LETTER PLACEMENT AND FORMAT

Because the appearance of the letter is important, the typist should make an effort to carefully position the material on the stationery. It really is a simple matter to center the letter, to provide attractive and adequate white space on all four sides, and to maintain a fairly even right-hand margin.

Every letter should be centered on the sheet of stationery with adequate margins provided.

Several different letter formats can be used. The most popular are the *full block, modified block,* and *modified block with indented paragraphs.* These are illustrated in Figures B–1, B–2, and B–3. Figure B–4 illustrates the simplified letter format of the Administrative Management Society, and Figure B–5 illustrates a format with a you-orientation.

Readers are influenced by a letter's appearance. If the initial reaction to the appearance of the letter is poor, that impression may linger as the letter is read. A ten-line letter jammed at the top or bottom of the page may indicate to the reader that the company it represents doesn't care, is poorly organized, and is ineptly administered. On the other hand, an attractive, well-balanced page with plenty of white space may indicate a company that takes pride in its effort, is well organized, and is carefully administered.

FIGURE B–1 Full Block Form

HEMISPHERE
INSURANCE

Mr. Leonard O. Hollmann
Executive Director
Trendex Engineering Company
1418 East LaSalle Street
Chicago, Illinois 60024

Dear Mr. Hollmann:

There are several different formats that may be used for typing business letters.

This is an example of a full block style where every line starts at the left margin. There are no paragraph indents. It is often preferred by typists because it is so easy to set up.

Note that the salutation is followed by a colon. In a more informal situation, where the addressee is a personal friend, the salutation could be followed by a comma.

Sincerely,

Robert J. Jennings

Robert J. Jennings
Sales Manager

RJ/db

Enclosure

9225 W. KENMORE, BLOOMINGTON, ILLINOIS   61701

FIGURE B–2   Modified Block Form

Letterhead.

CENTRAL STATES BANK

March 3, 198_

Inside Address.

Mr. T. Anthony Jones
336 Gales Street
Washington, D.C. 20002

Salutation.

Dear Mr. Jones:

Body.

This modified block form is very similar to the block style, except that the date and the complimentary close start near the center of the page.

Usually the date and the complimentary close are indented to align at the same horizontal point. This is because it is easy for the typist to set the tab once.

Sometimes the date must be placed in a different spot because of the nature of the letterhead. The modified block is popular because it has a balanced appearance compared to the full block style.

Complimentary
Close.

Sincerely,

Robert O. Casey

Signature.

Robert O. Casey
Administrative Aide

Identifying Initials.

RC/tm

Copy Notation.

cc: Alice McManus
     Midwest Sales Representative

39 HERITAGE DRIVE   INDIANAPOLIS, INDIANA   46202

FIGURE B–3   Modified Block Form with Indented Paragraphs

Washington & Washington, Ltd.
113 Wakefield Street
Memphis, Tennessee   38118

October 19, 198_

Ms. Pam C. Cartwright
Abbott Corporation
100 West Fifth Avenue
Los Angeles, CA 90009

Dear Ms. Cartwright:

   This letter is very similar to the modified block letter, except
that the first line of each new paragraph is indented five spaces.

   As shown, the date and the complimentary closing start near the
center of the page. However, in some cases, the date might have to be
realigned to conform with the letterhead.

   This type of letter is in common use today in many business
situations.

                              Cordially yours,

                              Clay S. Davis

                              Clay S. Davis
                              Customer Relations

CSD/mal

FIGURE B–4   The Administrative Management Society (AMS) Simplified Letter Format

Military-style date increases readability and reduces punctuation.

Salutation addresses the subject, not the receiver.

Receiver's name incorporated into the opening and, often, the closing paragraph.

Format moves directly to substance without extraneous matter.

Block form with minimal punctuation.

No closing.

Dictator's initials eliminated.

Pleasanton, California   95928

19 May 198_

R R Carlberg, President
Ames Industries, Inc
4102—92 Street SW
New York NY 10015

THE MODERN SIMPLIFIED LETTER

A productive letter format, Mr. Carlberg, that deserves your recognition
is the Modern Simplified Letter.

You are a competent business leader and an authority on information/word
processing. As the cost of the average business letter continues to
increase, you can appreciate the many advantages of a modern letter
style that saves time and results in various efficiencies. The format is
conducive to saving the writer and the reader time.

The Modern Simplified Letter is attractive and easy to type and
incorporates a no-nonsense, businesslike approach to business communication:

1   Block style eliminates tabulating; saves keystroking time
2   Standard placement for dateline and line length
3   Military-style date easier and quicker to type
4   Letter address positioned for window envelopes
5   Subject line shows the purpose of the letter; facilitates filing
6   Name of addressee in opening and closing paragraph adds friendliness
7   Periods omitted after abbreviations and enumerations
8   Name of writer presented for a correctly addressed response
9   Reference initials only for the typist

You will have success with Modern Simplified Letters, Mr. Carlberg. Your
associates will be impressed with your messages when they are presented
in this functional format.

Mary Nesbitt

Dr. Mary J. Nessbit
Professor
ds

FIGURE B–5   You-oriented Salutation Format

WISCONSIN FARM EQUIPMENT
Parkside, Wisconsin 53467

September 7, 198_

Mrs. Joan Fohr, Assistant Director
Personnel
The USA Tire & Rubber Co.
Akron, OH 44303

Your personnel conference was fun, Joan . . .

. . . and it was rewarding to address your colleagues on the topic of
innovations in businesss-letter writing. Your and many others inquired
about the letter with the "you-oriented" salutation. Here it is; some
special features of this letter include:

> • Avoidance of the traditional "Dear."

> • It works well for people you know.

> • The style is a bit less formal than the traditional format.

> • The format works well for "form" letters when individaul names
>   can be inserted in the salutation.

Some people may feel that this letter format is too "mod" and think the
only way to start a letter is with "Dear." However, when it can work,
and you want to deviate for the mode, give it a try. It's difficult to
read the salutation and not keep reading—therefore it also is an
advantageous form to use when attempting to quickly move the reader into
the message and incorporate a bit of the sales approach.

Thanks for your nice comments about the program—hope it will be possible
to talk with this group of personnel professionals again.

Sincerely,

Martin C. White, Manager
Internal Communications

MCW/jrb

A "you-oriented"
statement is
substituted for the
traditional "Dear
Joan."

The opening
phrases should
gain the reader's
attention move it
into the substance.

The letter can be
prepared in full
block or block with
indented
paragraphs.

The format works
well for people
known to you and
for sales letters.

THE SECTIONS OF THE BUSINESS LETTER

The usual business letter consists of six parts: the heading, which includes the letterhead and the date; the inside address; the salutation; the body of the letter; the complimentary close; and the signature. These six parts are labeled in Figure B–2.

Heading

The letterhead usually answers the question of who, where, and what. The *who* should indicate the exact legal name of the company (not *Corp.* if it is really *Inc.*). The *where* should include not only the street address but also the city, state, and zip code. The *what* may give the reader some indication of the organization's operations ("Makers of Quality Furniture for over 50 Years").

Letterhead design is selected very carefully by most organizations, since it is instrumental in presenting a certain image of the firm. A highly stylized letterhead design may convey the image of a forward-looking, innovative organization, while a very formal treatment may convey the image of a stable, reliable company. In selecting a letterhead design, the *image* to be conveyed must be considered just as much as the who, where, and what.

The date should be written using either of the following formats:

March 7, 1986   7 March 1986

The date should not be written as 3/7/86 (or 3-7-86) because of the possibility of misinterpretation. In the United States, 3/7/86 would be read as March 7, 1986, but in Latin America, Great Britain, and much of Europe, this date would be interpreted as July 3, 1986.

The format used in Figure B–6 is correct for plain stationery that does not have a letterhead. The address in the upper right corner is that of the writer.

The Inside Address

The inside address always includes basic information.

The inside address should duplicate the information on the envelope and should be derived from the letterhead of the correspondence to be answered. The company designation, name and title of addressee, and street address should be reproduced exactly as indicated on the original letter. If the firm is designated as *Inc.*, that should be used and not *Corporation*. If the street is listed as *Fourth*, the reply should not use *4th*.

The recipient's name in the inside address should always be preceded by a title (Mr., Ms., Mrs., Miss, Dr., Colonel, Reverend). If the individual holds a supervisory position, both title and position should be stated:

FIGURE B–6   Sender's and Receiver's Addresses on Plain Stationery

DEPARTMENT STORE

```
                                179 Marlborough Street
                                Boston, MA  02116
                                May 18, 198_

    Ms. Lydia Rand
    The Bentworth Corporation
    2700 Little River Turnpike
    Annandale, VA  22003

    Dear Ms. Rand:
```

Dr. James Stevenson, Director
Food Industry Management Program
University of Southern California
University Park
Los Angeles, California 90007

**Appropriate titles
should be used in all
inside address sec-
tions.**

Where the degree designation (initials) is the same as the individual's title, only one
should be used:

Incorrect:
Dr. Robert Coffey, Ph.D.
Dr. Frank Olsen, M.D.

Correct:
Dr. Martin Kelly
       or
Martin Kelly, M.D.

Dr. Tamara Gotz
       or
Tamara Gotz, Ph.D.

See Appendix A for suggestions on using numbers in written communications.

On the whole, abbreviations should not be used unless they also appear in the letterhead of the message being answered. Building or house numbers should be written in numerals except for *one.* Street names that are numbered should be written out from First to Tenth streets. Numerals should be used for street names past Tenth. And of course, zip codes should always be included.

The Salutation

Because most of us react much more favorably to our name than we do to an impersonal designation such as *Dear Friend, Dear Occupant, Dear Teacher, Dear Accountant,* names should be used whenever possible. Many organizations have found it advisable to type in, on hundreds or thousands of form letters, individual names and addresses. Marketing research indicates that most people respond favorably to that approach even if they are aware the letter is a form.

But what salutation should you use when you don't know the individual's name or you are writing to a company? There are no easy answers. However, this seems to be the trend today:

1. If you know the addressee's name, use it: *Dear Mr. French; Dear Ms. Kelly; Dear Dr. Lyons.*
2. If the letter is going to an organization, use *Ladies and Gentlemen.*
3. If the individual has a title and the name is not known or he or she is a high-level dignitary, use the appropriate salutation: *Dear Director; Dear Editor; Dear Mr. (or Madam) President; Your Eminence; Dear General.*

There also is a trend toward putting more life into the salutation with such openings as "Thank you, Mr. Britt," "I was delighted, Ahmed," or "Your Check, Ms. Bailey." The first line of the body of the letter then begins with a capital letter and completes the sentence begun in the salutation.

In the final analysis, the salutations that are used usually will be selected according to the firm's policy and/or the writer's common sense and sense of courtesy and good taste.

In business letters, the salutation is almost always followed with a colon. In personal letters *(Dear Marty, Dear Betty,)*, the mark of punctuation following the salutation is a comma.

The Body

Chapters 7 through 12 of the text are largely concerned with different types of letters (sales, credit, inquiry, and others) which make up the body. However, it is important to note that the format of the letter's body should always be visually attractive: carefully centered, with adequate white space, and paragraphs that are relatively short.

The Complimentary Close

Like several other parts of the business letter, the complimentary close has changed slowly. Thomas Jefferson, in 1789, closed his letter to George Washington with "Your most obedient and humble servant." Even when Aaron Burr challenged Alexander Hamilton to the fatal duel, he closed with "I have the honor to be Yours respt."

Today the more common closes are *Yours truly, Sincerely, Sincerely yours,* and *Yours sincerely.* To a lesser degree, *Cordially* or *Cordially yours* are used. But the logic of these is questionable. Is he or she "truly yours"? or even "sincerely yours"? Perhaps that is why many individuals are following the recommendation of dropping the complimentary close or are turning to such phrases as *Best regards, Warm regards,* or even *See Your Ford Dealer, Ford for the Best.*

Various styles in the complimentary close are acceptable.

The Signature Section

In most instances, the signature section is made up of three or four parts. The four-part signature includes the name of the company (usually typed in capital letters) and the writer's signature, typed name, and title. The name of the company (which appears in the letterhead) is usually omitted in a three-part signature.

When the writer is not available to sign the letter, a substitute (such as a secretary) may sign and add initials. However, this practice should be discouraged as much as possible. Most readers are offended by the implication that the writer could not spare a few seconds to sign the letter. Also, the use of *per* or *by,* placed in front of the signature, is obsolete and should be avoided.

The signature portion of the business letter is made up of three or four parts.

MISCELLANEOUS ITEMS

Aside from knowing the basic format and parts of business letters, a good letter writer must be familiar with the use of attention lines, subject lines, identifying initials, enclosure lines, and carbon copies.

The Attention Line

Quite often an *attention line* is used in business letters. This is done when the writer wants the letter to go to a specific individual in a firm because that person either is familiar with the writer's needs or is handling the project with which the letter is concerned.

If the letter is *addressed* to a particular person and that individual is no longer with the company, the letter may be returned to the sender. However, if the letter is sent to *the attention of* a person and that individual is no longer with the organization, the letter will be opened and processed by the individual's successor. Figure B–7 shows an example of an attention line.

An attention line often will speed the processing of a letter.

FIGURE B–7 **Attention Line**

```
PHILLIP TRUCKENBROD CONCERT ARTISTS
                 A DIVISION OF TRIAD CORPORATION
       15 High Street, Suite 621 • Hartford, Connecticut 06103 • (203) 728-1096


       Bailey Brick Company
       1212 West Detroit Street
       Detroit, Michigan  48224

       Attention:  Mrs. K. Korm, Treasurer

       Ladies and Gentlemen:
```

The Subject Line

The subject line can shorten a letter because it may contain reference information often placed in the first paragraph.

The *subject line* also is used to improve efficiency and speed in handling correspondence. When carefully worded, it can replace the first paragraph usually used to introduce the transaction about which the letter is concerned. Figure B–8 shows an example of a subject line.

Identifying Initials

Initials placed after the signature may prove useful when identification of the writer or typist is desired.

The usual custom is to place the dictator's and typist's initials in the lower left corner of the letter as in Figure B–1. However, there is a growing trend toward dropping this custom. The signature makes it unnecessary to use the writer's initials. And if the letter was typed in a word-processing center or in a typing pool, the typist's initials seem somewhat meaningless.

However, there are frequent instances in which a department or division head signs *all* the letters emanating from the department, even though six different people may be writing them. This is usually done so that he or she may know something about all areas' activities. In addition, it may be wise to have most of "this department's" letters signed by a vice-president rather than an assistant sales manager.

FIGURE B–8   Subject Line

Editorial Services
P.O. Box 1891
Tubac, Arizona 85646

William Best, Jr.

Tel: (602) 398-2322

Mr. Richard Norris
1803 North Parkway Drive
Portland, ME 04104

SUBJECT: Invoice No. 1303-A

Dear Mr. Norris:

In such cases, the actual writer's initials appear in the left corner (with the typist's), but not the signer's initials. Some companies use all three sets of initials. And in some instances, a firm uses only the typist's initials.

Enclosure Line

The notation *Enclosure* is usually placed just below the identifying initials. It tells the reader that items in addition to the letter may be found in the envelope. This could be an article, check, invoice, or sample of a product.

> **An *enclosure* notation may prove very useful to the reader in checking the completeness of the envelope's content.**

The abbreviation *Encl.* is used or *Enclosure.* If more than one item is enclosed, the number is usually stated. Government agencies often identify each enclosure so that if one is withdrawn it can be easily identified. Figure B–1 shows a sample enclosure line.

Copies

When a copy of a letter sent to Mr. Hillman is also sent to another party, Mr. Hillman should be told that fact. Quite obviously, he would be offended if a copy were sent and

The notation *cc* is helpful in informing the letter's reader of the names of other recipients of the same letter.

he was not told. The notation *cc:,* at the bottom of the letter, informs the reader of copies sent (see Figure B–2).

In the event a copy of the letter is sent to Ms. Adjani without Mr. Hillman's being informed, the initials *bc* or *bcc* (blind copy) are used. Of course, that designation is placed only on the copy and not on the original letter.

CONCLUDING COMMENTS

It should again be emphasized, in this discussion on the mechanics of business letters, that there is no one correct method. Every organization develops a style it prefers that is consistent with its image. It may agree in whole or in part with the suggestions above. But for that company, the style makes sense.

A Sample Long Report

**Mature Women Graduates
<u>Can</u> Re-enter the Professions**

A Special Report Prepared for the State-Wide Managers Association
Analyzing the Employment Opportunities in the Aerospace Industry
in Southern California for Mature Female Graduates

MANAGEMENT OPPORTUNITIES FOR
RE-ENTERING MATURE FEMALE GRADUATES
IN THE
AEROSPACE INDUSTRY IN SOUTHERN CALIFORNIA

Prepared for

Mr. Leonard L. Evans
Executive Director
Sate-Wide Managers Association

Prepared by

Jacquie B. Lyndon and Lorraine K. Baldwinson
Research Associates
Reynolds Association Management Company
Chicago, Illinois

May 198_

May 3, 198_

Mr. Leonard L. Evans
Executive Director
State-Wide Managers Association
35 Bruce Street
Los Angeles, CA 90013

Dear Mr. Evans:

With the changing demographics of our society and the rapidly expanding
proportion of well-educated women entering the professions, doing the
research for the report you requested on March 11, 198_, was intriguing
and enjoyable. As you specified, the report explores the management
opportunities for mature female college graduates in the aerospace
industry in Southern California.

Purposes.—The primary purposes of the study were to determine:

1. Employment Opportunities: Are female graduates over the age of
   30 considered for entry-level positions in management?

2. Employment Compensation: What is the salary range offered to
   re-entering, mature female graduates?

3. Employment Procedures: What are the best ways for the mature
   re-entering female to pursue professional employment?

Research.—The primary research consisted of (1) interviews with mature
female graduates, potential employers, and job placement personnel, and
(2) a survey of 100 corporations in the aerospace industry in Southern
California. Secondary research used government reports, statistical
information provided by California University at Southwold, published
reports on women's sudies, and articles from the relevant literature.

The recommendations in this report are practical and workable, and you
should find them useful in facilitating the re-entry of mature females.
If you have questions or comments on this study, its methods, or its
recommendations, please call on us.

Cordially yours,

Lorraine K. Baldwinson

Jacquie B. Lyndon   Lorraine K. Baldwinson
Research Associate   Research Associate

TABLE OF CONTENTS

TABLE OF TABLES

<u>Synopsis</u>

<u>Problems Women Face</u>

Anyone attempting to re-enter the employment market is going to perceive problems, some of them real. For the mature female re-entering the employment market, the problems are heightened. There are some steps women can take to succeed in entering a profession. They must recognize that many of the problems the mature female faces are self-imposed.

<u>Employment Keys</u>

Anyone seeking employment needs to think clearly and do some intelligent research; the same applies to mature women, who are the focus of this study. Recommendations for this group include:

<u>Know Thyself.</u> The individual must know herself; this responsibility should not be foisted upon others. To avoid a multitude of problems that no potential employer will be able to solve, she must look at her values, skills, and interests before selecting a college major.

<u>Is There a Job?</u> Is there really a job at the end of the education? The older adult does not have many options for retooling if the incorrect path is chosen.

<u>Landing on One's Feet.</u> Correctly or incorrectly, it is assumed that mature women (and men, too) have more and better skills than their younger counterparts. They should develop their skills so that they can immediately implement them on the job.

<u>Professional Assistance.</u> Although it is generally unwise for the young college graduate to use an outside employment agency to secure a job, such agencies can be most helpful for the mature female in making appropriate linkages with realistic and satisfying employment opportunities.

At different times in the history of our society various groups have found it difficult to maximize their employment opportunities; currently, the older female is facing some problems, but the problems are not insurmountable. If the woman thinks, plans, and is aggressive, she will find many employment options. She has much to offer—but her skills and abilities need to be honed and carefully marketed.

Introduction

The Problem

More and more women in their mid-life years are returning to colleges and universities to prepare for re-entry into the job market. There are several reasons for this phenomenon, all generally having an ecomomic cause.

Mature female graduates manifest two common attitudes. The woman who has been at home raising a family is generally full of fears and anxieties about her future. On the other hand, the woman already in her chosen field is confident and self-assured and has returned to school to enable her to secure a management position. However, there are a number of roadblocks, self-imposed and imposed by others, that the woman must identify and hurdle if she is to achieve her goal of obtaining rewarding employment.

The Purposes

To explore the opportunities and problems of the mature female seeking to re-enter the professional employment market in the aerospace industry in Southern California.

To recommend workable procedures for women making the transition from "housewife" to professional manager.

The Research Methods

Primary Research.—The primary sources of data included:

- A survey of 100 major California corporations in the aerospace industry in Southern California.

- Personal interviews with potential employers, job placement agencies, and mature female graduates.

Secondary Research.—The secondary sources included:

- Published reports from governmental agencies and commissions, plus articles concentrating on women's studies.

- Statistical information provided by California University at Southwold.

2

<u>The Research Limitations</u>

Because recommendations were needed in fewer than two months and because of the imposed budgetary limits, more comprehensive research methods were not employed. However, as the results will indicate, the selected methods were not only workable, but produced useful and reliable results. <u>The Terminology</u>

<u>Mature female</u>.—A woman between the ages of 35 and 50.

<u>Seeking</u>.—Actively pursuing full-time employment in a management position.

<u>Re-enter</u>.—Returning to full-time employment after not working for a number of years.

<u>Professional employment market</u>.—Jobs calling for at least a four-year college degree where conceptual knowledge is a requisite.

<u>Procedures</u>.—Steps for obtaining meaningful employment.

<u>Transition</u>.—Moving from home-making to full-time professional employment.

<u>Opportunities and problems</u>.—The challenges and pitfalls (positive and negative aspects) of re-entering the employment marketplace.

<u>Aerospace industry</u>.—Profit-making organizations and governmental or quasi-governmental agencies engaged in air or space manufacturing, technology, or support services.

<u>Housewife</u>.—An uncompensated female who cares for the family's home and has primary duties probably related to the raising of children.

<u>Southern California</u>.—The metropolitan areas between Los Angeles and San Diego.

<u>The Employment Context for the Mature Female</u>
<u>Re-Entering Professional Employment in the Aerospace Industry in</u>
<u>Southern California</u>

<u>Job Availability and Conditions</u>

<u>Unsought</u>.—It does not appear that women are necessarily discrimi-
nated against in employment, but recruiters state that their firms
rarely specifically seek women to fill management slots. Representatives
of executive search firms report that they can successfully represent
and present female candidates for professional positions. When the
female is "properly introduced," often a "match" can be achieved.
However, employers are not going out of their way to bring women into
management. The situation is changing, and with one-third of all MBA
graduates being women, the change will continue. At the same time,
successful employment is not going to automatically occur—the mature
female will have to make it happen. (8:5)

<u>Economics</u>.—When all women are considered, a Harris poll shows that
nearly 75% do not receive pay equal to men's for comparable work. (2:6)
However, those data reflect all women. It is generally assumed that when
the more recent hires are isolated, the economic differences between men
and women in similar professional positions narrows very quickly; there
are numerous cases where firms seem to be paying a premium to bring
competent females into the executive office.

Economic independence and security for the mature woman is an
attainable goal. (7:1) If women in the middle years use their educational opportunities before re-entering the job market, the chances of
obtaining suitable employment in the mangement levels will increase.

<u>Availability vs. Security</u>.—Job availability in management positions
for women is no longer a major issue. However, job security for women
over 40 in management is not good. In 1980, top-management women
represented 4% of fired clients at Hinchey and Company in New York, job-
placement consultants. But by 1985, thet percentage had quadrupled, to
16%. "It will continue to increase in the next few years," says Susan
Walker, the firm's executive vice-president. She adds, "Among our firm's
clients, the average age of top fired women is 40 and the average salary
is $47,000. Both of these statistics are lower than those for men."
(1:9)

One, however, must put these data into the context (the economic
turmoil) of the late 1980's. The economy and general employment in the
United States are going through tremendous change. Thousands of
professional employees are being fired or subjected to early retirement.
This is the current economic phenonmenon, and the "new" person attempting to re-enter and remain in a demanding job is going to find the
conditons tough—regardless of sex.

3

4

Discrimination or Entry Time?

   Economic Necessity.—Because many families find it impossible to
survive on one salary, more and more women are working outside the home.
When the woman attempts to re-enter the employment market, sex discrimination and occupational segregaton can severely limit the woman's
opportunities for economic independence.

   Double Edged Sword.—Re-entering women in mid-life find that their
opportunities for employment and economic security are severely limited.
Throughout our society, the demands from the factory floor to the
executive suite are for eonomic independence. However, it is tougher for
everyone to achieve economic security today. Carrying the "baggage" of
sex, age, and inexperience, the woman finds it very difficult to
automatically eliminate these problems. (7:5)

   Assumed Discrimination.—The actual citations of discrimination are
being reduced as more women enter the professions, but it remains true
that most of the employment policy makers are men. These men moved
through the management ranks when morality virtually dictated that women
belonged in the home. Therefore, perhaps even unaware of their own male
dominance, those males make it difficult for women to easily enter the
"corporate club." Further, the discrimination is silent and manifests
itself in many ways, dependent upon the level of education and position
of authority in the job for which the woman is applying. The problems
for the female escalate as she attempts to enter a management position
customarily held by men. (6:121)

Educational Building Blocks

   As the discriminatory sanctions decrease, and they *are* decreasing,
it appears that women will most likely find it easier to achieve the
employment goals for which they qualify. This is because women are
rapidly gaining solid educations in professions other than teaching;
that educational base will serve as an excellent launch pad into future
managerial positions.

   The current generation of mid-life women differs considerably from
the generation of women who are now elderly, just as they contrast
strongly in a number of ways with today's younger women. For example,
women over 40 in today's society have achieved a higher level of
education than their predecessors, and yet their younger sisters have
surpassed them.

   Women most likely will vault ahead on the basis of their educational acomplishments. Seventy-two percent of today's mid-life women
have completed high school. This figure compares with 84% of the younger
group and only 53% of the older group. (7:26)

5

<u>The Employment Trend</u>

Although it is difficult for the re-entering mature woman to quickly achieve her rightful place, the "winds" seem to be very much in her favor. Each day more competent women are entering the management ranks right out of college and also from the previous "housewife" roles. Younger women are finding the transition relatively easy. The trends seem to indicate that these two groups of women (the young woman entering the profession directly from college and the mature re-entering female) have clearly charted their trails, and as younger women move up in the organization the possibilities for the mature re-entering woman should be enhanced. This is because these "groups" will eventually merge, networks will be established, and inherent discrimination will be substantially reduced. (14)

<u>The Current Situation In Southern California</u>

<u>The Survey</u>

<u>Methodology</u>.—Besides just relying on general data collected for the entire nation, a survey was designed and implemented that focused specifically on the aerospace industry in Southern California. Over an 18-day period, from March 28, 198_ to April 15, 198_, questionnaires were distributed. (See Appendix I for the "Cover Letter for the Instrument" and Appendix II for "The Survey Instrument.") The question- naires were mailed to the directors of Human Resource Departments at 100 corporations in the aerospace industry in Southern California. These corporations were seleacted from The Career Opportunity Index. (5)

<u>Survey Purpose</u>.—The instrument was designed to answer two major questions:

<u>Opportunity</u>: Are female graduates over the age of 30 considered for entry-level management positions?

<u>Income</u>: What is the range of compensation offered to mature female graduates?

<u>Survey Returns</u>.—By the cutoff date, 322 responses had been returned from the 100 that had been mailed.

<u>The Survey Results</u>.—Many firms prefer to promote from within, which can make it difficult for anyone on the outside to get a responsible management position. Generally, fewer than 20% of all women employees are over the age of 30. Therefore, firms may have second thoughts about bringing in people who may be "out of step." And firms prefer work experience. Although these graduates may be forgiven in the case of the young woman, older job applicants, regardless of 15-20 years of

6

housewife duties, may be expected to bring some employment experience to the job. Three points from the survey that need further amplification follow.

Available Positions: Regardless of the age of the graduate, work experience within the field in question is manadatory for a person to be considered for management positions, even at the entry level. The opportunities available to mature women are greater if some time is involved in the work force prior to graduation.

Inside Promotions: The results show that the majority of companies promote from within; therefore, there are very few mid-level management positions available to outsiders. Only a small percentage of women hired are promoted to managerial positions.

Salary Situation: A majority of the corporations responding to the survey indicated that the annual income offered for entry-level management positions is between $20,000 and $30,000. Prior work experience is the determining factor in the salary offered for a position.

Table A provides a summary of the most frequent responses in the survey, and Appendix III presents a full tabulation of the survey results. (See Table A.)

The Interviews

Methodology.—Six people in six different positions were interviewed. Of the six, three were mature female graduates, one was a personnel director, and the remaining two were employed by California University at Southwold. (See Appendix IV, "The Interview Questions.")

The Purposes.—The primary purposes in the interviews were:

To determine how age and prior experience of the applicant affects the hiring process.

To discover techniques the mature female can employ to obtain professional employment.

To ascertain realistic salary levels for the mature female re-entering the employment arena.

TABLE A.

MOST FREQUENT RESPONSES IN SURVEY

Item	Most frequent response	Percentage of respondents
1. Number of people employed?	over 500	59
2. Percentage of women over 30?	10-20%	47
3. Of women employed, how many are in managerial or executive positions?	0-5%	59
4. How many managerial positions were filled outside in the past year?	0-3%	53
5. Of these, what percentage was filled by mature females?	0-5%	56
6. Does your firm participate in the job placement program at California University?	no	69
7. Are recent graduates with degrees in marketing considered for management positions in your firm?	no	84
8. What income is offered for entry-level management positions?	$20-30,000	47
9. How important is work experience to securing a managerial position in your firm?	very important	66

7

8

The Questions.—The questions asked during the interviews were designed to elicit information on the five major questions:

1. Age: Is age a major factor in seeking desired positions?

2. Experience: What is the importance of job experience prior to graduation?

3. Strategy: What are realistic salary expectations for a mature graduate?

5. Recommendation: What do you recommend for a mature female graduate seeking an entry-level management position?

Age is not a factor in itself. The underlying difficulty mature women face upon graduation is indirectly related to their age. The expectations of the mature woman are drastically different from those of younger graduates.

Re-entry women who had been homemakers prior to graduation suffered from insecurities and did not feel that they had a solid basis for seeking professional positions. In contrast, the mid-life women who were changing careers held an attitude of superiority. Both perspectives were a detriment in seeking employment.

Job experience, regardless of the targeted career, was considered mandatory in order to seek employment in that field before receiving a degree. This "job training" was considered invaluable in obtaining a position in entry-level management.

All of the candidates interviewed agreed that mature women, even more than younger women graduates, should have prior work experience to be competitive. Classroom experience is not an adequate substitute for practical job experience. (10;11;13)

Ways to obtain the position varied among the interviewees. There was a difference of opinion concerning the best method for a mature female graduate to use in finding suitable employment opportunities. This conflict was between the graduates interviewed and those professional counselors connected with the University Placement Center.

Placement Counselors associated with the California University believed that the Job Placement Center was instrumental in helping mature women find employment. It was admitted, however, that the number of women who use the job placement services was very small.

9

In contrast, the mature graduates felt that the on-campus interviews were a source of higher-paying positions, but they did not feel that these positions were aviailable through this source. All three mature graduates believed that employers who were interviewing on campus were looking for younger people without preconceived expectations. (9;13;14)

Income opportunities are primarily determined by how the graduate targets the salary and by the individual's grade point average and prior work experience. The graduates interviewed applied only for the positions offering $25,000 or more per year.

Recommended strategies for obtaining the job the individual desires include the following (the most useful suggestions were submitted by the University Placement Center):

Know yourself, your values, skills, and interests.

Look ahead at the job market before selecting your major.

Make the match between your career, skills, and prior work experience.

Become the best at what you are doing, and sell yourself that way.

Be realistic and open-minded, and keep a positive attitude.

Use professional guidance in seeking employment.

Research potential employers.

Develop a cover letter and resume that present your best case.

<u>Conclusions and Recommendations</u>

<u>Conclusions</u>

The data seem to fall into natural categories and are thought to be representative of the population.

<u>Homemaker Background</u>.—The typical mature female student has been a homemaker and has returned to school in order to better prepare herself for the job market.

<u>Work Experience Vital</u>.—Earlier work experience affects the opportunities and the wages offered to the mature female graduate. On the other hand, work experience has less influence on jobs offered to the younger female graduate.

<u>Get Guidance</u>.—Professsional assistance can increase the chances for success in obtaining a suitable job for the mature female graduate.

<u>Opportunities Available</u>.—No age descrimination in itself is directed at the mature female graduate. The aggressive, confident, educated, experienced woman has an opportunity to secure an entry-level management position in her mid-life years.

<u>Recommendations</u>

Based upon the primary and secondary research, it is suggested that the mature female desiring to re-enter the professions:

<u>Know Herself</u>.—The individual should know herself—her values, skills, and interests—before selecting a major.

<u>Conduct Research</u>.—The woman should research job availability in her chosen field.

<u>Obtain Re-Entry Skills</u>.—The female should use the counseling and guidance available at the re-entry centers on college campuses to develop the skills required for re-entering the job market.

<u>Gain Professional Employment Expertise</u>.—The woman graduate should use professional employment placement services.

10

Bibliography

<u>Publications</u>

1. "The Ax Falls Increasingly on Top Management Women." <u>Wall Street Journal</u> (September 1986), p. 9.

2. "Comparable Worth." <u>Wall Street Journal</u> (September 1986), p. 6.

3. <u>CPC Annual</u>. College Placement Council, Inc., Pittsburgh, Pennsylvania, 1986.

4. Fader, Shirley. "When You Are Doing the Hiring." <u>Working Woman</u> (February 1985), pp. 52-59.

5. Leverett, Donna M. "Career Opportunity Index." California Career Research Systems, Inc., 1986.

6. Rendell, Margherita. "Educating Women for Leadership." Working Papers. The Rockefeller Foundation, 1986.

7. <u>The Status of Mid-Life Women and Options for Their Future</u>. Select Committee on Aging. Committee Publication Number 96-215. Washington: GPO, 1980.

8. "Women Are Seldom the Focus of Executive Searches." <u>Wall Street Journal</u> (September 1986), p. 5.

<u>Interviews</u>

9. Anderson, Dolores. Family Support Officer, Ventura County, Ventura, CA, March 20, 198_.

10. Clarke, Clara. Counselor, Job Placement Center. California State University, Northwold, Northwold, CA, April 19, 198_.

11. Hanks, Dana. Public Relations Director, Archival Medical Center. Los Angeles, CA, April 2, 198_.

12. Newlon, Lorraine. Admissions and Records Director. California State University Northwold, Northwold, CA, April 2, 198_.

13. Rayford, Glenda. Loan Officer, World Savings and Loan. Ventura, CA, March 29, 198_.

14. Taft, Pat. Regional Personnel Director, Shield Healthcare. Camarillo, CA, April 10, 198_.

11

APPENDIXES

 I. The Cover Letter for Survey Instrument

 II. The Survey Instrument

 III. The Survey Results

 IV. The Interview Questions:
   For Placement Service Professionals
   For Mature Female Graduates

APPENDIX I

The Cover Letter for Survey Instrument

March 28, 198_

Personnel Administrator's Name
Company Name
Address

Dear (insert name):

Not only are more women entering the professions for the first time,
many are also attempting, after years of housewife duties, to re-enter
the employment market. Your asssistance is needed in determining the
managerial opportunities for mature female college graduates in the
aerospace industry in Southern California. This information will be
valuable for the mature woman re-entering the job market or entering for
the first time. It will also be valuable for employers in the aerospace
industry.

Your opinion, as a professional in personnel, will help us evaluate
available opportunities for these women. We would be very grateful if
you would take a few moments to complete the attached questionnaire and
return it by April 15, 198_, in the enclosed stamped envelope.

If you would like a copy of this report, please contact us after June 1,
198_.

Your assistance in completing this questionnaire is sincerely appreciated, and your answers will remain confidential.

Cordially,

Lorraine Baldwinson
Research Associate

Jacquie B. Lyndon

Jacquie B. Lyndon
Research Associate

Enc. 2

13

APPENDIX II
The Survey Instrument

QUESTIONNAIRE

Please answer the questionnaire and return in the enclosed self-addressed
stamped envelope by April 10, 198_. All answers will remain confidential.
Thank you for your assistance.

1.   How many people are employed by your company?

     under 50 _____   50-200 _____   200-500 _____   over 500 _____

2.   What percentage of these employees are mature women? (over 30)

     5-10% _____   10-20% _____   over 20% _____

3.   Of these mature female employees, how many hold managerial or
     executive positions?

     0-5% _____   5-10% _____   10-20% _____   over 20% _____

4.   How many executive or managerial positions have been filled from
     outside sources within the last year?

     0 _____   1-3 _____   3-7 _____   7-10 _____   over 10 _____

5.   What percentage of these positions were filled by mature females?

     0-5% _____   5-10% _____   10-20% _____   over 20% _____

6.   Does your firm participate in the job placement program at
     California University at Southwold?

     yes _____   no _____

7.   Are recent graduates with a degree in business considered for
     managerial positions within your firm?

     yes _____   no _____

14

APPENDIX III
The Survey Results

32 responses form a sample of 100 (32% return)

1. How many people are employed by your company?

50-200	200-500	over 500	N/A
4	9	19	0
13%	28%	59%	0

2. What percentage of these employees are mature women? (over 30)

5-10%	10-20%	over 20%	N/A
3	15	4	10
9%	47%	13%	31%

3. Of these mature female employees, how many hold managerial or executive positions?

0-5%	5-10%	10-20%	over 20%
19	3	4	6
59%	9%	13%	19%

4. How many executive or managerial positions have been filled from outside sources within the last year?

0-3	3-7	7-10	N/A
17	5	3	7
53%	16%	9%	22%

5. What percentage of these positions were filled by mature females?

0-5%	5-10%	over 20%	N/A
18	6	3	5
56%	19%	9%	16%

6. Does your firm participate in the job placement program at California University at Southwold?

yes	no
5	27
16%	84%

7. Are recent graduates with a degree in business considered for managerial positions within your firm?

yes	no
19	13
66%	34%

15

APPENDIX IV

<u>The Interview Questions: For Placement Service Professions</u>

1. Do many mature women utilize the job placement services?
2. Approximately what percentage of these women are business majors?
3. Do you find that mature women have different expectations?
4. In your opinion, is age a factor in receiving job offers?
5. What are some reasons, in your opinion, that women over 30 return
    to school?
6. Do you recommend professional guidance in getting a job?
7. What are the salary ranges of the jobs offered to business majors?
8. How important is prior managerial work eperience in securing a
    desirable position?
9. Are employers willing to interview mature women for managerial
    positions?
10. Besides the job placement services on campus, are there other means
    of securing a position that you would recommend?
11. How important is GPA to prospective employers?
12. What recommendations do you have for women over thirty who are
    entering the job market?

<u>The Interview Questions: For Mature Female Graduates</u>

1. What is your educational background?
2. What means did you use to find a position?
3. How many interviews did you participate in?
4. Do you feel you were passed over because of your age?
5. Do you feel that men were considered more qualified than you for
    any positions based solely on their sex?
6. Do you feel younger women were considered more qualified than you
    for any positions based on their age?
7. Why did you return to school?
8. What were your reasons for returning to the job market?
9. Did you secure professional guidance in getting a job?
10. What salary range jobs did you apply for?
11. Did you receive any job offers that you didn't accept?
12. Based on your experience, what advice would you give to mature women
    re-entering school with the goal of securing a managerial position
    upon graduation?

INDEX